STATE CONTROL OVER PRIVATE MILITARY AND SECURITY COMPANIES IN ARMED CONFLICT

The past two decades have witnessed the rapid proliferation of private military and security companies (PMSCs) in armed conflicts around the world, with PMSCs participating in, for example, offensive combat, prisoner interrogation and the provision of advice and training. The extensive outsourcing of military and security activities has challenged conventional conceptions of the state as the primary holder of coercive power and raised concerns about the reduction in state control over the use of violence.

Hannah Tonkin critically analyses the international obligations on three key states – the hiring state, the home state and the host state of a PMSC – and identifies the circumstances in which PMSC misconduct may give rise to state responsibility. This analysis will facilitate the assessment of state responsibility in cases of PMSC misconduct and set standards to guide states in developing their domestic laws and policies on private security.

HANNAH TONKIN completed a masters and doctorate in international law at the University of Oxford on a Rhodes Scholarship, after having previously completed degrees in science and law at the University of Adelaide, Australia. She has worked as a lawyer at the UN International Criminal Tribunal for the former Yugoslavia in The Hague and taught international law at the University of Oxford. She is now a lawyer at the UN International Criminal Tribunal for Rwanda in Arusha, Tanzania.

D1734377

CAMBRIDGE STUDIES IN INTERNATIONAL AND COMPARATIVE LAW

Established in 1946, this series produces high quality scholarship in the fields of public and private international law and comparative law. Although these are distinct legal sub-disciplines, developments since 1946 confirm their interrelations.

Comparative law is increasingly used as a tool in the making of law at national, regional and international levels. Private international law is now often affected by international conventions, and the issues faced by classical conflicts rules are frequently dealt with by substantive harmonisation of law under international auspices. Mixed international arbitrations, especially those involving state economic activity, raise mixed questions of public and private international law, while in many fields (such as the protection of human rights and democratic standards, investment guarantees and international criminal law) international and national systems interact. National constitutional arrangements relating to 'foreign affairs', and to the implementation of international norms, are a focus of attention.

The Series welcomes works of a theoretical or interdisciplinary character, and those focusing on the new approaches to international or comparative law or conflicts of law. Studies of particular institutions or problems are equally welcome, as are translations of the best work published in other languages.

General Editors   James Crawford SC FBA
Whewell Professor of International Law, Faculty of Law, University of Cambridge

John S. Bell FBA
Professor of Law, Faculty of Law, University of Cambridge

A list of books in the series can be found at the end of this volume.

STATE CONTROL OVER PRIVATE MILITARY AND SECURITY COMPANIES IN ARMED CONFLICT

HANNAH TONKIN

CAMBRIDGE
UNIVERSITY PRESS

CAMBRIDGE UNIVERSITY PRESS
Cambridge, New York, Melbourne, Madrid, Cape Town,
Singapore, São Paulo, Delhi, Mexico City

Cambridge University Press
The Edinburgh Building, Cambridge CB2 8RU, UK

Published in the United States of America by Cambridge University Press, New York

www.cambridge.org
Information on this title: www.cambridge.org/9781107613140

© Hannah Tonkin 2011

First published 2011
3rd printing 2012
First paperback edition 2013

A catalogue record for this publication is available from the British Library

Library of Congress Cataloguing in Publication Data
Tonkin, Hannah, 1981–
State control over private military and security companies in armed conflict /
Hannah Tonkin.
p.   cm. – (Cambridge studies in international and comparative law ; 80)
Includes bibliographical references and index.
ISBN 978-1-107-00801-4 (hardback)
1. Combatants and noncombatants (International law)   2. Mercenary troops –
Legal status, laws, etc.   3. Private military companies – Law and legislation
4. Private security services – Law and legislation   I. Title.
KZ6418.T66   2011
355.3′5 – dc22   2011013507

ISBN 978-1-107-61314-0 Paperback

CONTENTS

ACKNOWLEDGEMENTS

I could not have produced this book without the assistance and support of others. It began life as a doctoral thesis completed at the University of Oxford under the supervision of Dapo Akande and Professor Guy Goodwin-Gill. Dapo's sharp intellect, close attention to detail and extensive knowledge of international law undoubtedly pushed me to produce a better thesis and book. He regularly went beyond the call of duty by providing feedback from the other side of the world, whether by email between Yale and The Hague or by skype between Oxford and Australia, and his flexibility and tireless availability enabled me to pursue a range of endeavours while still maintaining a strong level of supervision throughout my doctorate. I am also extremely grateful to my supervisor during the final term of my doctorate, Professor Guy Goodwin-Gill, who invested a considerable amount of time and energy to comprehend the entire project at a late stage. His feedback on the final drafts of my thesis and his general advice on the road to publication were invaluable.

Dr Sarah Percy and Dr Roger O'Keefe examined my masters thesis at the University of Oxford, and their exacting standards helped me to improve my work and develop it into a doctoral proposal. My doctoral thesis examiners, Professors Vaughan Lowe and Nigel White, also provided helpful comments, and I am grateful for their assistance.

The Rhodes Scholarship funded my studies at Oxford for three full years. I will forever be indebted to the Rhodes Trust for the financial support, self-confidence and phenomenal professional and personal opportunities that the Scholarship provided. I was also fortunate to receive a Wingate Scholarship during the final stages of my doctorate.

Parts of Chapters 3, 4 and 5 of this book develop work that appeared in 'Common Article 1: A Minimum Yardstick for Regulating Private Military and Security Companies' (2009) 22 *Leiden Journal of International Law* 779–99. I gratefully acknowledge the journal's permission to reprint the relevant passages.

During my time at Oxford, I was lucky to have the support of numerous friends, colleagues and family members. I would particularly like to thank those who reviewed various sections of the draft, namely, David Tonkin, Dr Jeni Whalan, Dr Will Feldman and Dr Carsten Hoppe. Finally, I would like to thank my family for the tireless love and support that they provided throughout my many years of study.

ABBREVIATIONS

AJIL	American Journal of International Law
CEDAW	Convention on the Elimination of All Forms of Discrimination Against Women
CETS	Council of Europe Treaty Series
CFR	Code of Federal Regulations
CIA	Central Intelligence Agency
Consol TS	Consolidated Treaty Series
CPA	Coalition Provisional Authority
DOD	Department of Defense
ECHR	European Convention on Human Rights
EComHR	European Commission on Human Rights
ECOMOG	Economic Community of West African States Military Observer Group
ECtHR	European Court of Human Rights
EJIL	European Journal of International Law
EO	Executive Outcomes
GCI	First Geneva Convention for the Amelioration of the Condition of the Wounded and Sick in Armed Forces in the Field
GCII	Second Geneva Convention for the Amelioration of the Condition of Wounded, Sick and Shipwrecked Members of Armed Forces at Sea
GCIII	Third Geneva Convention relative to the Treatment of Prisoners of War
GCIV	Fourth Geneva Convention relative to the Protection of Civilian Persons in Time of War
Hague III	Convention Relative to the Opening of Hostilities
Hague IV	Convention Respecting the Laws and Customs of War on Land
Hague V	Convention Respecting the Rights and Duties of Neutral Powers and Persons in Case of War on Land
Hague XIII	Convention Concerning the Rights and Duties of Neutral Powers in Naval War
HC	House of Commons
HCJ	High Court of Justice (Israel)

HRL	Human Rights Law
IAComHR	Inter-American Commission on Human Rights
IACtHR	Inter-American Court of Human Rights
ICCPR	International Covenant on Civil and Political Rights
ICJ	International Court of Justice
ICLQ	International and Comparative Law Quarterly
ICRC	International Committee of the Red Cross
ICTY	International Criminal Tribunal for the former Yugoslavia
IHL	International Humanitarian Law
ILC	International Law Commission
ILM	International Legal Materials
ILR	International Law Reports
Iran–US CTR	Iran–United States Claims Tribunal Reports
LNTS	Law of Nations Treaty Series
MEJA	Military Extraterritorial Jurisdiction Act
MPRI	Military Professional Resources Incorporated
NGO	Non-Governmental Organisation
OAU	Organisation of African Unity
PCIJ	Permanent Court of International Justice
PMC	Private Military Company
PMSC	Private Military and Security Company
PNG	Papua New Guinea
Protocol I	First Additional Protocol to the Geneva Conventions of 12 August 1949, and relating to the Protection of Victims of International Armed Conflicts
Protocol II	Second Additional Protocol to the Geneva Conventions of 12 August 1949, and relating to the Protection of Victims of Non-International Armed Conflicts
PSC	Private Security Company
Recueil des Cours	Recueil des Cours de l'Academie de Droit International de la Haye
Res.	Resolution
RIAA	Reports of International Arbitral Awards
RUF	Revolutionary United Front
UCIHL	University Centre for International Humanitarian Law
UCMJ	Uniform Code of Military Justice
UNCAT	United Nations Convention Against Torture
UNGA	United Nations General Assembly
UNHRC	United Nations Human Rights Committee
UNSC	United Nations Security Council
UNTS	United Nations Treaty Series
WTO	World Trade Organization

TABLE OF CASES

International Court of Justice/Permanent Court of International Justice

European Court of Human Rights/European Commission on Human Rights

Inter-American system

UN Human Rights Committee

International Criminal Tribunal for the former Yugoslavia

International arbitral decisions

World Trade Organization

United Kingdom

United States

Other jurisdictions

TABLE OF STATUTES

TABLE OF INTERNATIONAL TREATIES
AND CONVENTIONS

~

Introduction

The past two decades have witnessed the rapid growth and consolidation of the global private security industry. Tens of thousands of contractors working for private military and security companies (PMSCs) now provide a wide range of services to states, international organisations, corporations and non-governmental organisations around the world. Many PMSCs operate in zones of armed conflict, where they carry out functions that were formerly the exclusive domain of the armed forces. In this context, PMSCs have performed coercive activities such as offensive combat, armed security and the detention and interrogation of prisoners, as well as non-coercive activities such as military advice and training, transport, housing and intelligence collection and analysis. Some PMSCs provide a wide range of military and security services, whilst others specialise in a small number of specific activities.

Nowhere has the scale and scope of PMSC activity been more evident than in Iraq and Afghanistan, where the US has become dependent on private contractors to carry out its operations. During the period from 2003 to 2007, US agencies awarded around US$85 billion in contracts for work to be performed in the Iraqi theatre alone.[1] By 2007, the number of contractors working for the US in the Iraqi theatre was at least 190,000 – more than the number of US troops – and the ratio of contractors to US troops was at least 2.5 times higher than it had been during any other major US conflict.[2] Subsequently, as the Obama administration shifted its focus from Iraq to Afghanistan, the number of contractors working for the US in Iraq began to decline, while the number in Afghanistan increased significantly.[3] In 2010, contractors made up around 54 per cent of the

---

1 US Congressional Budget Office, 'Contractors' Support of US Operations in Iraq' (August 2008). The following countries are considered to be part of the Iraqi theatre: Iraq, Bahrain, Jordan, Kuwait, Oman, Qatar, Saudi Arabia, Turkey and the United Arab Emirates.
2 *Ibid.*
3 US Commission on Wartime Contracting, 'At What Cost? Contingency Contracting in Iraq and Afghanistan' (10 June 2009).

US Department of Defense (DOD) workforce in Iraq and Afghanistan, with the total number of DOD contractors in those countries hovering around 250,000 and additional contractors working for other government agencies.[4]

The extensive outsourcing of military and security activities calls into question twentieth-century paradigms of interstate warfare and conventional conceptions of the state as the primary holder of coercive power.[5] Indeed, although private force is by no means a new phenomenon in historical terms, the recent proliferation of private, profit-driven military and security actors signals a clear shift in the modern conceptualisation and delivery of security. This presents significant challenges for the normative frameworks and accountability structures of traditional international law, which largely assume that the use of force in the international arena falls within the mandate of state institutions. Of particular concern is the reduction in state *control* over military and security activities, as well as the lack of adequate *accountability* mechanisms for PMSC misconduct in the field. Whilst there is no evidence that private contractors are more likely to misbehave than national troops, private contractors certainly can, like national soldiers, engage in inappropriate or harmful behaviour in the course of performing their functions. Yet states often fail to take the same measures to control PMSC personnel that they would ordinarily take to control national soldiers, and many of the accountability mechanisms that exist for the national armed forces are weak or absent in the case of PMSCs.

Notwithstanding these challenges, this book argues that the state-centred frameworks of traditional international law are in fact sufficiently flexible to accommodate the modern private security industry. The extensive use of PMSCs has certainly reduced reliance on national

---

4 Schwartz, 'Department of Defense Contractors in Iraq and Afghanistan: Background and Analysis', Congressional Research Service Report for Congress R40764 (2 July 2010); see also US Office of the Under Secretary of Defense for Acquisition, Technology and Logistics, 'Contractor Support of US Operations in the USCENTCOM Area of Responsibility, Iraq, and Afghanistan' (May 2010); US Government Accountability Office, 'Contingency Contracting: Improvements Needed in Management of Contractors Supporting Contract and Grant Administration in Iraq and Afghanistan' (April 2010).

5 Max Weber's classic definition of the modern nation-state as 'a human community that (successfully) claims the monopoly of the legitimate use of physical force' has been conventional wisdom since the mid-nineteenth century and remains the obvious point of reference for most contemporary inquiries: see, e.g., Gerth and Mills, *From Max Weber: Essays in Sociology* (1948), 77–8; Weber, *The Theory of Social and Economic Organization* (1964).

armed forces, but it has not undermined the role of the state *per se* in regulating contemporary armed conflict. In general, for every PMSC working in a conflict zone, three states retain a significant capacity to influence company behaviour and to promote accountability in cases of contractor misconduct: first, the state that hires the PMSC (the hiring state); secondly, the state in which the PMSC operates (the host state); and thirdly, the state in which the PMSC is based or incorporated (the home state). This book critically analyses the principal international obligations on these three states and discusses how PMSC misconduct may give rise to state responsibility in each case. In addition, this book evaluates the recent laws and practices of certain key states in order to ascertain the extent to which those states appear to be fulfilling their international obligations. This two-way analysis fills a critical gap in the existing private security literature, as there is currently little in-depth analysis of the relationship between states' domestic frameworks on the one hand and states' international legal obligations and responsibility on the other.

Chapter 1 presents the historical, normative and factual background of the private security industry. It traces the historical evolution of private military actors and assesses how perceptions of their legitimacy and utility have shifted over time. It then critically examines the moral and practical objections that consistently arose in relation to private military actors in the past, and considers the extent to which similar concerns have arisen in relation to modern PMSCs. Within this historical and normative context, Chapter 1 scrutinises the facts surrounding the contemporary private security industry, first locating PMSCs on the broader spectrum of military and security service provision, and then examining their general character and the main activities that they perform in armed conflict today.

Chapter 2 lays the theoretical groundwork for the book by outlining the basic normative structure of the international legal system and explaining how the law of state responsibility operates within that systemic context. It discusses the general nature of international obligations and the conditions for breach, and identifies the key categories of obligations on the hiring state, the home state and the host state of a PMSC. Within this conceptual framework, Chapter 2 identifies the different ways in which states may violate their obligations through state organs or other individuals acting as state agents, and it then outlines the general circumstances that may justify or excuse states' otherwise wrongful acts. This paves the way for a detailed analysis of the obligations and responsibility of the hiring state, the host state and the home state in the subsequent chapters of the book.

Chapter 3 critically examines the attribution of PMSC misconduct to the hiring state. It identifies three situations in which such attribution may occur: first, in rare cases the contractor may form part of the hiring state's armed forces; secondly, and more commonly, the contractor may be empowered by the law of the hiring state to exercise elements of governmental authority; and, thirdly, the contractor may be acting on the instructions or under the direction or control of the hiring state when he or she engages in the relevant misconduct. Chapter 3 argues that a large proportion of PMSC activity in armed conflict will fall within at least one of these three categories. In practice, however, it will frequently be more difficult to prove the responsibility of the hiring state for violations committed by a PMSC employee than it would be if a national soldier of that state were to behave in the same way, and some PMSC conduct may fall outside the rules of attribution altogether. This reveals a potential responsibility gap between states that act through their national armed forces and states that hire PMSCs.

Chapters 4, 5 and 6 closely analyse the obligations on the host state, the hiring state and the home state to take positive steps to prevent, investigate, punish and redress PMSC misconduct in the field. Where such an obligation applies and a state fails to take the necessary measures to control PMSC behaviour, contractor misconduct may give rise to the responsibility of that state under international law. Although it is the PMSC employee's misconduct that triggers state responsibility in such cases, it is the state's *own failure* to take adequate preventive or remedial measures that in fact constitutes the basis for the state's responsibility, and not the PMSC activity itself. The obligations discussed in these three chapters may provide a pathway to state responsibility that is independent of the attribution of PMSC misconduct to the hiring state, thus helping to bridge the attribution gap (identified in Chapter 3) between PMSCs and national soldiers.

The legal analysis in this book focuses on PMSCs operating in armed conflict, including situations of military occupation. In this context, international humanitarian law (IHL) will be applicable and may influence the interpretation of other international legal frameworks, such as human rights law. Yet it is important to bear in mind that many PMSCs also operate in other contexts, such as peacekeeping, territorial administration and post-conflict reconstruction, where IHL will not apply and where other frameworks will assume primary importance. Although non-conflict situations are not the principal focus of this book, certain parts of the analysis are highly relevant in those contexts, particularly the assessment of the law of state responsibility in Chapters 2–3 and of human rights law in Chapters 4–6.

Overall, this book may facilitate the assessment of state responsibility in cases of PMSC misconduct, by identifying and expounding the content of states' obligations to control PMSCs in armed conflict and the precise circumstances in which contractors' misconduct may give rise to state responsibility. This book does *not* argue that the law of state responsibility is sufficient in itself to address the control and accountability concerns surrounding the private security industry; on the contrary, any response should incorporate a range of strategies targeting various actors including individual contractors, PMSCs and states.[6] Nonetheless, the law of state responsibility provides a useful mechanism for addressing some of these concerns and, in doing so, it provides a significant legal incentive to states themselves to exert greater control over PMSC activity. More generally, by highlighting and clarifying the pertinent international obligations on states, this book could play an important standard-setting role to encourage and assist states in developing their domestic laws and practices on private security, with a view to improving overall PMSC compliance with international law.

6 Similarly, the UN Working Group that is studying the private security industry supports a 'three-tier approach' to the regulation of PMSCs, including self-regulation, regulation at the national level, and international regulatory legal standards and oversight mechanisms: see Report of the Working Group on the Use of Mercenaries as a Means of Violating Human Rights and Impeding the Exercise of the Right of Peoples to Self-Determination (2 July 2010), UN Doc. A/HRC/15/25.

1

The private security industry uncovered

Private, profit-driven military actors are almost as old as warfare itself, and were a central component of most wars until the mid-nineteenth century. Throughout history, these individuals triggered various moral and practical objections which ultimately affected their success in the international system. Whilst the modern private security industry is unprecedented in its scale and sophistication, it shares a number of characteristics with past markets for force, and some PMSCs have attracted social stigma similar to that borne by their historical counterparts. An understanding of this historical and normative backdrop provides a key foundation for the analysis of states' international obligations to control PMSCs in contemporary armed conflict.

Accordingly, this chapter provides a critical overview of the private security industry in its historical and normative context. The first section traces the historical evolution of private military actors, and assesses how perceptions of the legitimacy and utility of those actors shifted over time. The second section draws on that historical analysis in order to identify three recurring objections to private force, and considers the extent to which those objections have arisen in response to modern PMSCs. The third section scrutinises the contemporary spectrum of military/security service provision, and locates modern PMSCs on that spectrum by reference to other actors such as mercenaries and national soldiers. Finally, the fourth section examines the private security industry in depth. What exactly are PMSCs and what do they do? It first considers the nature of the companies themselves, the conflicts in which they operate and the clients for whom they work, and it then develops a typology of the private security industry by classifying PMSC services into four categories. This typology is central to the legal analysis in subsequent chapters because the scope of states' international obligations to control a PMSC in armed conflict depends primarily on the services provided by that company in a particular case.

1.1 History of private military actors in international relations

Max Weber's classic definition of the modern nation-state as 'a human community that (successfully) claims the monopoly of the legitimate use of physical force' has been conventional wisdom since the mid-nineteenth century.[1] Twentieth-century paradigms of interstate warfare between standing national armies reflect this model of the state as the primary holder of coercive power. Even as states privatised many core public services during the latter half of the twentieth century, the military continued to be regarded as *qualitatively* different and thus remained one of the last bastions of government monopoly. Indeed, as Samuel Huntington noted in 1957, 'while all professions are to some extent regulated by the state, the military profession is monopolised by the state'.[2]

Although Weber's conception of the state has been the obvious reference point for most modern debates about international security, in historical terms state monopoly over force is actually an anomaly. States have a long history of reliance on the private sector for military operations, going right back to the armies of ancient China, Greece and Rome.[3] Twelfth-century feudal lords supplemented their forces by hiring foreign, independent and profit-motivated fighters, as did the Pope, the Renaissance Italian city-states and most of the European forces during the Thirty Years' War of 1618–48. Reliance on private force essentially persisted in various forms until the nineteenth century, when the modern paradigm of interstate warfare between citizen armies prevailed. Thomson explains:

> The contemporary organisation of global violence is neither timeless nor natural. It is distinctively modern. In the six centuries leading up to 1900, global violence was democratised, marketised, and internationalised. Non-state violence dominated the international system.[4]

This section critically examines how the 'contemporary organisation of global violence' evolved from the twelfth century to today, and considers

---

1 See Gerth and Mills, *From Max Weber* (1948), 77–8; Weber, *The Theory of Social and Economic Organization* (1964); Weber, *Economy and Society: An Outline of Interpretive Sociology* (1978), 54.
2 Huntington, *The Soldier and the State: The Theory and Politics of Civil–Military Relations* (1957), 37.
3 For a detailed history of private military service, see Mockler, *The New Mercenaries* (1985), ch. 1; Thomson, *Mercenaries, Pirates, and Sovereigns: State-Building and Extraterritorial Violence in Early Modern Europe* (1994); Percy, *Mercenaries: The History of a Norm in International Relations* (2007); France (ed.), *Mercenaries and Paid Men: The Mercenary Identity in the Middle Ages* (2008).
4 Thomson, *Mercenaries, Pirates, and Sovereigns*, 3.

how changing perceptions of the legitimacy and utility of private force can help to explain that evolution. This discussion focuses on the *perceived* legitimacy of private military actors, and does not attempt to assess their actual legitimacy on the basis of some moral, political and/or legal criteria. In other words, the notion of legitimacy is used in this chapter in a descriptive rather than a normative sense.[5] This is appropriate as it is the *perception* of illegitimacy that can influence the responses of states and the international media, and this in turn can hinder the success of the private military actors themselves.

Private force in twelfth- to seventeenth-century Europe

Foreign, independent and profit-motivated fighters – known in common parlance as mercenaries[6] – were widespread in Europe between the twelfth and seventeenth centuries. These individuals freely sold their military services to the highest bidder on the international stage. Some mercenaries joined together to offer a collective form of military service known as 'free companies'. Perhaps the earliest example was the Grand Catalan Company hired by the Byzantine Emperor to fight the Turks around 1300.[7] Free companies played a crucial role in the Hundred Years' war of 1337–1453, and continued to provide military services on the European market for some time thereafter. Far from being accepted as legitimate actors on the international stage, these companies gained notoriety as quasi-criminal, loosely organised bands whose members often behaved reprehensibly whilst performing their contracts and then worked for themselves pillaging Europe in between formal employment.[8] Fowler notes that the free companies were 'an affront to order'[9] and 'one of the major problems facing those responsible for government and the rule of law in western Europe'.[10]

In Renaissance Italy, instead of hiring free companies, the northern city-states contracted with independent commanders known as *condottieri*

---

5 For a discussion of legitimacy in the normative sense, see Buchanan, *Justice, Legitimacy and Self-Determination: Moral Foundations for International Law* (2004).

6 The term 'mercenary' is used in the first two sections of this chapter in a non-technical and non-legal sense to refer to any foreign, independent and profit-motivated fighter. The legal definition of a mercenary, on the other hand, is discussed in the third section of this chapter, and in greater detail in the first section of Chapter 5.

7 Mockler, *The Mercenaries* (1969), 9–10.

8 Mallett, *Mercenaries and Their Masters* (1974), 27–9.

9 Fowler, 'War and Change in Late Medieval France and England', in Fowler (ed.), *The Hundred Years War* (1971), 171.

10 Fowler, *Medieval Mercenaries* (2001), vol. I, 1.

to supply specific numbers of troops for particular military services.[11] Although the *condottieri* were less problematic than the free companies in other parts of Europe, the system nonetheless caused periodic difficulties for the Italian city-states, particularly during the pause in the Hundred Years' War between 1360 and 1369.[12]

The use of private fighters enabled rulers to further foreign policy interests abroad without having to accept responsibility if their endeavours failed. This contributed much to rulers' political, territorial and economic goals, at little cost to themselves.[13] Nonetheless, this international system of marketised force had serious practical shortcomings, as the *ad hoc* delegation of violence to freelance mercenaries led to a lack of legitimate control over force – that is, a lack of control imposed by the entity that was understood to have the authority to wage war, be it a sovereign state, a king, a prince or even the Pope.[14] The practice of privateering, whereby rulers authorised private naval actors to carry out hostilities at sea, led to organised piracy. Mercenaries' activities overseas threatened to drag their home states into foreign conflicts to which they were not a party. Empowered mercantile companies used violence against each other and even against their home states.[15] In short, states and other rulers proved unable to control the independent fighters that they hired, and then simply disclaimed responsibility when their private endeavours produced negative consequences. The post-Westphalian rise of the nation-state did not immediately reverse this trend, leading to a situation that Thomson describes as 'probably the closest the modern state system has come to experiencing real anarchy'.[16]

The first shift away from mercenary use: state troop exchange

Between the fifteenth and seventeenth centuries, many European rulers addressed these practical problems of control by formally integrating foreign fighters into their standing armies and buying or leasing army units from other rulers. As Percy explains, '[t]he challenges posed by independent companies of mercenaries were overcome by bringing the use of force under centralised control and creating more permanent armies'.[17] The practice of states officially buying and leasing troops from other states

---

11 Mockler, *The Mercenaries*, 44.   12 Mallett, *Mercenaries and Their Masters*, 27.

13 Thomson, *Mercenaries, Pirates, and Sovereigns*, 21, 32–3, 43, 84–8; Avant, *The Market for Force: The Consequences of Privatizing Security* (2005), 27.

14 See Percy, *Mercenaries: The History of a Norm*, 57.

15 Thomson, *Mercenaries, Pirates, and Sovereigns*, 67–8.   16 *Ibid.*, 43.

17 Percy, *Mercenaries: The History of a Norm*, 83.

became so common that, by the eighteenth century, foreigners constituted between 25 and 60 per cent of regular European standing armies.[18] Accompanying this increase in official state-based troop exchange was a decrease in states' use of independent mercenaries hired on the open market. In fact, by the eighteenth century, independent mercenaries freely selling their services to the highest bidder had virtually disappeared.[19] This broad shift in practice towards the formal exchange of foreign fighters within state-based institutions eliminated many of the practical problems of control and accountability that had been associated with the independent mercenaries of earlier years.

The second shift away from mercenary use: citizen armies

It was not until the nineteenth century, however, that states shunned the use of foreign fighters altogether by ending the official exchange of military units with other states. The Napoleonic Wars separated the 'wars of kings' from the 'wars of people', and this led to a remarkable change in the conduct of European warfare as states began to fight wars using exclusively their own citizens. As Avant observes, '[m]ercenaries went out of style in the nineteenth century . . . It became common sense that armies should be staffed with citizens.'[20]

A combination of material and ideational changes had preceded the French Revolution and laid the groundwork for the shift towards citizen armies.[21] Material changes arose from the pressures of population growth, which required territorial expansion and organisational and technological changes in military institutions. Armies of nationalistic soldiers fighting for their country gradually came to be seen as more effective than armies of mercenaries.[22] Ideational changes arose from Enlightenment ideas which motivated military and constitutional reformers to advocate

18 Mockler, *The New Mercenaries*, 8.
19 Percy, *Mercenaries: The History of a Norm*, ch. 3.
20 Avant, 'From Mercenaries to Citizen Armies: Explaining Change in the Practice of War' (2000) 54(1) *International Organization* 41, 41.
21 The term 'citizen army' is sometimes used to refer to an army of conscripts and at other times to an army of citizens fighting for their own country (even if they volunteer). For the purposes of this discussion, the latter definition is more important.
22 E. Cohen, *Citizens and Soldiers: The Dilemmas of Military Service* (1985); Gooch, *Armies in Europe* (1980); Posen, 'Nationalism, the Mass Army, and Military Power' (1993) 18(2) *International Security* 80; McNeill, *The Pursuit of Power: Technology, Armed Force, and Society Since AD 1000* (1982); Rothenberg, *The Art of Warfare in the Age of Napoleon* (1977).

citizen armies as part of a new relationship between citizen and state. No longer were the armed forces regarded solely as a 'military' institution; they were now regarded as central to the construction and consolidation of national identities. The new connection between citizen and state meant that it was increasingly considered dishonourable for states to hire foreign soldiers and, conversely, for soldiers to serve in a foreign army.[23] States also had to accept some responsibility to control private violence emanating from their territory, since citizens were increasingly considered representatives of their home state. The international law of neutrality thus developed, which encouraged states to prevent their citizens from serving in foreign armies and thereby helped to dry up the supply of private foreign fighters.[24]

The practice of hiring foreign fighters was clearly delegitimised by the nineteenth century, and states ceased buying or leasing troops from other states.[25] In addition, states moved to prohibit foreign recruitment in state territory, and many passed municipal neutrality laws prohibiting the enlistment of their citizens in foreign armies. Britain was the last major power to shun the use of foreign fighters, thereby signifying the general acceptance of a new paradigm of international warfare and paving the way for the nationalistic World Wars of the twentieth century.

Private force in the twentieth century

Private, profit-motivated military participation in foreign conflicts was relatively infrequent for several decades into the twentieth century, as the

---

23 Thomson, *Mercenaries, Pirates, and Sovereigns*; Avant, 'From Mercenaries to Citizen Armies', 45; Leander, 'Drafting Community: Understanding the Fate of Conscription' (2004) 30(4) *Armed Forces & Society* 571; Mockler, *The New Mercenaries*, 6–7; Avant and Sigelman, 'Private Security and Democracy: Lessons from the US in Iraq' (2010) 19(2) *Security Studies* 230.

24 See Convention Respecting the Rights and Duties of Neutral Powers and Persons in Case of War on Land (adopted 18 October 1907, entered into force 26 January 1910), 205 Consol TS 299, Arts. 4–6. The German delegation to the Hague Conference of 1907 put forward a proposal to take neutrality law one step further by prohibiting belligerent states from accepting the service of foreigners, but that proposal was rejected: see de Bustamente, 'The Hague Convention Concerning the Rights and Duties of Neutral Powers and Persons in Land Warfare' (1908) 2 *AJIL* 95, 100.

25 Avant also highlights the importance of domestic politics and path dependency in accounting for the fact that different countries shifted towards citizen armies at different times: see Avant, 'From Mercenaries to Citizen Armies', 67. Percy argues that mercenaries were considered inherently objectionable because they fought for financial gain rather than for a cause: see Percy, *Mercenaries: The History of a Norm*, chs. 4–5.

citizen army was the clear model for international warfare. That model came under serious challenge, however, in the Spanish Civil War (1936–9) when a large number of foreigners known as 'volunteers' fought in the International Brigade for ideological reasons.[26] Like mercenaries in other conflicts, the volunteers in the Spanish Civil War were foreign to the conflict and posed serious problems of control and accountability because they were not part of the regular armed forces of any state. These factors led virtually every European government to take positive action to deter volunteer recruitment. Nonetheless, the volunteers did not attract the same degree of moral opprobrium as mercenaries had attracted in other conflicts. The international community appeared to consider profit-motivated mercenaries to be more morally problematic than ideologically motivated volunteers, despite the fact that both actors were foreign to the conflicts in which they fought and operated outside formal state control.[27]

Foreign, independent and profit-motivated fighters re-entered the spotlight during Africa's post-colonial wars of the 1960s, this time associated with the lone mercenary 'thug' who lacks morals and restraint and who is motivated solely by personal profit. The most notable examples were Les Affreux ('The Terrible Ones'), who included the infamous Irishman 'Mad' Mike Hoare and Frenchman Bob Denard.[28] Mercenaries suppressed national liberation movements and directly challenged nascent state regimes in Africa, and even fought against the UN during its operation in Congo (1960–4),[29] provoking widespread disgust in the international community – a reaction Mockler notes had become 'almost instinctive'.[30] In 1977, states incorporated their abhorrence for mercenaries into international humanitarian law through Article 47 of the First Additional Protocol to the Geneva Conventions (Protocol I), which denies

---

26 Although commonly labelled 'volunteers', many of these individuals were in fact paid for their military service. The crucial point is that they were motivated by political ideals rather than profit.

27 See A. V. W. Thomas and A. J. Thomas Jr, 'International Legal Aspects of the Civil War in Spain, 1936–1939', in Falk (ed.), *The International Law of Civil War* (1971); Brownlie, 'Volunteers and the Law of War and Neutrality' (1956) 5 *ICLQ* 570; Burmester, 'The Recruitment and Use of Mercenaries in Armed Conflicts' (1978) 72 *AJIL* 37, 38.

28 Singer, 'War, Profits, and the Vacuum of Law: Privatised Military Firms and International Law' (2004) 42 *Columbia Journal of Transnational Law* 521, 527.

29 Cassese, 'Mercenaries: Lawful Combatants or War Criminals?' (1980) 40 *Zeitschrift für ausländisches öffentliches Recht und Völkerrecht* 1.

30 Mockler, *The New Mercenaries*, 7.

mercenaries the right to prisoner-of-war status.[31] Also in 1977, the Organization of African Unity (OAU) concluded a regional convention which criminalised mercenarism in Africa.[32] Yet, despite repeatedly denouncing mercenaries during the 1960s and 1970s, the international community failed to establish a broad prohibition of mercenarism in international law.[33]

The modern private security industry emerged in the early 1990s. Singer argues that three converging dynamics can largely account for the rapid growth and consolidation of the industry at that time.[34] First, the end of the Cold War (and, on a local level, the end of apartheid in South Africa) led states to downsize their armed forces, and this released a flood of professional soldiers available for hire, many with little to offer on the open market but their military skills.[35] Secondly, the increase in the supply of military skills coincided with an increase in the demand for those skills on the private market. As superpower support diminished in various parts of the world, many weak states collapsed into civil war, and embattled governments sought private outside assistance to restore and maintain security.[36] Non-state actors operating in those states, such as private corporations and humanitarian groups, also sought private security services to guard installations and personnel. At the same time, demand for private security came from militarily strong states seeking to develop leaner, more efficient and more flexible national forces by focusing on core capabilities and outsourcing non-core services to the private sector. Kinsey also notes that the growing technical complexity of military equipment created a strong need for specialist civilian contractors to provide maintenance and support, due to the difficulty of developing

---

31 First Additional Protocol to the Geneva Conventions of 12 August 1949, and relating to the Protection of Victims of International Armed Conflicts (adopted 8 June 1977, entered into force 7 December 1979), 1125 UNTS 3.

32 Convention of the OAU for the Elimination of Mercenarism in Africa (adopted 3 July 1977, entered into force 22 April 1985) OAU Doc. CM/433/Rev.L.Annex 1.

33 For a more detailed discussion of international mercenary law, see Chapter 5, section 5.1.

34 Singer, 'Outsourcing War', *Foreign Affairs* (1 March 2005); see also Avant, *Market for Force*, 30–8.

35 For statistics about the downsizing of armed forces from the late 1980s to 2003, see Bonn International Center for Conversion, *Global Disarmament, Demilitarization and Demobilization* (2003).

36 In some regions, the number of conflict zones and the incidence of civil wars doubled: see Seybold, 'Major Armed Conflicts', in *Stockholm International Peace Research Institute Yearbook 2000*, 15–75.

and retaining the relevant skills in the military.[37] Thirdly, Singer argues that perhaps the most important factor leading up to the rise of the private security industry was the neo-liberal revolution that had taken place during the preceding decades – that is, the normative shift towards the marketisation of the public sphere.[38]

The private security industry burst into the international spotlight in the mid-1990s when the South African firm Executive Outcomes (EO) and the London-based firm Sandline International[39] provided offensive combat services to the governments of Angola and Sierra Leone. These companies' operations proved crucial in quelling hostilities and compelling the rebels in each country to negotiate respective settlements. The impressive military capabilities of EO and Sandline, combined with their readiness to take on messy tasks of intervention that developed states and multilateral institutions were unable or unwilling to tackle, led some commentators to suggest that PMSCs could play a key role in helping to end otherwise intractable civil conflicts.[40] Supporters of the industry further proposed that PMSCs could undertake peacekeeping operations to assist governments of developing countries.[41] Even former UN Secretary-General Kofi Annan admitted that he had seriously considered hiring a private firm to assist with the 1994 Rwandan crisis.[42]

---

37 Kinsey, *Corporate Soldiers and International Security: The Rise of Private Military Companies* (2006), 96–7.

38 Singer, *Corporate Warriors: The Rise of the Privatized Military Industry*, updated edn (2008), 49–70; see also Avant, *Market for Force*, 30–8; Shearer, *Private Armies and Military Intervention* (1998), 26–34.

39 Sandline was registered in the Bahamas but had its head office in the UK.

40 See, e.g., 'We're the Good Guys These Days', *Economist* (29 July 1995) 32; Brooks, 'Help for Beleaguered Peacekeepers', *Washington Post* (2 June 2003); Brooks, 'Write a Cheque, End a War' (2000) 6 *Conflict Trends*; Mallaby, 'Think Again: Renouncing Use of Mercenaries Can Be Lethal', *Washington Post* (5 June 2001); see also Shearer, *Private Armies and Military Intervention*.

41 See, e.g., Mallaby, 'Mercenaries Are No Altruists, But They Can Do Good', *Washington Post* (4 June 2001); Fidler and Catan, 'Private Military Companies Pursue the Peace Divide', *Financial Times* (23 July 2003); see also UN Commission on Human Rights, 'Report on the Question of the Use of Mercenaries as a Means of Violating Human Rights and Impeding the Exercise of the Right of Peoples to Self-Determination' (20 February 1997), UN Doc. E/CN4/1997/24, 19–20.

42 Annan ultimately decided against that option, declaring that 'the world may not be ready to privatise peace': see Ditchley Foundation lecture (26 June 1998); see also Human Rights Committee Executive Committee, 'Operationalizing the "Ladder of Options"' (27 June 2000), UN Doc. EC/50/SCINF.4. On the use of PMSCs by the United Nations, see Østensen, *Outsourcing Peace?: The United Nations' Use of Private Security and Military Companies* (2009); Patterson, *Privatising Peace: A Corporate Adjunct to United Nations Peacekeeping and Humanitarian Operations* (2009).

It soon became clear, however, that there remained strong international opposition to private, offensive warfare. As in the past, critics focused both on moral concerns about private force *per se* and on more pragmatic concerns relating to the way in which private force is utilised, particularly the lack of state control over PMSCs and the absence of adequate accountability mechanisms for PMSC misconduct.[43] Widespread media reports describing private security contractors as 'mercenaries' or 'dogs of war' tarnished the image of PMSCs,[44] and in 1998 South Africa enacted legislation severely restricting PMSC activities in a deliberate attempt to crush the local private security industry.[45] The provision of offensive combat services became bad for business, eventually leading both EO and Sandline to dissolve and deterring other companies from offering offensive combat services on the open market.[46] In the shadow of these relatively few instances of private offensive combat, a wider private security industry has burgeoned around the globe.

Lessons from history

This study has revealed two broad historical shifts against the use of foreign, independent and profit-motivated fighters. A closer examination of the reasons behind each shift illustrates how changing perceptions of the legitimacy and utility of private fighters can influence their prominence in the world system. The first historical shift took place between the fifteenth and seventeenth centuries as rulers tried to bring independent fighters under greater state control. Whilst this shift was largely a functional attempt by states to minimise the practical problems of control and accountability posed by freelance mercenaries, it also had a normative dimension: the independent mercenaries were seen as morally problematic *per se* because they fought for their own interests rather than for the legitimate sovereign. The functional and normative objections were

---

43 See, e.g., Musah and Fayemi (eds.), *Mercenaries: An African Security Dilemma* (2000); Silverstein, *Private Warriors* (2000).

44 See, e.g., 'Papua New Guinea Hires Mercenaries', *Washington Times* (28 February 1997); Waugh, '"Mercenaries as Peacekeepers" Plan under Fire', *Independent* (14 February 2002); Adams, 'Straw to Back Controls over British Mercenaries', *Financial Times* (2 August 2002); van Niekerk, 'Africa's Diamond Dogs of War', *Observer* (13 August 1995); Pech and Beresford, 'Corporate Dogs of War Grow Fat in Africa', *Guardian Weekly* (26 June 1997).

45 Regulation of Foreign Military Assistance Act (1998) No. 18912.

46 EO dissolved in 1999 and Sandline dissolved in 2004, but most commentators agree that both companies later re-emerged in different forms: see, e.g., Silverstein, *Private Warriors*, 165.

sometimes linked through the assumption that independent mercenaries would behave badly on the battlefield precisely because they were not attached to a just cause. The official state-based exchange of troops helped to address both the functional and the normative objections by bringing freelance fighters under formal state control and, at the same time, compelling them to fight for a cause that was widely perceived as legitimate.[47] The second shift in the nineteenth century saw states shun the use of foreign fighters altogether – even foreign fighters operating under tight state control – and embrace national armies made up exclusively of citizens, thus establishing the centrality of the citizen–state military relationship to the modern state system.

Throughout history, in making decisions about private force, states appear to have been influenced both by material factors and by the relevant standards of behaviour in existence at the time. These standards can be broadly labelled 'norms', a wide category which includes, but is not limited to, legal rules.[48] Changing perceptions of the legitimacy of private force can help to explain why states gradually stopped using private military services and why individuals gradually stopped offering such services. In other words, the associated stigma helped to discourage both the demand and the supply of private force, and this contributed to the eventual abandonment of private force by the nineteenth century. In some cases, normative reservations may have deterred states from using mercenaries even when private force appeared to be the best response in functional terms. Krasner acknowledges that 'a utilitarian calculus alone' struggles to explain the virtual absence of mercenaries from the present world system, since mercenaries would seem to be an optimal solution for states (such as the US) that have material and financial resources but lack citizens willing to fight.[49]

---

47 Percy, *Mercenaries: The History of a Norm*, 79.
48 There is broad agreement on the general definition of a norm: see, e.g., Philpott, *Revolutions in Sovereignty: How Ideas Shaped Modern International Relations* (2001), 21; Price, 'A Genealogy of the Chemical Weapons Taboo' (1995) 49(1) *International Organization* 73. However, theorists disagree fundamentally on what norms do. Structural realists argue that norms have no independent effect on state behaviour, whereas the other main streams of international relations theory agree that norms can influence state behaviour but disagree as to the nature and extent of that influence: see Percy, *Mercenaries: The History of a Norm*, ch. 1.
49 Krasner is a leading structural realist: see Krasner, 'Sovereignty: An Institutional Perspective', in Caporaso (ed.), *The Elusive State: International and Comparative Perspectives* (1989), 92.

Without understanding the influence of norms, it is difficult to understand the negative international reaction to the combat operations of EO and Sandline in the 1990s and the subsequent market shift in the private security industry away from the provision of offensive combat services.[50] Despite their apparent military successes, these companies triggered hostile reactions in their hiring states (such as Papua New Guinea), their home states (South Africa and the UK) and the broader international community. The continuing stigma attached to private offensive combat ultimately led to the dissolution of EO and Sandline, and deterred other companies from offering offensive combat services on the open market. Percy argues that 'the reaction to these companies, and the evolution of the industry from one that openly promoted the use of active combat to one that actively avoids it, demonstrates that the anti-mercenary norm is still influential'.[51]

The next section seeks to identify the primary components of this 'anti-mercenary norm' by identifying the main reasons *why* private force was considered morally objectionable in the past. It then discusses the extent to which those past objections have arisen in relation to modern PMSCs.

1.2 Objections to private force, mercenaries and modern PMSCs

Why are we instinctively averse to the idea of private warfare? The various definitions (both legal and non-legal) of a mercenary provide some clues as to the characteristics that render these individuals objectionable. These definitions usually include at least two basic criteria: that mercenaries are foreign or external to the conflict in which they fight, and that mercenaries are motivated to fight primarily by financial gain.[52] Some definitions add a third criterion: that mercenaries are not part of the armed forces of any state.[53] Far from being a mere checklist for assessing the status of a

---

50 For a detailed discussion of the influence of norms on the modern private security industry, see Percy, *Mercenaries: The History of a Norm*, ch. 7.

51 *Ibid.*, 207.

52 For non-legal definitions of a mercenary see, e.g., Burmester, 'The Recruitment and Use of Mercenaries in Armed Conflicts', 37; Thomson, *Mercenaries, Pirates, and Sovereigns*, 26; Musah and Fayemi (eds.), *Mercenaries*, 16; Singer, *Corporate Warriors*, 41; Mockler, *The Mercenaries*, ch. 1; 'Report of the Ad Hoc Committee on the Drafting of an International Convention Against the Recruitment, Use, Financing and Training of Mercenaries' (June 1982), UN Doc. A/37/43. For the international legal definition of a mercenary, see Protocol I, Art. 47.

53 See, e.g., Hampson, 'Mercenaries: Diagnosis Before Proscription' (1991) 3 *Netherlands Yearbook of International Law* 1, 5–6; Protocol I, Art. 47(e).

particular fighter, these criteria are in fact indicative of deeper objections to private force. Three such objections are particularly common: first, private military actors do not fight for an appropriate cause; secondly, they undermine democracy by fighting outside the citizen–state military relationship; and, thirdly, they are not subject to adequate control and accountability mechanisms. Whereas the first and second objections stem from the *status* of private fighters – that is, what these fighters *are* – the third objection stems from the *activities* of private fighters – that is, what these fighters actually *do* on the battlefield.

There are echoes of each of these objections in contemporary private security literature. Indeed, despite considerable investment in public relations, modern PMSCs have been dogged by accusations that they are merely mercenaries packaged in corporate form. PMSCs are fully aware that perceptions of their legitimacy are crucial to their commercial success, and they have worked hard to distance themselves from the mercenaries of past eras. They emphasise that they do not provide offensive combat services, that they work only for 'legitimate' clients such as states, NGOs and registered corporations, and that they work alongside and in co-operation with national armed forces. Many PMSCs belong to industry associations such as the British Association of Private Security Companies[54] and the International Peace Operations Association,[55] which have developed codes of conduct and which welcome a degree of formal regulation in the knowledge that it may improve business prospects.[56] Notwithstanding these efforts, the same basic objections have continued to impede the industry's quest to achieve full public acceptance. This section considers these three objections in turn.

Lack of attachment to a cause

The principal 'status' objection to private force stems from the idea that taking human life in warfare is only morally justified by some attachment

---

54 See www.bapsc.org.uk.   55 See www.ipoaworld.org/eng.
56 See de Nevers, '(Self) Regulating War?: Voluntary Regulation and the Private Security Industry' (2009) 18(3) *Security Studies* 479; de Nevers, 'The Effectiveness of Self-Regulation by the Private Military and Security Industry' (2010) 30(2) *Journal of Public Policy* 219; Ranganathan, 'Between Complicity and Irrelevance? Industry Associations and the Challenge of Regulating Private Security Contractors' (2010) 41(2) *Georgetown Journal of International Law*; Cockayne, Speers Mears, Cherneva, Gurin, Oviedo and Yaeger, *Beyond Market Forces: Regulating the Global Security Industry* (2009). Conversely, some opponents of the industry have argued that formal regulation would bestow unwarranted legitimacy on PMSCs: see, e.g., Musah and Fayemi (eds.), *Mercenaries*; Campaign Against Arms Trade, *Comments on the Green Paper on Private Military Companies* (August 2002).

to a cause bigger than oneself.[57] As the UK government explained in its 2002 Green Paper, 'there is a natural repugnance towards those who kill (or help kill) for money ... To encourage such activity seems contrary both to our values and to the way in which we order society.'[58] This objection is reflected in most definitions of a mercenary through the requirement that the individual be motivated to fight principally by financial gain. National soldiers are assumed to be motivated by patriotism rather than personal profit (although this assumption is perhaps questionable in an era when many soldiers join the army at least in part for the salary and benefits), and they are therefore assumed to be fighting for a cause bigger than themselves. Other participants in the conflict might be motivated by the ideological, political or religious goals of the group for which they fight, or they might be peacekeepers fighting for the goals and values of the UN or a regional body such as the African Union. Morally, it is generally considered more acceptable to fight for such causes than to fight for money. This provides some clues as to why the international community reacted with less aversion to the ideologically motivated foreign volunteers who fought in the Spanish Civil War than to the profit-motivated mercenaries who fought in post-colonial Africa. The volunteers were generally considered morally superior to the mercenaries because they were motivated to fight for a cause larger than themselves, even though both categories of fighters caused serious practical problems of control and accountability.[59]

The notion that individuals should fight for a cause also helps to explain why well-established and permanently integrated foreign forces, such as the French Foreign Legion[60] and the Brigade of Gurkhas in the British

---

57 See Percy, 'Morality and Regulation', in Chesterman and Lehnardt (eds.), *From Mercenaries to Market: The Rise and Regulation of Private Military Companies* (2007), 14–18. For a discussion of the difference between justifications and excuses in this context, see Lynch and Walsh, 'The Good Mercenary' (2000) 8(2) *Journal of Political Philosophy* 133, 139.

58 UK Foreign and Commonwealth Office Green Paper, 'Private Military Companies: Options for Regulation' (February 2002), para. 53.

59 Some commentators point out the unsatisfactory nature of this position, e.g. Lynch and Walsh note that there is little proof that 'organized violence centred on strong group identification is in itself morally better': see Lynch and Walsh, 'The Good Mercenary', 134; see also Percy, *Mercenaries: History of a Norm*, 54–7.

60 The French Foreign Legion was established in 1831 as a unit of foreign fighters, since foreigners were forbidden to enlist in the French Army after the July Revolution of 1830. Today, the Legion comprises around 60 per cent French citizens and continues to play an important role in the French army as an elite unit: see www.legion-etrangere.com; Porch, *The French Foreign Legion: A Complete History* (1991).

army,[61] are generally considered morally superior to mercenaries. Indeed, during discussions at the diplomatic conference that led to the creation of Protocol I, states made it clear that they did not consider permanently incorporated foreigners to be mercenaries.[62] Far from roaming around the world fighting for foreign clients on an *ad hoc* basis, French Legionnaires and Gurkhas are assumed to have permanently adopted the goals and values of France and Britain as their own. They are long-term employees of the state regardless of whether the state is at war, and in the case of Legionnaires after a certain period of service they are offered French citizenship.[63] Thus, although they may not be citizens of a party to the conflict, these fighters are not 'external' in the same way as a freelance foreign fighter who is recruited especially to fight in a particular conflict.[64]

In addition to arguing that individuals who fight for money rather than a cause are morally inferior *per se*, some commentators object to mercenaries' lack of a cause on a more instrumental level. According to this argument, financially motivated fighters might be more likely to misbehave than national soldiers precisely because the former are not motivated to fight for a cause. Other commentators argue, however, that there is no reason to assume that a financially motivated fighter is more likely to misbehave than a patriotically motivated one; in fact, in some cases the reverse might be true.[65] In states engaged in civil wars, foreign PMSC personnel might be more professional than local soldiers and might encourage proper behaviour in local forces.[66] Sierra Leone's national army in the 1990s, for example, consisted largely of untrained, underpaid and

61 The Brigade of Gurkhas is the collective term for British army units that are composed of Nepalese soldiers: see www.army.mod.uk/brigade_of_gurkhas/index.htm; Parker, *The Gurkhas: The Inside Story of the World's Most Feared Soldiers* (2005).

62 See *Official Records of the Diplomatic Conference on the Reaffirmation and Development of International Humanitarian Law Applicable in Armed Conflicts, Geneva (1974–1976)* (1978), paras. 99–100.

63 Thomson, *Mercenaries, Pirates, and Sovereigns*, 91; Percy, *Mercenaries: History of a Norm*, 61. Members of the Gurkhas and the French Foreign Legion are also considered more acceptable because they operate under tighter state control than freelance fighters, as will be discussed below.

64 Burmester, 'The Recruitment and Use of Mercenaries in Armed Conflicts', 38; Musah and Fayemi (eds.), *Mercenaries*, 16.

65 See, e.g., Sandoz, 'Private Security and International Law', in Cilliers and Mason (eds.), *Peace, Profit, or Plunder: The Privatisation of Security in War-Torn African Societies* (1999), 210.

66 Avant, *Market for Force*, 60–1; Zarate, 'The Emergence of a New Dog of War: Private International Security Companies, International Law, and the New World Disorder' (1998) 34 *Stanford Journal of International Law* 75, 150–2.

underage soldiers, many addicted to drugs and alcohol, and some even known to moonlight as rebel troops.[67]

The objection that it is morally wrong to kill or fight for money also arises in relation to modern PMSCs which, as private corporations, are assumed to be motivated by profit rather than by a cause. Whilst this objection is highly pertinent to the offensive combat PMSCs of the 1990s, it does not apply as strongly to PMSCs that provide only peripheral support services (such as cooking food for soldiers) or security services that are not directly linked to ongoing hostilities. In light of these considerations, it is perhaps unsurprising that industry representatives promote themselves as 'security' contractors rather than 'military' contractors. The latter term tends to evoke images of killing on the battlefield, and such images are morally problematic when linked to a profit-driven corporation rather than a national soldier fighting for his or her country.[68]

Fighting outside the citizen–state military relationship

The second common 'status' objection to mercenaries is that they might undermine democracy because they fight outside the context of the citizen–state relationship.[69] According to this argument, which can be traced at least as far back as Machiavelli, the citizen army may constrain the state from going to war. Conversely, the use of foreign mercenaries may impede the development of a healthy relationship between citizen and state, and may even corrupt the citizens themselves if mercenaries fight without regard for the public good. Thus, in order to prevent tyranny, the army should be recruited from and at one with the people.[70] In a related objection, private fighters are often said to threaten democratic control over force because they are not part of the national armed forces of the hiring state, since states' democratic mechanisms to control warfare are generally directed towards their national militaries.

---

67 Venter, 'Sierra Leone's Mercenary War Battle for the Diamond Fields' (1995) 28 *International Defence Review* 65, 67; Rubin, 'An Army of One's Own' (February 1997) *Harper's Magazine* 44, 49.

68 See Pfanner, 'Interview with Andrew Bearpark' (2006) 88(863) *International Review of the Red Cross* 449, 451; www.bapsc.org.uk; see also the discussion of terminology in the fourth section of this chapter.

69 See Percy, 'Morality and Regulation', 18–22; Krahmann, *States, Citizens and the Privatisation of Security* (2010).

70 Grundy, 'On Machiavelli and the Mercenaries' (1968) 6(3) *Journal of Modern African Studies* 295.

These ideas were central to the nineteenth-century shift towards the exclusive use of citizen armies, as discussed in the first section of this chapter. Most definitions of a mercenary reflect these ideas through the inclusion of two criteria: that the individual be foreign to the conflict in which he or she fights, and that the individual not be part of the armed forces of a state party to the conflict.

The objection to individuals fighting outside the democratic citizen–state military relationship might help to explain why members of the French Foreign Legion and Gurkhas are often regarded with some suspicion, even though they are integrated into the French and British forces and are assumed to have adopted the goals of France and Britain as their own. Equally, this objection might help to explain why the Netherlands abandoned its own foreign legion (the Koninklijk Nederlandsch–Indische Leger (KNIL), or Royal Netherlands–Indian Army), which was created in 1830 around the same time as the French Foreign Legion but which ceased recruiting foreigners (with the exception of Dutch colonials) around 1900.

Various permutations of these arguments are evident in the contemporary literature on the private security industry. For example, the 2002 UK Green Paper on Private Military Companies argues that '[i]n a democracy it seems natural that the state should be defended by its own citizens since it is their state'.[71] During the 1990s, failing governments in Sierra Leone, Angola and Papua New Guinea hired foreign PMSCs to assist in fighting civil wars, and many commentators feared that this might threaten indigenous police and military forces, which are crucial to the social contract.[72] Both Avant and Singer highlight the reduction of democratic control over war, arguing that the use of PMSCs instead of national militaries may make it easier for states to go to war and may hide the true costs of war from the public.[73] Indeed, it is easier to sustain an unpopular war when it is private contractors who are coming home in body bags rather than national troops.[74] Avant and Sigelman predict that the shift away from a citizen-based army towards a market-based system 'should chip away at demands by legislative institutions for a check on policy and by citizens

---

71 UK Green Paper, para. 53.
72 See, e.g., *ibid.*, paras. 46–9; 1997 UN Mercenaries Report; Leander, 'The Market for Force and Public Security: The Destabilizing Consequences of Private Military Companies' (2005) 42 *Journal of Peace Research* 605, 615–18; Holmquist, 'Private Security Companies: The Case for Regulation' (2005), 15–17.
73 Singer, *Corporate Warriors*, 206–15; Avant, *Market for Force*, 155–6.
74 Walker and Whyte, 'Contracting Out War? Private Military Companies, Law and Regulation in the United Kingdom' (2005) 54 *ICLQ* 651.

for transparency, and it should make securing public consent to use force easier'.[75] Singer also points out that PMSCs can seriously disrupt the civil–military balance and thus threaten domestic stability.[76] In extreme cases, PMSCs may even act as foreign policy proxies for governments wishing to intervene in foreign conflicts unofficially, just as the American firm MPRI 'undoubtedly functioned as an instrument of US policy' in the Balkans conflict of the 1990s.[77]

Fighting outside state control

In addition to objections based on the status of private fighters as morally problematic *per se*, critics often raise more pragmatic objections to the *activities* of these individuals in armed conflict. One common contention is that private fighters might be more likely than national soldiers to desert or otherwise misbehave in the field. This is sometimes linked to the first 'status' objection outlined above, in the sense that private fighters might misbehave precisely because they are not attached to a cause. Yet there is also a more practical explanation for this objection: private fighters are not subject to the same mechanisms of state control and accountability as national soldiers. The historical overview in the first section of this chapter illustrated how the lack of state control over independent mercenaries caused serious practical problems in the past, eventually leading states to incorporate foreign fighters into their national armies. In a similar vein, contemporary commentators have raised concerns about the lack of state control over PMSCs.

The hiring state's lack of control over PMSC activities

When states outsource military and security tasks to PMSCs, the screening, selection and training of individual contractors shift into the hands of the firm, together with the locus of judgment on how operations are carried out on the ground. Commercial subcontracting practices exacerbate this loss of hiring state control. Individuals can work as independent contractors for PMSCs, which are themselves subcontractors of larger companies, which are subcontractors of prime contractors, which may have been hired by a government agency. These convoluted relationships

---

75 Avant and Sigelman, 'Private Security and Democracy', 242.
76 Singer, *Corporate Warriors*, 191–205.
77 UK Green Paper, para. 50; see also Silverstein, *Private Warriors*, 145; Zarate, 'The Emergence of a New Dog of War', 148; Singer, *Corporate Warriors*, 48. MPRI's operations in the Balkans are discussed in the fourth section of this chapter.

often mean that the government has no real control over the PMSC personnel who are performing military and security tasks on its behalf.[78]

The hiring state's lack of control over PMSCs can lead to inadequate screening and training standards for contractors. For example, following the 2003 invasion of Iraq, the US government contracted the American firm CACI to provide a number of interrogators to work at Abu Ghraib prison, as well as contracting the firm Titan to provide interpreters. An official report into the Abu Ghraib prisoner abuse scandal of 2003–4 found that employees of both CACI and Titan had participated in the abuse.[79] It further emerged that approximately 35 per cent of the contract interrogators working at the prison lacked formal interrogation training, and their hiring firm CACI had failed to conduct adequate background investigations prior to their employment.[80] Similarly, in 2009, serious deficiencies in contractor qualifications and training surfaced in relation to ArmorGroup security guards hired by the US in Afghanistan and Iraq.[81] A US Senate report on the ArmorGroup contract to guard the American embassy in Kabul revealed that a large proportion of the guards could not speak English and had no security training or experience, leaving the US embassy in Kabul vulnerable to a possible attack.[82] Investigations into ArmorGroup contractors working at the embassy also revealed numerous incidents of sexual misconduct, which one former company manager attributed to a failure to screen potential employees.[83] In an unrelated

78 See US Commission on Wartime Contracting Hearing, 'Subcontracting: Who's Minding the Store?' (26 July 2010); Isenberg, 'A Fistful of Contractors' (2004), 16.

79 Fay, 'Investigation of the Abu Ghraib Detention Facility and 205th Military Intelligence Brigade' (2004). A class action brought against CACI and Titan under the Alien Tort Statute charged the companies with torture and other heinous and illegal acts committed against Iraqi detainees. On 11 September 2009, in a 2–1 decision, a panel of the Court of Appeals for the District of Columbia affirmed the dismissal of all claims against Titan and, reversing the decision of the District Court, dismissed all claims against CACI: see *Saleh* v. *Titan*, 580 F 3d 1.

80 See also Schooner, 'Contractor Atrocities at Abu Ghraib: Compromised Accountability in a Streamlined, Outsourced Government' (2005) 16 *Stanford Law and Policy Review* 549, 556–7; Gibson and Shane, 'Contractors Act as Interrogators', *Baltimore Sun* (4 May 2004); Borger, 'Cooks and Drivers Were Working as Interrogators', *Guardian* (7 May 2004).

81 ArmorGroup was acquired by the Danish company G4S plc in April 2008: see www.armorgroup.com and www.g4s.com.

82 Senate Committee on Homeland Security and Governmental Affairs, Subcommittee on Contracting Oversight, 'New Information about the Guard Force Contract at the US Embassy in Kabul' (June 2009).

83 Project on Government Oversight, Letter to Secretary of State Hillary Clinton Regarding US Embassy in Kabul (1 September 2009); 'Ex-Managers: Security Firm Cut Corners at Embassy', *New York Times* (11 September 2009); Sherman and DiDomenico, 'The

incident in Baghdad in August 2009, an ArmorGroup security guard allegedly shot and killed two fellow guards and wounded at least one Iraqi. It subsequently emerged that the guard had a criminal record and was described by one co-worker as 'a walking time-bomb', raising serious concerns about the company's vetting process.[84]

The reduction in hiring state control over PMSC activities can also create serious practical problems on the ground. PMSC personnel fall outside the military chain of command, and this can make it difficult to sort out lines of authority and communication. For PMSCs hired by the US, a civilian contracting officer is designated to administer and monitor the contract in the field, but he or she 'is not always colocated with the military commander or the contractor personnel and may not even be within the theater of operations'.[85] Moreover, the contracting officer is authorised only to monitor the details of contractual performance, and cannot modify the scope or size of the contract. This reflects a broader problem in that the contractual instrument provides little flexibility to adjust to changes in government objectives or practical conditions on the ground. This rigidity can pose a constant challenge for the hiring state as it seeks to maintain effective operations in a fluid conflict environment.[86]

The home state's lack of control over PMSC activities

In addition to reducing the hiring state's control over its military and security activities, the privatisation of security may reduce the ability of the PMSC's home state to control violence that emanates from its territory. This is particularly pertinent to states such as the US and the UK, in which most of the major PMSCs are based or incorporated. In many cases where a firm provides military services to a foreign actor, it shares skills learned in its home state's military in a transaction that its home state might want

Public Cost of Private Security in Afghanistan' (2009). A number of company guards and supervisors resigned or were fired in connection with the investigations: see Alexander, 'US Says 16 Guards Removed in Afghan Embassy Scandal', *New York Times* (10 September 2009); Cole, 'Firm Fires US Embassy Guards in Kabul', *Wall Street Journal* (5 September 2009).

84 'Briton Held in Iraq over Shooting', *BBC News* (10 August 2009); Haynes and Ford, 'Briton Facing Iraq Murder Trial on Probation for Gun Offence' (13 August 2009).

85 US Congressional Budget Office, 'Contractors' Support of US Operations in Iraq' (August 2008), 20 (references omitted); see also US Commission on Wartime Contracting, 'At What Cost? Contingency Contracting in Iraq and Afghanistan' (10 June 2009), 7–13; US Commission on Wartime Contracting Hearing, 'Reliance on Contingency Services Contracts: Where Is the Management and Oversight?' (19 April 2010).

86 Avant, *Market for Force*, 85.

to control.[87] Furthermore, if the PMSC wishes to provide services to one side in a foreign civil war, it must make a complex and highly political decision as to which party is the 'legitimate' government and is therefore entitled to request outside military assistance. The home state of a PMSC might prefer to handle such decisions itself in deciding whether to provide official military assistance.

Another potential concern for the home state of a PMSC is that the company's behaviour overseas may affect the state's reputation. Although most companies claim that they work only for legitimate clients such as governments, international organisations, NGOs and corporations, there have been reports of firms working for dictatorships, rebel groups, drug cartels and even radical jihadist groups.[88] In extreme cases, PMSC behaviour overseas could even implicate the home state in foreign conflicts to which it is not a party, particularly if other states interpret the company's behaviour to be effectively an act of the home state. There are reports from the seventeenth and eighteenth centuries of states being implicated in conflicts by virtue of private violence emanating from their territory.[89] In more recent times, some members of the British government were worried that the involvement of British firm Gurkha Security Guards in Sierra Leone in 1995 might be interpreted as British intervention.[90] There are also historical examples of empowered private actors using violence against each other and against other states with which their home states were at peace. Thomson cites one extreme case in which the British East India Company actually blockaded British troops in relation to a dispute over Indian territory.[91]

Close links between PMSCs and their home governments generally increase the likelihood that firms will act in line with international norms and with the national interest of their home state. In addition, states that are themselves significant consumers of PMSC services can provide strong market incentives for local companies to conform to foreign policy objectives. In the US, many of the same firms that sell military and security services to foreign clients also sell services to the US government – and the US government is an excellent customer. The desire to preserve their government contracts gives US firms a strong market incentive to

87 See *ibid.*, 143.
88 Singer, *Corporate Warriors*, 170, 180–2; Silverstein, *Private Warriors*.
89 Thomson, *Mercenaries, Pirates, and Sovereigns*, 43–68.
90 Vines, 'Gurkhas and the Private Security Business in Africa', in Cilliers and Mason (eds.), *Peace, Profit, or Plunder*, 128–30.
91 Thomson, *Mercenaries, Pirates, and Sovereigns*, 67.

conform to US foreign policy, even when working overseas for foreign actors.[92] US regulations supplement this market control. In other states, however, in the absence of significant governmental consumption and/or formal regulation of the local private security industry, the risk remains that company actions overseas might conflict with national interests. The scandal surrounding the actions of British company Sandline International in Sierra Leone, discussed in the fourth section of this chapter, illustrates this danger.

General lack of transparency in the private security industry

A more general concern is the lack of transparency in the private security industry. Transparency is fundamental to democratic practice as it allows informed action on the part of both citizens and governments. Yet, in many cases, there is no ongoing duty of disclosure on PMSCs to divulge information about their operational activities, and corporate confidentiality privileges often exempt company documents from freedom of information laws.[93] Estimates of the cost of the industry and the number of contractors working in a particular conflict can vary widely, and casualty figures routinely released by the military exclude private contractors, thus reducing information about the human costs of war.[94]

This lack of information impedes effective oversight of the private security industry and diminishes states' capacity to make informed and sound decisions about private force.[95] Avant and Sigelman explain:

> Because Congress has less information about contractors than troops, it has also been less able to control them. Using contractors avoids an important veto point and thus both speeds policy making and limits the number and variety of inputs into the policy process. Furthermore, because the use of PMSCs has garnered less attention than the use of troops, this tool has reduced the political costs of using force.[96]

Whilst Congress has taken steps to improve access to information about PMSCs in the US, the lack of transparency remains a serious problem.[97] Private security contracts have implications that go far beyond those

---

92 Zarate, 'The Emergence of a New Dog of War', 148; Avant, *Market for Force*, 146–57.
93 Singer, *Corporate Warriors*, 214.
94 Avant and Sigelman, 'Private Security and Democracy', 245.
95 Percy, *Regulating the Private Security Industry* (2006), 21.
96 Avant and Sigelman, 'Private Security and Democracy', 262.
97 See National Defense Authorization Act for FY 2009, S 3001, 110th Cong., 2nd Sess.; National Defense Authorization Act for FY 2010, HR 2647, 111th Cong., 1st Sess.; see also Avant and Sigelman, 'Private Security and Democracy', 253–4.

of other transactions, as they can entail the use of violence and can impact upon stability within a country or a region. The nature of the private security industry therefore demands a significantly *higher* level of transparency in order to facilitate informed decision-making about PMSCs and to enhance control and accountability in the industry.

Historically, mercenaries were considered less threatening when placed under state control. As in the past, contemporary objections to private security that are based on the lack of control and accountability might be resolved, or at least diminished, through greater state regulation aimed at controlling PMSC activities. In contrast, regulation cannot easily resolve the first two objections discussed above – PMSCs' lack of attachment to a cause and the fact that they fight outside the context of the citizen–state relationship – since those objections stem from the *status* of the companies as morally problematic actors *per se*.[98]

1.3 The spectrum of private military and security activity today

A broad spectrum of actors may be involved in the supply of military and security services, and these actors tend to attract varying degrees of social stigma. Mercenaries lie at one end of the spectrum, bearing the strongest social stigma, and national soldiers lie at the other end of the spectrum, perceived to be the most legitimate military actors in the international system. This section locates modern PMSCs on the spectrum of military/security service provision by reference to other actors such as mercenaries and national soldiers. This contextual analysis is particularly important since, unlike the terms 'mercenary' and 'armed forces', the term 'PMSC' and its variants[99] have no *legal* definition, and the designation of a particular entity as a PMSC carries no legal consequences in itself. The outer contours of the PMSC category are largely shaped by what PMSCs are *not* rather than what they are; most PMSC personnel are not mercenaries within the international legal definition (although some PMSC personnel may fall within non-legal conceptions of a mercenary), they are not volunteers, they are not soldiers working permanently for another state, and they are not national soldiers. Accordingly, this section delineates the PMSC category by reference to the broader spectrum of contemporary private military and security activity.

---

98 Percy, 'Morality and Regulation', 23.
99 Some commentators label all PMSCs 'private military companies' (PMCs), whilst others label all PMSCs 'private security companies' (PSCs), and still others distinguish between PMCs and PSCs. This terminology is discussed in the fourth section of this chapter.

Mercenaries

Mercenaries lie at the far end of the spectrum, as they generally bear the strongest social stigma. These individuals constituted a major problem in the African wars of decolonisation, but their activities today are more limited and sporadic. As discussed in the second section of this chapter, although there is some variation between the different definitions of a mercenary, there is general agreement that the term in its ordinary, non-legal sense refers to a foreign, independent and profit-motivated fighter.

Despite broad consensus on the general characteristics of a mercenary, it has proved difficult for states to translate this common understanding into a workable *legal* definition. Article 47 of Protocol I sets out the accepted international definition of a mercenary as any person who:

(a) Is specially recruited locally or abroad in order to fight in an armed conflict;

(b) Does, in fact, take a direct part in the hostilities;

(c) Is motivated to take part in the hostilities essentially by the desire for private gain and, in fact, is promised, by or on behalf of a Party to the conflict, material compensation substantially in excess of that promised or paid to combatants of similar ranks and functions in the armed forces of that Party;

(d) Is neither a national of a Party to the conflict nor a resident of territory controlled by a Party to the conflict;

(e) Is not a member of the armed forces of a Party to the conflict; and

(f) Has not been sent by a State which is not a Party to the conflict on official duty as a member of its armed forces.

Whilst this provision accurately captures the norm against mercenary use, discussed in the second section of this chapter, it constitutes a flawed *legal* definition as it creates a series of loopholes by which individuals can exclude themselves from the mercenary classification with relative ease.[100] Chapter 5 examines this definition in detail and considers how it applies to modern PMSC personnel.[101] One of the principal defects of the definition is that it focuses on the *motivation* of the individual; it identifies mercenaries not by reference to *what* they do, but *why* they do it. Yet human motives are highly complex. In many cases (including

---

100 Percy, 'Mercenaries: Strong Norm, Weak Law' (2008) 61(2) *International Organization* 367.
101 See Chapter 5, section 5.1.

national soldiers), monetary reward will be one of several factors motivating an individual to take part in a conflict, but it will rarely be the sole
or even the 'essential' motivation, and in any event motivation can be
extremely difficult to prove. Paragraphs (d) and (e) create further loopholes: where a state hires a foreign individual to fight in a conflict, it can
easily circumvent paragraph (d) by granting the individual citizenship, or
it can circumvent paragraph (e) by temporarily enrolling the individual
in its national military forces. The combination of these factors has led
to a general consensus that any mercenary who cannot exclude himself
from this definition 'deserves to be shot – and his lawyer with [him]'.[102]
Thus, many of the individuals who qualify as mercenaries as the term
is commonly understood in ordinary parlance – as foreign, independent
fighters who are motivated by profit – would not qualify as mercenaries
under the strict legal definition in Article 47 of Protocol I.

Private military and security companies

Further along the continuum of private force lies the broad category of
'private military and security companies'. This category encompasses a
wide range of firms providing services intricately linked to armed conflict, including Sandline and EO providing combat-ready battalions in
the 1990s, DynCorp providing military training and advice, Blackwater
providing armed security, and Brown & Roots providing military support, as discussed in the fourth section of this chapter. Some PMSCs also
work outside the context of armed conflict, but such activities are not the
primary focus of this book.

Many modern PMSC personnel cannot reasonably be described as
mercenaries, particularly those individuals who perform military support services like preparing food or doing laundry. Nonetheless, there is
undoubtedly some overlap between the PMSC and mercenary categories,
and many of the same objections tend to arise in relation to both. A
small number of PMSC personnel would probably fall within the legal
definition of a mercenary, as discussed in Chapter 5, and a larger number
would probably qualify as mercenaries as the term is generally understood
in common parlance.

---

102 Best, *Humanity in Warfare: The Modern History of the International Law of Armed
Conflicts* (1980), 375; see also Hampson, 'Mercenaries: Diagnosis Before Proscription',
29; Singer, 'War, Profits', 531; Kwakwa, 'The Current Status of Mercenaries in the Law of
Armed Conflict' (1990) 14(1) *Hastings International and Comparative Law Review* 67,
73–4.

That said, it is important to highlight certain differences between those PMSC personnel who might reasonably be labelled mercenaries, on the one hand, and the archetypal independent mercenaries such as those who fought in post-colonial Africa, on the other. First, unlike freelance mercenaries soliciting business in seedy African bars, modern PMSCs are registered corporations which operate above ground and which are bound to their home state in various official and unofficial ways.[103] For Zarate, this is crucial since 'state accountability is the key to distinguishing mercenaries from other combatants'.[104] The second commonly cited difference between PMSC personnel and mercenaries is the legitimacy of their clients. Whereas modern PMSCs claim to work only for legitimate clients such as governments, NGOs, corporations and the UN, '[m]ercenaries will sell their services to the highest bidder and are usually unconcerned about the nature of their clientele'.[105] The mercenaries of the 1960s and 1970s worked largely for ex-colonial powers in Africa, often against national liberation movements and sometimes against other developing countries; essentially, they represented racist, exploitative, colonial interests.[106] The third key distinguishing feature applies only to the combat PMSC personnel of the 1990s: those individuals generally enlisted in their client state's armed forces, and this helped to increase state control and accountability.[107]

Whatever the precise degree of overlap between mercenaries and PMSCs, it is clear that the latter category as a whole lies further along the spectrum of military/security activity as it is generally considered more legitimate than the former.

Volunteers

The next category along the spectrum consists of foreign fighters known as 'volunteers' who fight for political, religious or ideological reasons rather than for monetary reward. Perhaps the most well-known actors in this category are the foreigners who fought in the Spanish Civil War for ideological reasons.[108] More recent examples include the foreigners

---

103 See Percy, *Mercenaries: History of a Norm*, ch. 2.
104 Zarate, 'The Emergence of a New Dog of War', 124–5.
105 Percy, 'Morality and Regulation', 14.   106 See Cassese, 'Mercenaries'.
107 See Dinnen, May and Regan (eds.), *Challenging the State: The Sandline Affair in Papua New Guinea* (1997); UK Green Paper, para. 6; Zarate, 'The Emergence of a New Dog of War', 124.
108 The 1997 UN Mercenaries Report refers to voluntary service as 'altruistic voluntary enlistment', which cannot be considered criminal (para. 75).

who fought in the *mujahedeen* in Afghanistan and those who fought with the Bosnian forces in the Balkan conflict. Volunteers have generally borne less social stigma than mercenaries because they are motivated by a cause rather than by money, notwithstanding the fact that volunteers (like mercenaries) are external to the conflicts in which they fight and pose problems of control and accountability because they are not permanently integrated into the armed forces of a state party.[109]

Soldiers integrated into a foreign force

Still further along the spectrum lie individual soldiers who are foreign to a conflict but who are under state control permanently or almost permanently. This category includes members of the French Foreign Legion and the Gurkhas, who are permanently integrated into the armed forces of France and Britain respectively, as well as national soldiers who are on secondment to another force.[110] Although these actors are not citizens of a state party to the conflict, they are generally regarded as more legitimate than mercenaries. They are assumed to have adopted their employer state's goals and values as their own; indeed, they are employees of the state regardless of whether the state is at war, and after a certain period of service Legionnaires are even offered French citizenship.[111] Moreover, compared with volunteers fighting overseas on an *ad hoc* basis or joining the forces of another state for the duration of a particular conflict, French Legionnaires and Gurkhas operate under tighter and more long-term state control. These permanently integrated foreign fighters can still be controversial, however, as demonstrated in 1982 when Argentina protested to the government of Nepal that a battalion of Gurkha 'mercenaries' was being sent to the Falkland Islands.[112]

National soldiers fighting for their home state

Finally, national soldiers lie at the far end of the spectrum as the most legitimate military actors in contemporary international relations. National

109 Burmester, 'The Recruitment and Use of Mercenaries in Armed Conflicts', 37–41; Thomas and Thomas, 'International Legal Aspects of the Civil War in Spain'; Brownlie, 'Volunteers and the Law of War and Neutrality'.
110 During the discussions of the 1970s about mercenaries and international law, states made it clear that they did not consider permanently incorporated soldiers such as the French Foreign Legion and the Gurkhas to be mercenaries: see, e.g., *Official Records of the Diplomatic Conference, Geneva (1974–1976)*, paras. 99–100.
111 Thomson, *Mercenaries, Pirates, and Sovereigns*, 91.
112 See Marston, 'UK Materials in International Law' (1982) 53 *British Yearbook of International Law* 519.

soldiers are presumed to be motivated by some sense of patriotism rather than by profit, they fight in the context of the citizen–state military relationship, and they are subject to tight control and accountability mechanisms.

1.4 What are PMSCs and what do they do?

Having positioned modern PMSCs in the broader military and security context, this section critically examines the nature and activities of PMSCs themselves. This provides the final element of background to contextualise the legal analysis in the remainder of this book.

Terminology

Within the modern private security industry there has been an ongoing debate about terminology, which is linked both to functional considerations about the companies' activities and to normative considerations about the legitimacy of private force *per se*. This section begins by identifying and explaining the principal terminological approaches evident in the literature and outlining the reasons for the approach adopted in this book. When considering the question of terminology, it is important to bear in mind that the precise label given to a company has no legal consequences in itself, and it is preferable to focus upon the substantive analysis of the company's activities in armed conflict.

Some commentators divide the private security sector into two categories of private military companies (PMCs) and private security companies (PSCs).[113] This division is problematic, however, as there is no clear definition of the two terms and the line between them is unclear. Companies often perform different services under different contracts. DynCorp and Aegis, for example, provided protective security services in Afghanistan as well as military advisory services in Liberia.[114] Another difficulty with the PMC/PSC division is that in low-intensity conflicts lacking a clear frontline (such as Iraq and Colombia), it can be extremely difficult to distinguish between military and security actors. Private contractors providing mere 'security' can have a significant impact on the local conflict and can be exposed to combat threats.

---

113 See, e.g., UK Green Paper; Percy, *Mercenaries: History of a Norm*; Schreier and Caparini, *Privatising Security: Law, Practice and Governance of Private Military and Security Companies* (2005).

114 See O'Brien, 'What Should and What Should Not Be Regulated?', in Chesterman and Lehnardt (eds.), *From Mercenaries to Market*, 38–9.

For these reasons and for general convenience it is preferable to adopt a single term to encompass the entire industry. Some commentators and virtually all industry representatives use the term PSCs to encompass the entire industry.[115] Andrew Bearpark, director general of the British Association of Private Security Companies, explains this decision in the following terms:

> In the UK, we refer to private security companies rather than private military companies. It better expresses the wide range of services companies are offering, but it also obviously has to do with cultural reservations with the term private military companies, which may imply that services at the front lines in conflicts are included.[116]

Yet the term PSCs by itself does not adequately convey the military nature of many company services and the fact that many 'security' operations are conducted in the context of an armed conflict, where contractors can easily be drawn into combat.

For these reasons, some commentators prefer to use the term PMCs to encompass the entire industry. The editors of a leading 2007 book explain that they adopt this approach because

> semantically the term 'military' better captures the nature of these services as it points to the qualitative difference between firms operating in conflict zones in a military environment and 'security firms' that primarily guard premises in a stable environment.[117]

This approach is also unsatisfactory, however, as the term PMCs by itself does not adequately convey the full range of company services and the fact that companies often work for civilian clients instead of militaries.

The final terminological strand in the literature represents a combination of the above approaches. The International Committee of the Red

---

115 See, e.g., Avant, *Market for Force*; Holmquist, 'Private Security Companies'; Spearin, 'Private Security Companies and Humanitarians: A Corporate Solution to Securing Humanitarian Spaces?' (2001) 8(1) *International Peacekeeping* 20.

116 Pfanner, 'Interview with Andrew Bearpark', 451; see also www.bapsc.org.uk.

117 Chesterman and Lehnardt (eds.), *From Mercenaries to Market*, 3; but note that many of the contributing authors use the term PSCs in their other publications: see, e.g., Dickinson, 'Accountability of Private Security Contractors under International and Domestic Law' (2007) 11(31) *ASIL Insight*; Avant, *Market for Force*; Cockayne, *Commercial Security in Humanitarian and Post-Conflict Settings* (2006). Singer refers to 'private military firms': see Singer, *Corporate Warriors*.

Cross (ICRC) uses the single term PMSCs to encompass the entire industry but does not distinguish between companies within that category.[118] This reflects the traditional definitional approach of international humanitarian law, which focuses not on the label given to a particular group but rather on its actual activities, objectives and internal structures. The UN Working Group on the use of mercenaries as a means of violating human rights and impeding the exercise of the right of peoples to self-determination, which was established in 2005 to replace the prior mandate of the UN Special Rapporteur on the use of mercenaries, also adopts the term PMSCs.[119] The same terminology appears in the 2008 Montreux Document, which was produced by seventeen states as a result of an initiative launched jointly by Switzerland and the ICRC.[120] Paragraph 9(a) of the Montreux Document states:

> 'PMSCs' are private business entities that provide military and/or security services, irrespective of how they describe themselves. Military and security services include, in particular, armed guarding and protection of persons and objects, such as convoys, buildings and other places; maintenance and operation of weapons systems; prisoner detention; and advice to or training of local forces and security personnel.

This book adopts the same terminological approach, utilising the single term PMSCs to encompass the entire industry and then proceeding directly to the substantive analysis of the companies' activities. The term PMSCs is deliberately vague since the focus of the legal analysis ought to be on each company's activities rather than its title.

General nature of PMSCs

What, then, are PMSCs? Like other corporations, most PMSCs are registered corporate bodies with legal personalities, hierarchical structures,

---

118 See www.icrc.org.
119 See Report of the Working Group on the Use of Mercenaries as a Means of Violating Human Rights and Impeding the Exercise of the Right of Peoples to Self-Determination (2 July 2010), UN Doc. A/HRC/15/25.
120 Montreux Document on Pertinent International Legal Obligations and Good Practices for States Related to Operations of Private Military and Security Companies during Armed Conflict (17 September 2008), UN Doc. A/63/467-S/2008/636 ('Montreux Document'). The seventeen states were Afghanistan, Angola, Australia, Austria, Canada, China, France, Germany, Iraq, Poland, Sierra Leone, South Africa, Sweden, Switzerland, the UK, Ukraine and the US.

websites and public relations officials. Some are part of larger multi-national conglomerates with extensive economic interests, and their behaviour in one region can affect their reputation worldwide.[121] As service-orientated businesses in a global industry, PMSCs are generally capital-intensive with limited infrastructure. They utilise a flexible workforce, drawing on databases of individuals in order to assemble a suitable group of employees for each contract. Many PMSC employees are former military or security personnel, including some elite members of the special forces such as the Rangers, Delta Force and SEALs in the US and the Special Air Service in the UK.

Most of the PMSCs working in armed conflict are based or incorporated in militarily advanced countries. US-based PMSCs easily constitute the largest share of the global market, with a very high percentage of their revenues coming from US government contracts. In the Iraqi theatre alone, the US Congressional Budget Office reports that US agencies awarded US$85 billion in private contracts for the period 2003–7, comprising approximately US$76 billion for the Department of Defense (DOD), US$5 billion for the US Agency for International Development, and US$4 billion for the Department of State.[122] This trend continued into 2010, when contractors made up around 54 per cent of the DOD's workforce in Iraq and Afghanistan, numbering about 250,000 in total in those countries.[123] UK-based PMSCs constitute the second major group, with most of their revenues coming from private clients such as the extractive industries. Israeli firms are also increasingly significant players in the global industry. Whilst PMSCs from these states clearly dominate the

---

121 EO had close connections with the Branch-Heritage group of energy and mining companies. A director of several of those companies reportedly made the initial introductions leading to EO's employment in Angola and Sierra Leone, and EO was allegedly paid partly in oil and mining concessions: see 1997 UN Mercenaries Report; O'Brien, 'Freelance Forces: Exploiters of Old or New-Age Peacebrokers?' (August 1998) *Jane's Intelligence Review* 42, 43; Howe, 'Private Security Forces and African Stability: The Case of Executive Outcomes' (1998) 36(2) *Journal of Modern African Studies* 307, 309–10.

122 US Congressional Budget Office, 'Contractors' Support of US Operations in Iraq' (August 2008), 15.

123 Schwartz, 'Department of Defense Contractors in Iraq and Afghanistan: Background and Analysis', Congressional Research Service Report for Congress R40764 (2 July 2010); see also US Office of the Under Secretary of Defense for Acquisition, Technology and Logistics, 'Contractor Support of US Operations in the USCENTCOM Area of Responsibility, Iraq, and Afghanistan' (May 2010); US Government Accountability Office, 'Contingency Contracting: Improvements Needed in Management of Contractors Supporting Contract and Grant Administration in Iraq and Afghanistan' (April 2010).

market, there are also a growing number of companies based in Eastern Europe, Latin America, the Middle East and Africa.[124]

PMSCs working in foreign conflicts in the 1990s hired mainly nationals of their home state or of other developed (usually Western) states foreign to the conflict. For example, EO hired mainly South African nationals for its operations in Angola and Sierra Leone, whilst Military Professional Resources Inc. (MPRI) and Sandline hired mainly American and British nationals for their overseas operations. In contrast, foreign PMSCs currently operating in Iraq and Afghanistan employ a large number of locals. The British firm Erinys, for example, hired over 14,000 Iraqis to guard Iraq's petroleum infrastructure.[125] PMSCs today also tend to recruit actively from developing third-states in an attempt to lower their operating costs and thus compete for lucrative contracts on the global market.[126] According to one UN official, a commonly used business model in the lucrative guarding sector in Afghanistan is the 'colonial model', which utilises foreign managers from developed states with local or developing third-state regular guards. Some PMSC services, however, such as guarding embassies, close protection of expatriate staff, and security assessments and training, tend to be performed primarily by staff from the home country of the PMSC or from other similar countries.[127]

PMSC clients include states, NGOs, international organisations and corporations. States that hire PMSCs range from strong states like the US, the UK and Russia to failing states like Sierra Leone in the mid-1990s. The US in particular has found it expedient to transfer many of its military and security activities to the private sector, arguing that PMSCs provide operational benefits to the overstretched national military by augmenting the total force and freeing up uniformed personnel to perform combat

---

124 See Cockayne, Speers Mears, Cherneva, Gurin, Oviedo and Yaeger, *Beyond Market Forces*, 17.
125 Isenberg, 'Challenges of Security Privatisation in Iraq', in Bryden and Caparini (eds.), *Private Actors and Security Governance* (2007), 155. This practice has been criticised as it deprives the nascent public forces of skilled personnel and constructs security as a private commodity rather than a public good, and this in turn may undermine the state-building process: see Leander, 'The Market for Force and Public Security', 616–17.
126 This practice has been criticised as exploitative and destabilising, particularly for war-torn countries that are struggling to move beyond their violent past: see Hanes, 'Private Security Contractors Look to Africa for Recruits', *Christian Science Monitor* (8 January 2008).
127 Rimli and Schmeidl, 'Private Security Companies and Local Populations: An Exploratory Study of Afghanistan and Angola' (2007), 16–17.

missions.[128] According to the DOD, since contractors can be hired faster than the military can develop internal capabilities, contractors can be quickly deployed to provide critical support when necessary. They can also provide expertise in specialised fields that the military may not possess. The DOD further argues that the use of PMSCs can help to reduce overall military spending as contractors can be hired when a particular need arises and then released when their services are no longer needed, although it acknowledges the flipside of this practice that the military loses in-house capabilities and is then forced to rely even further on contractor support in the future.[129]

Much of the literature tends to focus upon PMSCs working for states and thus overlooks or ignores the large number of PMSCs working for private corporations, international organisations and humanitarian groups in zones of conflict. Like public workers, non-state groups need to protect their installations and their personnel, and in many cases private security is the only available solution. Many humanitarian organisations – including Save the Children, CARE, the International Rescue Committee and World Vision – are increasingly turning to private companies for the protective security necessary to deliver humanitarian aid. Likewise, the UN High Commissioner for Refugees, the UN Children's Fund, the UN Development Programme and the World Food Programme have all used private security services.[130] As one official in the UN Office for the Coordination of Humanitarian Affairs explained,

> where before the only people you'd expect to see occasionally with an armed guard were a high-level UN official guarded by the government or UN armed guards, or indeed the occasional journalist wandering around with some thug, nowadays you've got a lot of local aid workers walking around with armed individuals taking care of their security and safety.[131]

Leander points out that the increasing use of PMSCs by a variety of actors in weak states can perpetuate 'Swiss cheese' security coverage – full of holes – where security is covered only for those who have the means to pay for it. The trouble is that those actors tend to be unevenly distributed

128 Schwartz, 'Department of Defense Contractors in Iraq and Afghanistan'.   129 *Ibid.*
130 Stoddard, Harmer and DiDomenico, *The Use of Private Security Providers and Services in Humanitarian Operations* (2008); Spearin, 'Private Security Companies and Humanitarians'; Cockayne, *Commercial Security*; Avant, 'NGOs, Corporations, and Security Transformation in Africa' (2007) 29(2) *International Relations* 143.
131 Cockayne, *Commercial Security*, 5; Isenberg, 'Dogs of War: Blue Helmets and Bottom Lines', www.upi.com (17 February 2009); Lynch, 'UN Embraces Private Military Contractors', *Foreign Policy* (17 January 2010).

in space and there is no guarantee that their security needs will lead them to cover the economically and socially weak in the area.[132] On the other hand, even where aid workers and corporations dislike reliance on PMSCs (as is frequently the case), the alternative is often to stay out of the conflict zone altogether. This would prevent humanitarian groups from working where they are most needed, as well as preventing private firms from taking advantage of valuable investment opportunities around the world. It is not surprising, therefore, that many corporations and aid organisations rely extensively on PMSCs.

PMSC services

PMSCs perform a wide variety of activities in armed conflict, including some that are generally considered core military functions.[133] For analytic purposes it is useful to organise the industry into logical categories rather than simply examining PMSC action on a case-by-case basis. Since a single PMSC often provides different services under different contracts, it is preferable to classify the individual PMSC *activities* rather than classifying the companies themselves.[134] This typology aids the legal analysis in the remainder of the book, since the international obligations on states to control PMSCs depend primarily on the activities performed by the companies in a particular case.

Singer uses a common military analogy to distinguish between PMSC services according to their proximity to the 'tip of the spear' or the tactical battlefield.[135] Those services closest to the tip of the spear are typically the most controversial and, in some cases, dangerous to provide. PMSC personnel engaged in offensive combat will of course be extremely close to the tip of the spear. PMSC personnel providing armed guarding services may also lie relatively close to the tip of the spear, particularly if they guard a military objective in a region that is likely to experience hostile fire. Yet this notion of the 'tip of the spear' encompasses not only the contractors' physical proximity to the frontline, but also their influence on the strategic and tactical environment. PMSC personnel providing high-level advice

---

132 Leander, 'The Market for Force and Public Security', 617.
133 Many PMSCs also operate in non-conflict contexts such as peacekeeping, territorial administration and post-conflict reconstruction, but those situations are not the focus of this book.
134 Avant, *Market for Force*, 16–22.
135 Singer, *Corporate Warriors*, 91, although Singer uses this analogy to classify the PMSCs themselves rather than classifying each individual PMSC contract.

or training to military forces may be close to the tip of the spear even if they are not physically close to the frontlines of battle. This is especially true if the PMSC provides advice/training in relation to specific aspects of an ongoing conflict. In contrast, the delivery of food to troops may bring PMSC personnel into the physical theatre of the conflict and may even expose them to combat threats, but it has little direct influence on the strategic balance of the conflict and it therefore lies further from the tip of the spear.

This analogy helps to divide PMSC activities performed in armed conflict into four logical categories: (1) offensive combat; (2) military and security expertise; (3) armed security; and (4) military support. This provides a useful conceptual framework for the legal analysis in subsequent chapters of the book.

Offensive combat

The first category of PMSC contracts involves the service at the very 'tip of the spear': offensive combat. This encompasses only those individuals who are armed and who are contractually authorised to use their weapons for offensive attacks. Although in practice it can sometimes be difficult to draw the line between offensive and defensive combat, particularly in low-intensity conflicts lacking a clear frontline (such as Iraq and Colombia), there is nonetheless a clear conceptual distinction which has important legal implications.

The offensive combat category includes conventional fighters located close to the frontline, such as ground troops fighting with machine guns or air pilots dropping bombs on enemy targets. It also includes individuals who launch attacks using technologically advanced weapons systems, such as the MQ-1 Predator, even if those individuals are located far from the frontline.[136] Indeed, in modern warfare an individual pushing a button on a distant computer can inflict far more lethal damage than an individual pulling the trigger at the frontline, and to describe only the latter as offensive combat would be to privilege the more technologically advanced party to the conflict.[137]

---

136 The Predator is an unmanned aerial vehicle which is remote-controlled by humans. It can serve in a reconnaissance role and it can also carry and use two AGM-114 Hellfire missiles. Where a contractor uses a weapons system such as the Predator solely for surveillance purposes, their activities will fall within the 'military expertise' category discussed below.

137 The notion of 'offensive combat' in this context is intended to be narrower than the notion of taking 'a direct part in hostilities' for the purposes of IHL: see Protocol I, Art. 51(3).

Several PMSCs performed offensive combat operations during the 1990s, the most famous being the operations of South African firm Executive Outcomes (EO) and British firm Sandline in Angola and Sierra Leone, as well as the planned operation of Sandline in Papua New Guinea. Generally speaking, the clients of these companies were governments that had relatively low military capabilities but were faced with civil war or some other immediate, high threat situation. These operations were extremely controversial and sparked vociferous debate about the legitimacy of the private security industry as a whole.

As discussed in the first section of this chapter, by the end of the 1990s the international community had clearly demonstrated its distaste for private offensive warfare, and consequently no company today will offer offensive combat services on the open market. Yet it is important to remember that a number of companies openly performed lucrative offensive combat contracts in relatively recent times, including EO, Sandline, NFD and Strategic Consultant International, and this extreme end of the private security spectrum could certainly resurface in the future. Moreover, there appears to be a continuing market for private offensive force in the context of *covert* operations. In August 2009, the *New York Times* reported that the Central Intelligence Agency (CIA) hired a number of Blackwater contractors in 2004 as part of a secret programme to locate and assassinate top operatives of Al Qaeda.[138] According to government officials, the CIA did not have a formal contract with Blackwater for the programme, but instead had individual agreements with top company officials. It is unclear whether the CIA had intended the contractors themselves to capture or kill Al Qaeda operatives, or simply to help with training and surveillance in the programme, but in any case this incident demonstrates that the extreme end of the private security industry may continue to exist underground.

In order to illustrate the general nature of PMSC offensive combat services, this discussion now provides an overview of the operations of EO and Sandline in Sierra Leone in the 1990s, as well as the planned operation of Sandline in Papua New Guinea.

Executive Outcomes in Sierra Leone The EO story began when Eben Barlow, a former assistant commander of the 32nd Battalion of the South

138 Mazzetti, 'CIA Sought Blackwater's Help to Kill Jihadists', *New York Times* (19 August 2009); Warrick, 'CIA Assassination Program Had Been Outsourced to Blackwater, Ex-Officials Say', *Los Angeles Times* (20 August 2009); MacAskill, 'CIA Hired Blackwater for Al-Qaida Assassination Programme, Sources Say', *Guardian* (20 August 2009). Blackwater has since changed its name to Xe Services LLC: see www.xecompany.com.

African Defence Force and former top official at the Civil Cooperation Bureau in South Africa, founded the company in 1989.[139] By 1999, EO's website advertised strategic and tactical military advisory services, sophisticated military training packages in land, peacekeeping and 'persuasion' services, sea and air warfare, advice on the selection of weapons systems and acquisition, and paramilitary services.[140] Drawing on a database of over 2,000 former members of the South African Defence Force and the South African Police, EO worked in a number of states including Angola, Sierra Leone, Uganda, Kenya, South Africa, Congo and Indonesia.[141]

EO's operations in Sierra Leone began in March 1995 when, following EO's success in Angola,[142] the embattled government of Captain Valentine Strasser hired the company to help the national army fight the rebels of the Revolutionary United Front (RUF). The RUF had grown in the 1980s sponsored by Liberian warlord Charles Taylor, and had waged a campaign of terror against the people of Sierra Leone since 1991.[143] Although 70 per cent of state revenue was being spent fighting the rebels during the early 1990s, the Sierra Leone regime continued to lose ground as the RUF seized valuable mining territories. Sierra Leone's national army consisted of untrained and underpaid soldiers, many of whom were underage and/or addicted to drugs and alcohol, and some of whom even moonlighted as rebel troops.[144] In early 1995, after attacking two diamond mines that were the last major source of state revenue, the rebels advanced towards the capital, Freetown.[145]

---

139 The South African military intelligence formed the Civil Cooperation Bureau as a covert assassination and espionage unit to eliminate enemies of the apartheid state: see Rubin, 'An Army of One's Own'; Cawthra, 'The Security Forces in Transition', in Cawthra, Cilliers and Mertz, *The Future of Security and Defence in South Africa* (1998), 2; Seegers, *The Security Forces and the Transition in South Africa: 1986–1994* (1995).

140 www.eo.com, cited in Avant, *Market for Force*, 18 (accessed by Avant on 14 January 1999).

141 Singer, *Corporate Warriors*, 115; Goulet, 'Mixing Business with Bullets' *Jane's Intelligence Review* (September 1997).

142 The Angolan government hired EO in 1993 for US$40 million to help its army defeat the rebel movement, Unita. EO's involvement helped the Angolan army to regain crucial mining and oil territory and to gain the upper hand over Unita, eventually compelling the Unita leader to sign the UN-brokered Lusaka Protocol in November 1995: see Howe, 'Private Security Forces and African Stability'; Spicer, *An Unorthodox Soldier: Peace and War and the Sandline Affair* (1999), 44; Hooper, *Bloodsong: An Account of Executive Outcomes in Angola* (2002).

143 Abdullah, 'Bush Path to Destruction: The Origin and Character of the Revolutionary United Front/Sierra Leone' (1998) 36(2) *Journal of Modern African Studies* 203.

144 Venter, 'Sierra Leone's Mercenary War Battle for the Diamond Fields', 67; Rubin, 'An Army of One's Own', 49.

145 Van Niekerk, 'Africa's Diamond Dogs of War'; Reno, 'Privatising War in Sierra Leone' (1997) 97 *Current History* 610.

Under the contract of hire, the government delegated significant authority to EO over training, logistics and command and control of government forces. EO initiated an intensive training programme for government forces, established intelligence and effective radio communications, and assumed operational control over offensives.[146] It also deployed its own battalion-sized unit on the ground, supplemented by artillery, transport and combat helicopters and aircraft, a transport ship and various ancillary specialists.[147] Soon after their arrival, EO personnel led the army on a counter-offensive and drove the rebels away from Freetown. In early 1996, as the RUF retreated and EO recaptured key territories, the government held parliamentary and presidential elections. The newly elected President Kabbah negotiated a cease-fire and held peace talks with the RUF. Acknowledging that EO was essentially responsible for their defeat, the RUF leaders demanded the expulsion of the company before they would continue negotiations.[148] The parties finally signed the Abidjan peace agreement on 30 November 1996, and EO departed at the end of January 1997.[149]

Sandline International in Sierra Leone   In May 1997, just six months after the conclusion of the peace agreement in Sierra Leone, the RUF backed a military coup which ousted the new civilian government and forced President Kabbah to flee to Guinea.[150] As Sierra Leone collapsed into chaos once again, the Economic Community of West African States sent a military force – the Economic Community of West African States Military Observer Group (ECOMOG) – to maintain law and order and, eventually, to oust the junta responsible for the coup.[151] However, ECOMOG was unable to stabilise the situation or to recapture Freetown, and in July 1997 President Kabbah turned to Sandline for help.[152] Although the precise extent of Sandline's support remains shrouded in mystery,

---

146 Howe, 'Private Security Forces and African Stability', 316.
147 Singer, *Corporate Warriors*, 93.
148 Musah, 'A Country under Siege: State Decay and Corporate Military Intervention in Sierra Leone', in Musah and Fayemi (eds.), *Mercenaries*, 93–5; Hooper, 'Peace in Sierra Leone: A Temporary Outcome?' (February 1997) *Jane's Intelligence Review* 91; see also McCormack, 'The "Sandline Affair": Papua New Guinea Resorts to Mercenarism to End the Bougainville Conflict' (1998) 1 *Yearbook of International Humanitarian Law* 292.
149 Kinsey, *Corporate Soldiers*, 73.
150 Douglas, 'Fighting for Diamonds: Private Military Companies in Sierra Leone', in Cilliers and Mason (eds.), *Peace, Profit or Plunder*, 188–9; Musah, 'A Country under Seige', 95–6.
151 Douglas, 'Fighting for Diamonds', 188–9; Hirsch, *Sierra Leone: Diamonds and the Struggle for Democracy* (2001), 65.
152 Reportedly at the suggestion of Peter Penfold, the British High Commissioner to Sierra Leone: see Douglas, 'Fighting for Diamonds', 189.

it seems that the company provided the Sierra Leone government with weapons and a wide range of military services including offensive combat, military training and advice.[153] Sandline's operations in support of the countercoup were successful, and by February 1998 ECOMOG troops had driven the junta away from Freetown. Kabbah returned to power in March 1998.[154]

The aftermath of Sandline's operations in Sierra Leone proved embarrassing for the UK government as it emerged that Sandline's shipment of weapons to Sierra Leone had violated a UN arms embargo.[155] It further transpired that Sandline had fully briefed senior UK officials, including the High Commissioner to Sierra Leone, about its operations in Sierra Leone and had therefore assumed that the contract had governmental approval.[156] Although a parliamentary inquiry ultimately characterised the so-called 'arms to Africa' affair as a function of governmental incompetence rather than a deliberate violation,[157] the UK government's 'ethical foreign policy' nonetheless lay in tatters. The controversy also tarnished Sandline's business reputation and set back the efforts of other PMSCs to be seen as legitimate actors in international relations.

Sandline International in Papua New Guinea   In addition to its contracts in Africa, in 1997 Sandline concluded a controversial one-year contract with the government of Papua New Guinea (PNG). Under the contract, the company was both to be a 'force multiplier' and to lead the assault against the secessionist Bougainville Revolutionary Army.[158] Sandline subcontracted most of the work to EO. The contract was approved by the PNG National Security Council (an executive body) with no public discussion or parliamentary notice.[159] When the private troops arrived on the ground, the PNG army mutinied, and violent public riots broke out

---

153 *Ibid.*, 190.
154 Hirsch, *Sierra Leone: Diamonds and the Struggle for Democracy*, 65–73.
155 UNSC Res. 1132 (8 October 1997), UN Doc. S/RES/1132, para. 6.
156 Douglas, 'Fighting for Diamonds', 186–95.
157 Legg and Ibbs, 'Report of the Sierra Leone Arms Investigation', Return to an Address of the Honourable House of Commons dated 27 July 1998.
158 See Agreement for the Provision of Military Assistance between the Independent State of Papua New Guinea and Sandline International (31 January 1997), available at www.c-r.org/our-work/accord/png-bougainville/key-texts14.php; see also 1997 UN Mercenaries Report; Ashworth, 'PNG's Private Army Spurs Australia into Action', *Independent* (13 March 1997); 'Papua New Guinea Hires Mercenaries', *Washington Times* (28 February 1997).
159 Singer, *Corporate Warriors*, 193.

in support of the army. Australia condemned the proposed operation,[160] with the Australian media branding the contractors 'mercenaries', 'dogs of war' and 'assassins', and several other nations also lodged protests against the contract.[161] The controversy forced the PNG Prime Minister, Sir Julius Chan, to resign, and the PNG government then cancelled the contract and the PMSC personnel quickly left the country.[162]

The hostile reaction to the PNG/Sandline contract demonstrated a deep-seated opposition within the international community to the direct involvement of foreign, private military actors in civil strife. The various protests lodged by foreign nations in relation to the PNG affair focused on the direct *offensive* role to be played by Sandline soldiers, especially the alleged plan to assassinate the leaders of the Bougainville Revolutionary Army.[163] Of course, PMSCs are only too aware that their survival depends upon the positive perceptions of their home states and of the international community. The controversy surrounding Sandline's operations in PNG and Sierra Leone marred the company's business reputation and undermined public perceptions of the private security industry as a whole. As both Sandline and EO disbanded, other PMSCs sought to set themselves apart from those companies by disclaiming any involvement in private offensive combat. Consequently, no company today will offer offensive combat services on the open market.

Military and security expertise

Military and security expertise contracts involve the provision of high-level technical or strategic capabilities to military/security forces, including the maintenance of technical weapons systems, the collection and analysis of intelligence, and the provision of military/security advice and training. Whilst these contractors are unarmed and are not authorised to use force, the application of their expertise may nonetheless have an immense strategic impact on the conflict. There is a particularly strong demand for technical support services, as the growing sophistication of

---

160 Shearer, *Private Armies and Military Intervention*, 11–12.
161 Zarate, 'The Emergence of a New Dog of War', 99.
162 Shearer, *Private Armies and Military Intervention*, 12. Sandline sued the PNG government and the parties went to international arbitration. The panel agreed with Sandline's submission that a change of regime did not relieve the new PNG government of the previous government's contractual obligations, notwithstanding the fact that the contract was signed without parliamentary approval. PNG eventually paid the full amount: see 'Payout Ends Mercenary War', *Australian* (1 May 1999); 'PNG Pays up to Mercenaries', *BBC News* (1 May 1999).
163 Zarate, 'The Emergence of a New Dog of War', 99.

military equipment has greatly increased the need for specialist contractors to maintain technical systems. In Iraq, for example, the US has hired a large number of private contractors to maintain complex weapons systems such as the F-117 Nighthawk fighter, the B-2 Spirit bomber and the TOW missile system.[164]

Many PMSCs provide specialist intelligence services including satellite and aerial reconnaissance and photo interpretation and analysis.[165] Demand for private intelligence services has been particularly strong in the US since the attacks of 11 September 2001. In a report published three days after those attacks, the Senate Select Committee on Intelligence expressly encouraged a 'symbiotic relationship between the Intelligence Community and the private sector',[166] a policy which has led to a dramatic increase both in dollars spent on intelligence and in the extent of outsourcing in this area.[167] Private contractors reportedly represent the majority of personnel in the Pentagon's Counterintelligence Field Activity unit, the CIA's National Clandestine Service and the National Counterterrorism Center.[168]

In some cases, PMSCs may even be involved in the interrogation of prisoners. Virginia-based firm CACI notes on its website that it 'assist[s] our government and commercial clients in developing integrated solutions that close gaps between security, intelligence and law enforcement to address complex threats to their security'.[169] Following the 2003 invasion of Iraq, the US government hired CACI to provide several interrogators to work at detention centres in Iraq, including the notorious Abu Ghraib prison. In February 2008, CIA Director Michael Hayden testified before the Senate Select Intelligence Committee and confirmed that the CIA continued to use private contractors at its secret detention facilities.[170]

---

164 Singer, 'The Private Military Industry and Iraq: What Have We Learned and Where to Next?' (2004), 4–5. Where contractors use unmanned aerial vehicles such as the Predator to drop missiles, their activities would fall within the 'offensive combat' category discussed above.

165 Chesterman, '"We Can't Spy . . . If We Can't Buy!": The Privatization of Intelligence and the Limits of Outsourcing "Inherently Governmental Functions"' (2008) 19(5) *EJIL* 1055.

166 US Senate Report on Intelligence Authorization Act for Fiscal Year 2002 (14 September 2001).

167 Chesterman, 'We Can't Spy . . . If We Can't Buy!', 1056.

168 Pincus, 'Lawmakers Want More Data on Contracting Out Intelligence', *Washington Post* (7 May 2006); Keefe, 'Don't Privatize Our Spies', *New York Times* (25 June 2007).

169 See www.caci.com/fcc/isis.shtml.

170 Hearing of the Senate Select Committee on Intelligence: Annual Worldwide Threat Assessment (5 February 2008), 26.

Another PMSC service involving a high degree of expertise is mine clearance, which is performed by both specialist demining companies such as Minetech and generalist companies such as ArmorGroup and Saracen.[171] For example, the US firm Ronco Consulting Group cleared cluster bombs and other unexploded weapons in Kosovo, as well as mines in Namibia and Mozambique.[172] The Australian firm Milsearch is the predominant demining operator in Indochina.[173] Some demining companies also provide mine risk education and consultancy, including the Israeli firm MAAVERIM.[174]

The final category of military/security expertise contracts involves the provision of advice and training to military/security forces. Client states may be seeking to establish democratic control over the armed forces, to develop policies and procedures for long-term defence planning, to restructure their forces, or otherwise to increase their military/security capabilities. For example, the Coalition Provisional Authority hired Vinnell Corp to train the Iraqi army,[175] Hungary hired the US firm Cubic to help it to restructure its military to meet the standards required to become part of NATO,[176] and the Indonesian government hired Strategic Communication Laboratories to help it to respond to internal outbreaks of secessionist and religious violence.[177] Perhaps the most prominent military advice and training operation thus far is that of US firm MPRI to train the Croatian armed forces during the Balkans conflict of the 1990s.

MPRI in Croatia   MPRI has long been one of the leading companies in the military advising and training sector.[178] Most of MPRI's corporate officers are former top-ranked US military leaders, and the company draws on a database of thousands of former military officers to fulfil its contracts. Essentially, this impressive pool of military expertise is MPRI's product.[179] Although MPRI, like other American PMSCs, must compete for its contracts on the open market and must obtain a licence from the US government in order to work for foreign governments, its close ties

---

171 See UK Green Paper, para. 10; Landmine Monitor website, www.icbl.org/lm/.
172 See www.roncoconsulting.com.   173 See www.milsearch.com.au.
174 Schreier and Caparini, *Privatising Security*, 25.
175 Daragahi, 'Use of Private Security Firms in Iraq Draws Concerns', *Washington Times* (10 June 2003); Steele, 'Last Stop Before Iraq', *Army* (1 May 2004), 54.
176 Avant, 'Privatizing Military Training' (2000) 5(17) *Foreign Policy in Focus*.
177 Schreier and Caparini, *Privatising Security*, 23.   178 See www.mpri.com.
179 Schreier and Caparini, *Privatising Security*, 23; Thompson, 'Generals for Hire', *Time* (15 January 1996), 34.

to the US military and government give it a distinct advantage over its rivals.[180] This arrangement can enable the US government to conduct 'foreign policy by proxy', using MPRI to provide US military expertise overseas where conventional US military assistance programmes would not be appropriate for political or tactical reasons.[181]

MPRI's most controversial operations were those in the Balkans conflict of the 1990s.[182] In September 1994, with Serbian forces occupying 30 per cent of Croatian territory,[183] the Croatian government hired MPRI to provide a 'Democracy Training Assistance Program', which included advice and training to the Croatian military in the areas of leadership, management and civil–military operations. The US government authorised the contract and deemed it not to be in violation of the existing UN arms embargo, since it did not involve battlefield strategy, tactics or weapons.[184] Shortly after MPRI began its programme, Croatian forces enjoyed an unprecedented surge in military success and regained several key territories.[185] In August 1995, Croatian forces launched 'Operation Storm' to recapture the Krajina region, rapidly overpowering the Serbian forces with a devastating offensive and regaining the entire territory within one week in a 'textbook' US-style operation.[186] For Croatia, the offensive represented a crucial turning point in the war.[187] Although both MPRI and the US government insist that the company limited its programme to general advice and training, many commentators and UN

---

180 E.g., the Colombian government reportedly hired MPRI after a senior US government official recommended the firm to the Colombian Minister of Defence: see Singer, *Corporate Warriors*, 121.

181 Silverstein, 'Privatising War: How Affairs of States are Outsourced to Private Corporations', *The Nation* (28 July 1997), 4. The UK Green Paper states that MPRI 'undoubtedly functioned as an instrument of US policy in the Balkans' (para. 50).

182 For a detailed account of MPRI's operations in the Balkans, see Avant, *Market for Force*, 101–13; Singer, *Corporate Warriors*, 125–30; Shearer, *Private Armies and Military Intervention*, 56–63.

183 R. Cohen, 'US Cooling Ties to Croatia after Winking at Its Buildup', *New York Times* (28 October 1995); Cowell, 'Conflict in the Balkans', *New York Times* (1 August 1995).

184 R. Cohen, 'US Cooling Ties to Croatia after Winking at its Buildup'.

185 Cowell, 'Conflict in the Balkans'; Fox, 'Fresh War Clouds Threaten Ceasefire', *Sunday Telegraph* (15 October 1995).

186 Power *et al.*, 'The Croatian Army's Friends', *US News and World Report* (21 August 1995); Eagar, 'Invisible US Army Defeats Serbs', *Observer* (5 November 1995); Fox, 'Fresh War Clouds Threaten Ceasefire'; Silber and Little, *Yugoslavia: Death of a Nation* (1997), 357.

187 R. Cohen, 'US Cooling Ties to Croatia after Winking at Its Buildup'; Zarate, 'The Emergence of a New Dog of War', 108. Although deemed a massive success for Croatia, the offensive violated the UN cease-fire and created 170,000 refugees: see Singer, *Corporate Warriors*, 126.

officers believe that MPRI played a direct role in the Croatian offensives, and Croatian forces openly credited the company as the reason for their victory.[188]

Armed security

Armed security contracts involve the physical protection of persons or property in zones of armed conflict. Examples include ArmorGroup's provision of site security to a large number of mining and petroleum companies,[189] DynCorp's protection of the Afghan president Hamid Karzai, and the provision of site security in Iraq by various PMSCs including Vinnell, Global Risk and Erinys.[190] The protection of the US embassy in Iraq, together with the associated multitude of diplomats and US personnel travelling through the Green Zone following the 2003 invasion, required a particularly large armed force which was comprised almost exclusively of contractors from Blackwater, DynCorp and Triple Canopy. In 2010, US government officials announced that the State Department would more than double its private security force in Iraq in 2010–11, to fill the hole left by the departure of US troops.[191]

A related activity sometimes performed by PMSCs is armed border and immigration control. In 2006, for example, Israel privatised both the Sha'ar Ephraim crossing in the northern West Bank and the Erez crossing between Gaza and Israel.[192] Some PMSCs also provide private police. DynCorp, for example, has provided the police in American contributions to several international missions.[193]

---

188 See, e.g., Fox, 'Fresh War Clouds Threaten Ceasefire'; Power *et al.*, 'The Croatian Army's Friends'; R. Cohen, 'US Cooling Ties to Croatia after Winking at Its Buildup'; 'Croatia: Tudjman's New Model Army', *Economist* (11 November 1995), 148; Silverstein, *Private Warriors*, 172–3; Singer, *Corporate Warriors*, 5.

189 See www.armorgroup.com. ArmorGroup is now part of the Danish company G4S: see www.g4s.com.

190 See, e.g., Daragahi, 'Use of Private Security Firms in Iraq Draws Concerns'; 'US Firm to Rebuild Iraqi Army', *BBC News* (26 June 2003); Traynor, 'The Privatisation of Warfare', *Guardian* (10 December 2003); www.dyn-intl.com; www.globalgroup.com; www.erinys.net.

191 Hodge, 'Doubling the State Department's Private Army in Iraq?', *Wall Street Journal* (12 July 2010); Gordon, 'Civilians to Take US Lead after Military Leaves Iraq', *New York Times* (18 August 2010).

192 'Erez Crossing Will Be Operated by Private Company Starting Thursday', *Haaretz* (18 January 2006); Foundation for Middle East Peace, 'Settlement Time Line' (2006) 16(2) *Report on Israeli Settlement in the Occupied Territories* 5.

193 See www.dyn-intl.com/policemissions/police-missions-home.aspx.

Whilst these security contractors are armed, they are restricted in the types of weapons that they may carry and they are authorised to use force only in limited circumstances including self-defence, the defence of people or property specified in their contracts, and the defence of civilians.[194] Unlike offensive combat operations, armed security operations are not generally designed to shift the strategic landscape of the conflict beyond the immediate situations at hand.[195] Nonetheless, armed security guards often work 'in and amongst the most hostile parts of a conflict or post-conflict scenario', and at times it can be extremely difficult to distinguish between national troops and armed security guards.[196] Senator Jack Reed, a member of the US Armed Services Committee, has described 'security in a hostile fire area' as 'a classic military mission'.[197] Moreover, PMSCs often guard facilities or personnel that are themselves strategic centres of gravity and are therefore highly likely to be attacked.

Armed security guards working in this environment sometimes face combat-like situations. For example, in 2004 a number of Blackwater contractors, hired to guard the US headquarters in Iraq, repelled insurgent attacks in ways that closely resembled combat.[198] In a separate incident, four Blackwater contractors were killed and mutilated in Fallujah whilst guarding a convoy.[199] In September 2007, Blackwater contractors guarding a US State Department motorcade in Baghdad were involved in a shooting incident in which thirty-four Iraqi civilians were killed or injured.[200] These incidents illustrate how the traditional line between

194 US Office of the Under Secretary of Defense for Acquisition, Technology and Logistics, 'Contractor Support of US Operations in the USCENTCOM Area of Responsibility, Iraq, and Afghanistan' (May 2010); US Department of Defense Instruction 3020.41 (3 October 2005); Federal Acquisition Regulation 52.225-19(b)(3)(ii); Defense Federal Acquisition Regulation Supplement 252.225-7040(b)(3)(ii).

195 O'Brien, 'What Should and What Should Not Be Regulated?', 38.

196 Michael Battles, co-founder of the PMSC Custer Battles, cited in Barstow, 'Security Companies: Shadow Soldiers in Iraq', New York Times (19 April 2004).

197 Ibid.

198 Priest, 'Private Guards Repel Attack on US Headquarters', Washington Post (6 April 2004).

199 Elsea, Schwartz and Nakamura, 'Private Security Contractors in Iraq: Background, Legal Status and Other Issues', Congressional Research Service Report for Congress RL 32419 (updated 25 August 2008), 11; Gettleman, '4 From US Killed in Ambush in Iraq: Mob Drags Bodies', New York Times (1 April 2004); 'Americans Mutilated after Iraqi Ambush', Washington Post (4 April 2004); Mlinarcik, 'Private Military Contractors and Justice: A Look at the Industry, Blackwater and the Fallujah Incident' (2006) 4 Regent Journal of International Law 129.

200 US Department of Justice Press Release 08-1068, 8 December 2008; see also Tavernise, 'US Contractor Banned by Iraq over Shootings', New York Times (18 September 2007);

military and security tasks can easily become blurred on the ground, particularly in low-intensity conflicts where there is no clear frontline. In some cases, there may also be a risk of 'mission creep' if private guarding activities assume an offensive character. A September 2009 report of the Project on Government Oversight, an independent watchdog group in the US, cites one example involving ArmorGroup contractors who were hired by the US to guard the US embassy in Kabul. These private security guards were reportedly sent on a reconnaissance mission outside the embassy perimeter, taking them beyond the terms of their contract and creating the danger that they could be drawn into a military incident with enemy forces.[201]

Military support

Military support contracts involve the provision of general logistics and other support services to military forces in conflict zones. These services include transport, food, laundry, the assembly and disassembly of military bases and camps, and the repatriation of bodies. According to one Western diplomat, it takes ten to twelve individuals to support each American or British soldier in combat, and this support is increasingly provided by PMSCs.[202] The US army's logistics civil augmentation contract paid out US$22 billion between 2003 and 2007 in Iraq alone.[203]

Although military support services are not generally associated with the use of deadly force, they are crucial to the overall success of military operations. Military support contractors effectively serve as private 'enablers' to public troops, freeing up national forces to concentrate on the primary business of fighting.[204] Indeed, if a state could not mobilise these services through the private security industry, it would either have to mobilise them through the national military or reassess the extent of its presence in the conflict zone.[205] Moreover, military support operations must be designed to survive and operate under attack, and at

Sevastopulo, 'Iraqis Pull Security Contractor's Licence', *Financial Times* (17 September 2007).

201 Project on Government Oversight, Letter to Secretary of State Hillary Clinton Regarding US Embassy in Kabul (1 September 2009).

202 Rimli and Schmeidl, 'Private Security Companies and Local Populations', 18.

203 US Congressional Budget Office, 'Contractors' Support of US Operations in Iraq' (August 2008).

204 Singer, *Corporate Warriors*, 97–8, 137.

205 Bianco and Anderson Forest, 'Outsourcing War', *Business Week* (15 September 2003).

times these contractors may face combat threats whilst performing their functions.[206]

1.5 Conclusion

Private military actors were a prominent feature of an earlier international system which persisted for around five centuries. However, a combination of functional and normative factors led states gradually to abandon the international marketisation of military activities, and by the nineteenth century state monopoly over force through citizen armies had become the paradigm of international warfare. The emergence and rapid proliferation of PMSCs in the early 1990s challenged that paradigm and signalled an important shift in the modern understanding of international security. In the past two decades, hundreds of thousands of private contractors have provided military and security services to states, international organisations, corporations and NGOs around the world. PMSCs' activities have ranged from offensive combat in the 1990s to advice, training, armed security and logistics today. A strong market for military and security services now exists alongside, and intertwined with, national military and police forces.

This private security boom has revived many of the long-standing debates about the utility and legitimacy of private force. Throughout history, three objections consistently arose in relation to private fighters: first, they fight for money rather than for a cause; secondly, they challenge the democratic relationship between the citizen and the state; and, thirdly, they do not operate under adequate state control. Each of these objections contributed to the social stigma attached to private fighters in the international system. Variations of these objections frequently arise in the modern private security debate, particularly in relation to the combat PMSCs of the 1990s, and this has undermined the companies' efforts to establish themselves as legitimate actors in international relations.

Nonetheless, the trend towards the privatisation of security is unlikely to be reversed in the near future, and states and their citizens need to determine for themselves the most effective and appropriate response to the industry. The remainder of this book analyses the international legal aspects of this debate from the perspectives of three key states: the host

---

206 Avant notes that a number of private contractors died whilst driving through a combat zone under contract to transport fuel to troops: see Avant, *Market for Force*, 22.

state, the hiring state and the home state of a PMSC. The discussion in this chapter has provided the critical historical, normative and factual background for the subsequent legal analysis, and this may ultimately help states to choose the most effective and appropriate means by which they can fulfil their international obligations to control PMSCs in armed conflict.

2

State obligations and state responsibility

This book examines both primary and secondary rules of international law. It identifies the pertinent primary obligations on three categories of states – the hiring state, the home state and the host state of a PMSC – and assesses how particular PMSC misconduct may give rise to the international responsibility of these states for a violation of their obligations.[1] This chapter lays the general theoretical groundwork for the book by outlining the basic normative structure of the international legal system and critically examining how the law of state responsibility operates within that systemic context.

This chapter is divided into six sections. The first section discusses the nature of international obligations and the general conditions for breach. It identifies the key categories of primary obligations on the hiring state, the host state and the home state of a PMSC, and critically analyses the conceptual differences between each category. Within this conceptual framework, the second, third and fourth sections critically analyse the circumstances in which PMSC activities may give rise to state responsibility. The fifth section then outlines the conditions that may justify or excuse states' otherwise wrongful acts. Finally, the sixth section examines the consequences of state responsibility for the wrongdoing state and for the claimant party. An understanding of this general framework paves the way for the discussion of the specific obligations and responsibility of the hiring state, the host state and the home state in the subsequent chapters of this book.

---

1 The term 'misconduct' in this context encompasses any inappropriate or harmful PMSC conduct. The term is not intended to denote the illegality of the conduct under international or domestic law.

2.1 The nature of international obligations and conditions for breach

Every violation by a state of its international obligations entails the international responsibility of that state.[2] State responsibility is thus the corollary of state obligation under international law. Two elements must be present to establish that a state has violated its international obligations: first, there must be an action or omission that is attributable to the state under international law; and, secondly, that act must constitute a breach of an international obligation of the state.[3] These two elements derive from two normatively distinct facets of international law. The question of whether a particular act or omission is internationally wrongful is governed by the *primary* rules of international law, which determine the substantive obligations on states. These rules make up the bulk of international law, both conventional and customary. On the other hand, the question of whether a particular act or omission constitutes an 'act of a state' is governed by the *secondary* rules of international law, which determine the general circumstances in which a state will be considered responsible for wrongful conduct and the legal consequences that flow from such responsibility. As a whole, these secondary rules comprise the law of state responsibility.[4] The designation of a particular rule as primary or secondary expresses the distinction between the content of rules and the result of their breach.

The study of state responsibility is inextricably linked to the work of the International Law Commission (ILC), which has been examining the topic since 1953. In 2001, the ILC adopted a complete text of the Articles on Responsibility of States for Internationally Wrongful Acts ('ILC Articles'), together with accompanying Commentaries.[5] The UN General Assembly took note of the ILC Articles, recommended them to the attention of governments, and annexed them to Resolution 56/83

---

2 International Law Commission Articles on Responsibility of States for Internationally Wrongful Acts with Commentaries (2001) *Yearbook of the International Law Commission*, vol. II(2), Art. 1.

3 *Ibid.*, Art. 2.

4 See Combacau and Alland, '"Primary" and "Secondary" Rules in the Law of State Responsibility: Categorising International Obligations' (1985) 16 *Netherlands Yearbook of International Law* 81.

5 ILC Articles on Responsibility of States for Internationally Wrongful Acts with Commentaries (2001) *Yearbook of the International Law Commission*, vol. II(2).

of 2001.[6] The General Assembly again commended the ILC Articles in 2004,[7] and again in 2007 when it noted that the ILC Articles were being extensively referred to in practice.[8] To a large extent the ILC Articles reflect existing law, whilst in some respects they progressively develop that law.[9] Although the ILC Articles have not been adopted as a treaty and thus are not binding, they represent the views of a large number of well-recognised publicists and are generally considered to be highly persuasive.[10]

The basic tenet of state responsibility is that a state is only responsible for its *own* acts; it is not responsible for the acts of all its nationals or of all persons in its territory. Indeed, if it were otherwise, the state would effectively be the guarantor of all transactions concluded within its national borders and all acts committed by its citizens abroad. As the state itself is an abstract entity which can only act through its human agents and representatives, the law of state responsibility delineates which persons should be deemed to be acting on behalf of a state, such that their misconduct may give rise to state responsibility.[11]

Whilst the general rule is that states are *not* responsible for the acts of private persons, in certain circumstances misconduct by a private actor may give rise to the international responsibility of a state. There are essentially two ways in which this may occur. First, the private actor's misconduct may be directly attributable to the state by virtue of an agency relationship between the state and the private actor, in which case the private actor's misconduct may itself constitute an internationally wrongful act of the state giving rise to state responsibility. Secondly, irrespective of the question of attribution, the state may incur responsibility if it fails

---

6 UNGA Res. 56/83 (10 December2001), UN Doc. A/RES/56/83.

7 UNGA Res. 59/35 (2 December 2004), UN Doc. A/RES/59/35.

8 UNGA Res. 62/61 (6 December 2007), UN Doc. A/RES/62/61. The General Assembly deferred once again any decision on whether the Articles should be adopted as a multilateral convention: see Crawford and Olleson, 'The Continuing Debate on a UN Convention on State Responsibility' (2005) 54 *ICLQ* 959.

9 This helps the General Assembly to fulfil its task under Art. 13 of the UN Charter to 'initiate studies and make recommendations for the purpose of ... encouraging the progressive development of international law and its codification'.

10 See Report of the Secretary-General, 'Responsibility of States for Internationally Wrongful Acts: Compilation of Decisions of International Courts, Tribunals and Other Bodies' (1 February 2007), UN Doc. A/62/62; Report of the Secretary-General, 'Responsibility of States for Internationally Wrongful Acts: Comments and Information Received from Governments' (9 March 2007), UN Doc. A/62/63; Caron, 'The ILC Articles on State Responsibility: The Paradoxical Relationship between Form and Authority' (2002) 96 *AJIL* 857.

11 *German Settlers in Poland* (Advisory Opinion) PCIJ (1923), 22.

to fulfil a primary obligation to take certain positive action in relation to the private actor. For example, a state may have an obligation to exercise due diligence to prevent particular private misconduct, in which case it may incur responsibility for a failure to take adequate preventive steps. The key question in such cases is not whether the private misconduct is itself attributable to the state, but whether the overall state system of administration failed to take adequate steps to prevent that misconduct.[12] Whatever the mode of responsibility, a finding of state responsibility does not preclude the responsibility of the private actors themselves under international or domestic law.[13] The next two sections of this chapter examine these two pathways to state responsibility in sequence.

2.2 The attribution of private misconduct to the state

International law imposes numerous obligations on states requiring them to refrain from committing (through their officials or agents) internationally wrongful acts such as war crimes or violations of human rights. Like national soldiers, PMSC personnel working in zones of armed conflict may engage in wrongful conduct of this nature. In such cases, if the wrongful PMSC conduct is attributable to the hiring state, it will give rise to the responsibility of that state under international law. A crucial question, therefore, is under what circumstances will PMSC conduct be attributable to the hiring state? Chapter 3 examines this question in detail, but it is useful at this point to identify the three principal situations in which such attribution may occur.

Article 4 of the ILC Articles sets out the basic rule governing the core cases of attribution: all acts of state organs are deemed to be acts of the state.[14] Thus, if a state hires a PMSC and formally enlists the PMSC personnel in the national armed forces, the acts of those individuals will be deemed acts of the hiring state. The practice of the hiring state enlisting PMSC personnel in its national armed forces was common for the combat

---

12 See Jennings and Watts (eds.), *Oppenheim's International Law*, 9th edn (1992), 501; Higgins, *Problems and Process: International Law and How We Use It* (1994), 153–4.

13 See ILC Articles, Art. 58; Nollkaemper, 'Concurrence between Individual Responsibility and State Responsibility in International Law' (2003) 52 *ICLQ* 615. For a discussion of the possible criminal liability of PMSCs and PMSC employees under international law, see 8 *Journal of International Criminal Justice*, Special Issue on Transnational Business and International Criminal Law (2010).

14 ILC Articles, Art. 4; see also *LaGrand (Germany v. US)* (Merits) ICJ Reports 2001, para. 81; Brownlie, *State Responsibility* (1983), 132–66; Jennings and Watts (eds.), *Oppenheim's International Law*, 539–48.

PMSCs of the 1990s, such as Executive Outcomes and Sandline,[15] but that practice is virtually unheard of today. Even where the hiring state does not formally enrol PMSC personnel into its armed forces, there may be exceptional cases in which the PMSC personnel are so highly integrated into the state's armed forces that they constitute a part of those forces *de facto* for the purposes of state responsibility, as discussed in Chapter 3. In reality, however, very few PMSCs will form part of the hiring state's armed forces, and in most cases the attribution of PMSC misconduct to the state will fall to be determined under either Article 5 or Article 8 of the ILC Articles.

Article 5 encompasses PMSC employees who are 'empowered by the law of [the hiring] state to exercise elements of the governmental authority', provided that they are 'acting in that capacity in the particular instance'. As noted in Chapter 3, it is generally agreed that a PMSC contracted by a state to engage in offensive combat, to conduct interrogations or to operate a detention centre, for example, is exercising governmental authority'.[16] The situation is less clear-cut with regard to other PMSC services such as military/security advice and training, intelligence collection and analysis, and guarding and protection services. Chapter 3 argues that a contextual analysis of these activities points to their inclusion within the notion of 'governmental authority' in Article 5.

Article 8 encompasses PMSC employees who are in fact acting on the instructions or under the direction or control of the hiring state. As the hiring state will rarely instruct a PMSC explicitly to violate international law, it is the second category of state 'direction or control' that is most relevant for present purposes. The controversy surrounding this category is well known. Commencing with the *Nicaragua* case of 1984, the International Court of Justice (ICJ) has consistently propounded a test of 'effective control', which excludes responsibility in cases where a state exercises overall control over an individual but does not exercise control over the particular act in question.[17] In the *Tadić* case of 1999, in

---

15 See Dinnen, May and Regan (eds.), *Challenging the State: The Sandline Affair in Papua New Guinea* (1997); Zarate, 'The Emergence of a New Dog of War: Private International Security Companies, International Law, and the New World Disorder' (1998) 34 *Stanford Journal of International Law* 75, 124; UK Foreign and Commonwealth Office Green Paper, 'Private Military Companies: Options for Regulation' (February 2002), para. 6.

16 See Chapter 3, section 3.2.

17 *Military and Paramilitary Activities In and Against Nicaragua (Nicaragua v. USA)* (Merits) ICJ Reports 1986, para. 115; see also the Separate and Concurring Opinion of Judge Ago, para. 18.

assessing individual criminal responsibility, the Appeals Chamber of the International Criminal Tribunal for the former Yugoslavia rejected the ICJ's 'effective control' test in favour of a more lenient standard of 'overall control' to attribute the acts of an organised armed group to a state.[18] Chapter 3 critically analyses the requirements for attribution under Article 8 and assesses how this rule applies to the modern private security industry.

2.3 States' obligations to take positive steps to control PMSCs

In addition to their obligations to refrain from committing wrongful acts such as war crimes, states have a number of obligations to take certain *positive* action prescribed by international law. Within this latter category, it is helpful to make a further distinction between obligations of result and obligations of diligent conduct. This distinction derives from the civil law systems of various states, particularly France, and has been strongly propounded on the international plane by Professor Dupuy.[19] Obligations of result require states to guarantee that they will achieve a particular outcome, irrespective of the means. Obligations of diligent conduct (*'obligations de s'efforcer'*), on the other hand, are 'best efforts' obligations requiring states only to take those measures that are reasonably within their power in order to achieve the desired result.

The ICJ explained the difference between these two categories in the *Genocide* case, in relation to the obligation to prevent genocide in Article 1 of the Genocide Convention.[20] According to the Court,

> it is clear that the obligation in question is one of conduct and not one of result, in the sense that a State cannot be under an obligation to succeed, whatever the circumstances, in preventing the commission of genocide:

18 *Prosecutor* v. *Tadić*, Judgment, ICTY-94-1-A, Appeals Chamber, 15 July 1999.

19 Dupuy is highly critical of the formulation adopted by the former special rapporteur Robert Ago: see Dupuy, 'Reviewing the Difficulties of Codification: On Ago's Classification of Obligations of Means and Obligations of Result in Relation to State Responsibility' (1999) 10 *EJIL* 371; see also Combacau, 'Obligations de Résultat et Obligations de Comportement: Quelques Questions et Pas de Réponse', *Mélanges Offerts à P. Reuter* (1981); Crawford, 'Revising the Draft Articles on State Responsibility' (1999) 10 *EJIL* 436, 439; Pisillo-Mazzeschi, 'The Due Diligence Rule and the Nature of the International Responsibility of States' (1992) 35 *German Yearbook of International Law* 9, 47–8.

20 Convention on the Prevention and Punishment of the Crime of Genocide (adopted 9 December 1948, entered into force 12 January 1951), 78 UNTS 277.

> the obligation of States parties is rather to employ all means reasonably available to them, so as to prevent genocide so far as possible.[21]

A state that takes all measures reasonably within its power to prevent genocide will thus fulfil its obligation, irrespective of whether genocide ultimately takes place.[22]

The distinction between obligations of result and obligations of diligent conduct provides a useful analytic framework within which to assess states' obligations to control PMSCs, although this classification is not exclusive and does not in itself bear direct consequences for state responsibility.[23] The remainder of this section will examine these two categories in turn.

Obligations of result

A state that is under an obligation of result is obliged to *guarantee* that a particular act will be performed to the standard required by international law. If the state fails to perform that act to the requisite standard, or otherwise to ensure that the act is so performed, the state will incur international responsibility for its failure. These are termed 'obligations of result' because the ultimate question in assessing responsibility is whether or not, in the result, the state has met the requisite standard. The fact that a state has exerted its best efforts and taken all reasonable measures in the circumstances is not enough; the state is judged by its ultimate success or failure.

The four Geneva Conventions of 1949 (GCI–GCIV) impose a number of obligations of result on state parties.[24] For example, GCIII lays down

---

21 *Case Concerning the Application of the Convention on the Prevention and Punishment of the Crime of Genocide (Bosnia and Herzegovina* v. *Serbia and Montenegro)* (Merits) (26 February 2007), para. 430; see also ILC Articles, Commentary to Art. 14, para. 14.

22 See Pisillo-Mazzeschi, 'The Due Diligence Rule', 30.

23 See ILC Articles, Commentary to Art. 12, para. 11; Dupuy, 'Reviewing the Difficulties of Codification'.

24 First Geneva Convention for the Amelioration of the Condition of the Wounded and Sick in Armed Forces in the Field (adopted 12 August 1949, entered into force 21 October 1950), 75 UNTS 31 ('GCI'); Second Geneva Convention for the Amelioration of the Condition of Wounded, Sick and Shipwrecked Members of Armed Forces at Sea (adopted 12 August 1949, entered into force 21 October 1950), 75 UNTS 85 ('GCII'); Third Geneva Convention relative to the Treatment of Prisoners of War (adopted 12 August 1949, entered into force 21 October 1950), 75 UNTS 135 ('GCIII'); Fourth Geneva Convention relative to the Protection of Civilian Persons in Time of War (adopted 12 August 1949, entered into force 21 October 1950), 75 UNTS 287 ('GCIV').

the standards of treatment that a detaining state must meet in the internment of prisoners of war, and GCIV lays down the requisite standards of treatment for interned civilians during armed conflict. In relation to the latter, Article 89 of GCIV provides:

> Daily food rations for internees shall be sufficient in quantity, quality and variety to keep internees in a good state of health and prevent the development of nutritional deficiencies. Account shall also be taken of the customary diet of the internees.
>
> Internees shall also be given the means by which they can prepare for themselves any additional food in their possession.
>
> Sufficient drinking water shall be supplied to internees. The use of tobacco shall be permitted.
>
> Internees who work shall receive additional rations in proportion to the kind of labour which they perform.
>
> Expectant and nursing mothers and children under fifteen years of age shall be given additional food, in proportion to their physiological needs.

A state might choose to hire a PMSC to work in a prisoner of war or civilian internment camp,[25] just as the US outsourced certain activities at Abu Ghraib prison in Iraq to the PMSCs Titan and CACI.[26] In such a case, if the company failed to provide the prisoners/internees with adequate health care or nutrition, the state would be responsible for its failure to ensure that the relevant standards of treatment were met. Such responsibility would arise regardless of whether the PMSC conduct was attributable to the state under the secondary rules of state responsibility, and regardless of any action the state may have taken to ensure that the PMSC would perform its functions properly.[27]

That is not to say, however, that the hiring state would automatically be responsible for any violations of IHL committed by the PMSC whilst working at the camp. On the contrary, the hiring state would incur direct

---

25 Although the state could not outsource the overall operation of a prisoner of war camp, since Art. 39 of GCIII requires that such camps remain under the immediate authority of an officer of the regular armed forces of the Detaining Power.

26 See Fay, 'Investigation of the Abu Ghraib Detention Facility and 205th Military Intelligence Brigade' (August 2004); Schooner, 'Contractor Atrocities at Abu Ghraib: Compromised Accountability in a Streamlined, Outsourced Government' (2005) 16 *Stanford Law and Policy Review* 549, 556–7.

27 Gillard, 'Business Goes to War: Private Military/Security Companies and International Humanitarian Law' (2006) 88(863) *International Review of the Red Cross* 525, 549–50; University Centre for International Humanitarian Law, 'Expert Meeting on Private Military Contractors' (Geneva, August 2005), 44–5.

responsibility for particularly instances of PMSC misconduct only to the extent that such misconduct was attributable to the state under the rules of state responsibility. The hiring state's obligations of result under IHL are governed by the *primary* rules of international law, whereas the state's responsibility for any PMSC misconduct carried out whilst performing those obligations falls to be assessed under the *secondary* rules of attribution. Article 29 of GCIV highlights this distinction in the context of civilian internees, providing that '[t]he Party to the conflict in whose hands protected persons may be is responsible for the treatment accorded to them *by its agents*'.[28]

Like IHL, international human rights law (HRL) also imposes certain obligations of result on states. For example, the right to a fair trial under Article 6(1) of the European Convention on Human Rights (ECHR) provides that '[i]n the determination of his civil rights and obligations or of any criminal charge against him, everyone is entitled to a fair and public hearing within a reasonable time by an independent and impartial tribunal established by law'.[29] States have a duty to ensure that their legal systems meet this overall standard of fairness, although they have a broad discretion as to the means that they adopt to achieve this end. In the *Colozza* case, the European Court of Human Rights (ECtHR) explained the nature of the obligation as follows:

> The Contracting States enjoy a wide discretion as regards the choice of the means calculated to ensure that their legal systems are in compliance with the requirements of article 6 § 1 in this field. The Court's task is not to indicate those means to the States, but to determine whether the result called for by the Convention has been achieved.[30]

The Court thus considered that Article 6(1) imposes an obligation of result.

In short, the hiring state of a PMSC will always be responsible for any failure by the company to fulfil the state's obligations of result under international law, and this provides the state with a legal incentive to ensure that PMSCs fulfil the obligations with which they have been entrusted.

---

28 Emphasis added; cf the situation relating to prisoners of war under Art. 12 of GCIII, which provides that '[p]risoners of war are in the hands of the enemy Power, but not of the individuals or military units who have captured them. Irrespective of the individual responsibilities that may exist, the Detaining Power is responsible for the treatment given them.'

29 European Convention on Human Rights (4 November 1950), CETS No. 005.

30 *Colozza* v. *Italy* (1985), para. 30, citing *De Cubber* v. *Belgium* (1984), para. 35.

Obligations of diligent conduct

Obligations of diligent conduct require states to exercise due diligence and employ all reasonable means in order to achieve a specific result, as far as possible. The most pertinent obligations in this category are those that require states to exercise due diligence to prevent and punish particular private activities. The Commentaries to the ILC Articles explain that obligations of prevention 'are usually construed as best efforts obligations, requiring States to take all reasonable or necessary measures to prevent a given event from occurring, but without warranting that the event will not occur'.[31] If a state fails to take the requisite positive steps and the prohibited private activity takes place, the state's failure will constitute an international wrong giving rise to state responsibility. Although it is the prohibited PMSC activity that triggers state responsibility in such cases, it is the state's *own failure* to take adequate measures of prevention (or punishment) that in fact constitutes the basis for the state's responsibility, and not the PMSC activity itself.[32]

The *Home Missionary Society Claim* of 1920 illustrates the nature of these obligations. The British administration of the protectorate of Sierra Leone had imposed a tax on the native population, and this led to rioting during which missionaries were killed and property was destroyed. The US brought a claim against Great Britain, alleging that 'in the face of the native danger the British Government wholly failed to take proper steps for the maintenance of order and the protection of life and property'. The Tribunal rejected the US's claim, since from the outbreak of the insurrection the British authorities took every measure available for its repression. According to the Tribunal, a government 'cannot be held liable as the insurer of lives and property under the circumstances presented in this case'.[33]

Due diligence obligations to prevent and punish private misconduct can play a key role in establishing state responsibility in cases where the misconduct cannot be attributed to a state. The *Genocide* case illustrates this scenario. The ICJ could not find Serbia responsible for actually committing genocide because there was no agency relationship between the Serbian state and the Bosnian Serb army. Nonetheless, the Court found Serbia responsible for failing to discharge its obligation to take positive

---

31 ILC Articles, Commentary to Art. 14, para. 14.
32 See Brownlie, *State Responsibility*, 150; Jennings and Watts (eds.), *Oppenheim's International Law*, 501.
33 *Home Missionary Society Claim (US v. UK)* (1920) 6 RIAA 42.

steps to prevent genocide under Article 1 of the Genocide Convention.[34] In a similar vein, the host state, the hiring state and the home state of a PMSC all have certain due diligence obligations to prevent and punish company misconduct in armed conflict, and these obligations could provide a pathway to state responsibility quite independent of the attribution of particular PMSC misconduct to a particular state.

2.4 A framework for analysing due diligence obligations

This section develops a five-step framework for the analysis of due diligence obligations in international law. The first step is to identify a pre-existing primary obligation on the state to exercise due diligence to prevent and punish particular private misconduct. Secondly, having identified such an obligation, what is the requisite mental element? Thirdly, what positive action is generally required of the state to meet the due diligence standard? Fourthly, what is the necessary causal connection between the state's failure to take action and the private misconduct? Finally, must the claimant show material or moral damage in order to establish responsibility? Whilst the answers to these questions may vary depending upon the particular primary obligation under consideration, it is nonetheless possible to identify the predominant trends in relation to each question.

Identifying a due diligence obligation of prevention and punishment

Due diligence obligations have long existed in international law.[35] In the *Alabama Claims* arbitrations of 1871, for example, the Tribunal applied a standard of due diligence to find Great Britain liable for failing to prevent individuals from violating British neutrality in the US civil war.[36] That obligation was essentially included in the Hague Conventions of

---

34 See *Genocide* case, paras. 425–50.
35 See generally Borchard, *Diplomatic Protection of Citizens Abroad* (1928), § 87; Dupuy, 'Due Diligence in the International Law of State Responsibility', in *Legal Aspects of Transfrontier Pollution* (1977); Pisillo-Mazzeschi, 'The Due Diligence Rule', 30; Pisillo-Mazzeschi, '*Due diligence' e Responsabilita Internazionale Degli Stati* (1989); Hessbruegge, 'The Historical Development of the Doctrines of Attribution and Due Diligence in International Law' (2004) 36 *New York University Journal of International Law and Politics* 265; Barnidge, *Non-State Actors and Terrorism: Applying the Law of State Responsibility and the Due Diligence Principle* (2007).
36 *Alabama Claims (US v. Britain)* (1871), in relation to the due diligence obligations contained in the Treaty of Washington (8 May 1871); see also Moore, *History and Digest of the International Arbitrations to Which the US Has Been a Party* (1898), ch. LXVIII.

1907.[37] Numerous international arbitral tribunals have since applied the due diligence principle in cases of a failure to prevent or punish private misconduct. In the *Youmans* case of 1926, for example, the claim of the US was predicated on two factors: first, the failure of the Mexican government to exercise due diligence to protect the father of the claimant from the fury of the mob at whose hands he was killed; and secondly, the government's failure to take proper steps towards the apprehension and punishment of the persons implicated in the crime.[38]

Particularly pertinent to the private security industry, HRL requires states to 'ensure' or 'secure' rights within state jurisdiction,[39] and this has been widely interpreted as requiring states to exercise due diligence to prevent, investigate, punish and redress human rights violations by private actors.[40] These obligations largely stemmed from the traditional duty of states to 'protect' aliens within state jurisdiction, which Robert Ago explained in the following terms:

> Prevention and punishment are simply two aspects of the same obligation to provide protection and have a common aim, namely to discourage potential attackers of protected persons from carrying out such attacks. The system of protection that the State must provide therefore includes not only the adoption of measures to avoid certain acts being committed but also provision for, and application of, sanctions against the authors of acts which the implementation of preventive measures has failed to avert.[41]

More recently, in the 2005 *Congo* case, the ICJ applied a standard of 'vigilance' to the obligation of an occupying power under Article 43 of the Hague Regulations 'to restore, and ensure, as far as possible, public order

---

37 Convention Concerning the Rights and Duties of Neutral Powers in Naval War (adopted 18 October 1907, entered into force 26 January 1910), 205 Consol TS 395 ('Hague XIII'), Arts. 8 and 25.
38 *Youmans* case (1926) 4 RIAA 110; see also the cases in Moore, *US Arbitrations*, 4027–56.
39 See, e.g., ECHR, Art. 1; International Covenant on Civil and Political Rights (adopted 16 December 1966, entered into force 23 March 1976), 999 UNTS 171 (ICCPR), Art. 1(2); American Convention on Human Rights (adopted 22 November 1969, entered into force 18 July 1978), 1144 UNTS 123 ('American Convention'), Art. 1.
40 See, e.g., *Velásquez Rodríguez v. Honduras* (Merits), Judgment of 29 July 1988, IACtHR Ser. C No. 4, paras. 148 and 172; *Kaya v. Turkey* (App. No. 22535/93), ECHR, 28 March 2000, paras. 101 and 108–9; Human Rights Committee, General Comment 6, UN Doc. A/37/40(1982); General Comment 31, UN Doc. CCPR/C/21/Rev.1/Add.13 (2004), para. 10. For a recent analysis of these obligations, see Hakimi, 'State Bystander Responsibility' (2010) 21 *EJIL* 341.
41 Ago, 'Fourth Report on State Responsibility' (1972) *Yearbook of the International Law Commission*, vol. II, 71.

and safety' in the occupied territory.[42] The Court held that such vigilance (essentially synonymous with due diligence) requires the occupying power to take positive steps 'to secure respect for the applicable rules of international human rights law and international humanitarian law, to protect the inhabitants of the occupied territory against acts of violence, and not to tolerate such violence by any third party'.[43]

The language of a particular obligation provides clues as to whether a due diligence standard of conduct applies.[44] Best efforts obligations requiring a state to use 'all means at its disposal'[45] or 'to employ all means reasonably available'[46] to prevent and punish a particular activity clearly involve the due diligence principle, as does an obligation to take safeguards that are 'as satisfactory as possible'.[47] Obligations not to 'allow' or 'tolerate' certain private activities have also been interpreted as entailing a due diligence duty to prevent and punish the private activities in question. Examples include the obligation on neutral states not to allow their territory to be used as a base of hostile operations by belligerents,[48] and the obligation on all states not to tolerate violent interventions into other states.[49] Likewise, the ICJ's statement in the *Corfu Channel* case that every state has an obligation 'not to allow knowingly its territory to be used for acts contrary to the rights of other states' signified a due diligence assessment based on knowledge.[50] In that case, Albania's knowledge of the mines in its territorial waters gave rise to an obligation to take certain measures to prevent the mines from causing harm to the vessels of other states, namely, to notify shipping generally of the existence of the minefield and to warn the approaching British ships of the imminent danger. Albania's failure to take those measures gave rise to its international responsibility for the damage caused to UK vessels by the explosion of the mines.[51]

---

42 *Case Concerning Armed Activities in the Territory of the Congo (DRC v. Uganda)* (Merits) ICJ Reports 2005, paras. 178–9.
43 *Ibid.*, para. 178.
44 For a discussion of the importance of language in identifying due diligence obligations, see Barnidge, *Non-State Actors and Terrorism*, 114–15.
45 Hague XIII, Arts. 8 and 25.   46 *Genocide* case, para. 430.
47 *Lake Lanoux (Spain v. France)* (1957) 24 ILR 123.
48 Convention Respecting the Rights and Duties of Neutral Powers and Persons in Case of War on Land (adopted 18 October 1907, entered into force 26 January 1910), 205 Consol TS 299, Arts. 4, 5 and 6.
49 UNGA Res. 2625 (XXV) (24 October 1970), UN Doc. A/8028, para. 2.
50 *Corfu Channel (UK v. Albania)* (Merits) ICJ Reports 1949, 22; see also Barnidge, *Non-State Actors and Terrorism*, 114–15; Brownlie, *State Responsibility*, 42–4, 181–2.
51 *Corfu Channel*, 20–2.

The above survey illustrates the wide range of due diligence obligations in international law and the types of language that generally denote an obligation of this nature. This provides a useful frame of reference for identifying the due diligence obligations on the host state, the hiring state and the home state of a PMSC to prevent and punish company misconduct in armed conflict.

Mental element

Having identified a due diligence obligation to prevent and punish a particular private activity, it is necessary to ascertain the mental element that the obligation entails. In other words, what degree of state *knowledge* of the prohibited activity must exist before the obligation will arise? The law of state responsibility does not require fault before an act or omission may be characterised as internationally wrongful.[52] Nonetheless, the relevant primary obligation may require a certain degree of fault as a necessary condition for responsibility *in relation to that particular obligation.*

An obligation of prevention and punishment will usually arise where the state actually knows that the prohibited activity has occurred or is occurring, or that there is a real and immediate risk that the activity will occur in the near future. At the other end of the spectrum, international law will not generally impose responsibility on a state for failing to prevent or punish covert or unforeseeable activities of which the state was not aware and which could not have been discovered through diligent detection. But what about cases where the state *ought* to have known that the prohibited activity was occurring, or ought to have foreseen that the activity would occur in the near future? It would appear incongruous if a state could avoid responsibility by claiming its lack of knowledge if it could have discovered the prohibited activity through diligent detection. Even so, it is not possible to state a general rule and it will always be necessary to examine the primary obligation in question in order to determine the requisite mental element.

In the *Corfu Channel* case, the ICJ based its finding of responsibility on the obligation of every state 'not to allow *knowingly* its territory to

---

52 See ILC Articles, Arts. 2 and 12, Commentary to Art. 2, paras. 3 and 10. For many years there was a major debate about whether international law has a general requirement of fault: see Brownlie, *State Responsibility*, 37–48; Higgins, *Problems and Process*, 159–61. It now appears to be settled that international responsibility is neither based on fault nor independent of fault; rather, the requisite degree of fault will always depend on the primary rule in question.

be used for acts contrary to the rights of other states'.[53] The Court was careful to state that the mere fact of the control exercised by a state over its territory does not, by itself, lead to the conclusion that the state knew or ought to have known of a prohibited activity carried out in that territory. Nonetheless, the Court made it clear that territorial control will have an important bearing on the methods of proof available to the victim state to establish the knowledge of the territorial state. As the victim state will often be unable to produce direct evidence of facts giving rise to responsibility, the Court stated that it should be allowed a more liberal recourse to inferences of fact and circumstantial evidence.[54] After examining the evidence in the case, the Court concluded that Albania must have known about the laying of the minefields in Albanian territorial waters, and the Court went on to identify the specific obligations that arose from that knowledge.[55] Although in the circumstances the Court was able to impute actual knowledge of the mines to Albania, it did not exclude the possibility that an obligation of prevention could arise in other circumstances on the basis of what a state *ought* to have known.

According to the ECtHR in *Keenan* v. *UK*, in assessing responsibility for a failure to protect life under Article 2 of the ECHR, the Court employs a test of 'foreseeability of the event': the state is responsible if the authorities 'knew or ought to have known' of the risk to the life of a person, and yet they failed to take measures that 'judged reasonably' might have prevented the occurrence of the lethal event.[56] Likewise, in *Kilic* v. *Turkey* the Court found that Article 2 had been violated on the basis of a lack of measures that might have avoided a foreseeable risk.[57] The Court found that Turkey had failed to take adequate measures to protect the life of the applicant's brother, a journalist who was working in southeastern Turkey for a newspaper voicing Kurdish opinions and who was found shot dead on his way home from work. According to the Court, the victim's death was predictable due to the situation in the southeastern region where

---

53 *Corfu Channel*, 22 (emphasis added); see also *Lighthouses Arbitration (France* v. *Greece)* (1956) 12 RIAA 217; *In re Rizzo* (1955) 12 ILR 317.

54 *Corfu Channel*, 18.

55 *Ibid.*, 22. Brownlie notes that the principles in the *Corfu Channel* case also apply to cases where the harm to another state occurs beyond the boundaries of the state harbouring the source of danger, provided that liability is based on a failure to control rather than on actual control or complicity: see Brownlie, *State Responsibility*, 182. This analysis has important implications for the home state of a PMSC, as discussed in Chapter 6.

56 *Keenan* v. *UK* (App. No. 27229/95), ECHR, 3 April 2001, para. 89, quoting *Osman* v. *UK* (App. No. 23452/94), ECHR, 28 October 1998, para. 116.

57 *Kilic* v. *Turkey* (App. No. 22492/93), ECHR, 28 March 2000, paras. 65–8.

security forces were accused of eliminating alleged supporters of the Kurdistan Workers' Party.[58] In a similar vein, in the *Genocide* case the ICJ held that the obligation to prevent genocide applies wherever a state is aware, *or should normally be aware*, of a serious risk that genocide will occur.[59] The ILC's Commentary to its 2001 Draft Articles on the Prevention of Transboundary Harm from Hazardous Activities couch the mental element in analogous terms: 'The degree of harm itself should be foreseeable and the State must know or should have known that the given activity has the risk of significant harm.'[60]

Thus, whilst the law of state responsibility imposes no general requirement of fault, primary obligations of prevention and punishment frequently entail some degree of state knowledge or constructive knowledge of the prohibited activity before demanding positive state action.

Positive action to discharge the obligation

What exactly does the 'due diligence' standard require and how much positive action can reasonably be expected of a state in a particular case? Clearly, the notion of due diligence refers to an international standard of behaviour, which is not to be determined solely by a state's own national law or practice. Thus, in the *Alabama Claims* arbitrations the Tribunal rejected the UK's proposed definition of due diligence as 'such care as Governments *ordinarily* employ in their domestic concerns'.[61] Nonetheless, the due diligence principle contains a strong element of subjectivity. As Pisillo-Mazzeschi explains, whilst the due diligence principle references itself against an objective international standard, it 'undoubtedly' has 'an elastic and relative nature'.[62] Barnidge similarly describes due diligence as a 'flexible reasonableness standard adaptable to the particular facts and circumstances'.[63]

---

58 *Ibid.*, paras. 65–8; see also Conforti, 'State Responsibility for Breach of Positive Obligations', in Fitzmaurice and Sarooshi (eds.), *Issues of State Responsibility before International Judicial Institutions* (2004).

59 *Genocide* case, para. 431; see also the cases in Moore, *US Arbitrations*, 4027–56, in which the Tribunal held the state responsible for a failure to prevent certain activities on its territory which the state *ought* to have discovered through diligent investigation.

60 ILC Draft Articles on the Prevention of Transboundary Harm from Hazardous Activities with Commentaries (2001) *Yearbook of the International Law Commission*, vol. II(2), Commentary to Art. 3, para. 18.

61 *Alabama Claims*, 612 (emphasis added).

62 Pisillo-Mazzeschi, 'The Due Diligence Rule', 44.

63 Barnidge, *Non-State Actors and Terrorism*, 138.

Although the requirements of due diligence must always be assessed by reference to the particular primary obligation in question, generally speaking states will need to undertake two distinct forms of action to fulfil an obligation of prevention and punishment. First, states will need to equip themselves in advance with the general *means* to prevent, detect, restrain and punish the prohibited activities. This may require the enactment of legislation or regulations and the establishment of an effective' administrative and judicial apparatus. Secondly, states will need to *use* that apparatus diligently in order to prevent particular prohibited activities and to detect, investigate and punish such activities where they occur or are about to occur.[64] The investigation and punishment of offenders serves a critical preventive function by reinforcing the state's legislation and deterring potential future wrongdoers.

A violation of a state's obligation may result either from broad inadequacies in the state system or from the failure of state agents to use that system diligently to prevent or punish prohibited activities in a particular case.[65] Thus, where a wrongful activity occurs, the state cannot escape liability simply because it had previously failed to enact laws to enable its administrative and judicial authorities to prevent or suppress that activity.[66] In *Alabama Claims*, for example, Britain could not plead the insufficiency of its neutrality legislation to escape liability to the US for the violation by private individuals of British neutrality.[67]

Whilst these observations provide guidance as to the general content of the due diligence principle, a number of factors may alter the precise demands of due diligence in a particular case. Three variables are particularly important: first, the capacity of the state to influence the private individual; secondly, the resources available to the state to perform its obligations; and, finally, the risk that the individual's activities will give rise to a violation of international law.

---

64 In human rights law, states have an explicit obligation to enact legislative and other measures to protect human rights: see, e.g., American Convention, Art. 2; ICCPR, Art. 2. In international environmental law, see ILC Draft Articles on Transboundary Harm, Commentary to Art. 3, para. 10. More generally, see Pisillo-Mazzeschi, 'The Due Diligence Rule', 26–30; Borchard, *Diplomatic Protection of Citizens Abroad*, § 86; UNGA Res. 60/147 (16 December 2005), UN Doc. A/RES/60/147, paras. 2–3.

65 See *Noyes* (1933) 6 RIAA 308, 311; Hall, *International Law*, 8th edn (1924), 641–2; *Kennedy* (1927) 4 RIAA 194, 198.

66 See Lauterpacht, 'Revolutionary Activities by Private Persons Against Foreign States' (1928) 22 *AJIL* 105, 128; Borchard, *Diplomatic Protection of Citizens Abroad*, § 86.

67 *Alabama Claims*; see also *Baldwin (US)* v. *Mexico* (11 April 1838) in Moore, *US Arbitrations*, 2623; *Noyes* case, 311; *Kennedy* case, 198; Hall, *International Law*, 641–2.

State's capacity to influence the private actor

A key consideration in assessing the requirements of due diligence is the extent to which the state is able to influence the particular private individual in question. The due diligence standard becomes more demanding as the relationship between the state and the individual becomes closer and the potential for state influence over the individual's activities increases. In the *Genocide* case, for example, the ICJ noted that the measures required to discharge the obligation to prevent genocide depend largely on the state's 'capacity to influence effectively the action of persons likely to commit, or already committing, genocide'.[68] Conversely, a state will not incur responsibility for a failure to take preventive action if it in fact lacks the capacity to influence potential perpetrators effectively.

A state's capacity to influence a PMSC in armed conflict may derive from the state's exercise of control over the territory in which the company is based or incorporated (in the case of the home state) or the territory in which the company operates (in the case of the host state). Alternatively, a state's capacity to influence a PMSC may derive from some special relationship between the state and the company, as in the case of the hiring state which has a clear means of influencing company behaviour through the contract of hire. Where a state falls into two or even three of these categories (home state, host state, hiring state) in relation to the same PMSC, its capacity to influence the company will be particularly strong.

Resources available to the state

A related consideration is the extent of the resources that are available to the state to perform its obligation of prevention and punishment. In the *Genocide* case, the ICJ emphasised that the obligation to prevent genocide requires each state to employ all means that are 'reasonably available' and 'within its power', so as to prevent genocide so far as possible.[69] Similarly, in the *Hostages* case, in finding that Iran was responsible for failing to protect the American diplomats, the Court stated that the authorities 'were fully aware of their obligations . . . *had the means at their disposal* to perform their obligations; [and] completely failed to comply with these obligations'.[70] In international environmental law, it is well accepted that

---

68 *Genocide* case, para. 430 (emphasis added).   69 *Ibid.*, para. 430.
70 *US Diplomatic and Consular Staff in Tehran (US v. Iran)* (Merits) ICJ Reports 1980, para.
     68 (emphasis added).

the measures expected of states with highly evolved systems and structures of governance may differ from those expected of states that are not so well placed, although 'a State's economic level cannot be used to dispense the State from its obligation'.[71]

Risk of violation

The final variable for due diligence obligations of prevention and punishment is the risk that the private activities will take place. A state will generally need to take more vigorous measures of prevention, investigation and punishment where there is a greater risk of violations, at least where the state is aware or ought to be aware of that increased risk. Where a particular situation gives rise to a serious risk of violations of the law, a state may need to exercise special diligence and devise special methods to target that situation. This reflects the general position put forward by the US and accepted by the Tribunal in *Alabama Claims* that the requisite standard of due diligence is that which is proportional to the degree of risk in the particular case.[72]

Courts will generally be unwilling to find that a state has violated its due diligence obligation of prevention where there was an unsubstantiated risk of harm, or a real but remote risk of harm. One example of an unsubstantiated risk is the ECtHR case of *LCB* v. *UK*.[73] The applicant claimed that she had developed leukaemia during her childhood, due both to her father's exposure to radiation and to the failure of authorities in the UK to warn her parents of the possible risks for the health of their subsequently conceived children. The Court rejected the claim, stating:

> Having examined the expert evidence submitted to it, the Court is not satisfied that it has been established that there is a causal link between the exposure of a father to radiation and leukaemia in a child subsequently conceived . . . The Court could not reasonably hold, therefore, that, in the late 1960s, the United Kingdom authorities could or should, on the basis of this unsubstantiated link, have taken action in respect of the applicant.[74]

An example of harm that is too remote is the case of *Tugar* v. *Italy*, in which the European Commission of Human Rights declared inadmissible

---

71 ILC Draft Articles on Transboundary Harm, Commentary to Art. 3, para. 13; see also paras. 12 and 17; Report of the UN Conference on Environment and Development (Rio de Janeiro, 3–14 June 1992), UN Doc. A/CONF151/26/Rev.l, vol. I: Resolutions Adopted by the Conference, Res. 1, Annex I.

72 *Alabama Claims*, 572–3, 613; see also ILC Draft Articles on Transboundary Harm, Commentary to Art. 3, para. 11; Sibert, *Traité de Droit International Public* (1951), vol. I, 317.

73 *LCB* v. *UK* (App. No. 23413/94), ECHR, 9 June 1998.   74 *Ibid.*, para. 39.

the claim of an Iraqi national who stepped on a mine while clearing a minefield in the Chowman Valley in Iraq after the first Gulf war. The severely injured applicant contended that, since Italy was the state that had permitted the sale of mines to Iraq without adopting any controls or establishing an effective arms transfer licensing system, it had failed to take adequate preventive measures against the risk of an 'indiscriminate' use of such arms. The Commission stated:

> There is no immediate relationship between the mere supply, even if not properly regulated, of weapons and the possible 'indiscriminate' use thereof in a third country, the latter's action constituting the direct and decisive cause of the accident which the applicant suffered.[75]

In these circumstances, Italy could not reasonably have been expected to take positive preventive action in response to such a remote risk of harm.

Causation

Where a state has the requisite knowledge of the risk that the prohibited private activity will occur and yet the state fails to take diligent preventive steps, will the mere occurrence of that activity give rise to state responsibility? Or must there also be a causal nexus between the state's failure to take preventive steps and the subsequent occurrence of the prohibited private activity?

The answer to this question depends on the particular primary rule under consideration, and not upon the secondary rules of state responsibility. This is presumably why causation is not discussed in Part I of the ILC Articles dealing with 'the internationally wrongful act of a State'. The Commentary to an earlier draft of the ILC Articles stated in Article 23, which was expressly devoted to the breach of an obligation to prevent a given event, that the internationally wrongful event must have occurred 'because the State has failed to prevent it by its conduct', and that 'for there to be a breach of the obligation, a certain causal link – indirect, of course, not direct – must exist between the occurrence of the event and the conduct adopted in the matter by the organs of the State'.[76] Article 23 was not included in the final version of the ILC Articles, and the only reference to causation is now in Article 31 dealing with reparation: the responsible state is under an obligation to make full reparation only for

---

75 *Tugar* v. *Italy* (App. No. 22869/93), Decision 22869 (18 October 1995) DR, vol. 83A, 29.
76 R Ago, 'Seventh Report on State Responsibility' (1978) *Yearbook of the International Law Commission*, vol. II(2), Commentary to Art. 23, para. 6.

the injury 'caused by' the internationally wrongful act. The notion of causation in Article 31 parallels that found in domestic tort law. This is clearly different from the notion of causation presently under discussion, which pertains to the structure of the internationally wrongful act itself, like the parallel concept in domestic criminal law.[77]

These two distinct notions of causation are evident in the ICJ's judgment in the *Genocide* case. The Court stated that responsibility for a failure to prevent genocide is incurred 'if the State manifestly failed to take all measures to prevent genocide which were within its power, and which *might have contributed* to preventing the genocide'.[78] The Court explained that

> it is irrelevant whether the State whose responsibility is in issue claims, or even proves, that even if it had employed all means reasonably at its disposal, they would not have sufficed to prevent the commission of genocide. *As well as being generally difficult to prove, this is irrelevant to the breach of the obligation of conduct in question,* the more so since the possibility remains that the combined efforts of several States, each complying with its obligation to prevent, might have achieved the result averting the commission of genocide which the efforts of only one State were insufficient to produce.[79]

This notion of causation corresponds to the structure of the internationally wrongful act – that is, to the content of the primary obligation to prevent genocide. Later in the judgment, in assessing the claim for reparation, the Court examined whether and to what extent the alleged injury was the consequence of wrongful conduct by the respondent, such that the respondent should be required to make reparation for the injury. In this context, 'the question whether the genocide would have taken place even if the Respondent had attempted to prevent it by employing all means in its possession, becomes directly relevant'.[80] This notion of causation corresponds to Article 31 of the ILC Articles and to the parallel concept in domestic tort law.

The ICJ's 'might have contributed' test for causation could provide a useful model for the assessment of other obligations of prevention in international law. Indeed, the ECtHR has adopted a similar test in relation to the protection of the right to life. Article 2 of the ECHR requires member states not only to refrain from the intentional and unlawful taking of life,

---

77 See Conforti, 'State Responsibility for Breach of Positive Obligations', 136.
78 *Genocide* case, para. 430 (emphasis added).   79 *Ibid.*, para. 430 (emphasis added).
80 *Ibid.*, para. 462.

but also to take appropriate steps to safeguard the lives of those within their jurisdiction. The ECtHR stated in the *Keenan* case:

> For a positive obligation to arise, it must be established . . . that the authorities knew or ought to have known at the time of the existence of a real and immediate risk to the life of an identified individual from the criminal acts of a third party and that they failed to take measures within the scope of their powers which, judged reasonably, *might have been expected to avoid that risk*.[81]

For other obligations, it may be necessary to establish a more direct causal relationship between the state's omission and the wrongful private conduct in order to establish a violation. It will always be necessary to examine the precise content of the relevant primary obligation in order to identify the requisite causal relationship.

Damage

There is no general requirement that the victim state show material or moral damage in order to establish state responsibility. In many cases, the legal injury is deemed inherent in the wrongdoing state's breach of its international obligation towards the claimant state. For example, the obligation under a treaty to enact a uniform law is breached by the failure to enact the law, and it is not necessary for another state party to point to any specific damage caused by that failure.[82] In other cases, the particular primary obligation in question may require the claimant state to prove damage in order to establish responsibility. For example, states may be held liable for the environmental damage caused by their failure to prevent certain private activities in state territory, in which case the existence of damage is a crucial component of the internationally wrongful act itself. The relevance of damage in assessing breach depends on the primary rule under consideration, and not on the secondary rules of state responsibility, although in any case damage will frequently be taken into account when assessing the modalities and quantum of reparation.

2.5 Circumstances precluding wrongfulness

In certain limited circumstances, a state that has engaged in internationally wrongful conduct may be able to rely on some defence or excuse to

---

81 *Keenan* v. *UK*, para. 89 (quoting *Osman* v. *UK*, para. 116) (emphasis added).
82 See ILC Articles, Commentary to Art. 2, para. 9.

absolve itself of international responsibility. Part I, Chapter 5, of the ILC Articles catalogues six such 'circumstances precluding wrongfulness': consent,[83] self-defence,[84] countermeasures,[85] *force majeure*,[86] distress[87] and necessity.[88] This list is not exhaustive, as specific defences or excuses may be recognised for particular obligations. Article 26 makes it clear that a state cannot rely on any of these circumstances if such reliance would conflict with a peremptory norm of general international law.

These circumstances will only justify or excuse the otherwise wrongful act for as long as they continue to exist. For example, if State A takes countermeasures in response to a breach of obligations by State B owed to State A, and State B then recommences performance of its obligations, State A must terminate its countermeasures; if it does not, it will incur responsibility for the period after State B resumed performance of its obligations.[89]

2.6 Consequences of state responsibility

Finally, turning to the consequences of state responsibility, in general the commission of an internationally wrongful act of a state gives rise to certain secondary obligations on the part of the wrongdoing state. These are codified in Part II, Chapter 1, of the ILC Articles. Article 30 identifies two principal legal consequences of an internationally wrongful act, namely, the wrongdoing state's obligation to cease the wrongful conduct and its obligation to make full reparation for the injury caused by that act.[90]

The obligation of reparation is the automatic corollary of a state's responsibility.[91] In essence, the law attempts to restore, as far as possible, the situation that existed prior to the state's failure to fulfil its obligation.[92] The Permanent Court of International Justice explained this principle in the following terms:

> The essential principle contained in the actual notion of an illegal act . . . is that reparation must, as far as possible, wipe out all the consequences of the illegal act and re-establish the situation which would, in all probability, have existed if that act had not been committed. Restitution in kind, or, if this is not possible, payment of a sum corresponding to the value which a

---

83 *Ibid.*, Art. 20.   84 *Ibid.*, Art. 21.   85 *Ibid.*, Art. 22.   86 *Ibid.*, Art. 23.
87 *Ibid.*, Art. 24.   88 *Ibid.*, Art. 25.
89 *Ibid.*, Art. 27(a); see also Arts. 52(3)(a) and 53.   90 *Ibid.*, Arts. 30 and 31.
91 *Factory at Chorzów* (Merits) PCIJ Ser. A No. 17 (1927), 29; *Spanish Zone of Morocco Claims (Spain v. Great Britain)* (1925) 2 RIAA 615, 641; *SS Wimbledon* PCIJ Ser. A No. 1 (1923), 3; ILC Articles, Commentary to Art. 31, para. 4.
92 See comments of UN special rapporteur (1987), UN Doc. A/CN.4/405, 17 para. 55; *Factory at Chorzów*, 47–8.

restitution in kind would bear; the award, if need be, of damages for loss sustained which would not be covered by restitution in kind or payment in place of it – such are the principles which should serve to determine the amount of compensation due for an act contrary to international law.[93]

Where a court has jurisdiction to determine a dispute, it will generally also have jurisdiction to determine the nature and extent of reparation.[94] Restitution in kind is the primary method of providing reparation, since it aims to re-establish the situation that existed before the commission of the wrongful act.[95] Insofar as the damage is not made good by restitution, the wrongdoing state is under an obligation to provide compensation. The basic requirement is that compensation should cover any 'financially assessable damage' flowing from the breach,[96] and this may be supplemented by interest.[97]

Although international tribunals are gradually developing the international law of remedies, many international disputes retain a distinctly symbolic element.[98] Frequently, the claimant will seek non-monetary compensation, known as 'satisfaction', such as 'an acknowledgment of the breach, an expression of regret, an apology or another appropriate modality'.[99] In many cases before international tribunals, an authoritative finding of the breach will be held to be sufficient satisfaction.[100] Such a finding serves to clarify the precise contours of the international obligation, and this then feeds back into the internal political processes of states where it can shape domestic laws and policies in accordance with international law.

Specialist treaties may also provide for specific forms of redress or other legal consequences.[101] In HRL, for example, in addition to an obligation of 'substantive' reparation (restitution, compensation, satisfaction and guarantees of non-repetition), a 'procedural' obligation of reparation may arise. This constitutes an obligation on the wrongdoing state, owed to other states, to give the injured individual an effective domestic remedy against the violation.[102]

---

93 *Ibid.*, 47.   94 See, e.g., Statute of the International Court of Justice, Art. 36.
95 For a detailed discussion of the forms and functions of reparation, see Brownlie, *State Responsibility*, ch. XIII.
96 ILC Articles, Art. 36.   97 *Ibid.*, Art. 38.
98 See Evans, *International Law*, 2nd edn (2006), 472.   99 ILC Articles, Art. 27(2).
100 See Shelton, *Remedies in International Human Rights Law* (1999), 199–213.
101 See ILC Articles, Introduction to Part Two, para. 2.
102 See, e.g., ECHR, Art. 13; American Convention, Art. 25; ICCPR, Art. 2(3); see also Pisillo-Mazzeschi, 'International Obligations to Provide for Reparation Claims', in Randelzhofer and Tomuschat (eds.), *State Responsibility and the Individual: Reparation in Instances of Grave Violations of Human Rights* (1999), 155–6.

The responsible state is only liable for injury that is 'caused by' its internationally wrongful act.[103] There must therefore be a causal link between the internationally wrongful act and the injury, and the injury must not be too 'remote' or 'consequential' to be the subject of reparation. In some cases, the injury may be attributable to a combination of causes, or to one of several concurrently operating causes, only one of which is to be ascribed to the responsible state. Nonetheless, the responsible state may be held responsible for the totality of the injury, provided that it is not too remote to be the subject of reparation.[104] In the *Hostages* case, for example, although the initial seizure of the hostages by Iranian students was not attributable to Iran, the Court held that Iran was fully liable for the hostages' ordeal from the moment of its failure to protect them.[105] Similarly, in the *Corfu Channel* case the Court did not find that Albania had laid the mines that damaged the British ships, but instead found Albania responsible for its failure to warn the UK of the presence of the mines. Nonetheless, the UK recovered the full amount of its claim against Albania.[106]

In addition to the consequences outlined above, certain serious breaches of peremptory norms of general international law (*jus cogens*) give rise to an obligation on all other states to refrain from recognising as lawful the situation thereby created or from rendering aid or assistance in maintaining it.[107] States must also cooperate to bring the serious breach to an end 'through any lawful means'. A breach is serious if it involves a 'gross or systematic failure by the responsible state to fulfil' such an obligation.[108]

2.7 Conclusion

The hiring state, the host state and the home state of a PMSC have a range of international obligations which indirectly encourage and, in some cases, directly oblige them to take positive steps to control company behaviour in armed conflict. Where a PMSC engages in inappropriate or harmful behaviour or otherwise fails to act in accordance with the standard required by international law, in certain circumstances that PMSC misconduct may lead to the international responsibility of any or all of

---

103 ILC Articles, Art. 31.   104 See *Ibid.*, Commentary to Art. 31, paras. 10 and 12–13.
105 *Hostages* case, paras. 60–8.
106 See *Corfu Channel* (Merits); *Corfu Channel* (Assessment of Amount of Compensation) ICJ Reports 1949, 244, 250.
107 See ILC Articles, Art. 41(2).   108 *Ibid.*, Art. 40(2).

these three categories of states. Some instances of PMSC misconduct may be directly attributable to the hiring state, such that the misconduct itself is deemed to be an act of the state giving rise to its responsibility under international law. Moreover, irrespective of the attributability of the PMSC misconduct itself, in certain circumstances it may indirectly give rise to the responsibility of the hiring state, the host state and/or the home state for a failure to fulfil a primary obligation to prevent, investigate, punish or redress.

The remainder of this book utilises the general framework set out in this chapter in order to examine the specific obligations on the hiring state, the host state and the home state of a PMSC. A clear understanding of these obligations may assist in the determination of state responsibility following an allegation of PMSC misconduct, either by facilitating formal dispute resolution proceedings or, more commonly, by providing a legal framework within which states can resolve their disputes diplomatically through negotiation. More generally, the analysis in this book may encourage and assist states to develop their internal laws and policies on private security in accordance with international standards, and this could help to improve overall PMSC compliance with international law.

3

The attribution of PMSC conduct to
the hiring state

PMSCs often work in zones of armed conflict alongside and in conjunction with the armed forces of their hiring state, performing many of the same functions in the context of the same overall mission. Like national soldiers, PMSC personnel may engage in inappropriate or harmful conduct that is inconsistent with the primary obligations of their hiring state; they may commit war crimes, for example, or violate human rights. Yet it will generally be more difficult to establish the responsibility of the hiring state for violations committed by a PMSC employee than it would be if a national soldier of that state were to engage in the same conduct. This discrepancy could provide an incentive for states to outsource their military and security activities in order to reduce the risk that they will incur responsibility for violations of international law in armed conflict.[1]

Nonetheless, this chapter argues that states *cannot* simply outsource their international responsibility by conducting their military and security functions through private contractors rather than regular soldiers. On the contrary, the traditional law of state responsibility is sufficiently broad and flexible to accommodate the majority of PMSC activities performed for a state in armed conflict. This chapter critically analyses each of the three principal ways in which PMSC conduct may be attributable to the hiring state under the secondary rules of state responsibility. The first section examines the rare case in which a PMSC is so highly integrated into the hiring state's armed forces that it is deemed to form part of those forces for the purposes of state responsibility. The second section assesses the more common scenario in which a PMSC is empowered by the law of the hiring state to exercise elements of governmental authority. The third section considers attribution based on the hiring state's instructions, direction or

---

1 See Hoppe, 'Passing the Buck: State Responsibility for Private Military Companies' (2008) 19(5) *EJIL* 989; University Centre for International Humanitarian Law, 'Expert Meeting on Private Military Contractors' (Geneva, August 2005) ('UCIHL Expert Meeting'), 20–2.

control. A close analysis of the rules of state responsibility reveals that a large proportion of PMSC activities in armed conflict will fall within one of these three categories.

3.1 PMSCs forming part of the armed forces

In rare cases, a PMSC may be so highly integrated into the armed forces of its hiring state that it actually forms part of those forces for the purposes of state responsibility. Such a finding would be highly significant for the hiring state, as it is much easier to establish state responsibility for acts of state organs than for acts of private individuals. This section identifies the circumstances in which a PMSC will form part of the hiring state's armed forces and discusses the attribution of PMSC conduct to the state in such cases, both in international and in non-international armed conflict.

Definition of the armed forces

International armed conflicts

Traditionally, international humanitarian law (IHL) relied upon states' domestic definitions of their armed forces in order to prescribe the rights and obligations associated with membership of those forces. Article 4A(1) of the Third Geneva Convention (GCIII) reflects this approach.[2] Article 43 of the First Additional Protocol to the Geneva Conventions (Protocol I), on the other hand, provides an *international* definition of the armed forces, which focuses upon the factual circumstances of an individual's participation in the conflict and not upon their legal status under domestic law.[3]

Article 4A of the Third Geneva Convention   Article 4A(1) of GCIII identifies one category of individuals entitled to prisoner of war status, namely, '[m]embers of the armed forces of a Party to the conflict as well as members of militias or volunteer corps forming part of such armed forces'. The term 'armed forces' in this provision encompasses only those individuals who form part of the armed forces *de jure* under the domestic law of the state in question. The International Committee of

---

2 Third Geneva Convention relative to the Treatment of Prisoners of War (adopted 12 August 1949, entered into force 21 October 1950), 75 UNTS 135.
3 First Additional Protocol to the Geneva Conventions of 12 August 1949, and relating to the Protection of Victims of International Armed Conflicts (adopted 8 June 1977, entered into force 7 December 1979), 1125 UNTS 3.

the Red Cross (ICRC) Commentary to GCIII explains that the reference to 'militias or volunteer corps forming part of such armed forces' refers to groups that form part of the armed forces under domestic law but are nonetheless 'quite distinct from the army as such'. Although the reference to such groups was strictly speaking 'probably not essential', since 'these were covered by the expression "armed forces"', for the sake of clarity the drafters chose to maintain this reference as it appears in the Hague Regulations.[4]

Article 4A(2) identifies a second category of individuals also entitled to prisoner of war status, namely, '[m]embers of other militias and members of other volunteer corps, including those of organised resistance movements, belonging to a Party' who fulfil the following four conditions:

(a) that of being commanded by a person responsible for his subordinates;

(b) that of having a fixed distinctive sign recognizable at a distance;

(c) that of carrying arms openly;

(d) that of conducting their operations in accordance with the laws and customs of war.

Thus, under Article 4A there are two ways by which a PMSC employee could qualify as a combatant entitled to prisoner of war status: he or she could be formally incorporated into the armed forces of the hiring state (Article 4A(1)) or, in the absence of such *de jure* incorporation, he or she could fulfil the criteria *de facto* set out in Article 4A(2). Article 4A has nothing to say, however, on the criteria for membership of a state's armed forces *per se*.

Article 43 of Protocol I   In contrast to Article 4A of GCIII, Article 43 of Protocol I lays down an *international* definition of the 'armed forces', which is not dependent upon domestic law. Given that a large majority of states have ratified Protocol I, Article 43 will be applicable in a substantial proportion of international conflicts.[5] This definition of the armed forces is central to the assessment of state responsibility in such conflicts because Article 91 of Protocol I provides a special rule of attribution for the conduct of a state's 'armed forces', as will be discussed below. Given that

4 Pictet (ed.), *Commentary to the Geneva Convention Relative to the Treatment of Prisoners of War* (1960), 52.

5 For the list of states parties, see www.icrc.org/ihl.nsf/WebSign?ReadForm&id=470&ps=P/.

Article 91 was adopted after Article 43, the relevant definition of the armed forces for the purpose of Article 91 is presumably that contained in Article 43. In other words, the acts of PMSC personnel who fall within Article 43 will be attributable to the hiring state pursuant to Article 91.[6]

Article 43(1) provides:

> The armed forces of a Party to a conflict consist of all organized armed forces, groups and units which are under a command responsible to that Party for the conduct of its subordinates, even if that Party is represented by a government or an authority not recognized by an adverse Party. Such armed forces shall be subject to an internal disciplinary system which, *inter alia*, shall enforce compliance with the rules of international law applicable in armed conflict.

Article 43(2) then provides that all members of the armed forces so defined (other than medical personnel and chaplains) are combatants.

Article 43 effectively abolishes the distinction between regular and irregular forces in Article 4A of GCIII and brings all combatants within the general category of the 'armed forces'. The definition of the armed forces in Article 43(1) is considerably broader than the definition of combatants in Article 4A of GCIII, since the former does *not* stipulate that individuals must wear a fixed distinctive sign, carry their arms openly and comply with the laws and customs of war (criteria (b) to (d) of Article 4A(2)). These three requirements continue to attach to the armed forces as a whole and must therefore be enforced through the state's 'internal disciplinary system', and (b) and (c) are incorporated into Article 44 as potential bases for forfeiting prisoner of war status.[7] These criteria do not, however, form part of the definition of the armed forces in Article 43(1). The second sentence of Article 43(1) is an additional rule applicable to the armed forces as defined in the first sentence, rather than a component of the definition of the armed forces *per* se; this is clear from the use of the word 'such' at the beginning of the second sentence. The result of this formulation is that some PMSC personnel may form part of the armed

---

6 See Kamenov, 'The Origin of State and Entity Responsibility for Violations of International Humanitarian Law in Armed Conflicts', in Kalshoven and Sandoz (eds.), *Implementation of International Humanitarian Law* (1989), 174–6.

7 Art. 44 specifies that any combatant who falls into the power of an adverse party shall be a prisoner of war. It goes on to specify that combatants must distinguish themselves from the civilian population with some sort of external sign; where this is not possible, combatants must carry their arms openly during the preparation and commission of each military engagement. If they fail to do so, they forfeit their right to prisoner of war status.

forces under Protocol I even though they do not qualify as combatants under GCIII.[8]

Thus, there are two situations in which PMSC personnel hired by a state to work in armed conflict would fall within the hiring state's armed forces under international law: first, the PMSC personnel could be incorporated *de jure* by the hiring state into its regular armed forces; or, secondly, the PMSC personnel could fall within those forces *de facto* because they qualify as members of organised armed forces, groups or units under a command responsible to the hiring state within Article 43 of Protocol I.

Essentially the same interpretation appears in the 2008 Montreux Document, which was produced by seventeen states as a result of an initiative launched jointly by Switzerland and the ICRC.[9] Part I of the Montreux Document, which sets out the existing international obligations of states, PMSCs and their personnel under international law, provides that PMSC violations of international law are attributable to the hiring state where the companies or their personnel are 'incorporated by the State into its regular armed forces in accordance with its domestic legislation' or 'members of organised armed forces, groups or units under a command responsible to the State'.[10] The Montreux Document is highly significant not only because it has triggered considerable discussion and support,[11] but also because it represents a clear expression of *opinio juris* of the states involved in its drafting (Afghanistan, Angola, Australia, Austria, Canada, China, France, Germany, Iraq, Poland, Sierra Leone, South Africa, Sweden, Switzerland, the UK, Ukraine and the US), a list that includes many of the states most affected by PMSC activity.[12]

---

8 See Sandoz, Swinarski and Zimmermann (eds.), *Commentary to the Additional Protocols of 8 June 1977 to the Geneva Conventions of 12 August 1949* (1987) ('*ICRC Commentary to the Additional Protocols*'), paras. 1659–81.

9 Montreux Document on Pertinent International Legal Obligations and Good Practices for States Related to Operations of Private Military and Security Companies during Armed Conflict (17 September 2008), UN Doc. A/63/467-S/2008/636 ('Montreux Document').

10 *Ibid.*, Part I, para. 7.

11 See, e.g., European Commission for Democracy through Law, 'Report on Private Military and Security Firms and Erosion of the State Monopoly on the Use of Force' (2009), para. 65.

12 For a discussion of the significance of the Montreux Document, see Cockayne, 'Regulating Private Military and Security Companies: The Content, Negotiation, Weaknesses and Promise of the Montreux Document' (2009) 13(3) *Journal of Conflict and Security Law* 401; del Prado, 'Private Military and Security Companies and the UN Working Group on the Use of Mercenaries' (2009) 13(3) *Journal of Conflict and Security Law* 429, 441–9.

Membership *de jure* **of the hiring state's armed forces**   A PMSC would certainly fall within Article 43 if the hiring state formally incorporated the company into its armed forces. Most countries have formal procedures for enlistment with which PMSCs would need to comply in order to acquire *de jure* membership of the armed forces, although some states have minimal procedures and might even permit individuals to become members of the armed forces merely by joining in the fighting.[13] A state hiring a foreign PMSC for combat or armed security might choose to incorporate the company into its armed forces in order to bring the contractors within the military chain of command, whilst also ensuring that they fall outside the definition of a mercenary in Article 47 of Protocol I.[14] Indeed, the government of Sierra Leone incorporated Executive Outcomes personnel into its armed forces before they fought in the civil war in 1995–6, just as the Papua New Guinea government incorporated Sandline personnel into its national forces as 'special constables' in 1997.[15] This practice, however, is virtually unheard of today.

A small number of commentators maintain that formal incorporation into a state's armed forces is the only way by which a group such as a PMSC could form part of those forces for the purposes of IHL. Those advancing this interpretation sometimes point to the requirement in Article 43(3) of Protocol I that a state notify the other parties to the conflict whenever it 'incorporates a paramilitary or armed law enforcement agency into its armed forces', arguing that this implies an obligation on the state to incorporate such groups formally into its armed forces.[16] However, an examination of the drafting history of Article 43(3) reveals that this argument is erroneous. The ICRC Commentary makes it clear that this provision was directed at domestic police forces, and was designed to ensure that there is no confusion between combatants in the armed forces

---

13 Schmitt notes that this was the case for the Taliban in Afghanistan: see Schmitt, 'Humanitarian Law and Direct Participation in Hostilities by Private Contractors or Civilian Employees' (2004–5) 5 *Chicago Journal of International Law* 511, 524.

14 For a discussion of the definition of a mercenary in Art. 47, see Chapter 1, section 1.3, and Chapter 5, section 5.1.

15 Dinnen, May and Regan (eds.), *Challenging the State: The Sandline Affair in Papua New Guinea* (1997); Zarate, 'The Emergence of a New Dog of War: Private International Security Companies, International Law, and the New World Disorder' (1998) 34 *Stanford Journal of International Law* 75, 124; UK Foreign and Commonwealth Office Green Paper, 'Private Military Companies: Options for Regulation' (2002), para. 6.

16 See, e.g., ICRC, 'Report of the Third Expert Meeting on the Notion of Direct Participation in Hostilities' (October 2005), 77; UCIHL Expert Meeting, 11–12.

and state officials performing internal law-keeping functions.[17] Where a state has converted the *de jure* status of the latter to that of the former, it has an obligation to notify the adverse party 'so that there is no confusion on its part'. This obligation applies only in relation to *de jure* state organs that can be equated with domestic police forces; it does not apply more generally to groups (such as PMSCs) that constitute private entities under the domestic law of the state.

Membership *de facto* of the hiring state's armed forces   According to the Commentary by Bothe, Partsch and Solf, Article 43(1) was intended to include any organised group that in fact 'acts on behalf of the party to the conflict in some manner', so long as 'that party is responsible for the group's operations'.[18] This leaves open the possibility that a PMSC could form part of the hiring state's armed forces by virtue of its *de facto* incorporation. The recognition of *de facto* state organs in international law is not unique to Article 43; on the contrary, the ICJ acknowledged in the *Nicaragua* and *Genocide* cases that groups may be treated as state organs under the general law of state responsibility even where they are not classified as such under domestic law.[19] States are not free to decide entirely subjectively who forms part of their armed forces under international law.

The key criterion in Article 43 is that the group be 'under a command responsible' to that state. The ICRC Commentary explains that '[a]ll armed forces, groups and units are necessarily structured and have a hierarchy, as they are subordinate to a command which is responsible to one of the Parties to the conflict for their operations'.[20] The Commentary adds that, in general, 'the exercise of such responsibility implies

---

17 *ICRC Commentary to the Additional Protocols*, para. 1682.
18 Bothe, Partsch and Solf, *New Rules for Victims of Armed Conflict: Commentary on the Two 1977 Protocols Additional to the Geneva Conventions of 1949* (1982), 234. During the drafting of Protocol I, many developing countries argued for this definition because they did not have substantial regular armed forces and had to rely largely on guerrilla troops: see *ICRC Commentary to the Additional Protocols*, para. 1672; Henckaerts and Doswald-Beck (eds.), *Customary International Humanitarian Law* (2005) ('*ICRC Customary Law Study*'), vol. I, rule 4, 14–16.
19 *Military and Paramilitary Activities In and Against Nicaragua (Nicaragua* v. *USA)* (Merits) ICJ Reports 1986, paras. 109–10; *Case Concerning the Application of the Convention on the Prevention and Punishment of the Crime of Genocide (Bosnia and Herzegovina* v. *Serbia and Montenegro)* (Merits) (26 February 2007), paras. 396–7. The recognition of *de facto* state organs under customary international law will be discussed below in relation to non-international armed conflicts.
20 *ICRC Commentary to the Additional Protocols*, para. 1672.

the exercise of effective control over subordinates', referring to Article 87 which governs the duty of commanders to prevent, suppress and report breaches of IHL committed by members of the armed forces under their command.[21] States have an obligation under Article 87(2) 'to require that ... commanders ensure that members of the armed forces under their command are aware of their obligations under the Conventions and this Protocol.'

The Appeals Chamber of the International Criminal Tribunal for the former Yugoslavia (ICTY) has likewise emphasised the need for state control in assessing whether a group in fact forms part of a state's armed forces. In the *Tadić* case of 1999, the ICTY Appeals Chamber developed its test of 'overall control' in relation to the rule of attribution in Article 8 of the International Law Commission's Articles on Responsibility of States for Internationally Wrongful Acts (ILC Articles),[22] as applied to 'an organised and hierarchically structured group' such as a military unit or armed bands of irregulars.[23] The Appeals Chamber noted that this test is also 'indispensable for determining when individuals who, formally speaking, are not military officials of a State may nevertheless be regarded as forming part of the armed forces of such a State'.[24]

Article 43 does not specifically require 'military' command, leaving open the possibility of command by civilian officials. Thus, although PMSCs generally fall outside the military chain of command and control, in theory they could still fulfil the requirement of responsible command if they were acting within a hierarchical structure that was answerable to the hiring state. For a PMSC to fulfil this criterion, government officials (civilian or military) would need to exercise control over the company's operations, as well as taking measures to prevent, suppress and report breaches of IHL committed by the company in the field. The terms of the PMSC's contract could provide some indicia that the company was acting within a hierarchical system of control and accountability, particularly if the contract included provisions specifying oversight by a particular government official, accompanied by regular reporting requirements and consequences for violation such as contractual termination, monetary penalties and exclusion from future contracts. One factor complicating

---

21 *Ibid.*, para. 1672, note 20.
22 ILC Articles on Responsibility of States for Internationally Wrongful Acts with Commentaries (2001) *Yearbook of the International Law Commission*, vol. II(2).
23 *Prosecutor* v. *Tadić*, Judgment, ICTY-94-1-A, Appeals Chamber, 15 July 1999 ('*Tadić* appeal judgment'), para. 120, discussed in section 3.3 of this chapter.
24 *Ibid.*, para. 98, note 117.

this analysis is the complex web of subcontracting arrangements that is common in the private security industry.[25] A 2006 directive of the US Department of Defense (DOD) requires 'contractors to institute and implement effective programs to prevent violations of the law of war by their employees *and subcontractors*, including law of war training and dissemination'.[26] Yet the reality is that the more convoluted the contractual relationship between the state and the company, the more difficult it will be to establish responsible command within Article 43(1).

An examination of US practice suggests that the oversight and disciplinary arrangements for PMSCs hired by the US would generally fail to meet the threshold for Article 43(1). For example, according to an official report into the Abu Ghraib prisoner abuse scandal, in 2003–4 in Iraq a small number of contracting officers were responsible for administering and monitoring numerous PMSC contracts involving 100 or more PMSC employees, sometimes in several locations. These contracting officers 'do well to keep up with the paper work, and simply have no time to actively monitor contractor performance'.[27] In some cases, the control relationship between the US and the PMSCs was even reversed, with contractors supervising public personnel rather than the other way around.[28]

The DOD subsequently attempted to improve these practices, and published a range of policy documents in 2005–6 with a view to increasing state control and accountability within the private security industry.[29] Serious problems nonetheless persisted. An August 2008 report of Congress explained the general supervisory arrangements for contractors in the field, noting that the civilian contracting officer who is designated to administer and monitor a particular PMSC contract

> is not always colocated with the military commander or the contractor personnel and may not even be within the theater of operations. The contracting officer may not have access to the place of performance if that place is remote or dangerous or if it covers a large geographic area. Instead,

25 See US Commission on Wartime Contracting Hearing, 'Subcontracting: Who's Minding the Store?' (26 July 2010).
26 US Department of Defense Directive 2311.01 E (9 May 2006), para. 5.11.9 (emphasis added).
27 Fay, 'Investigation of the Abu Ghraib Detention Facility and 205th Military Intelligence Brigade' (August 2004), 50–2.
28 *Ibid.*, 51. A similar reversal in the supervisory relationship was reported in relation to Blackwater operations in Najaf in 2004: see 'Contractors in Combat: Firefight from a Rooftop in Iraq', *Virginia Pilot* (25 July 2006); Scahill, *Blackwater* (2007), 123.
29 See, e.g., US Department of Defense Instruction 3020.41 (3 October 2005); US Department of Defense Directive 2311.01 E (9 May 2006).

he or she may rely on a technical representative, usually a military officer on the staff of the military unit being supported and colocated with the contractor. The technical representative interacts frequently, sometimes daily, with the contractor about details of performance but not about the scope or size of the contract.[30]

In some cases, the military commander may have a degree of authority over the PMSC by virtue of 'a task-order arrangement', which enables the commander to add new tasks to an existing contract within overall resource bounds. But the contractors still remain outside the military chain of command and control, and the contractual instrument provides little flexibility to adjust to rapid changes in government objectives or practical conditions on the ground. Furthermore, a 2009 report of the Commission on Wartime Contracting found that many civilian contracting officers lack adequate skills and training, and frequently have insufficient time to perform their duty to administer and monitor PMSC contracts in the field.[31]

Even broad governmental oversight of PMSC contracts with the US is sometimes lacking. For example, a June 2009 Senate report on the ArmorGroup–State Department contract to guard the US embassy in Kabul describes the contract as 'a case study of how mismanagement and lack of oversight can result in poor performance'.[32] The report details numerous deficiencies in ArmorGroup's performance including a severe, ongoing security guard shortage, the provision of substandard equipment, inadequate English language skills and security training amongst guards, and overworking of guards resulting in chronic sleep deprivation. These contractual violations continued throughout 2007 and 2008 despite

---

30 US Congressional Budget Office, 'Contractors' Support of US Operations in Iraq' (August 2008) (references omitted).
31 US Commission on Wartime Contracting, 'At What Cost? Contingency Contracting in Iraq and Afghanistan' (10 June 2009), 10; see also Government Accountability Office, 'Rebuilding Iraq: DOD and State Department Have Improved Oversight and Coordination of Private Security Contractors in Iraq, But Further Actions Are Needed to Sustain Improvements', GAO-08-966 (31 July 2008); Special Inspector General for Iraq Reconstruction, 'Field Commanders See Improvements in Controlling and Coordinating Private Security Contractor Missions in Iraq', SIGIR 09-022 (28 July 2009); US Government Accountability Office, 'Contingency Contracting: Improvements Needed in Management of Contractors Supporting Contract and Grant Administration in Iraq and Afghanistan' (April 2010); US Commission on Wartime Contracting Hearing, 'Reliance on Contingency Services Contracts: Where Is the Management and Oversight?' (19 April 2010).
32 US Senate Committee on Homeland Security and Governmental Affairs, Subcommittee on Contracting Oversight, 'New Information about the Guard Force Contract at the US Embassy in Kabul' (June 2009), 9.

the issuance of almost one written warning per month from the US State Department, jeopardising the security of the embassy and demonstrating the Department's chronic inability to compel contractual compliance. Nonetheless, the State Department renewed ArmorGroup's contract in June 2009.[33] Further reports in September 2009 detailed lewd behaviour and sexual misconduct by the ArmorGroup contractors and supervisors at their living quarters at a base in Kabul, pointing to a pervasive breakdown of discipline amongst the guard force and further emphasising the inability of the State Department to control private security contractors in the field.[34]

Recent DOD measures have included the establishment of a Joint Contracting Command in both Iraq and Afghanistan to provide a more centralised management system and to enforce contracting support requirements during ongoing operations.[35] The DOD has also increased the number of civilian contracting offers sent to administer complex contracts, developed programmes to improve the training of uniformed personnel to manage contractors during contingency operations, and prescribed procedures for incident reporting and discipline or removal of contractors.[36] As things stand, however, most PMSC personnel working under US contracts would be unlikely to fall within Article 43(1).

International conflicts not governed by Protocol I   Protocol I has been ratified by a large majority of states, including Afghanistan and Iraq, but certain key states (most notably the US and Israel) are not parties thereto.[37] In international conflicts not governed by Protocol I, such as the conflict in Afghanistan in 2001, customary international law will dictate whether a PMSC forms part of the hiring state's armed forces.

---

33 See Thompson and Landler, 'Company Kept Kabul Security Contract Despite Record', *New York Times* (11 September 2009).
34 See Project on Government Oversight, Letter to Secretary of State Hillary Clinton Regarding US Embassy in Kabul (1 September 2009); Cole, 'Firm Fires US Embassy Guards in Kabul', *Wall Street Journal* (5 September 2009); Alexander, 'US Says 16 Guards Removed in Afghan Embassy Scandal', *New York Times* (10 September 2009); 'Embassy Guard Photos Evoke Abu Ghraib Comparison', *New York Times* (14 September 2009).
35 Schwartz, 'Department of Defense Contractors in Iraq and Afghanistan: Background and Analysis', Congressional Research Service Report for Congress R40764 (2 July 2010), 13.
36 *Ibid.*, 13–15; US Department of Defense Instruction 3020.50, 'US Government Private Security Contractors Operating in a Designated Area of Combat Operations' (22 June 2009).
37 Afghanistan ratified Protocol I on 10 November 2009 and Iraq ratified it on 1 April 2010: see www.icrc.org/ihl.nsf/WebSign?ReadForm&id=470&ps=P/.

Much of Protocol I is considered to be reflective of customary law. For example, Article 91 reproduces Article 3 of the Hague Convention Concerning the Laws and Customs of War on Land of 1907,[38] which reflects the customary rule.[39] The ICRC also classifies Article 43(1) as essentially reflective of customary law, noting that it mirrors the definitions in many military manuals and 'is supported by official statements and reported practice', including practice of states not, or not at the time, party to Protocol I.[40] The ICRC's recent study on customary IHL notes that the definition in Article 43(1)

> is now generally applied to all forms of armed groups who belong to a party to an armed conflict to determine whether they constitute armed forces. It is therefore no longer necessary to distinguish between regular and irregular armed forces. All those fulfilling the conditions in Article 43 of Additional Protocol I are armed forces.[41]

Many commentators question whether the process of assimilation of regular and irregular armed forces, as exemplified by Protocol I, has in fact reached the level of customary law as the ICRC asserts. In the 'practice' section of the ICRC study, most of the military manuals cited are those of states parties to Protocol I, and even some of those still contain references to the conditions for militias and resistance movements laid down by the Hague Regulations and GCIII. Of the non-parties' manuals cited in the ICRC study, only the Indonesian air force manual and the US naval handbook seem to accord with Article 43(1).[42] What is more, it is well known that the US and Israel continue to object to the Protocol's relaxation of the criteria for lawful combatancy.[43] These objections relate less to Article 43's definition of the armed forces *per se* than to Article

38 Convention Respecting the Laws and Customs of War on Land (adopted 18 October 1907, entered into force 26 January 1910), 205 Consol TS 277.

39 See *Case Concerning Armed Activities in the Territory of the Congo (DRC v. Uganda)* (Merits) ICJ Reports 2005, para. 214.

40 *ICRC Customary Law Study*, vol. I, rule 4, 14.   41 *Ibid.*, rule 4, 16.

42 *ICRC Customary Law Study*, vol. II, Part I, 88–97; see also Rogers, 'Combatant Status', in Wilmshurst and Breau (eds.), *Perspectives on the ICRC Study on Customary International Humanitarian Law* (2007), 110.

43 For the US position on Protocol I, see Memorandum for Mr John H. McNeill, Assistant General Counsel (International), '1977 Protocols Additional to the Geneva Conventions: Customary International Law Implications' (8 May 1969); Gasser, 'Agora: The US Decision Not to Ratify Protocol I to the Geneva Conventions in the Protection of War Victims' (1987) 81 *AJIL* 912; Parks, 'Remarks, Customary Law and Additional Protocol I to the Geneva Conventions for Protection of War Victims' (1987) 81 *American Society of International Law and Procedure* 27.

44's removal of the requirement that a combatant comply with IHL and distinguish him- or herself from the population at all times in order to retain status as a combatant. Even so, it might be somewhat unrealistic to insist upon a customary definition of the armed forces on the basis of a provision that is not recognised by the world's major military power, at least in the absence of evidence of widespread consensus amongst other states not party to Protocol I.[44]

Given the uncertainty surrounding the customary status of Article 43(1), in international conflicts not governed by Protocol I it will be necessary to examine the domestic law of the relevant state in order to delineate membership of the state's armed forces for the purpose of attribution. In rare cases, individuals who are not *de jure* members of the armed forces under domestic law may nonetheless be deemed *de facto* members of those forces under customary international law. Essentially, the same analysis applies in this context as in non-international armed conflicts, to which this discussion now turns.

Non-international armed conflicts

A government fighting rebel forces in its territory may choose to hire a local or foreign PMSC to help it to maintain authority, or it may request a foreign state to hire a PMSC to assist in defeating the insurgents. In each case, the company's activities will be governed both by the domestic law of the warring state and by the rules of IHL applicable in non-international armed conflicts – most importantly Common Article 3 of the Geneva Conventions and, for those states that are parties to it, the Second Additional Protocol to the Geneva Conventions (Protocol II).[45]

On the other hand, where a foreign state sends a PMSC to support the *insurgents* in the non-international conflict, rather than supporting the government, this may trigger the application of the more detailed rules of IHL governing international conflicts.[46] The regime of IHL that governs non-international armed conflicts may still be applicable to certain

---

44 See ICRC, 'Report of the First Expert Meeting on the Notion of Direct Participation in Hostilities' (September 2003), 77; Schmitt, 'Humanitarian Law and Direct Participation', 527, note 65.

45 Second Additional Protocol to the Geneva Conventions of 12 August 1949, and relating to the Protection of Victims of Non-International Armed Conflicts (adopted 8 June 1977, entered into force 7 December 1987), 1125 UNTS 609.

46 Such action may also constitute an unlawful intervention into the internal affairs of the warring state: see Chapter 6, section 6.2.

hostilities, since the conflict may be 'mixed' in the sense that an international conflict may be taking place alongside a non-international conflict in the same state.[47] It will therefore be necessary to assess the status of the particular hostilities under consideration in order to determine which regime of IHL applies.

In non-international armed conflicts, a state's armed forces are defined by reference to the same general rules that define the other organs of the state. The starting point will always be the domestic law of the state in question. Article 4 of the ILC Articles makes this clear by providing in paragraph two that a state organ 'includes any person or entity which has that status in accordance with the internal law of the State'. Yet domestic law by itself is not sufficient to identify all state organs for the purposes of state responsibility. The notion of a 'state organ' under general international law encompasses 'all the individual or collective entities which make up the organisation of the state and act on its behalf'.[48] There may be some entities falling within this description that are not classified as state organs under the domestic law of the state. The use of the term 'includes' in Article 4(2) of the ILC Articles leaves open the possibility that such entities might nonetheless be characterised as state organs under international law. As the Commentary to Article 4(2) explains, 'a State cannot avoid responsibility for the conduct of a body which does in truth act as one of its organs merely by denying it that status under its own law'.[49]

The ICJ considered the issue of *de facto* state organs in the *Nicaragua* case, holding that a person, group or entity that does not have the status of a state organ under domestic law may nonetheless be equated with a state organ if its relationship with the state is one of 'complete dependence' on the one side and control on the other.[50] On the facts, however, the Court found that the Nicaraguan *contras* were not completely dependent on the US.

The ICJ reiterated this principle in the *Genocide* case of 2006, making it clear that there are two categories of attribution based on the *de facto* status or conduct of a private actor: Article 4 encapsulates private actors (persons, groups or entities) that in fact *constitute* a state organ, whereas Article 8 encapsulates private actors that act under the instructions, direction or control of the hiring state in a particular

---

47 See *Prosecutor* v. *Tadić*, Decision on the Defence Motion for Interlocutory Appeal on Jurisdiction, ICTY-94-1-AR72, Appeals Chamber, 2 October 1995.
48 ILC Articles, Commentary to Art. 4, para. 1.
49 *Ibid.*, Commentary to Art. 4, para. 11.   50 *Nicaragua*, paras. 109–10.

instance.[51] The test governing the former category is considerably more stringent than that governing the latter. According to the Court, an entity that does not have the status of a state organ under the internal law of the state may nonetheless be equated to a *de facto* organ if its relationship with the state is one of 'complete dependence'. The Court emphasised the 'exceptional' nature of this situation: the entity must be 'merely the instrument' of the state, such that its supposed independence is 'purely fictitious'.[52]

Whilst it is possible to envisage exceptional cases in which a PMSC's supposed independence is merely fictitious,[53] most companies would fail this stringent test by virtue of their independent corporate structure and the fact that they generally have at least some autonomy in planning and performing their operations. A different conclusion might result, however, by focusing on the particular team of contractors that is actually performing the contract in question, rather than focusing on the PMSC as a whole. This would appear to be consistent with the ICJ's reference to 'persons, groups or entities' as potential units of analysis.[54] Chapter 1 explained that many PMSCs are global entities which recruit a unique team of personnel for each contract from an international database of names. Many contractors do not even enter the hiring state of the PMSC, but travel straight from their own home state to the host state with the sole purpose of performing their contract, lacking any personal interest in the conflict over and above financial gain. Hoppe distinguishes this scenario from that of the Nicaraguan *contras*, which the ICJ noted were not 'created' by the US, but instead had a prior existence and independent cause which the US simply exploited for its own purposes.[55] The Court explicitly identified this lack of state 'creation' as a relevant factor in rejecting the *de facto* organ status of the *contras*.[56] Similarly, in the *Congo* case, the ICJ was unable to find that Uganda had created the rebel group under consideration, and this was highly pertinent to the Court's conclusion that

---

51 *Genocide* case, paras. 396–7. This followed statements by the ICTY Appeals Chamber in the *Tadić* appeal judgment of 1999 (at paras. 106–14) that the ICJ's notions of 'complete dependence' and 'effective control' in *Nicaragua* were simply spelling out the requirements of the same test under Art. 8 of the ILC Articles.

52 *Genocide* case, paras. 391–3.

53 Hoppe cites the example of Air America in Vietnam, which was an 'air proprietary' operated by the CIA during the Cold War: see Hoppe, 'State Responsibility for Violations of International Humanitarian Law Committed by Individuals Providing Coercive Services under a Contract with a State' (2008), 15.

54 *Ibid.*, 15–17. 55 *Ibid.*, 15–16. 56 *Nicaragua*, paras. 107–8.

the rebels were not an organ of the state.[57] Against this background, the fact that the contract between the PMSC and the hiring state effectively leads to the 'creation' of a new team of contractors appears significant, and in some cases this unique sub-unit of a PMSC might even qualify as a *de facto* state organ as defined by the ICJ.

Attributing acts of the armed forces to the state

International armed conflicts

In international armed conflicts, the chief provision governing the attribution of conduct of the armed forces is Article 91 of Protocol I, which provides:

> A Party to the conflict which violates the provisions of the Conventions or of this Protocol shall, if the case demands, be liable to pay compensation. It shall be responsible for all acts committed by persons forming part of its armed forces.

This essentially reproduces Article 3 of Hague IV,[58] which reflects the customary rule.[59] In the *Congo* case, the ICJ applied Article 91 not only to violations of Hague IV and Protocol I committed by the Ugandan armed forces, but also to violations of other rules of IHL and human rights law (HRL).[60] Likewise, Article 91 could be applied to hold the hiring state responsible for violations of IHL and HRL committed by PMSC personnel forming part of the state's armed forces.[61]

The rule in Article 91 applies to *all* acts committed by persons forming part of a state's armed forces, whereas the general rule governing the attribution of conduct of state organs in Article 4 of the ILC Articles applies only to acts committed by state organs acting 'in that capacity'.[62] In this sense, Article 91 provides a more specific interpretation of the general rule, applicable to the particular situation of the armed forces in an international armed conflict. Stated otherwise, Article 91 provides specific instructions as to the requirements of the general rule in this particular circumstance – such instructions being that *all* persons forming part of a state's armed forces are deemed to be acting in an official capacity for

---

57 *Congo* case, paras. 158–60.
58 Convention Respecting the Laws and Customs of War on Land (adopted 18 October 1907, entered into force 26 January 1910), 205 Consol TS 277.
59 *Congo* case, para. 214.   60 *Ibid.*, paras. 214–20.
61 See Hoppe, 'Passing the Buck', 1005.
62 See ILC Articles, Commentary to Art. 4, para. 13; see also Art. 7.

the entire period of their deployment in the international conflict zone. When viewed in this way, Article 91 can be described as a *lex specialis* rule of attribution – *lex specialis* in this context referring to a principle of more specific interpretation rather than a principle to solve conflicts of norms.[63]

The view that international law provides a special rule of attribution for soldiers in an international armed conflict has been authoritatively advanced by some members of the ILC. In discussing 'cases in which the armed forces of several countries had committed acts unrelated to military operations', Reuter stated in 1975 that '[i]t was now a principle of codified international law that States were responsible for all acts of their armed forces'.[64] In a similar vein, Ago stated that Article 3 of Hague IV 'made provision for a veritable guarantee covering all damage that might be caused by armed forces, whether they had acted as organs or as private persons'.[65] According to Ago, the 'very specialized' nature of Hague IV meant that Article 3 'could not provide a basis for the drafting of' the general rule of attribution for acts of state organs – the 'general rule' that eventually became Article 4 of the ILC Articles.[66] The ICJ hinted at a similarly broad view of Article 3 in the *Congo* case:

> In the Court's view, by virtue of the military status and function of Ugandan soldiers in the DRC, their conduct is attributable to Uganda. The contention that the persons concerned did not act in the capacity of persons exercising governmental authority in the particular circumstances, is therefore without merit.[67]

The ICTY Appeals Chamber also noted in its *Tadić* judgment of 1999 that the view that Article 91 of Protocol I encapsulates a special regime of state

---

63 See generally Koskenniemi, 'Study on the Function and Scope of the Lex Specialis Rule and the Question of "Self Contained Regimes"' (2004), UN Doc. ILC(LVI)/SG/FIL/CRD.1/Add.1 (2004), 4; ILC Study Group on Fragmentation of International Law, 'Difficulties Arising from Diversification and Expansion of International Law' (29 July 2005), UN Doc. A/CN.4/L.676, 6, para. 2.5.1; see also the discussion in Chapter 4, section 4.2, of this book.

64 Report to the General Assembly (1975) *Yearbook of the International Law Commission*, vol. II, 7, para. 5.

65 ILC, 1306th Meeting, 9 May 1975, 'State Responsibility' (1975) *Yearbook of the International Law Commission*, vol. I, 16, para. 4.

66 *Ibid.*

67 *Congo* case, para. 213; see also Kalshoven, 'State Responsibility for Warlike Acts of the Armed Forces' (1991) 40 *ICLQ* 827, 838; ILC, '1306th Meeting' (1975) *Yearbook of the International Law Commission*, vol. I, 16, para. 4.

responsibility applicable to the armed forces in international conflicts 'has been forcefully advocated in the legal literature.'[68]

It follows from this conception that *all* the acts of PMSC personnel forming part of their hiring state's armed forces in an international armed conflict will be attributable to that state pursuant to Article 91. There will be no need to establish that the particular contractor was acting 'in that capacity' at the relevant time.

Non-international armed conflicts

Where a PMSC forms part of the hiring state's armed forces in a non-international conflict – either because the state has incorporated the company *de jure* into its armed forces or because the company qualifies as a *de facto* state organ under the 'complete dependence' test established by the ICJ – attribution falls to be assessed under the general rules of state responsibility reflected in the ILC Articles.

Article 4 provides the basic rule of attribution: the conduct of any state organ shall be considered an act of that state under international law. The ILC Commentary makes it clear that this rule encompasses only those acts of state organs that are committed 'in that capacity'.[69] Generally speaking, state officials will be acting in that capacity if they are using the means and powers pertaining to the exercise of their official functions, such that they are 'cloaked with governmental authority' when they engage in the conduct in question.[70] On the other hand, state officials will not be acting in that capacity if their conduct 'has no connection with the official function' and is, in fact, merely the conduct of private individuals.[71]

Much will turn on how broadly the notion of an individual acting 'in that capacity' is construed in a particular situation. Unlike members of the armed forces in an international armed conflict, it is difficult to argue that members of the armed forces in a non-international conflict should be deemed to be acting in that capacity at all times. Since most of these soldiers will be fighting in their own country, their presence in the conflict zone will not be due to their status and functions as state

---

68 *Tadić* appeal judgment, para. 98, note 117.
69 ILC Articles, Commentary to Art. 4, para. 13; see also *Youmans* case (1926) 4 RIAA 110; *Caire* case (1929) 5 RIAA 516; *Velásquez Rodríguez* v. *Honduras* (Merits), Judgment of 29 July 1988, IACtHR Ser. C No. 4, para. 170; Brownlie, *State Responsibility* (1983), 145.
70 *Petrolane Inc.* v. *Iran* (1991) 27 Iran–US CTR 64, 92.
71 *Caire* case, 531; see also ILC Articles, Commentary to Art. 7, para. 7; Brownlie, *State Responsibility*, 145–50.

officials, and there will clearly be times when they are out of uniform and are not in any way using the means and powers pertaining to the exercise of their official functions. In such cases, they should be treated as acting in a purely private capacity, with the result that their conduct will not be attributable to the state pursuant to Article 4.

It is important to note that Article 4 covers all acts carried out by state organs when they are functioning in their official capacity, even if they are acting *ultra vires* their authority or in contravention of their instructions at the relevant time.[72] In the *Mallén* case, for example, whereas an act of private revenge by an off-duty American officer was not attributed to the US, a second act of private revenge which took place when the officer was in some sense on duty was held to be attributable to the US.[73] Similarly, in the *Caire* case, two Mexican officers murdered a French national after he refused to give them a sum of money. The French–Mexican Claims Commission held that the actions of the two men involved the responsibility of Mexico, since 'they acted under cover of their status as officers and used means placed at their disposal on account of that status'.[74]

If this rule were not in place, it would be virtually impossible for the claimant state to succeed in proving the responsibility of the defendant state.[75] The US–Mexican General Claims Commission recognised this difficulty in the *Youmans* case:

> Soldiers inflicting personal injuries or committing wanton destruction or looting always act in disobedience to some rules laid down by superior authority. There could be no liability whatever for such misdeeds if the view were taken that any acts committed by soldiers in contravention of instructions must always be considered as personal acts.[76]

Since a contract of hire will not generally authorise PMSC personnel to breach IHL or HRL, contractors who transgress in this way will usually be acting *ultra vires* the contract or in contravention of its terms. Nonetheless, the hiring state will incur responsibility pursuant to Article 4 unless the contractors' conduct was so far removed from their functions as part of the armed forces that it should be equated to the conduct of private individuals.

---

72 ILC Articles, Commentary to Art. 4, para. 13.   73 *Mallén* case (1925) 4 RIAA 173.
74 *Caire* case, 531.   75 ILC Articles, Commentary to Art. 10, para. 19.
76 *Youmans* case, 116; see also *Congo* case, paras. 214 and 243, in relation to *ultra vires* acts of the armed forces.

3.2 PMSCs empowered by law to exercise governmental authority

Even where a PMSC is not a state organ, its conduct may be attributable to the hiring state if it has been authorised by the law of that state to exercise elements of governmental authority. Article 5 of the ILC Articles thus provides:

> The conduct of a person or entity which is not an organ of the state under article 4 but which is empowered by the law of that state to exercise elements of the governmental authority shall be considered an act of the state under international law, provided the person or entity is acting in that capacity in the particular instance.[77]

Like the rule in Article 4, this rule applies regardless of whether the entity committing the act has exceeded its authority or contravened its instructions.[78]

Article 5 is intended to encompass quasi-state entities that exercise elements of governmental authority in place of state organs, as well as former state corporations that have been privatised but retain certain public functions.[79] The ILC Commentary observes that 'in special cases' the principle may also extend to private companies,

> provided that in each case the entity is empowered by the law of the state to exercise functions of a public character normally exercised by state organs, and the conduct of the entity relates to the exercise of the governmental authority concerned.[80]

Prima facie, this would appear to be well suited to the situation where a state outsources traditionally public functions such as the military, the police and the operation of detention centres to PMSCs.

The jurisprudence of the Iran–US Claims Tribunal illustrates the application of this norm. In *Hyatt International Corporation v. Iran*, the Tribunal attributed to Iran certain conduct, namely, the expropriation of contract rights, carried out by a non-state charity group (the Foundation for the Oppressed). The Tribunal stated:

> In view of the circumstances of its establishment and mode of governance, and in view of the functions it fulfils, the Tribunal concludes that the Bonyad Mostazafan, or Foundation for the Oppressed, has been and

---

77 ILC Articles, Commentary to Art. 5, para. 1.   78 *Ibid.*, Art. 7.
79 *Ibid.*, Commentary to Art. 5, para. 1.
80 *Ibid.*, Commentary to Art. 5, para. 2; see also Ago, 'Fourth Report on State Responsibility' (1972) *Yearbook of the International Law Commission*, vol. II, para. 191.

continues to be an instrumentality controlled by the Government of the Islamic Republic of Iran.[81]

In contrast, in *Schering Corporation* v. *Iran*, the Tribunal did not consider the acts of a workers' council at the claimant company to be attributable to Iran, since

> [t]he constitution and regulatory framework for the creation of Workers'
> Councils do not indicate that the Councils were to have other duties than
> basically representing the workers' interest *vis-à-vis* the management of
> companies and institutions and to cooperate with the management. That
> the formation of the Councils was initiated by the State does not in itself
> imply that the Councils were to function as part of the State machinery.[82]

There are three requirements for the attribution of a wrongful PMSC act to the hiring state pursuant to Article 5. First, the PMSC operation during which the wrongful act takes place must constitute the exercise of governmental authority. Secondly, the PMSC must be 'empowered by the law of the state' to exercise that authority. Thirdly, the contractor must in fact be acting in the exercise of governmental authority, rather than in a purely private capacity, when he or she commits the wrongful act. Each of these criteria will now be addressed in turn.

What constitutes 'governmental authority'?

The basic criterion in Article 5 is that the activity must involve an exercise of governmental authority. There is no international consensus as to the precise scope of 'governmental authority'. Indeed, the very concept requires value judgments which themselves rest on political assumptions about the proper sphere of state activity, and this 'depends on the particular society in question, its history and traditions'.[83]

Nonetheless, certain functions appear to be commonly regarded as intrinsically 'public' in nature, meaning that their performance by a PMSC necessarily entails the exercise of governmental authority. The Commentary cites several such functions including policing,[84] immigration and quarantine, detention and discipline pursuant to a judicial sentence or to prison regulations, and the identification of property for seizure.[85] These categories would encompass, for example, the DynCorp employees

---

81 *Hyatt International Corporation* v. *Iran* (1985) 9 Iran–US CTR 72, 94.
82 *Schering Corporation* v. *Iran* (1984) 5 Iran–US CTR 361, 370.
83 ILC Articles, Commentary to Art. 5, para. 6.
84 *Ibid.*, Commentary to Art. 5, paras. 4–5.   85 *Ibid.*, Commentary to Art. 5, para. 2.

hired by the US as police in post-conflict Bosnia, the PMSC personnel hired by Israel as armed border guards at the Erez and Sha'ar Ephraim crossings, and the CACI employees hired by the US as prison guards and interrogators in Iraq.[86] In fact, the Commentary specifically states that 'private security firms' contracted by the government to act as prison guards would fall within Article 5.[87] The Iran–US Claims Tribunal has also classified detention[88] and the seizure of property[89] by para-statal forces as exercises of governmental powers by those forces. In addition, it is generally agreed that core military activities such as combat and interrogation entail the exercise of governmental authority.[90]

Whilst there is widespread agreement that certain PMSC activities – such as offensive combat, policing, detention and immigration – entail the exercise of governmental authority within Article 5, the status of other activities – such as armed security, military advice and training, and intelligence collection and analysis – is less clear-cut. Instinctively, it might seem that these activities would entail governmental authority when performed for a state in armed conflict. Yet such instinctive classifications tend to rely primarily on the fact that the activities have historically been carried out by the state, and this becomes increasingly unsatisfactory as more and more functions are privatised.[91] In the absence of an exhaustive list of state functions under international law, it is necessary to develop a general analytic framework to facilitate the distinction between those activities that entail governmental authority and those that do not.

Private person test

A useful starting point in assessing whether a particular activity is inherently governmental is to ask whether the activity is one that a private individual could perform without the government's permission. In the present context, one might simply ask whether the activity is one that a PMSC could lawfully perform pursuant to a contract with a private client rather than a state. This resembles the criterion used in some civil law countries to divide competence between the civil and administrative

---

86 See Chapter 1, section 1.4.   87 ILC Articles, Commentary to Art. 5, para. 2.

88 *Rankin* v. *Iran* (1987) 17 Iran–US CTR 135; *Yeager* v. *Iran* (1987) 17 Iran–US CTR 92.

89 *Hyatt International Corporation* v. *Iran* (1985) 9 Iran–US CTR 72.

90 See, e.g., UCIHL Expert Meeting, 16–18; Hoppe, 'State Responsibility', 18–19.

91 See UCIHL Expert Meeting, 16–17.

courts.[92] Private persons could not lawfully engage in offensive combat, for example, pursuant to a contract with another private party; but they could certainly prepare food or do laundry. Equally, private persons could not lawfully contract with another private party to run a detention centre or interrogate prisoners; but they could contract to act as armed guards at an oilfield in a conflict zone. A PMSC could not lawfully provide strategic military advice and training to non-state forces in an armed conflict, and it would be unable to perform many of the activities necessary to collect and analyse intelligence for a private party without violating privacy laws. The fact that a PMSC could not lawfully perform an activity for a private party tends to indicate that the activity is inherently 'public' in nature and that it therefore entails governmental authority.

However, this test does not necessarily work the other way – that is, the mere fact that a PMSC could lawfully perform an activity for a private party does not, in itself, exclude the possibility that the activity may entail governmental authority. For example, the provision of armed security to a military convoy or a senior political figure (such as DynCorp's protection of Hamid Karzai) may well entail governmental authority, notwithstanding the fact that a PMSC could lawfully provide armed security to a private company operating in a conflict zone. The 'private person' test is therefore helpful but insufficient by itself to delimit the concept of governmental authority for the purpose of Article 5.

ILC guidelines

The ILC Commentary to Article 5 provides further guidance by identifying, in addition to the content of the power in question, three factors which may assist in determining whether particular powers involve the exercise of governmental authority: first, the way the powers are conferred on an entity; secondly, the purposes for which the powers are to be exercised; and, thirdly, the extent to which the entity is accountable to the government for the exercise of the powers.[93]

In relation to the first factor, the instinctive assumption might be that a state would be more likely to confer governmental authority on a private entity via statute rather than contract or executive order. Whilst this may be the case in some systems, recent practice shows that many states

---

92 A similar test is frequently utilised in the law of state immunity to distinguish between those state acts that involve sovereign authority and those state acts that do not, as will be discussed below.
93 ILC Articles, Commentary to Art. 5, para. 6.

empower private entities to perform clearly 'public' functions – such as the operation of domestic prisons and the interrogation of prisoners in armed conflict – simply by concluding a contract with the entity in question. This is certainly true for the states that most commonly hire PMSCs, particularly the US. In some situations, a government may be even *more* likely to use contractual mechanisms to confer public powers in order to evade the scrutiny of the legislature, in which case the rationale for the attribution of PMSC misconduct to the state would be particularly strong. The first factor identified by the ILC is therefore of little use in assessing whether PMSC activities entail governmental authority.

The third factor identified by the ILC is more useful. The Commentary refers not simply to the existence of *legal* accountability mechanisms, but more generally to 'the extent to which the entity is accountable to government' for the exercise of the powers in question.[94] This requires a broader analysis of the relationship between the PMSC and the government, including reporting duties and other oversight mechanisms.[95] Where the contract of hire includes provisions for monitoring PMSC activities and consequences for errant behaviour, this might provide some support for a finding that the company is exercising governmental authority. However, the absence of effective accountability mechanisms should not exclude the attribution of PMSC conduct to the state pursuant to Article 5, since it is precisely in those cases where the government authorises a PMSC to carry out a particular function, and yet fails to hold that PMSC accountable for its actions, that the rationale for the attribution of PMSC misconduct to the state is strongest.[96] A state should not benefit from its own failure to ensure that adequate oversight mechanisms are in place when it hires a PMSC in armed conflict.

The second factor, the purposes for which the powers are to be exercised, is the most useful in assessing whether PMSC activities entail governmental authority. This criterion endeavours to capture the notion that governmental authority involves some attempt to fulfil the sovereign objectives of the government, which undoubtedly include, in the words of the preamble to the US Constitution, to 'provide for the common defense'.

The inclusion of 'purpose' as a relevant factor brings to mind the long-standing debate in the law of state immunity about the appropriate way to

---

94 *Ibid.*   95 See Hoppe, 'State Responsibility', 22.
96 Lehnardt, 'Private Military Companies and State Responsibility', in Chesterman and Lehnardt (eds.), *From Mercenaries to Markets: The Rise and Regulation of Private Military Companies* (2007), 145.

identify state activities that are immune from the jurisdiction of another state.[97] In that context, international law distinguishes between the acts of a state in its sovereign capacity (*acta jure imperii*), which are immune from jurisdiction, and acts that are performed in a private capacity (*acta jure gestionis*), which are not immune. The former category includes foreign and military affairs, the enactment of legislation, the exercise of police power and the administration of justice. The latter category, on the other hand, is often described in terms of 'acts that a private person may perform', particularly in civil law countries which are able to apply by analogy the criterion for allocating competence between the civil and administrative domestic courts.[98] The largest and most important component of the 'private acts' category comprises the commercial activities of states.[99]

One of the principal justifications for this 'restrictive' theory of immunity is that certain disputes involving the sovereign functions of states should be settled on the international plane, whereas other disputes involving the private or commercial functions of states are more appropriately decided in municipal courts.[100] Thus, like the classification of an activity as one involving governmental authority for the purpose of state responsibility, the classification of an activity as one involving governmental authority for the purpose of state immunity signifies that it should be assessed on the international judicial plane under the law of state responsibility. Although there is no requirement that the criteria for

97 See generally Crawford, 'International Law and Foreign Sovereigns: Distinguishing Immune Transactions' (1983) 54 *British Yearbook of International Law* 74; Fox, *The Law of State Immunity* (2002); Schreuer, *State Immunity: Some Recent Developments* (1988); Sornarajah, 'Problems in Applying the Restrictive Theory of Sovereign Immunity' (1982) 31 *ICLQ* 661; Trooboff, 'Foreign State Immunity: Emerging Consensus of Principles' (1986) 200 *Recueil des Cours* 235.

98 See, e.g., *Banque Camerounaise de Développement* v. *Société des Etablissement Rolber* (1987) RCDIP 76, 773 (French Court of Cassation); European Convention on State Immunity (adopted 16 May 1972, entered into force 11 June 1976), CETS No. 074, Art. 7; *I Congreso del Partido* [1983] 1 AC 244, 262 (Lord Wilberforce); US House of Representatives Report No. 94-1487, (1976) 15 ILM 1398, 1406, discussing the US Foreign Sovereign Immunities Act 1976, s. 1605.

99 See, e.g., European Convention on State Immunity, Art. 7; US Foreign Sovereign Immunities Act 1976, s. 1605; UK State Immunity Act 1978, s. 3; Sinclair, 'The Law of Sovereign Immunity: Recent Developments' (1980) 167(ii) *Recueil des Cours* 113, 121–34, 146–96; UN Legislative Series, *Materials on Jurisdictional Immunities of States and their Property* (ST/LEG/SER.B/20, 1982).

100 See Brownlie, *Principles of Public International Law*, 7th edn (2008), 327–9; Crawford, 'Execution of Judgments and Foreign Sovereign Immunity' (1981) 75 *AJIL* 820, 856–8; Crawford, 'Immune Transactions', 75; Australian Law Reform Commission Report No. 24, 'Foreign State Immunity' (1984), para. 40.

classifying the relevant activity in each context be exactly the same, it is in the interests of logic and consistency that similar considerations be applied to both analyses. It is therefore helpful for present purposes to examine the criteria used to distinguish between public and private acts in the law of state immunity.

Before one can classify a particular activity for the purpose of state immunity, it is necessary to *identify* the activity with precision – that is, to isolate the specific facts that are relevant to the classification of the activity as public or private.[101] In fact, the classification of a particular activity will frequently turn on how that activity is initially defined. Any activity can be defined broadly, such as 'hiring a security guard', or narrowly, such as 'hiring an armed security guard to defend a US military convoy in a conflict zone'. Whilst both are accurate descriptions, the latter clearly identifies additional information that is legally relevant. The initial task of identification is often said to require one to 'distinguish' between the nature and purpose of the activity, and to concentrate only on the former; for, if one focuses on purpose, virtually all state transactions can ultimately be traced back to the public interest. Yet it is not possible to draw a clear-cut distinction between the nature and purpose of a particular act. Commentators often point out, for example, that signing a legally binding contract can be described simply as signing paper unless one considers the purpose of the act. It is clearly necessary to consider the whole context of the claim against the state.

The twentieth-century jurisprudence in the field of state immunity illustrates these difficulties. Although the earliest cases accepted immunity as a plea wherever it was shown that the act was performed for a sovereign purpose,[102] that approach proved over-inclusive and courts instead began to focus on the nature of the act in order to distinguish between the public and private spheres of state action.[103] In the House of Lords case of *I Congreso del Partido*, Lord Wilberforce agreed with the Federal Constitutional Court of Germany that in distinguishing between public and private acts, 'one should rather refer to the nature of the State transaction or the resulting legal relationships, and not to the motive or

---

101 See Crawford, 'Immune Transactions', 94–9; Schreuer, *State Immunity*, 15–22.
102 See, e.g., *Berizzi Bros* v. *SS Pesaro*, 271 US 562 (1925).
103 See, e.g., *United Arab Republic* v. *Mrs X* (10 February 1960) 65 ILR 385 (Swiss Federal Tribunal); *Holubek* v. *US Government* (10 February 1961) 40 ILR 73 (Austrian Supreme Court); *Empire of Iran* (30 April 1963) 45 ILR 57 (German Federal Constitutional Court). This approach is also expressly laid out in the US Foreign Sovereign Immunities Act 1976, s. 1603(d).

purpose of the State activity'.[104] Yet Lord Wilberforce also stressed that the nature of the act must not be viewed in isolation. On the contrary, the court 'must consider the whole context in which the claim against the State is made',[105] in which case 'the purpose . . . is not decisive but it may throw some light upon the nature of what was done'.[106] The ILC adopted a similar approach in its 1991 Draft Articles on Jurisdictional Immunities of States and their Property,[107] which formed the basis for the 2004 UN International Convention on Jurisdictional Immunities of States and their Property.[108]

English courts have applied Lord Wilberforce's contextual approach in deciding a number of state immunity cases, both under the State Immunity Act 1978 and under the common law. Two cases are particularly pertinent to this discussion. First, in *Littrell* v. *US (No. 2)*, the plaintiff, a US citizen, claimed damages for personal injuries arising from medical treatment he had received at a US military hospital in the UK whilst a serving member of the US Air Force.[109] The Court of Appeal upheld a plea of immunity at common law, the case falling outside the scope of the State Immunity Act 1978 by virtue of section 16(2). Lord Hoffmann stated:

> The context in which the act took place was the maintenance by the United States of a unit of the United States Air Force in the United Kingdom. This looks about as imperial an activity as could be imagined. But it would be facile to regard this context as determinative of the question. Acts done within that context range from arrangements concerning the flights of the bombers – plainly jure imperii – to ordering milk for the base from a local dairy or careless driving by off-duty airmen on the roads of Suffolk. Both of the latter would seem to me to be jure gestionis, fairly within an area of private law activity. I do not think that there is a single test or 'bright line' by which cases on either side can be distinguished. Rather, there are a number of factors which may characterise the act as nearer to or further from the central military activity . . . Some acts are wholly military in character, some almost entirely private or commercial and some in between.[110]

---

104 *I Congreso del Partido*, 263 (Lord Wilberforce), quoting from *Empire of Iran*, 80.
105 *Ibid.*, 267.   106 *Ibid.*, 272.
107 ILC Draft Articles on Jurisdictional Immunities of States and Their Property, with Commentaries, (1991) 30 ILM 1554, Art. 2(2).
108 UN Convention on Jurisdictional Immunities of States and Their Property (adopted 2 December 2004), 44 ILM 803, UN Doc. A/RES/59/38.
109 *Littrell* v. *US (No. 2)* [1995] 1 WLR 82.   110 *Ibid.*, 94–5.

Secondly, the House of Lords applied *Littrell* in the 2000 case of *Holland* v. *Lampen-Wolfe*.[111] The plaintiff was a US national who as part of her employment at an American university was seconded to give lectures in international relations at a US military base in England. The defendant, also a US national, worked as an education services officer at the base, and in that capacity he wrote a memorandum concerning the plaintiff's conduct as a lecturer. The plaintiff claimed that the defendant's memorandum was defamatory. The House of Lords upheld a plea of immunity at common law. Lord Hope stated:

> In the present case the context is all important. The overall context was that of the provision of educational services to military personnel and their families stationed on a US base overseas. The maintenance of the base itself was plainly a sovereign activity . . . But that is not enough to determine the issue. At first sight, the writing of a memorandum by a civilian educational services officer in relation to an educational programme provided by civilian staff employed by a university seems far removed from the kind of act that would ordinarily be characterised as something done *iure imperii*. But regard must be had to the place where the programme was being provided and to the persons by whom it was being provided and who it was designed to benefit . . . The whole activity was designed as part of the process of maintaining forces and associated civilians on the base by US personnel to serve the needs of the US military authorities . . . On these facts the acts of the respondent seem to me to fall well within the area of sovereign activity.[112]

One can apply similar considerations to the question of whether PMSCs providing military or security services to a state are exercising governmental authority within Article 5. Certain PMSC activities – such as armed security, intelligence collection and analysis, and military/security advice and training – may not necessarily be governmental in nature when viewed in isolation, but may in fact entail governmental authority when viewed in their overall context. Relevant factors include the location of the PMSC activity (an armed conflict zone), the persons whom the activity is provided to benefit (national military/security forces or senior government officials) and, as noted in the ILC Articles, the overall purpose of the act.

The application of this logic to armed guarding services clearly indicates that PMSC personnel who guard *military* persons or objects in armed conflict are exercising governmental authority, the assumption being that such contractors have been hired to repel military attacks by enemy forces.

---

111 *Holland* v. *Lampen-Wolfe* [2000] 1 WLR 1573.   112 *Ibid.*, 1577.

But what about the protection of *civilian* officials of the hiring state, such as high-level politicians or diplomats? The Blackwater employees involved in the Baghdad shooting incident in September 2007, in which thirty-four unarmed Iraqi civilians were killed or injured, were defending a US State Department motorcade;[113] were they exercising governmental authority for the purposes of Article 5? A consideration of the overall context of their activities suggests that the answer would be in the affirmative.[114] On the other hand, a PMSC that is hired by a state to guard the installations or personnel of a private company in a conflict zone would be unlikely to fall within Article 5, since the purpose of the activities is to protect civilian employees of a private firm rather than to protect a high-level government official visiting the theatre of conflict on state business.[115]

US law and policy regarding 'inherently governmental' functions

Many aspects of the above analysis resemble the US government's attempts to determine which military and security functions are appropriate for outsourcing.[116] The overarching US policy is that tasks that are 'inherently governmental' are to be performed by government personnel.[117] An inherently governmental function is defined in the Federal Activities Inventory Reform Act of 1998 ('FAIR Act') as a 'function that is so intimately related to the public interest as to require performance

---

113 US Department of Justice Press Release 08–1068, 8 December 2008; see also Tavernise, 'US Contractor Banned by Iraq over Shootings', *New York Times* (18 September 2007); Sevastopulo, 'Iraqis Pull Security Contractor's Licence', *Financial Times* (17 September 2007).

114 Blackwater (now Xe Services) itself has argued that the 'shooters' should be considered US government employees and therefore that the US should assume any liability for the company's actions: see *In Re Xe Services Alien Tort Litigation*, 665 F Supp 2d 569 (ED Va 2009). In January 2010, Blackwater settled one series of lawsuits arising from the shootings: see Risen, 'Interference Seen in Blackwater Inquiry', *New York Times* (2 March 2010); Gallagher, 'Civil Litigation and Transnational Business: An Alien Tort Statute Primer' (2010) 8 *Journal of International Criminal Justice* 745, 754.

115 Hoppe, 'State Responsibility', 21–2.

116 See generally, Commission on Wartime Contracting Hearing, 'Are Private Security Contractors Performing Inherently Governmental Functions?' (18 June 2010); Luckey, Grasso and Manuel, 'Inherently Governmental Functions and Department of Defense Operations: Background, Issues, and Options for Congress', Congressional Research Service Report for Congress R40641 (22 July 2009).

117 Office of Management and Budget Circular A-76 (Revised), 'Performance of Commercial Activities' (29 May 2003).

by Federal Government employees'.[118] This definition includes services that bind the US to action, advance US interests by military or diplomatic action, or significantly affect the life, liberty or property of private persons.[119]

In March 2010, under congressional direction,[120] the Office of Management and Budget (OMB) released a draft policy letter setting out the Obama Administration's proposed position on the question of 'when work performed for the Federal government must be carried out, in whole, or in part, by Federal employees'.[121] The letter endorses the FAIR Act definition of 'inherently governmental' functions, provides basic guidance for judging whether a function is inherently governmental, and lists examples of such functions including the command of military forces, the direction and control of intelligence operations, and the award, administration and termination of contracts. The letter also advises government agencies to avoid overreliance on contractors for functions that are 'critical' for their missions or 'closely associated' with inherently governmental functions, although it notes that contractors may perform such functions if government agencies can provide increased oversight and management.[122] Examples of functions falling within this 'critical' or 'closely associated' category include assistance in contract management and the provision of non-law enforcement security activities that do not directly involve criminal investigations, such as prisoner detention or transport.[123]

Whereas the OMB policy letter provides relatively general government-wide guidance, the DOD has developed more specific criteria for characterising PMSC activities in armed conflict. A 2006 DOD Instruction classifies certain military activities as inherently governmental *per se*, including

---

118 31 USC 501, § 5(2)(A). This statutory definition closely resembles the more policy-oriented definition contained in Office of Management and Budget Circular A-76 (Revised), 'Performance of Commercial Activities' (29 May 2003), Attachment A: Inventory Process, B(1).

119 FAIR Act, § 5(2)(B).

120 Duncan Hunter National Defense Authorization Act for FY2009, PL 110-417, § 321, 122 Stat 4411-12 (14 October 2008).

121 Office of Management and Budget, 'Work Reserved for Performance by Federal Government Employees' (31 March 2010): 16196–7.

122 In a similar vein, Nagel and Fontaine propose the concept of 'core competencies', which involve work that may not be inherently governmental but is nonetheless so essential that it should be performed by government employees as far as possible: see Nagl and Fontaine, 'Contracting in Conflicts: The Path to Reform' (2010).

123 See Brodsky, 'Inherently Governmental Rule Sparks Little Consensus', *Government Executive* (3 June 2010).

combat operations, interrogations to the extent that they entail substantial discretion,[124] and activities that require 'military-unique knowledge and skills' such as the administration of US military correctional facilities, the provision of military advice and training, and the direction and control of intelligence operations.[125] The Instruction recognises that protective security services may be inherently governmental in certain circumstances, but emphasises that a fact-specific analysis will be required in each case. The Instruction explains:

> Security is IG [inherently governmental] if it involves unpredictable international or uncontrolled, high threat situations where success depends on how operations are handled and there is a potential of binding the United States to a course of action when alternative courses of action exist.[126]

This includes 'security operations that are performed in highly hazardous public areas where the risks are uncertain', since such operations 'could require deadly force that is more likely to be initiated by US forces than occur in self defense'.[127] Security is not inherently governmental, on the other hand, if it does not require the exercise of substantial discretion; examples include the security of buildings in secure compounds in hostile environments and security for 'other than uniquely military functions'.[128] It follows that PMSC contracts

> shall be used cautiously in contingency operations where major combat operations are ongoing or imminent. In these situations, contract security services will not be authorized to guard US or coalition military supply routes, military facilities, military personnel, or military property except as specifically authorized by the geographic Combatant Commander (non-delegable).[129]

Of course, national assessments of the appropriateness of outsourcing particular functions are quite distinct from the international legal question of attribution. Nonetheless, an examination of US law and policy serves to illustrate the importance of context in determining whether a particular PMSC activity entails governmental authority, and a similar approach can be applied to the assessment of attribution pursuant to Article 5.[130]

---

124 US Department of Defense Instruction 1100.22, 'Guidance for Determining Workforce Mix' (7 September 2006), E2.1.
125 *Ibid.*, E2.5.   126 *Ibid.*, E2.1.4.1.   127 *Ibid.*, E2.1.4.1.4.   128 *Ibid.*, E2.1.4.
129 US Department of Defense Instruction 3020.41, 6.3.5.2.
130 See also Commission on Wartime Contracting Hearing, 'Are Private Security Contractors Performing Inherently Governmental Functions?' (18 June 2010).

What constitutes 'the law of the state'?

The above analysis has argued that a large proportion of PMSC activities in armed conflict will entail the exercise of governmental authority. That is not sufficient in itself, however, to attribute contractor misconduct to the hiring state pursuant to Article 5. In addition, the contractor must be 'empowered by the law of the state' to exercise governmental authority, in the sense that such authority must have been conferred on the PMSC pursuant to some internal *legal* framework of the hiring state. This is not to suggest that the law must dictate every aspect of the PMSC's activities; on the contrary, the exercise of governmental authority by the PMSC may well involve an independent discretion or power to act.[131] This criterion is thus distinct from the criterion in Article 8 (discussed in the third section of this chapter) that the contractor must in fact be acting on the instructions or under the direction or control of the hiring state when he or she engages in the relevant misconduct.

Empowerment by law would clearly encompass the situation where a state enacts legislation specifically identifying and authorising a particular PMSC to exercise governmental authority. Such a situation would fit well with the example given in the ILC Commentaries of private entities that 'have delegated to them certain powers' entailing governmental authority.[132]

Yet the wording of Article 5 suggests that the provision is not limited to the legislative delegation of a power to a particular private entity. Since the PMSC must be 'empowered by *the* law of the state', rather than *a* law of the state, it would seem that the hiring state need not enact a specific law empowering a specific PMSC to undertake functions entailing governmental authority. Instead, Article 5 would in all likelihood be satisfied if the state established a general legislative or other legal framework empowering a government agency to delegate its powers to a private company, and the agency then contracted with a particular PMSC to perform certain activities.[133] Such a situation would fit well with the example given in the Commentaries of 'private security firms *contracted* to act as prison guards' to exercise 'powers of detention and discipline'.[134]

Under this analysis, Article 5 would also apply to situations where the contract of hire authorised the PMSC to subcontract other companies to

---

131 ILC Articles, Commentary to Art. 5, para. 7.
132 *Ibid.*, Commentary to Art. 5, para. 2.   133 See UCIHL Expert Meeting, 18.
134 ILC Articles, Commentary to Art. 5, para. 2 (emphasis added).

perform all or part of the work, provided that the subcontracted company exercised governmental authority pursuant to the subcontract.[135]

When is a PMSC employee 'acting in that capacity'?

The third criterion for attribution pursuant to Article 5 is that the private contractor must in fact be acting in the exercise of governmental authority, rather than in a purely private capacity, when he or she engages in the relevant misconduct.[136] Similar considerations apply to this analysis as to the analysis of whether a contractor who is part of the hiring state's armed forces is acting 'in that capacity' for the purposes of Article 4 of the ILC Articles, as discussed in the first section of this chapter, although the notion of acting 'in that capacity' will generally be broader for contractors who form part of the state's armed forces. In short, PMSC misconduct will only be attributable to the hiring state pursuant to Article 5 if the contractors are using the means and powers pertaining to the exercise of public power and are thus 'cloaked with governmental authority' at the relevant time.[137] On the other hand, contractors' misconduct will not be attributable if it 'has no connection with the official function' and is, in fact, merely the conduct of private individuals.[138]

If a contractor raped a civilian woman outside a pub, for example, while he was off-duty and out of uniform, that would not generally be attributable to the hiring state pursuant to Article 5. The contractor's misconduct would probably be deemed a purely private activity of an individual who happened to be a PMSC employee, rather than an act of the state. If, on the other hand, an off-duty armed security contractor shot a civilian woman whilst he was walking home from his shift, still in uniform and carrying his state-issued weapon, the shooting would in all likelihood be attributable to the hiring state. Everything will turn on the specific circumstances surrounding the contractor's misconduct in the particular case.

Article 5 encompasses all acts committed by PMSC personnel whilst they are exercising governmental authority, even those acts that are *ultra*

---

135 See UCIHL Expert Meeting, 20.
136 ILC Articles, Commentary to Art. 7, 10; *Youmans* case; *Caire* case; *Velásquez Rodríguez v. Honduras*, para. 170; *Royal Holland Lloyd v. US* (1931) 73 Ct Cl 722; Brownlie, *State Responsibility*, 145.
137 *Petrolane Inc. v. Iran* (1991) 27 Iran–US CTR 64, 92.
138 *Caire* case, 531; ILC Articles, Commentary to Art. 7, para. 7; Brownlie, *State Responsibility*, 145–50.

vires the contract of hire or in contravention of the contractual terms.[139] As discussed in the first section of this chapter, if this rule were not in place it would be virtually impossible for the claimant state to succeed in proving the responsibility of the hiring state pursuant to Article 5, since PMSC misconduct will rarely be authorised by the hiring state and may even be explicitly prohibited.[140] The contract authorising CACI to conduct interrogations at Abu Ghraib, for example, would not have authorised contractors to abuse the detainees; indeed, it may even have contained provisions expressly requiring the humane treatment of detainees. Nonetheless, the contractors' conduct would have been attributable to the US, as the contractors were clearly using the means and powers pertaining to their functions as prison guards and interrogators at the time of the offending conduct.

This discussion has shown that in many cases PMSC misconduct in armed conflict will be attributable to the hiring state pursuant to the rule in Article 5. This rule is therefore central to the analysis of state responsibility in the private security context. Some contractor misconduct, however, may fall outside the scope of Article 5 for one of two reasons: either the contractor engages in the misconduct whilst off-duty and thus not acting 'in that capacity' at the relevant time, or the contractor engages in the misconduct whilst performing an activity that does not entail governmental authority. In such cases, it may still be possible to attribute the misconduct to the hiring state pursuant to the rule in Article 8 of the ILC Articles if the wrongdoing contractor is in fact acting under the state's instructions, direction or control.

3.3 PMSCs acting under state instructions, direction or control

International law has long recognised that the conduct of a private person who is in fact acting on behalf of a state may be attributed to that state for the purposes of state responsibility. One early example is the *Zafiro* case, in which the Great Britain–US Arbitral Tribunal held the US responsible for looting by the civilian crew of a private ship that was being used as a supply vessel by American naval forces in the Spanish–American war.[141] In attributing the civilian conduct to the US, the Tribunal emphasised that the captain and crew were in fact under the command of a US naval officer who had come on board to control and direct the movements of

---

139 ILC Articles, Commentary to Art. 4, para. 13.
140 *Ibid.*, Commentary to Art. 10, para. 19; *Youmans* case, 116.
141 *Zafiro* (1925) 4 RIAA 160.

the ship. The Mexico–US General Claims Commission applied the same rule in the *Stephens* case, which involved a killing committed by a member of an auxiliary of the Mexican forces. The Commission found that the killing was attributable to Mexico, stating that 'it is difficult to determine with precision the status of these guards as an irregular auxiliary of the army, the more so as they lacked both uniforms and insignia; but at any rate they were "acting for" Mexico.'[142]

This principle of attribution *de facto* is reflected in Article 8 of the ILC Articles:

> The conduct of a person or group of persons shall be considered an act of a State under international law if the person or group of persons is in fact acting on the instructions of, or under the direction or control of that State in carrying out the conduct.

This rule identifies two situations in which PMSC misconduct will be attributable to the hiring state: first, where the PMSC is acting on the instructions of the state; and, secondly, where the PMSC is acting under the direction or control of the state. In either case, the particular PMSC conduct that is said to constitute an internationally wrongful act must fall within the scope of the state's instructions, direction or control.[143]

State instructions

In the rare case that a state hired a PMSC and actually instructed it to violate international law, the attribution of PMSC misconduct would be relatively straightforward. The state could incorporate such instructions into the terms of the contract of hire, for example, or it could issue the instructions to PMSCs in the field via an authorised contracting officer.[144] In either case, the hiring state would not need to exercise any particular level of practical control over the PMSC after the instructions had been given for the misconduct to fall within Article 8.

According to the ICJ in the *Genocide* case, for a state's instructions to fall within Article 8, they must have been given 'in respect of each

---

142 *Stephens* (1927) Mexico–US General Claims Commission.

143 See ILC Articles, Commentary to Art. 8, para. 8. This contrasts with Art. 5, which encompasses *all* acts performed by PMSC contractors whilst exercising governmental authority, even if they are acting *ultra vires* their contractual authority.

144 The US has contracting officers in the field to administer the contracts and act as the 'the liaison between the commander and the defense contractor for directing or controlling contractor performance because commanders have no direct contractual relationship with the defense contractor': see US Department of Defense Instruction 3020.41, 6.3.3.

operation in which the alleged violations occurred, not generally in respect of the overall actions taken by the persons or groups of persons having committed the violations'.[145] It is not clear from the Court's judgment how narrowly the notion of an 'operation' is to be construed. If a state hired a PMSC to perform interrogations at a detention centre, for example, and included a term in the contract instructing the company to use particular interrogation procedures that amounted to torture or ill-treatment, it would seem that such a scenario should fall within Article 8. It would be too restrictive to require the state to issue a specific instruction detailing the interrogation procedure for each detainee. The same logic would apply to other situations in which a state hired a PMSC to perform a narrowly defined activity (such as protective security) in a particular area for a reasonably limited period of time. On the other hand, if the PMSC contract covered a broader range of activities (such as the combat contracts of Executive Outcomes and Sandline in Sierra Leone and Angola), it might be necessary to distinguish between different 'operations' carried out pursuant to the same contract.

Another key question is how specific the instructions must be in order to fall within Article 8. Must there be a specific order directing *how* the particular wrongful act is to be performed, or will a general instruction suffice? Logic suggests the latter, provided that the order authorises wrongful conduct. Hoppe gives the example of a command to a contractor to 'get the prisoner to talk by any means necessary' as being sufficient to satisfy Article 8, since the order effectively authorises violations of IHL and HRL even though it does not specify precisely how the interrogation should take place.[146] Likewise, an instruction to a private security guard to shoot anyone who comes near the protected object would effectively authorise a violation, since it authorises the contractor to shoot indiscriminately without prior warning and without considering whether the person might be an innocent civilian.

In August 2009, the *New York Times* reported that the Central Intelligence Agency (CIA) hired a number of individual Blackwater contractors in 2004 as part of a secret programme to locate and assassinate top operatives of Al Qaeda.[147] It is unclear whether the CIA hired the contractors themselves to capture or kill Al Qaeda operatives, or simply to help with

---

145 *Genocide* case, para. 400.   146 Hoppe, 'State Responsibility', 24.

147 See Mazzetti, 'CIA Sought Blackwater's Help to Kill Jihadists', *New York Times* (19 August 2009); Warrick, 'CIA Assassination Program Had Been Outsourced to Blackwater, Ex-Officials Say', *Los Angeles Times* (20 August 2009); MacAskill, 'CIA Hired Blackwater for Al-Qaida Assassination Programme, Sources Say', *Guardian* (20 August 2009).

training and surveillance in the programme; if the former, this would certainly fall within the scope of state 'instructions' for the purposes of Article 8.

A more common scenario would be where a state gave overly vague or ambiguous instructions which, although not unlawful on their face, conveyed a lack of concern as to how the instructions were carried out and which could even be interpreted as implicitly authorising a violation. The ILC Commentary to Article 8 attempts to provide guidance for situations where a state has authorised a particular act and the private actor then engages in 'actions going beyond the scope of the authorization'. The Commentary states:

> Such cases can be resolved by asking whether the unlawful or unauthorized conduct was really incidental to the mission or clearly went beyond it. In general a State, in giving lawful instructions to persons who are not its organs, does not assume the risk that the instructions will be carried out in an internationally unlawful way.[148]

The notion of conduct that is 'really incidental to' the mission does little to clarify the situation in relation to overly vague or ambiguous instructions. For example, an instruction to a security guard to shoot anyone who approaches looking 'suspicious' might be interpreted as an implicit authorisation to shoot indiscriminately and without warning, but it might equally be interpreted as an instruction to shoot only those individuals who look like combatants. Is a civilian shooting really incidental to the security mission in these circumstances? PMSC shootings are certainly not uncommon in the context of 'defensive' security operations. For example, according to a Report of the US House of Representatives Committee on Oversight and Governmental Reform, Blackwater security guards were involved in an average of 1.4 shooting incidents per week between 2005 and 2007, firing the first shots in over 80 per cent of the incidents and in some cases killing apparently innocent civilians, despite the fact that their contracts only authorised the 'defensive' use of force.[149]

The best way for the hiring state to avoid responsibility under this rule would be to include in the contract of hire detailed rules complying with IHL, and to ensure that government representatives give clear and lawful instructions to PMSCs in the field. Having taken such action, the hiring

---

148 ILC Articles, Commentary to Art. 8, para. 8.
149 US House of Representatives Committee on Oversight and Governmental Reform, 'Additional Information about Blackwater USA' (1 October 2007), 1–2.

state would not incur responsibility if a contractor then carried out those instructions in an unlawful way.

State direction or control

Where no specific instructions exist but the hiring state is nonetheless linked to the PMSC actions through its actual direction or control of PMSC behaviour in the field, the question of attribution may be even more complex.

The ICJ considered this rule of attribution in the *Nicaragua* case, in assessing whether violations of IHL committed by various individuals during the Nicaraguan civil war were attributable to the US. For the purpose of assessing US responsibility, the Court distinguished between three categories of individuals. First, the acts of members of the US government administration (such as CIA operatives) and members of the US armed forces were undoubtedly attributable to the US. Secondly, certain acts of Latin American operatives (the UCLAs) were also attributable to the US, either because the UCLAs had been given specific instructions by US agents or officials and had acted under their supervision,[150] or because US agents had 'participated in the planning, direction and support' of specific operations.[151] Thirdly, and crucially for the present analysis, was the category of the *contras* (the rebels fighting against the Nicaraguan government). The Court rejected Nicaragua's claim that all the conduct of the *contras* was attributable to the US by reason of its control over them:

> United States participation, even if preponderant or decisive, in the financing, organising, training, supplying and equipping of the *contras*, the selection of its military or paramilitary targets, and the planning of the whole of its operation, is still insufficient in itself, on the basis of the evidence in the possession of the Court, for the purpose of attributing to the United States the acts committed by the *contras* in the course of their military or paramilitary operations in Nicaragua.[152]

According to the Court, for the violations of IHL committed by the *contras* to be attributed to the US, it was necessary to show that the US had '*effective control of the military or paramilitary operations in the course of which the alleged violations were committed*'.[153]

---

150 *Nicaragua*, paras. 75–80.   151 *Ibid.*, para. 86.   152 *Ibid.*, para. 115.
153 *Ibid.*, para. 115 (emphasis added); see also the Separate and Concurring Opinion of Judge Ago, para. 18.

In the *Tadić* case of 1999, the ICTY Appeals Chamber considered the issue of *de facto* state agents in a different context. The Appeals Chamber had to determine whether Bosnian Serb forces were in fact acting on behalf of the Federal Republic of Yugoslavia (FRY), such that the armed conflict was international in character and the more extensive rules of IHL applied. The Chamber dismissed the *Nicaragua* test of effective control and instead established a more flexible threshold of control, which can vary according to the circumstances of the case.[154] In relation to an organised and hierarchically structured group, such as a militia, the Chamber considered a more lenient standard of 'overall control' to be appropriate. This standard goes beyond the mere financing and equipping of the forces and also involves 'participation in the planning and supervision of military operations', but it does not require the issuance of specific orders or instructions relating to individual military actions.[155]

In his Separate and Dissenting Opinion in *Tadić*, Judge Shahabuddeen was highly critical of the majority's approach, emphasising the different contexts of the two decisions: *Nicaragua* had dealt with state responsibility whereas *Tadić* was dealing with individual criminal responsibility. Judge Shahabuddeen noted that the relevant question was not whether the FRY was responsible for breaches of IHL committed by the Bosnian Serb militia, but the separate question of whether the FRY had used force through the militia against Bosnia-Herzegovina.[156] The Commentaries to the ILC Articles favour the ICJ's test of effective control and appear to agree with Judge Shahabuddeen that the *Tadić* case involved a different question from that in issue in *Nicaragua*.[157]

Judge Shahabuddeen's view is highly persuasive when considered within the framework of primary and secondary rules of international law. There is no compelling reason why the same test must apply to, on the one hand, the question of whether a state is acting through a private individual for the purpose of ascertaining the applicable rules of IHL and, on the other hand, the question of whether a state is acting through a private individual for the purpose of establishing state responsibility. The former is determined by the primary rules of international law, which govern the substantive obligations on states, whereas the latter is determined by the secondary rules of international law, which govern the circumstances in which states will be considered

---

154 *Tadić* appeal judgment, para. 117.   155 *Ibid.*, 145.
156 *Ibid.*, Separate Opinion of Judge Shahabuddeen, para. 17.
157 ILC Articles, Commentary to Art. 8, para. 5.

responsible for wrongful conduct and the legal consequences flowing from that responsibility.[158]

The *Nicaragua* decision itself demonstrates the conceptual difference between the primary rules governing a state's use of force through private individuals and the secondary rules governing the attribution of private conduct to the state. The ICJ held that violations of IHL committed by the *contras* were not attributable to the US because the latter did not have effective control over the former. By contrast, the Court answered in the affirmative the question of whether the US had used force through the *contras*, effectively establishing a less stringent imputability test for the primary rule on the use of force than for the secondary rules of attribution.[159] The ICJ established an even higher threshold in relation to the question of when a state is acting through a private individual in launching an 'armed attack' giving rise to a right of self-defence in the victim state.[160] The requisite degree of imputability may therefore vary between different primary rules as well as between primary rules and secondary rules.

Since the *Tadić* decision of 1999, the ICJ has twice reaffirmed its effective control test: in the *Congo* case of 2005[161] and in the *Genocide* case of 2007.[162] In the latter case, the Court stated:

> It must however be shown that this 'effective control' was exercised . . . in respect of each operation in which the alleged violations occurred, not generally in respect of the overall actions taken by the persons or groups of persons having committed the violations.[163]

Although the decisions of the ICJ are binding only on the parties to the case at hand, in practice enormous weight is accorded to the settled jurisprudence of the Court, to the extent that the *Genocide* case can be taken virtually to have settled the matter.

The application of the ICJ's effective control test to PMSCs raises essentially the same question that arises in relation to state instructions, namely, how broadly the notion of an 'operation' is to be understood in the private security context. As argued above, a single PMSC contract for the performance of a particular activity (such as protective security) in a particular area for a reasonably limited period of time should be construed as one operation for the purposes of Article 8. The crucial issue will be whether

---

158 For a detailed discussion of this distinction, see Chapter 2.
159 *Nicaragua*, para. 228.   160 *Ibid.*, para. 195.   161 *Congo* case, para. 160.
162 *Genocide* case, para. 399.   163 *Ibid.*, para. 401.

the state exercises effective control over that PMSC activity during the relevant time.

It is clear from *Nicaragua* that a hiring state's general structural control over a PMSC (by financing, organising, training, supplying and equipping the company) would not suffice to establish attribution pursuant to Article 8, even if such control were 'preponderant or decisive'.[164] Most PMSCs are in any case independent entities with their own corporate structures and the ability to enter into contracts with different clients, with the result that these factors would be less significant for a PMSC than for an armed group such as the *contras*. Yet the elements of control identified by the Court would be highly significant if exercised over a single PMSC *operation*, rather than over the company itself. The hiring state will generally have a preponderant or decisive role in selecting, financing, organising and planning the particular PMSC operation to be performed under the contract, and in some cases the state will also supply and equip the contractors for the operation. The contract will ordinarily set out the specific goals of the operation, and in some cases it may also detail how the contractors must be trained, as well as identifying any specific weapons or equipment that must be supplied by the company itself. Any failure on the part of the company to comply with these terms may result in contractual penalties and even termination. When viewed in this way, a detailed contract of hire would appear to go a long way towards fulfilling the 'effective control' threshold.

On the other hand, where the contract of hire is relatively broad in scope and/or gives the company a high degree of discretion in planning, organising and performing its activities, it will be necessary to focus on the other mechanisms available to the hiring state to control PMSC conduct in the field. These mechanisms will also be crucial if one adopts a narrower view of the notion of an 'operation' than that propounded in this chapter. As discussed in the first section of this chapter, PMSC contracts with the US generally identify a government official (the contracting officer) who is responsible for administering and monitoring the contract in the field. If the contracting officer is unable to be within the theatre of operations, he or she has a military representative in the field who interacts frequently, sometimes daily, with the contractor about the details of performance.[165] In some cases, the military commander in the field may also have some

---

164 *Nicaragua*, para. 115.
165 See US Congressional Budget Office, 'Contractors' Support of US Operations in Iraq', 20.

authority over the PMSC by virtue of 'a task-order arrangement', which enables him or her to add new tasks to an existing contract within overall resource bounds.[166] The DOD has also established a centralised system to manage private security contracts in both Iraq and Afghanistan.[167] These arrangements for state control in the field, if implemented effectively, combined with the control exercised through the contract itself, could fulfil the ICJ's test of effective control for the purpose of Article 8.

3.4 Conclusion

The recent boom in private security raises the concern that states may be able to evade responsibility for violations of international law (such as war crimes and human rights abuses) simply by performing their military and security policy through private companies rather than public forces. This chapter has argued that such concerns are overstated, since a large proportion of PMSC activities performed for a state in armed conflict will in fact be attributable to that state under international law.

Occasionally, PMSC personnel may be so closely integrated into the hiring state's armed forces that they actually form part of those forces for the purposes of state responsibility. In most cases, however, PMSC personnel retain their independent status as private actors contracted by the hiring state, and attribution falls to be determined pursuant to Article 5 or Article 8 of the ILC Articles. The former provision applies to contractors who are exercising governmental authority when they engage in the relevant misconduct. This encompasses a large proportion of PMSC activities performed for a state in the overall context of an armed conflict, most clearly those activities that entail the threat or use of violence or coercion and those activities that entail the application of military expertise. Even where PMSC misconduct falls outside the scope of Article 5, it may be attributable to the hiring state pursuant to Article 8 by virtue of the factual relationship of control between the state and the company.

This chapter has demonstrated that a flexible and fact-specific interpretation of the rules of attribution serves to minimise the accountability gap that can arise between states that hire PMSCs and states that act through their national armed forces. The risk of incurring legal responsibility for PMSC misconduct provides a significant incentive to states to consider carefully the functions that they outsource and to take active

---

166 *Ibid.*, 20.
167 Schwartz, 'Department of Defense Contractors in Iraq and Afghanistan', 13.

steps to control PMSC behaviour in the field. The fact remains, however, that some PMSC misconduct may fall outside the scope of the rules of attribution, and in the fog of war it may in any event be difficult to prove attributability to the requisite standard. In such cases, the hiring state might still incur responsibility if it has failed to fulfil some primary obligation to take positive steps to control the PMSC, as discussed in Chapter 5. In short, states that outsource their military and security activities to PMSCs cannot simply disclaim responsibility when their private proxies engage in inappropriate or harmful behaviour in the field.

4

Obligations of the host state

International law imposes a number of obligations on states to take positive steps to prevent, investigate, punish and redress private misconduct in their territory. These obligations derive from the fundamental principle of state sovereignty: since every sovereign state is presumed to exercise exclusive control over its territory, it is also presumed to possess some capacity to control private acts committed in its territory in order to ensure that they accord with international law. It follows that the host state of a PMSC – that is, the state in which the company operates – will be obliged to take certain active measures to control company behaviour in armed conflict.

In reality, of course, a state in whose territory an armed conflict is taking place will often lack the capacity to exercise extensive control over PMSCs operating in that conflict. The state may have lost control over all or some of its territory, for example, or it may simply lack the resources and/or institutional capacity to control company behaviour. Where a state lacks the practical capacity to exercise effective control over a PMSC operating in its territory, the international obligations of the company's hiring state and home state – often highly developed states such as the US and the UK – will assume particular importance, as discussed in Chapters 5 and 6. Nonetheless, this will not relieve the host state of its obligation to exercise due diligence and take those measures that are reasonably within its power in the circumstances to control PMSCs in state territory.

This chapter critically analyses the most pertinent obligations on the host state to control PMSCs in armed conflict, first under international humanitarian law (IHL) and then under human rights law (HRL). The third section of this chapter then considers how, in some cases, immunity agreements such as Coalition Provisional Authority (CPA) Order No. 17 in Iraq can hinder the host state's ability to fulfil its international obligations by preventing the state from exercising jurisdiction over foreign PMSC personnel.[1]

---

1 CPA Order No. 17 of 2004, s. 4(2).

Where the host state fails to take adequate steps to control PMSC activity and a contractor engages in conduct that is inconsistent with the relevant norms of international law, in certain circumstances the state could incur responsibility for a failure to fulfil its international obligations. This provides a pathway to state responsibility that is *not* dependent on the direct attribution of particular PMSC misconduct to a state. More generally, the host state's obligations under IHL and HRL could play an important standard-setting role by mandating a baseline level of positive action for all states in whose territory PMSCs operate in armed conflict.

4.1 Obligations to control PMSCs under international humanitarian law

As the international legal framework specially tailored to armed conflict, IHL provides the obvious starting point for any consideration of the host state's obligations to control PMSCs in this context. This section considers three norms of IHL which are particularly pertinent to PMSCs: the obligation to ensure respect for IHL in all circumstances, the obligation to protect the civilian population, and the obligation to suppress or repress violations of IHL.

The obligation in Common Article 1 to 'ensure respect' for IHL

Article 1 common to the four Geneva Conventions (GCI–GCIV)[2] and Protocol I,[3] widely referred to as 'Common Article 1', establishes a general obligation on all states 'to respect and to ensure respect' for IHL 'in all circumstances'. The phrase 'and to ensure respect' indicates that this provision goes beyond a mere obligation to refrain from violating IHL, and requires states to take *positive* steps to promote compliance with IHL.

2 First Geneva Convention for the Amelioration of the Condition of the Wounded and Sick in Armed Forces in the Field (adopted 12 August 1949, entered into force 21 October 1950), 75 UNTS 31 ('GCI'); Second Geneva Convention for the Amelioration of the Condition of Wounded, Sick and Shipwrecked Members of Armed Forces at Sea (adopted 12 August 1949, entered into force 21 October 1950), 75 UNTS 85 ('GCII'); Third Geneva Convention relative to the Treatment of Prisoners of War (adopted 12 August 1949, entered into force 21 October 1950), 75 UNTS 135 ('GCIII'); Fourth Geneva Convention relative to the Protection of Civilian Persons in Time of War (adopted 12 August 1949, entered into force 21 October 1950), 75 UNTS 287 ('GCIV').
3 First Additional Protocol to the Geneva Conventions of 12 August 1949, and relating to the Protection of Victims of International Armed Conflicts (adopted 8 June 1977, entered into force 7 December 1979), 1125 UNTS 3 ('Protocol I').

Whilst in many cases the general obligation to ensure respect for IHL will overlap with more specific obligations of the host state under IHL and HRL, Common Article 1 may nonetheless play an important role as a residual obligation, filling in the gaps between those more specific rules and establishing a baseline standard of conduct for all states in whose territory an international or non-international armed conflict is taking place. The broad scope and universal applicability of Common Article 1 distinguish it from other pertinent rules of international law and certainly justify further analysis.

This section first examines the general nature and scope of Common Article 1, arguing that it constitutes a concrete legal obligation and not merely a statement of aspiration. The discussion then considers the application of Common Article 1 to private actors such as PMSCs, the positive measures the host state should take to fulfil the obligation, and the circumstances in which PMSC activity could give rise to the host state's responsibility for a violation of the obligation.

Nature and scope of Common Article 1

The phrase 'in all circumstances' indicates that Common Article 1 is unconditional and not constrained by the requirement of reciprocity.[4] The obligation applies not only to international conflicts, but also to non-international conflicts insofar as they fall within Common Article 3. Thus, in the *Nicaragua* case the ICJ characterised the conflict as non-international, and then went on to find that the US had violated Common Article 1 by virtue of its 'encouragement' of private actors engaged in the conflict to act in violation of Common Article 3.[5] The Court further noted that the obligation to ensure respect for IHL 'does not derive only from the Conventions themselves, but from the general principles of humanitarian law to which the Conventions merely give specific expression'.[6]

Irrespective of Common Article 1, states must clearly ensure that PMSC personnel who are acting as state agents respect the substantive rules

---

4 *Prosecutor* v. *Kupreškić*, Judgment, IT-95-16-T, Trial Chamber, 14 January 2000, para. 517; Pictet (ed.), *Commentary to the Geneva Convention Relative to the Protection of Civilian Persons in Time of War* (1958) ('*ICRC Commentary to GCIV*'), 15.
5 *Military and Paramilitary Activities In and Against Nicaragua (Nicaragua v. USA)* (Merits) ICJ Reports 1986, paras. 219–20 and 250; see also *Prosecutor* v. *Delalić*, Judgment, IT-96-21-A, Appeals Chamber, 20 February 2001 ('*Čelebići* case'), para. 164.
6 *Nicaragua*, para. 220.

of IHL.[7] This is a corollary of the general rules of state responsibility, according to which a state incurs responsibility for the acts of its armed forces and other persons or groups in fact acting on its instructions or under its direction or control. If Common Article 1 were limited to a duty to ensure respect for IHL by state agents, it would effectively be redundant as a legal obligation. Such an interpretation would be contrary to one of the fundamental principles of treaty interpretation, namely, the principle of effectiveness (*effet utile*) which requires that a treaty be interpreted 'in such a way that a reason and a meaning can be attributed to every word in the text',[8] so as to avoid a reading 'that would result in reducing whole clauses or paragraphs to redundancy or inutility'.[9]

It could perhaps be argued that Common Article 1 was intended to be an aspirational statement rather than an independent obligation carrying real legal weight;[10] but the use of the word 'undertake' in Article 1 goes against this interpretation. As the ICJ explained in the *Genocide case* in relation to the obligation to prevent and punish genocide in Article 1 of the Genocide Convention,[11] the ordinary meaning of the word 'undertake' is 'to give a formal promise, to bind or engage oneself, to give a pledge or promise, to agree, to accept an obligation. It is a word regularly used in treaties setting out the obligations of the Contracting Parties... It is not merely hortatory or purposive.'[12]

The International Committee of the Red Cross (ICRC) has long taken the position that the phrase 'and to ensure respect' in Common Article 1 is *not* redundant, but was included in order to 'emphasize and strengthen the

---

7 Henckaerts and Doswald-Beck (eds.), *Customary International Humanitarian Law* (2005) ('*ICRC Customary Law Study*'), vol. I, rule 139.

8 *Anglo-Iranian Oil Co. (UK v. Iran)* (Jurisdiction) ICJ Reports 1952, 93, 105.

9 World Trade Organization, *US – Standards for Reformulated and Conventional Gasoline,* Report of the Appellate Body (20 May 1996) WTO Doc. WT/DS2/AB/R, 23; see also *Corfu Channel (UK v. Albania)* (Merits) ICJ Reports 1949, 124; *Territorial Dispute Case (Libyan Arab Jamahiriya v. Chad)* (Merits) ICJ Reports 1994, 24; Jennings and Watts (eds.), *Oppenheim's International Law,* 9th edn (1992), 1280–1. This principle is one corollary of the general rule of interpretation in Art. 31 of the Vienna Convention on the Law of Treaties (adopted 23 May 1969, entered into force 27 January 1980), 1155 UNTS 331.

10 See University Centre for International Humanitarian Law, 'Expert Meeting on Private Military Contractors' (Geneva, August 2005) ('UCIHL Expert Meeting'), 43.

11 Convention on the Prevention and Punishment of the Crime of Genocide (adopted 9 December 1948, entered into force 12 January 1951), 78 UNTS 277.

12 *Case Concerning the Application of the Convention on the Prevention and Punishment of the Crime of Genocide (Bosnia and Herzegovina v. Serbia and Montenegro)* (Merits) (26 February 2007), para. 162.

responsibility of the Contracting Parties'.[13] The ICRC's 1960 Commentary to the Geneva Conventions explains the nature of the obligation in the following terms:

> The proper working of the system of protection provided by the Conventions demands in fact that the States which are parties to it should not be content merely to apply its provisions themselves, but should do everything in their power to ensure that it is respected universally.[14]

In fact, in the decades since 1949 this provision has been widely interpreted as imposing an obligation on all states to take positive steps to ensure that the rules of IHL are respected by all.[15] Perhaps the earliest significant illustration of this broad approach emanated from the 1968 Tehran Conference on Human Rights, at which delegates passed a resolution affirming that every state has an obligation to use all means at its disposal to promote respect for IHL by all, particularly by other states.[16] A more recent example is Security Council Resolution 681 of 1990 concerning the Arab territories occupied by Israel, which calls upon the contracting parties to GCIV 'to ensure respect by Israel, the occupying Power, for its obligations under the Convention in accordance with Article 1 thereof'.[17] The General Assembly has adopted several resolutions to the same effect in relation to the Arab–Israeli conflict.[18] Other international organisations have likewise called upon their member states to respect and ensure respect for IHL, in particular the Council of Europe, NATO, the Organization of African Unity and the Organization of American States.[19] More generally, in Resolution 60/47 of 2005 the General Assembly considered the scope of the obligation to ensure respect for IHL

---

13 *ICRC Commentary to GCIV*, 16.

14 Pictet (ed.), *Commentary to the Geneva Convention Relative to the Treatment of Prisoners of War* (1960), 18. Some commentators have argued that the drafters did not intend Common Art. 1 to impose an obligation on states not party to the conflict (third states) to take action to ensure that states party to the conflict ensure respect for IHL. The debate about third states is not relevant to the host state, but it is discussed in Chapter 5 in relation to the hiring state.

15 For a comprehensive review of state practice, see *ICRC Customary Law Study*, vol. II, rule 144.

16 Res. XXIII, International Conference on Human Rights, Tehran (12 May 1968), adopted with no opposing votes.

17 UNSC Res. 681 (20 December 1990), UN Doc. S/RES/681, para. 5.

18 See, e.g., UNGA Res. 32/91 A (13 December 1977), UN Doc. A/RES/32/91; UNGA Res. 37/123 A (16 December 1982), UN Doc. A/RES/37/123; UNGA Res. 38/180 A (19 December 1983), UN Doc. A/RES/38/180; UNGA Res. 43/21 (3 November 1988), UN Doc. A/RES/43/21.

19 See *ICRC Customary Law Study*, vol. I, 510.

and concluded that it entails, *inter alia*, a duty to take positive measures to prevent violations, to investigate violations and punish perpetrators, and to provide victims with access to justice and effective remedies.[20] The Resolution emphasises that the 'basic principles' contained therein 'do not entail new international or domestic legal obligations', but simply 'identify mechanisms, modalities, procedures and methods for the implementation of existing legal obligations'.[21]

The ICJ discussed the duty to ensure respect for IHL in its advisory opinion in the *Wall* case of 2004.[22] Considering Israel's actions in the occupied Palestinian territories under GCIV, the Court noted that all states party to the Convention have an obligation 'to ensure compliance by Israel with international humanitarian law as embodied in that Convention'.[23] The Court recalled Common Article 1 and concluded on that basis that every state party, 'whether or not it is a party to a specific conflict, is under an obligation to ensure that the requirements of the instruments in question are complied with'.

The above survey illustrates a general trend towards a broad and dynamic interpretation of Common Article 1, obliging all states to take reasonable steps within their power to promote compliance with IHL. Rule 144 of the ICRC's 2005 study on customary international law reflects this trend, affirming in relation to international armed conflicts that '[s]tates may not encourage violations of international humanitarian law by parties to an armed conflict. They must exert their influence, to the degree possible, to stop violations of international humanitarian law.'[24] Considerable doctrinal literature supports the view that this is a norm of customary international law applicable in both international and non-international armed conflicts.[25]

---

20 UNGA Res. 60/147 (16 December 2005), UN Doc. A/RES/60/147, para. 3.
21 *Ibid.*, 3.
22 *Legal Consequences of the Construction of a Wall in the Occupied Palestinian Territory* (Advisory Opinion) ICJ Reports 2004.
23 *Ibid.*, para. 163.   24 *ICRC Customary Law Study*, vol. I, 509.
25 See, e.g., Duquesne, 'La Responsabilité Solidaire des Etats aux Termes de l'Article 1 des Conventions de Genève' (1966) 15 *Annales de Droit International Médical* 83, 83; Boisson de Chazournes and Condorelli, 'Quelques Remarques à propos de l'Obligation des Etats de "Respecter et Faire Respecter" le Droit International Humanitaire en Toutes Circonstances', in Swinarski (ed.), *Studies and Essays on International Humanitarian Law and Red Cross Principles in Honour of Jean Pictet* (1984); Gasser, 'Ensuring Respect for the Geneva Conventions and Protocols: The Role of Third States and the United Nations', in Fox and Meyer (eds.), *Effecting Compliance* (1993); Palwankar, 'Measures Available to

Ensuring respect for IHL by private actors

Crucially for the host state of a PMSC, the obligation to ensure respect for IHL extends to ensuring respect *by private actors* (such as PMSCs) involved in armed conflict. As Fleck explains, the obligation applies to all states 'in their relations to state *and non-state parties* to the conflict'.[26] This aspect of the obligation in Common Article 1 is reflected in the 2008 Montreux Document, which states clearly that host states 'have an obligation, within their power, to ensure respect for international humanitarian law by PMSCs operating in their territory'.[27] The Montreux Document was produced by seventeen states (Afghanistan, Angola, Australia, Austria, Canada, China, France, Germany, Iraq, Poland, Sierra Leone, South Africa, Sweden, Switzerland, the UK, Ukraine and the US) as a result of an initiative launched jointly by Switzerland and the ICRC. Part I of the Document sets out the understanding of the drafting states of the existing obligations of states, PMSCs and their personnel under international law in relation to PMSCs in armed conflict, whilst Part II identifies seventy-three 'good practices' for states dealing with PMSCs. The Document has attracted considerable support[28] and provides a clear expression of *opinio*

States for Fulfilling Their Obligation to Ensure Respect for International Humanitarian Law' (1994) 298 *International Review of the Red Cross* 9; Azzam, 'The Duty of Third States to Implement and Enforce International Humanitarian Law' (1997) 66 *Nordic Journal of International Law* 55; Roberts, 'Implementation of the Laws of War in Late 20th Century Conflicts' (1998) 29(2) *Security Dialogue* 137, 142; Boisson de Chazournes and Condorelli, 'Common Article 1 of the Geneva Conventions Revisited: Protecting Collective Interests' (2000) 837 *International Review of the Red Cross* 67; Kessler, 'Die Durchsetzung der Genfer Abkommen von 1949 in nicht-internationalen bewaffneten Konflikten auf Grundlage ihres gemeinsamen Art. 1' (2001) 132 *Veröffentlichungen des Walther-Schücking-Instituts für Internationales Recht an der Universität Kiel* 26, 26; Kessler, 'The Duty to "Ensure Respect" under Common Article 1 of the Geneva Conventions: Its Implications on International and Non-International Armed Conflicts' (2001) 44 *German Yearbook of International Law* 498; Fleck, 'International Accountability for Violations of the Ius in Bello: The Impact of the ICRC Study on Customary International Humanitarian Law' (2006) 11 *Journal of Conflict and Security Law* 182, 182.

26 Fleck, 'International Accountability for Violations of the Ius in Bello', 181–2 (emphasis added); see also Kessler, 'Die Durchsetzung der Genfer Abkommen', 195.

27 Montreux Document on Pertinent International Legal Obligations and Good Practices for States Related to Operations of Private Military and Security Companies during Armed Conflict (17 September 2008), UN Doc. A/63/467-S/2008/636 ('Montreux Document'), Part I, para. 9.

28 See, e.g., European Commission for Democracy through Law, 'Report on Private Military and Security Firms and Erosion of the State Monopoly on the Use of Force' (2009), para. 65.

juris of the seventeen states involved in its drafting, many of which are particularly affected by PMSC activity.[29]

Ensuring respect for IHL by PMSCs would logically require the host state to take positive measures to prevent and punish any PMSC violations of which it is aware or ought to be aware. It is important to note, however, that no court to date has found a state responsible for a mere failure to take positive action to ensure respect for IHL by private actors. In *Nicaragua*, the US incurred responsibility for a violation of Common Article 1 on the basis of its 'encouragement' of the rebel *contras* to act in violation of Common Article 3. As there was sufficient evidence to prove that the US had actively supported the prohibited activities of the *contras*, the Court did not need to consider whether a state's mere failure to take positive action to prevent and punish those activities could constitute a violation of Common Article 1.[30] Nonetheless, the Court did not exclude the possibility of state responsibility on this basis, and in principle it is difficult to see how a state that failed to take such positive action could fulfil its obligation under Common Article 1 'to ensure that the requirements of the [Geneva Conventions] are complied with'.[31]

The obligation to ensure that private actors respect IHL in Common Article 1 shares a number of common features with the obligation to prevent and punish genocide in Article 1 of the Genocide Convention. In the *Genocide* case, Serbia's obligation to prevent genocide was crucial as it provided a mechanism to establish Serbia's responsibility even though the ICJ could not attribute the genocide itself to the state.[32] Likewise, where a PMSC employee violates IHL in armed conflict, the obligation to ensure respect for IHL could provide a pathway to state responsibility that is not dependent on the attribution of the PMSC misconduct to a particular state. This broadens the state responsibility analysis from a mere consideration of the agency relationship between the hiring state and the company, discussed in Chapter 3, to a consideration of whether the host state took adequate measures to prevent or punish PMSC violations in its territory. Moreover, as Common Article 1 is *not* territorially limited – revealing another similarity with the obligation to prevent and punish genocide[33] – it may also oblige other states (such as the hiring state and

29 Cockayne, 'Regulating Private Military and Security Companies: The Content, Negotiation, Weaknesses and Promise of the Montreux Document' (2009) 13(3) *Journal of
   Conflict and Security Law* 401.
30 See *Nicaragua*, paras. 220 and 255.   31 *Wall* advisory opinion, para. 158.
32 See *Genocide* case, paras. 425–50.   33 *Ibid.*, 183.

the home state) to take positive steps to control PMSCs, as discussed in Chapters 5 and 6.

Whilst Common Article 1 is not territorially limited and binds all states 'in all circumstances', common sense suggests that a state must have some capacity to influence a PMSC before the state will be required to take concrete action directed towards that particular company.[34] Conversely, a state will not incur responsibility for a failure to take positive action to ensure respect for IHL by a PMSC unless the state actually had some capacity to exert effective influence over that company. The requirement that a state have the 'capacity to influence effectively' a PMSC thus serves as a *de facto* precondition to the state's positive obligation to ensure respect for IHL by that company. This provides the crucial link between, on the one hand, the universal and somewhat vague obligation in Common Article 1 and, on the other hand, the need for particular states to take concrete action in relation to particular PMSCs.

A similar approach is evident in the ICJ's reasoning in the *Genocide* case in relation to the obligation to prevent genocide. The Court noted that the measures required to discharge the obligation depend largely on the state's 'capacity to influence effectively the action of persons likely to commit, or already committing, genocide'.[35] The corollary of the Court's reasoning is that a state will not incur responsibility for a failure to take preventive action directed towards particular individuals if the state in fact lacked the capacity to influence those individuals effectively.

Ordinarily, the host state of a PMSC will be presumed to possess some capacity to influence the company by virtue of the state's sovereignty and control over the territory in which the company operates. This gives rise to an obligation on the host state under Common Article 1 to take positive steps to prevent and punish PMSC violations of IHL. In many situations of armed conflict, however, the host state will lack the capacity to exert effective influence over PMSCs operating in its territory. Formal occupation represents the extreme case of this loss of host state control, since an occupying power by definition exercises a high degree of control over the occupied territory. The Montreux Document thus provides that

---

34 For a similar point in relation to the obligation to ensure respect by other states, see Kessler, 'The Duty to "Ensure Respect"', 505; Kessler, 'Die Durchsetzung der Genfer Abkommen', 118; Levrat, 'Les Conséquences de l'Engagement Pris par le HPC de "Faire Respecter" les Conventions Humanitaires' in Kalshoven and Sandoz (eds.), *Implementation of International Humanitarian Law* (1989), 279; Gasser, 'Ensuring Respect for the Geneva Conventions and Protocols', 28.

35 *Genocide* case, para. 430.

'[i]n situations of occupation, the obligations of [Host] States are limited to areas in which they are able to exercise effective control'.[36] Even in cases falling short of formal occupation, the host state may have lost control over parts of its territory or the situation may be so unstable that it is difficult to determine which party exercises control at a particular time. In the *Al-Skeini* case of 2007, for example, the House of Lords noted the large number of British troops deployed in southern Iraq in 2003 and described the situation as 'fluid', although it ultimately concluded that the UK did not exercise effective overall control over the territory in question.[37] Since the host state's obligation to ensure PMSC compliance with IHL is dependent on the state's capacity to influence PMSC behaviour effectively, it requires a fact-specific analysis of the territorial control exercised by the host state in each case.

Where the host state does in fact have the capacity to exert effective influence over a PMSC operating in its territory, the next step is to identify the positive measures the state should take in order to discharge its Common Article 1 obligation.

Positive action to discharge the obligation

The wording of the duty 'to ensure respect' in Common Article 1 suggests that it entails an obligation of a due diligence nature.[38] This aspect of the duty to ensure respect is reflected in rule 144 of the ICRC's study on customary IHL, quoted above, which provides that states 'must exert their influence, *to the degree possible*, to stop violations of international humanitarian law'.[39] Due diligence obligations are certainly not foreign to IHL. For example, Article 77(2) of Protocol I obliges states to 'take all feasible measures in order that children who have not attained the age of fifteen years do not take a direct part in hostilities', and Article 86(2) provides for penal or disciplinary responsibility of superior officers if they 'did not take all feasible measures within their power to prevent or repress' certain breaches of IHL by their subordinates.

A more explicit reference to the due diligence principle appears in the 1987 ICRC Commentary to Article 91 of Protocol I. Article 91 restates the customary rule that '[a] Party to the conflict which violates the provisions of the Conventions of this Protocol shall, if the case demands, be liable to

---

36 Montreux Document, Part I, para. 13.
37 *Al-Skeini* v. *Secretary of State for Defence* [2007] UKHL 26; [2008] 1 AC 153.
38 For a discussion of the importance of language in identifying due diligence obligations, see Chapter 2, section 2.4.
39 *ICRC Customary Law Study*, vol. I, 509 (emphasis added).

pay compensation'. The ICRC Commentary notes that Article 91 reflects the general principle of international law that the conduct of any state organ constitutes an act of state, provided that the organ acted in its official capacity. The Commentary then states:

> As regards damages which may be caused by private individuals, i.e., by persons who are not members of the armed forces (nor of any other organ of the State), legal writings and case-law show that the responsibility of the State is involved if it has not taken such preventive or repressive measures as could reasonably be expected to have been taken in the circumstances. In other words, *responsibility is incurred if the Party to the conflict has not acted with due diligence to prevent such acts from taking place, or to ensure their repression once they have taken place.*[40]

It is difficult to see how the due diligence obligation asserted by the ICRC could derive exclusively from Article 91, since that provision sets out only a secondary rule of attribution. The primary rule in Common Article 1 provides a far more convincing basis for a general due diligence obligation of this nature, requiring the host state to exert its best efforts and take all measures reasonably within its power to prevent and punish violations of IHL by PMSCs in its territory.

Chapter 2 explained that due diligence constitutes a 'flexible reasonableness standard adaptable to the particular facts and circumstances',[41] and it identified three factors that may affect the extent of positive action required of a state in a particular case: the capacity of the state to influence the PMSC, the resources available to the state to perform its obligations, and the risk that the company's activities will give rise to a violation of IHL.[42] The requirements of due diligence become more demanding as these factors increase.

In relation to the specific measures required to discharge the obligation, paragraph 9 of Part I of the Montreux Document provides that the host state is obliged to:

---

40 Sandoz, Swinarski and Zimmermann (eds.), *Commentary to the Additional Protocols of 8 June 1977 to the Geneva Conventions of 12 August 1949* (1987) ('*ICRC Commentary to the Additional Protocols*'), para. 3660 (emphasis added). In support of this contention, the ICRC cites a 1951 work by Marcel Sibert which states that the government 'doit exercer *toute la diligence nécessaire*, soit pour empêcher ces faits de se produire, soit pour assurer leur répression s'ils se sont produits': Sibert, *Traité de Droit International Public* (1951), vol. I, 317 (emphasis in the original).

41 Barnidge, *Non-State Actors and Terrorism: Applying the Law of State Responsibility and the Due Diligence Principle* (2007), 138.

42 See Chapter 2, section 2.4.

a) disseminate, as widely as possible, the text of the Geneva Conventions and other relevant norms of international humanitarian law among PMSCs and their personnel;

b) not encourage or assist in, and take appropriate measures to prevent, any violations of international humanitarian law by personnel of PMSCs;

c) take measures to suppress violations of international humanitarian law committed by the personnel of PMSCs through appropriate means such as military regulations, administrative orders and other regulatory measures as well as administrative, disciplinary or judicial sanctions, as appropriate.

These are characterised as concrete obligations implicit in the host state's general obligation to ensure respect for IHL. Part II of the Montreux Document then sets out a number of illustrative 'good practices', which provide guidance and assistance to the host state seeking to fulfil these obligations. Whilst generally speaking a host state's failure to implement any one of these practices will not, in itself, constitute a violation of Common Article 1, taken as a whole these practices provide a useful 'checklist' to ensure that the state has in fact discharged its obligation.[43] The diligent use of this checklist will also help the host state to comply with any applicable obligations under HRL, as discussed in the second section of this chapter.

Regarding the host state's obligation to 'take appropriate measures to prevent' violations of IHL, identified in paragraph 9(b) set out above, Part II of the Montreux Document recommends the development of a licensing scheme for PMSCs.[44] The envisaged scheme would require all PMSCs to obtain a licence from the host government in order to operate in state territory, such licences being valid for a specific time period (typically one year). As part of the authorisation process, the host government would lay down certain rules concerning PMSCs' weapons and services, among other factors, accompanied by procedures to monitor compliance. Sanctions would apply to any PMSCs that provided military or security services without a licence.

Coalition Provisional Authority Memorandum No. 17 of 2004 established a regulatory scheme of this nature for PMSCs operating in Iraq.[45] The CPA dissolved at the end of June 2004, but the Transitional Administrative Law provided that the CPA's decrees would remain in force unless

---

43 See Montreux Document, 12.   44 Ibid., Part II, paras. 25–48.
45 CPA Memorandum No. 17, 'Registration Requirements for Private Security Companies' (26 June 2004). This followed the establishment of a similar scheme in Sierra Leone in 2002: see National Security and Central Intelligence Act 2002, s. 19.

rescinded or modified by new legislation.[46] Two annexes to Memorandum No. 17 provide binding Rules for the Use of Force (Annex A) and a Code of Conduct (Annex B), which all PMSC personnel must follow. Section 9 prohibits PMSC employees from conducting law enforcement activities, although section 5 of Annex A permits PMSC employees to stop, detain, search and disarm civilians where the employees' safety so requires or if such functions are specified in the contract. Section 6 prohibits PMSC employees from joining Coalition or Multinational Forces in 'combat operations except in self-defense or in defense of persons as specified in [their] contracts'. The Private Security Company Association of Iraq helps PMSCs to register with the Iraqi Ministry of Interior and assists US contracting authorities to verify the PMSC registry.[47]

Similarly, in February 2008 the Afghan Ministry of Interior introduced an interim licensing procedure for PMSCs working in Afghanistan.[48] This regulation was enacted pursuant to the private security draft legislation that was before the parliament, in an effort 'to ensure transparency, accountability and quality services by private security companies in accordance with the laws of Afghanistan'.[49] Following a forty-five-day registration period, the Ministry of Interior issued operating licences to thirty-nine local and international PMSCs in a process that was monitored by the UN, NATO, the Combined Security Transition Command-Afghanistan and various embassies.[50] The regulation sets out prohibited PMSC activities, requirements for security companies to be issued operating and weapons licences, vetting procedures for employees, guidelines for uniforms, and restrictions on procurement of equipment and ammunition. PMSCs seeking registration are also required to disclose their organisational structure and their ownership. In August 2010, Afghan President Hamid Karzai took this even further by issuing a decree ordering all PMSCs in the country to disband within four months, with the sole exception being for private guards operating within embassy

46 See Law of Administration for the State of Iraq for the Transitional Period (8 March 2004); Katzman and Elsea, 'Iraq: Transition to Sovereignty', Congressional Research Service Report for Congress RS21820 (21 July 2004).
47 See Private Security Company Association of Iraq, *Baghdad MOI PSC Registration Guide 2006*, available at www.pscai.org.
48 Procedure for Regulating Activities of Private Security Companies in Afghanistan (2008).
49 *Ibid.*, 2.
50 See Sherman and DiDomenico, 'The Public Cost of Private Security in Afghanistan' (September 2009), 4–6.

compounds, consulates, NGOs and economic organisations such as the World Bank.[51]

The Montreux Document also characterises as implicit in Common Article 1 an obligation on the host state to suppress PMSC violations of IHL.[52] In international conflicts this reinforces the specific obligations in the Geneva Conventions to repress grave breaches and to suppress other breaches of IHL, discussed below. In non-international conflicts, on the other hand, the Common Article 1 obligation to suppress violations essentially stands alone. Ideally the host state would adopt *criminal* legislation to fulfil this obligation; in fact, the ICTY Appeals Chamber suggested in the *Čelebići* case that the absence of domestic legislation criminalising violations of Common Article 3 could in itself constitute a violation of Common Article 1.[53] The hiring state should also 'consider establishing corporate criminal responsibility for crimes committed by the PMSC'.[54] Whatever the precise means adopted by the host state to prohibit PMSC violations of IHL, it is clear that the state must investigate and, where warranted by the evidence, prosecute, extradite or otherwise punish any PMSC personnel suspected of having violated IHL in state territory. The host state should also 'provide for non-criminal accountability mechanisms for improper and unlawful conduct of PMSC and its personnel', including providing for civil liability.[55]

State responsibility for breach of Common Article 1

If the host state does not take adequate measures to control a PMSC and the company violates IHL in state territory, the state could incur international responsibility for its failure to ensure respect for IHL. Although no court to date has found a state responsible under Common Article 1 merely on the basis of such inaction, the above analysis has shown that this pathway to responsibility is certainly possible in principle.

Of course, the mere occurrence of a PMSC violation in state territory would not in itself establish that the host state had breached its preventive

---

51 See Vogt, 'Karzai Decree Ousts Private Security Firms', *Washington Times* (17 August 2010); Rubin, 'Karzai Orders Guard Firms to Disband', *New York Times* (17 August 2010); Partlow, 'Karzai Wants Private Security Firms Out of Afghanistan', *Washington Post* (17 August 2010).

52 Montreux Document, Part I, para. 9(c) (quoted above).

53 *Prosecutor* v. *Delalić*, Judgment, IT-96-21-A, Appeals Chamber, 20 February 2001 ('*Čelebići* case'), para. 167; see also Cassese, 'On the Current Trends towards Criminal Prosecution and Punishment of Breaches of International Humanitarian Law' (1998) 9(1) *EJIL* 2.

54 Montreux Document, Part II, para. 49.   55 *Ibid.*, Part II, para. 50.

obligation. The claimant would also need to prove that the state had failed to exercise due diligence to ensure company compliance with IHL. The claimant would not need to prove, however, that an exercise of due diligence by the host state would in fact have prevented the violation of IHL in question. This would be difficult to prove and, in any event, it is irrelevant to the breach of the state's obligation to exercise due diligence to prevent violations of IHL. In order to establish such a breach, it would suffice to prove that the host state had failed to take those measures within its power that *might* have been expected to prevent the violation in the circumstances.[56] The extent of the state's responsibility would then depend on an evaluation of, on the one hand, the preventive steps in fact taken by the state and, on the other hand, the state's capacity to influence the PMSC, the degree of risk associated with the PMSC activity, and the resources available to the state.

The host state's obligation to ensure respect for IHL not only provides a potential mechanism for establishing state responsibility *ex post facto* in cases of PMSC misconduct; it could also help to set minimum standards of conduct for all states in whose territory PMSCs operate in international or non-international conflict. In this way, the obligation to ensure respect in Common Article 1 could play a similar role to the rules in Common Article 3 which, according to the ICJ, 'constitute a minimum yardstick, in addition to the more elaborate rules which are also to apply to international conflicts'.[57]

Obligation to protect civilians in international armed conflict

In addition to the general obligation to ensure respect for IHL, the Geneva Conventions and Protocol I impose a number of more specific obligations on states parties to protect civilians in international armed conflict, particularly women and children. These obligations require states to take certain positive steps to control not only the conduct of state agents and officials, but also the conduct of private persons.

---

56 This essentially mirrors the test used by the ICJ in the *Genocide* case (para. 430), as well as that used by the European Court of Human Rights in assessing the obligation to safeguard the right to life in *Keenan* v. *UK* (App. No. 27229/95), ECHR, 3 April 2001 (para. 89) and *Osman* v. *UK* (App. No. 23452/94), ECHR, 28 October 1998 (para. 116).

57 *Nicaragua*, para. 218; see also *Prosecutor* v. *Tadić*, Decision on the Defence Motion for Interlocutory Appeal on Jurisdiction, ICTY-94-1-AR72, Appeals Chamber, 2 October 1995, para. 102.

Article 27 of GCIV provides that '[p]rotected persons . . . shall be protected especially against all acts of violence or threats thereof and against insults and public curiosity'. It further states that '[w]omen shall be especially protected against any attack on their honour, in particular against rape, enforced prostitution, or any form of indecent assault'. In a similar vein, Article 76 of Protocol I obliges states to protect women 'in particular against rape, forced prostitution and any other form of indecent assault', and Article 77 obliges states to protect children 'against any form of indecent assault'. These obligations are particularly important in light of the high rate of rape and sexual assault in armed conflict.[58]

It is possible to infer from these provisions a due diligence obligation on the host state to control PMSCs engaged in activities that could threaten the civilian population, especially women and children. This obligation is most relevant to those companies that bear weapons or otherwise operate in a coercive environment such as a detention centre. It is also possible to infer a due diligence obligation to minimise the risk that off-duty contractors (or off-duty soldiers) might engage in unlawful sexual activities with women or children. In international conflicts, these special obligations complement and reinforce the general obligation in Common Article 1 to ensure respect for IHL.

As part of its efforts to fulfil these obligations, the host state should take reasonable measures within its power to combat underage and forced prostitution in its territory. Such prostitution is common in zones of armed conflict and post-conflict reconstruction, in part due to the large presence of unaccompanied, highly paid and mostly male international workers. The 'sex-slave' scandal in Bosnia provides an example of PMSC misconduct in a post-conflict context. The American firm DynCorp provided a large number of personnel to the US government to meet its obligation to staff the UN police force in post-conflict Bosnia and Herzegovina. During 1999 and 2000, a number of DynCorp employees participated in a prostitution ring in Bosnia involving girls as young as twelve, many of whom were trafficking victims, and some contractors allegedly 'purchased' young prostitutes for personal use.[59]

---

58 See Askin, 'Prosecuting Wartime Rape and Other Gender-Related Crimes under International Law: Extraordinary Advances, Enduring Obstacles' (2003) 21 *Berkeley Journal of International Law* 288.
59 See Human Rights Watch, 'Hopes Betrayed: Trafficking of Women and Girls to Post-Conflict Bosnia and Herzegovina for Forced Prostitution' (26 November 2002); Maffai, 'Accountability for Private Military and Security Company Employees that Engage in Sex Trafficking and Related Abuses While under Contract with the United States Overseas' (2008–9) 26 *Wisconsin International Law Journal* 1095.

In non-international armed conflict, neither Common Article 3 nor Protocol II[60] contains a duty to take positive steps to protect the civilian population in general or women and children in particular. Articles 7–11 of Protocol II impose limited duties on states to protect the wounded, sick and shipwrecked, as well as medical units and religious personnel, and these duties entail a due diligence standard of conduct. Beyond these specific obligations, the only provision mandating a general level of host state action in non-international conflict is Common Article 1.

Obligation to repress or suppress violations of IHL

In international armed conflict, the substantive provisions of the Geneva Conventions and Additional Protocols explicitly oblige all states to take measures to repress or suppress breaches of IHL that have occurred or are ongoing. These obligations apply over and above the general obligation to suppress violations of IHL, which is implicit in Common Article 1.

The clearest obligations on states relate to 'grave breaches' of the Geneva Conventions. This category encompasses certain serious offences including wilful killing, torture or inhuman treatment, and wilfully causing great suffering or serious injury to body or health.[61] Article 49(1)/50(1)/129(1)/146(1) common to the Geneva Conventions explicitly requires all states, first, to enact any legislation necessary to criminalise grave breaches under domestic law and, subsequently, to prosecute or extradite suspects in the exercise of universal jurisdiction.

In rare cases PMSC personnel might commit offences of this nature. For example, employees of the American PMSCs Titan and CACI, working under contract with the US, were found to have participated in the prisoner abuse at Abu Ghraib prison in Iraq in 2003–4.[62] The host state of the PMSC will be the most obvious forum for prosecution in such cases, unless there is an agreement in place granting foreign contractors immunity from local laws, such as CPA Order No. 17 of 2004 in Iraq (discussed in the third section of this chapter).[63] Where such immunity applies or the host state is otherwise unable or unwilling to conduct the

---

60 Second Additional Protocol to the Geneva Conventions of 12 August 1949, and relating to the Protection of Victims of Non-International Armed Conflicts (adopted 8 June 1977, entered into force 7 December 1987), 1125 UNTS 609 ('Protocol II').

61 GCI, Art. 50; GCII, Art. 51; GCIII, Art. 130; GCIV, Art. 147.

62 See Fay, 'Investigation of the Abu Ghraib Detention Facility and 205th Military Intelligence Brigade' (August 2004).

63 CPA Order No. 17 of 2004, s. 4(2).

prosecution itself, the state could fulfil its obligation to repress grave breaches by handing the PMSC employees over for trial to another state (such as their state of nationality) that has made out a *prima facie* case, or to an international criminal tribunal.[64]

A more likely scenario would be where a PMSC employee committed a non-grave breach of IHL. All states have an obligation to 'take measures necessary for the suppression of' ('*faire cesser*') non-grave breaches of IHL under Common Article 49(3)/50(3)/129(3)/146(3). Whilst this provision (unlike the equivalent provision relating to grave breaches) does not impose an *explicit* obligation on states to enact legislation enabling criminal prosecution, it will generally be difficult for a state to fulfil its obligation to suppress non-grave breaches in the absence of domestic criminal legislation.[65] According to the ICRC Commentary to Article 146(3) of GCIV, 'there is no doubt that what is primarily meant is the repression [by criminal prosecution] of breaches other than the grave breaches listed and only in the second place administrative measures to ensure respect for the provisions of the Convention'.[66] The Commentary goes on to state more explicitly that

> all breaches of the Convention should be repressed by national legislation. The Contracting Parties who have taken measures to repress the various grave breaches of the Convention and have fixed an appropriate penalty in each case should at least insert in their legislation a general clause providing for the punishment of other breaches.[67]

The envisaged repression of non-grave breaches refers to prosecution by states in the exercise of ordinary jurisdiction, whereas the grave breaches regime explicitly provides for universal jurisdiction.[68]

In non-international conflicts there are no specific provisions equivalent to Common Article 49/50/129/146, but an obligation to suppress violations of IHL is implicit in the general obligation to ensure respect for IHL in Common Article 1.[69] In this context, the ICTY Appeals Chamber

---

64 See Montreux Document, Part I, para. 11.   65 UCIHL Expert Meeting, 46–7.

66 *ICRC Commentary to GCIV*, 594.

67 See also International Law Commission Draft Code of Crimes Against the Peace and Security of Mankind, UN Doc. A/SI/10 (1996), Art. 9; UNGA Res. 3074 (XXVIII) (3 December 1973), UN Doc. A/3074; Cassese, 'On the Current Trends towards Criminal Prosecution and Punishment of Breaches of International Humanitarian Law'.

68 See generally Meron, 'International Criminalization of Internal Atrocities' (1995) 89 *AJIL* 554, 569–70; Brownlie, *Principles of Public International Law*, 6th edn (2003), 303, 565.

69 See Montreux Document, Part I, para. 9(c).

explicitly stated in the *Čelebići* case that a state's failure to enact legislation criminalising violations of Common Article 3 would 'arguably' be inconsistent with the general obligation in Common Article 1.[70]

4.2 Obligations to control PMSCs under human rights law

HRL provides another key source of obligations on the host state to control PMSCs. Whilst HRL lacks the specificity of IHL in situations of armed conflict, it offers a significant advantage to victims by virtue of its sophisticated procedures for individual complaint and redress.[71] Moreover, all violations of civil and political rights give rise to an individual right to an effective procedural remedy and reparation under HRL, whereas no such individual right exists in IHL.[72]

This section critically examines the host state's obligations to take active steps to prevent, investigate, punish and redress human rights violations committed by PMSCs in armed conflict. Before analysing the content of these obligations, however, it is first necessary to confirm that the general regime of HRL applies in armed conflict, and to assess the relationship between HRL and IHL in this context.

Applicability of HRL in armed conflict

Unlike IHL, which is specially tailored to situations of armed conflict, HRL constitutes a general framework primarily designed to apply to ordinary life during peacetime. Any attempt to apply a general legal framework to the exceptional situation of armed conflict raises the question of how those general norms relate to the more specific norms of IHL.

Do the rules of IHL displace the rules of HRL in armed conflict?

Although IHL and HRL share a common humanist ideal, the two regimes differ in their historical origins, theoretical foundations and primary objectives.[73] IHL is designed to regulate the conduct of parties to an

---

70 *Čelebići* case, paras. 163–7.
71 See generally Symonides (ed.), *Human Rights: International Protection, Monitoring, Enforcement* (2003).
72 Zegveld, 'Remedies for Victims of Violations of International Humanitarian Law' (2003) 851 *International Review of the Red Cross* 497.
73 See Doswald-Beck and Vité, 'International Humanitarian Law and Human Rights Law' (1993) 293 *International Review of the Red Cross* 94; Vinuesa, 'Interface, Correspondence

armed conflict with the purpose of 'alleviating as much as possible the calamities of war'.[74] It attempts to strike a balance between consider- ations of military necessity and the requirements of humanity, and it imposes obligations both on states and individuals in furtherance of that objective.[75] The primary purpose of HRL, on the other hand, is the pro- tection of individuals from abuses of power by their own governments. Whereas IHL regulates armed conflict on the basis of formal equality between contestants, HRL applies to relationships between unequal par- ties. This traditional conception of human rights as a means of protecting the governed from the governing helps to explain why HRL imposes obli- gations only on states and not on individuals, and why it confers rights directly on individuals *per se* without the interposition of states. Victims of human rights violations may stand on their own rights without nec- essarily relying on the goodwill of their state to take up their case on the international plane. HRL also provides more advanced procedural safe- guards for the protection of individual rights than IHL. The corollary of the general applicability of HRL, however, is that states have some leeway in restricting rights in the interests of national security or public safety, and in the extreme circumstances of an armed conflict the main human rights treaties allow for derogations from certain rights.[76]

In light of the fundamental differences between IHL and HRL, one might assume that during armed conflict the war-oriented human rights contained in IHL simply supplant the peacetime rights contained in HRL. The drafters of the Universal Declaration of Human Rights of 1948[77] and

and Convergence of Human Rights and International Humanitarian Law' (1998) 1 *Year- book of International Humanitarian Law* 69; Droege, 'The Interplay between International Humanitarian Law and International Human Rights Law' (2007) 40 *Israel Law Review* 310, 312–17.

74 St Petersburg Declaration Renouncing the Use, in Time of War, of Explosive Projectiles under 400 Grammes Weight (1868) *Laws of Armed Conflicts* 101, 102.

75 Dinstein, *The Conduct of Hostilities under the Law of International Armed Conflict* (2004), 16–20.

76 See International Covenant on Civil and Political Rights (adopted 16 December 1966, entered into force 23 March 1976), 999 UNTS 171, Art. 4; European Convention on Human Rights (4 November 1950), CETS No. 005, Art. 15; American Convention on Human Rights (adopted 22 November 1969, entered into force 18 July 1978), 1144 UNTS 123, Art. 27. The African Charter contains no derogation clause, but limitations are possible pursuant to Art. 27(2) to take account of 'the rights of others, collective security, morality and common interest': African Charter on Human and Peoples' Rights (adopted 27 June 1981, entered into force 21 October 1986), OAU Doc. CAB/LEG/67/3 rev 5.

77 Universal Declaration of Human Rights (adopted 10 December 1948), UNGA Res. 217 A(III), UN Doc. A/810 at 71 (1948).

the Geneva Conventions of 1949 seemed to assume that the two regimes would have essentially distinct fields of operation, and this understanding of IHL and HRL as two separate legal regimes largely prevailed at least until the 1970s.[78] Yet the drafters of the 1950 European Convention on Human Rights (ECHR) and the 1969 American Convention on Human Rights ('American Convention') clearly envisaged that those instruments would continue to apply during armed conflict, since they included provisions stipulating that a situation of 'war' permits states to derogate from certain specified rights, but only to the extent and for the period of time strictly required by the exigencies of the situation.[79] Moreover, historical developments since that time have signified a gradual convergence of IHL and HRL, culminating in the decisions of the ICJ in the *Nuclear Weapons*, *Wall* and *Congo* cases, in a process Meron describes as the '"humanization" of humanitarian law'.[80]

It is now widely recognised that HRL continues to apply during both international and non-international armed conflict, and there is extensive state practice and *opinio juris* to that effect.[81] For example, General Assembly Resolution 2675 (XXV) of 1970 on 'basic principles for the protection of civilian populations in armed conflicts' refers in its preamble to the Geneva Conventions as well as to 'the progressive development of the international law of armed conflict'.[82] In its first operative paragraph, the Resolution states that 'fundamental human rights, as accepted in international law and laid down in international instruments, continue to apply fully in situations of armed conflict'. Since then, numerous resolutions of the General Assembly, the Security Council and the Commission on Human Rights have reaffirmed, either explicitly or implicitly, the continuing applicability of HRL in both international and non-international armed conflict.[83] Further demonstrating the convergence of IHL and HRL are a number of widely ratified international treaties that draw from both

---

78 See, e.g., Pictet, *Humanitarian Law and the Protection of War Victims* (1975), 15; Dinstein, 'The International Law of Inter-State Wars and Human Rights' [1977] *Israel Yearbook of Human Rights* 148; Meyrovitz, 'Le Droit de la Guerre et les Droits de l'Homme' (1972) 88 *Revue de Droit Public et de la Science Politique* 1059, 1104; Suter, 'An Enquiry into the Meaning of the Phrase "Human Rights in Armed Conflicts"' (1976) 15 *Revue de Droit Pénal Militaire et Droit de la Guerre* 393, 421.

79 ECHR, Art. 15; American Convention, Art. 27.

80 Meron, 'The Humanization of Humanitarian Law' (2000) 94 *AJIL* 239.

81 See *ICRC Customary Law Study*, vol. I, 303–5.

82 UNGA Res. 2675 (XXV) (9 December 1970), UN Doc. A/2675.

83 See *ICRC Customary Law Study*, vol. I, 303–5; Droege, 'The Interplay between International Humanitarian Law and International Human Rights Law', 316–17.

regimes, including the Convention on the Rights of the Child[84] and the Rome Statute of the International Criminal Court.[85]

International human rights bodies and courts, including the UN Human Rights Committee, the European Court of Human Rights (ECtHR) and the Inter-American Court of Human Rights (IACtHR), have applied human rights treaties in times of non-international armed conflict as well as international armed conflict.[86] In its *Nuclear Weapons* advisory opinion of 1995, the ICJ recognised that the protection of the International Covenant on Civil and Political Rights (ICCPR) 'does not cease in times of war, except by operation of Article 4 of the Covenant whereby certain provisions may be derogated from in a time of national emergency'.[87] The Court reaffirmed this statement in its 2004 *Wall* advisory opinion, and extended the principle to the general application of human rights in armed conflict:

> More generally, the Court considers that the protection offered by human rights conventions does not cease in case of armed conflict, save through the effect of provisions for derogation of the kind to be found in Article 4 of the International Covenant on Civil and Political Rights.[88]

The Court reiterated this conclusion in the *Congo* case of 2005,[89] thereby making it clear that its opinion in the *Wall* case cannot be explained by the 'unusual circumstances of Israel's prolonged occupation' in the occupied Palestinian territories, since Uganda did not have such a long-term and consolidated presence in the eastern DRC.[90]

---

84 Convention on the Rights of the Child (adopted 20 November 1989, entered into force 2 September 1990), 1577 UNTS 3, Art. 38.

85 Rome Statute of the International Criminal Court (adopted 17 July 1998, entered into force 1 July 2002), UN Doc. A/CONF.183/9, (1998) 37 ILM 999; see also UNGA Res. 60/147 (16 December 2005), UN Doc. A/RES/60/147.

86 See Heintze, 'On the Relationship between Human Rights Law Protection and International Humanitarian Law' (2004) 86(856) *International Review of the Red Cross* 789; Droege, 'The Interplay between International Humanitarian Law and International Human Rights Law', 320–2.

87 *Legality of the Threat or Use of Nuclear Weapons* (Advisory Opinion) ICJ Reports 1996, para. 25.

88 *Wall* advisory opinion, para. 106.

89 *Case Concerning Armed Activities in the Territory of the Congo (DRC v. Uganda)* (Merits) ICJ Reports 2005, para. 119.

90 Dennis suggested in 2005 that the ICJ's *Wall* advisory opinion could be attributed to this feature of the Israeli occupation: see Dennis, 'Application of Human Rights Treaties Extraterritorially in Times of Armed Conflict and Military Occupation' (2005) 99 *AJIL* 119, 122.

Whilst for the most part states have not objected to these interpretations, the governments of the US and Israel have contested the general applicability of HRL to armed conflict in recent years.[91] In light of this official US position, the Montreux Document of 2008 is highly significant as a public affirmation by the US that IHL and HRL apply concurrently in armed conflict. The preface to the Document sets out the 'understanding' of the drafting states that 'certain well-established rules of international law apply to States in their relations with [PMSCs] and their operation during armed conflict, *in particular under international humanitarian law and human rights law*'.[92] Part I of the Document then sets out the 'existing legal obligations' that bind states in times of armed conflict, including a number of obligations under HRL.[93] This can be taken to be a significant expression of *opinio juris* of the seventeen drafting states – including the US – as to the continuing applicability of HRL in times of armed conflict. In this regard, as Cockayne notes:

> Given the uncertainty around the US position on such issues between 2003 and 2008, this was no small achievement. Indeed, one US government participant in the process pronounced the Montreux Document 'a significant achievement of historic importance', for precisely this reason.[94]

Derogating from human rights in times of emergency

The principal human rights treaties allow states to derogate from certain rights in a time of emergency threatening the life of the nation. The emergency need not involve the whole nation, but it must be the case that the normal application of HRL – taking into account limitations that are permissible in relation to a number of rights for public safety

---

91 See, e.g., Human Rights Committee, Consideration of Reports Submitted by States Parties under Article 40 of the Covenant, 2nd and 3rd Periodic Reports of the United States of America (28 November 2005), UN Doc. CCPR/C/USA/3, Annex I: Territorial Scope of the Application of the Covenant; Summary Record of the 2380th Meeting: USA, 2, UN Doc. CCPR/C/SR2380 (27 July 2006); Summary Legal Position of the Government of Israel, Annex I to the Report of the Secretary-General Prepared Pursuant to UNGA Res., ES-10713, para. 4, UN Doc. A/ES-10/248 (24 November 2003). For a discussion of the Israeli government's position, see Ben-Naftali and Shany, 'Living in Denial: The Application of Human Rights in the Occupied Territories' (2003–4) 37 *Israel Law Review* 17, 25–40; but note the contrasting approach of the Israeli High Court of Justice in *Ma'arab* v. *The IDF Commander in Judea and Samaria*, 57(2) PD 349, HCJ 3239/02.
92 Montreux Document, Preface, para. 1 (emphasis added).
93 See, e.g., *ibid.*, Part I, paras. 4, 7 and 10.
94 Cockayne, 'Regulating Private Military and Security Companies', 403. Regarding the 'US government participant', Cockayne cites a '[c]onfidential statement to participants in the Swiss Initiative, made under the Chatham House rule, 2008'.

and order – can no longer be ensured.[95] Derogations are permitted only to the extent strictly required by the exigencies of the situation, and not in relation to the specified non-derogable rights such as the right to life and freedom from torture. The derogations clauses in Article 15 of the ECHR and Article 27 of the American Convention explicitly state that a situation of 'war' permits states to derogate from certain specified rights. The express reference to war in these provisions clearly supports the ICJ's opinion that HRL continues to apply during armed conflict in the absence of derogation; for, if IHL automatically displaced HRL during armed conflict, there would be no need to derogate from any rights in the relevant treaties in case of war. The derogation clause in Article 4 of the ICCPR does not expressly mention 'war', but it is widely accepted that war is one of the most important emergencies falling within that provision. Conversely, Article 2 of the UN Convention Against Torture (UNCAT) explicitly states that a situation of war may *not* be invoked as a justification of torture.[96]

Generally speaking, there are two procedural requirements for the lawfulness of derogations: they must be officially proclaimed and other states party to the treaty must be notified thereof. The ICJ adopted a strict approach to the notice requirements for derogation from the ICCPR in the *Wall* case. In applying the Covenant to Israel's occupation of the Palestinian territories, the Court held that, although Israel had formally derogated from Article 9, it had forfeited its right to derogate from other Articles because of its failure to notify other states parties of its intent. The Court concluded that Israel remained bound by the other Articles of the Covenant, not only in Israeli territory but also in relation to the occupied Palestinian territories.[97] In a similar vein, the ECtHR has insisted that strict adherence to the procedural requirements in Article 15 of the ECHR is a prerequisite for derogation from the Convention. In the *Isayeva* case concerning Russia's conduct in the non-international armed conflict in Chechnya, the Court stated that '[n]o martial law and no state of emergency has been declared in Chechnya, and no derogation has been

---

95 *ICRC Customary Law Study*, vol. I, 301–2; Vinuesa, 'Interface, Correspondence and Convergence of Human Rights and International Humanitarian Law', 76–81; McGoldrick, *The Human Rights Committee: Its Role in the Development of the International Covenant on Civil and Political Rights* (1991), ch. 7.

96 UN Convention Against Torture (adopted 10 December 1984, entered into force 26 June 1987), 1465 UNTS 85.

97 *Wall* advisory opinion, para. 127; see also paras. 136 and 140.

made under article 15 of the Convention . . . The operation in question therefore has to be judged against a normal legal background.'[98] The ICRC's study on customary IHL embraces the strict approach of the ICJ and ECtHR.[99]

In short, the host state of a PMSC will continue to be bound by HRL in relation to the company's activities in state territory during armed conflict, except to the extent that the state has formally derogated from its obligations as strictly required by the exigencies of the situation. The host state will always be bound by its obligation to respect and ensure non-derogable rights such as the right to life and freedom from torture. The remainder of this section takes the continuing applicability of HRL during armed conflict as an accepted starting point, and proceeds to analyse the requirements of HRL in this specific context.

Relationship between HRL and IHL

Although IHL is, by and large, more specific than HRL in relation to armed conflict, this does not lead to the conclusion that the former regime will simply override the latter in this context. Rather, the relationship between IHL and HRL must be assessed in each case in relation to the particular norm in question.[100] This contextual analysis is particularly important for modern military operations involving activities such as policing and the administration of territory, which are closer to regular government functions than traditional combat. In these circumstances, HRL may provide a more appropriate regulatory framework than IHL, notwithstanding the fact that the operations take place in a conflict zone.[101]

The principle of lex specialis

In the *Wall* case, the ICJ identified three situations that might govern the relationship between IHL and HRL in regard to a particular right:

---

98 *Isayeva* v. *Russia* (App. No. 57950/00), ECHR, 24 February 2005, 191.

99 *ICRC Customary Law Study*, vol. I, 300.

100 Lindroos, 'Addressing Norm Conflicts in a Fragmented Legal System: The Doctrine of Lex Specialis' (2005) 74 *Nordic Journal of International Law* 27, 49; Krieger, 'A Conflict of Norms: The Relationship between Humanitarian Law and Human Rights Law in the ICRC Customary Law Study' (2006) 11(2) *Journal of Conflict and Security Law* 265, 271. More generally, see Provost, *International Human Rights and Humanitarian Law* (2002).

101 Ratner, 'Foreign Occupation and International Territorial Administration: The Challenges of Convergence' (2005) 16 *EJIL* 696; Droege, 'The Interplay between International Humanitarian Law and International Human Rights Law'.

> [S]ome rights may be exclusively matters of international humanitarian law; others may be exclusively matters of human rights law; yet others may be matters of both these branches of international law. In order to answer the question put to it, the Court will have to take into consideration both these branches of international law, namely human rights law and, as *lex specialis*, international humanitarian law.[102]

Although the Court did not offer any specific guidance as to how to distinguish between these three categories, it is generally accepted that the conduct of hostilities is essentially a matter of IHL, whereas ordinary law enforcement by state authorities is essentially a matter of HRL. The two regimes will frequently overlap in relation to persons in the power of an authority (including persons in the power of a PMSC hired by a state), in which case it is necessary to undertake a more nuanced analysis. Where IHL and HRL overlap, in that they both have something to say about a particular right, the principle of *lex specialis* can guide the interplay between the two regimes.

The International Law Commission Study Group on the Fragmentation of International Law ('ILC Study Group') has found that the *lex specialis* principle can play two roles in relation to overlapping norms, depending on the factual situation and the particular norm in question.[103] First, the *lex specialis* rule may provide a more specific interpretation of the general rule, such that the two rules complement and reinforce one another. Secondly, the *lex specialis* rule may constitute an exception or limitation to the general rule, in the sense that the former modifies, derogates from or overrules the latter. Koskenniemi explains this distinction in the following terms:

> There are two ways in which law takes account of the relationship of a particular rule to general rule ... A particular rule may be considered an application of the general rule in a given circumstance. That is to say, it may give instructions on what a general rule requires in the case at hand. Alternatively, a particular rule may be conceived as an exception to the general rule. In this case, the particular derogates from the general rule. The maxim *lex specialis derogat lex generalis* is usually dealt with as a conflict rule. However, it need not be limited to conflict.[104]

102 *Wall* advisory opinion, para. 106.
103 See ILC Study Group on Fragmentation of International Law, 'Difficulties Arising from Diversification and Expansion of International Law' (29 July 2005), UN Doc. A/CN.4/L.676 ('ILC Study Group Report').
104 Koskenniemi, 'Study on the Function and Scope of the Lex Specialis Rule and the Question of "Self Contained Regimes"' (2004), UN Doc. ILC(LVI)/SG/FIL/CRD.1/Add.1, 4.

This twofold conception of *lex specialis* is broader than the common understanding of the principle as a technique for solving conflicts between norms. Each aspect of the principle will now be considered in turn.

Lex specialis as a specific interpretation of the general rule

The first conception of *lex specialis* – as a more specific interpretation of the general rule – can guide the interplay between IHL and HRL in a wide range of situations. On this understanding, the particular rule and the general rule operate side-by-side in a relationship of complementarity and mutual reinforcement. This promotes the notion of international law as a coherent system rather than a mere set of discrete regimes.[105] The more specific rule may develop the general rule or apply that rule to a particular circumstance, whilst the general rule may articulate a rationale or purpose of the more specific rule. The more specific rule should therefore 'be read and understood within the confines or against the background of the general standard, typically as an elaboration, updating or a technical specification of the latter'.[106]

Lex specialis as an exception or limitation to the general rule

The second conception of *lex specialis* identified by the ILC Study Group is simply an exception or limitation to the general rule. In this scenario, rather than reinforcing or explaining the general rule, the specific rule modifies, derogates from or overrides that rule. The right to life provides one example. Article 6 of the ICCPR states that '[n]o one shall be arbitrarily deprived of his life', and Article 4(2) provides that this right is non-derogable. IHL, on the other hand, effectively tolerates the killing and wounding of innocent civilians during hostilities as lawful collateral damage.[107] The two regimes also utilise different conceptions of proportionality in this context: HRL requires that any use of force be proportionate to the aim of protecting life,[108] whereas under IHL the incidental loss of civilian life caused by an armed attack must not be excessive in relation to the concrete and direct military advantage anticipated.[109] In light of these differences in the context of hostilities, the more specific

---

105 ILC Study Group Report; Droege, 'The Interplay between International Humanitarian Law and International Human Rights Law', 340–4; Human Rights Committee, General Comment 31, UN Doc. CCPR/C/21/Rev.1/Add.13 (2004), para. 11.
106 ILC Study Group Report, para. 56.
107 Meron, 'The Humanization of Humanitarian Law', 240.
108 See *McCann* v. *UK* (App. No. 18984/91), ECHR Ser. A No. 324 (1995), paras. 202–13.
109 See Protocol I, Art. 51(5)(b).

norm of IHL effectively modifies the more general norm of HRL. The ICJ explained this principle in its *Nuclear Weapons* advisory opinion. After affirming that the protections of the ICCPR continue to apply in armed conflict, the Court stated:

> In principle, the right not arbitrarily to be deprived of one's life applies also in hostilities. The test of what is an arbitrary deprivation of life, however, then falls to be determined by the applicable *lex specialis*, namely, the law applicable in armed conflict which is designed to regulate the conduct of hostilities. Thus whether a particular loss of life, through the use of a certain weapon in warfare, is to be considered an arbitrary deprivation of life contrary to Article 6 of the Covenant, can only be decided by reference to the law applicable in armed conflict and not deduced from the terms of the Covenant itself.[110]

In other words, the right to life still applies in armed conflict, but in relation to the conduct of hostilities the content of that right is tied to the rules of IHL. The notion of an 'arbitrary' deprivation of life under HRL provides an interpretive window which permits the two norms to be 'applied concurrently, or within each other'.[111] The *lex specialis* rule of IHL thus modifies or derogates from the general HRL standard. In the conduct of hostilities, acts that are lawful under IHL will not constitute arbitrary deprivations of life for the purposes of HRL, even if those acts lead to catastrophic losses of human lives.

The right to life in Article 27 of the American Convention has virtually identical wording to the equivalent right in Article 4 of the ICCPR, and the Inter-American Commission on Human Rights has essentially followed the ICJ's approach in interpreting this right in the context of hostilities.[112] This approach would also appear to be valid under the ECHR, in light of the unique wording of the derogation clause in that instrument: Article 15(2) prohibits derogation from (*inter alia*) the right to life and freedom from torture and ill-treatment, but in relation to the right to life it provides an explicit exception in times of declared emergency 'in respect of deaths resulting from lawful acts of war'. A similar interpretation also appears open under the African Charter on Human and Peoples' Rights ('African Charter'), which contains no derogation

---

110 *Nuclear Weapons* advisory opinion, para. 25; see also *ICRC Customary Law Study*, vol. I, 300; *Coard* v. *US*, IAComHR Rep. No. 109/99, Case 10.951, 29 September 1999, para. 42.

111 ILC Study Group Report, para. 96.   112 *Coard* v. *US*, para. 42.

clause but which permits limitations on rights on the basis of (*inter alia*) 'collective security'.[113]

In relation to some norms, however, it is not possible to harmonise IHL and HRL through a process of coordinated interpretation. Harmonisation 'may resolve apparent conflicts; it cannot resolve genuine conflicts'.[114] For example, Article 5 of the ECHR provides that '[e]veryone has the right to liberty and security of person. No one shall be deprived of his liberty save in the following cases and in accordance with a procedure prescribed by law.' The provision then enumerates six situations that permit the deprivation of individual liberty, but this list does not include the deprivation of liberty on account of a situation of war or other considerations of national security. There is therefore no interpretive window in Article 5 through which one could import the rules of IHL justifying the detention of individuals in certain situations of armed conflict, and in such situations the more specific rules of IHL will simply prevail over Article 5 to the extent of any inconsistency.

Yet that is not to say that IHL will always provide the more specific rule in the context of an armed conflict. The *lex specialis* principle is based on the notion of appropriateness: in any given situation, the rule that is more specific will be more appropriate and therefore more effective than its general counterpart.[115] IHL is certainly the more refined body of law in relation to the conduct of hostilities and other situations closely linked to the battlefield, but in relation to ordinary law enforcement by state authorities (including PMSCs hired by a state to carry out law enforcement functions), HRL will generally provide the more appropriate rule. The two regimes will frequently overlap in relation to persons in the power of an authority, in which case the closer the situation is to the battlefield, the more that IHL will take precedence.[116]

The assessment of which regime is more appropriate to the circumstances is essentially one of fact rather than law. Consider, for example, a lethal use of force by a PMSC employee working as an armed security

---

113 African Charter on Human and Peoples' Rights, Art. 27(2).

114 Borgen, 'Resolving Treaty Conflicts' (2005) 37 *George Washington International Law Review* 573, 640.

115 Akehurst, 'The Hierarchy of the Sources of International Law' (1974–5) 47 *British Yearbook of International Law* 273; Pauwelyn, *Conflict of Norms in Public International Law* (2003), 385; Lindroos, 'Addressing Norm Conflicts in a Fragmented Legal System', 42.

116 Droege, 'The Interplay between International Humanitarian Law and International Human Rights Law', 344.

guard in the host state. If the incident took place when the contractor was guarding an oilfield in a relatively stable part of the country and was attacked by criminal bandits, the question of whether the killing was 'arbitrary' for the purposes of the right to life would essentially be determined by the ordinary rules of HRL. But if the contractor was guarding a military target in the heart of the conflict zone and was attacked by enemy forces, the question of whether the killing was arbitrary would fall to be determined by the specific rules of IHL. This example illustrates how the decision as to which regime is the *lex specialis* in a particular case can be crucial in assessing the substantive scope of the host state's obligations and responsibility in relation to PMSCs.

Obligation to prevent human rights violations by PMSCs

All of the main human rights treaties contain general provisions requiring states to 'ensure' or 'secure' the rights of individuals within their jurisdiction.[117] Human rights bodies have interpreted these provisions as imposing an obligation on states to exercise due diligence to prevent, investigate, punish and redress human rights violations by private actors (such as PMSCs) within state jurisdiction. According to the IACtHR in *Velásquez Rodríguez* v. *Honduras*, states must take 'all those means of a legal, political, administrative and cultural nature that promote the protection of human rights and ensure that any violations are considered and treated as illegal acts'.[118] Other human rights bodies have adopted a similarly broad approach.[119]

In his reports to the Human Rights Council, the UN special representative on the issue of human rights and transnational corporations and other business enterprises, John Ruggie, confirms the existence of a state duty to protect against corporate-related human rights abuse, grounded

---

117 See ICCPR, Art. 1(2); American Convention, Art. 1; ECHR, Art. 1; see also African Charter, Art. 1, which requires states to adopt measures 'to give effect to' rights.

118 *Velásquez Rodríguez* v. *Honduras* (Merits), Judgment of 29 June 1988, IACtHR Ser. C No. 4, paras. 174–5.

119 Regarding the right to life, see Human Rights Committee, General Comment 6, UN Doc. A/37/40(1982), paras. 3–5; *LCB* v. *UK* (App. No. 23413/94), ECHR, 9 June 1998, para. 36. Regarding the prohibition of torture and ill-treatment, see Human Rights Committee, General Comment 20, UN Doc. HRI/GEN/1/Rev.1, paras. 2 and 8; *Costello-Roberts* v. *UK* (App. No. 13134/87), ECHR Ser. A No. 247-C (1993), paras. 26–8; *A* v. *UK* (App. No. 25599/94), ECHR 1998-VI, para. 22; *Z* v. *UK* (App. No. 29392/95), ECHR, 10 May 2001, para. 73; see also UNCAT, Arts. 1, 2, 4 and 16.

in international human rights law.[120] Ruggie's reports set out a 'protect, respect and remedy' policy framework for business and human rights, which emphasises that the duty to protect requires states to take appropriate steps not only to prevent corporate-related human rights abuse within their jurisdiction, but also to investigate, punish and redress such abuse. This duty to protect is measured against a due diligence standard of conduct, meaning that '[s]tates are not held responsible for corporate-related human rights abuse *per se*, but may be considered in breach of their obligations where they fail to take appropriate steps to prevent it and to investigate, punish and redress it when it occurs'.[121]

The obligation to prevent, investigate, punish and redress human rights violations by PMSCs is also reflected in the Montreux Document, discussed in the first section of this chapter, which provides that host states

> are responsible to implement their obligations under international human rights law, including by adopting such legislative and other measures as may be necessary to give effect to these obligations. To this end they have the obligation, in specific circumstances, to take appropriate measures to prevent, investigate and provide effective remedies for relevant misconduct of PMSCs and their personnel.[122]

A host state that fails to take the necessary measures to control PMSC behaviour could incur international responsibility if a contractor violates human rights in state territory.

In the unique context of an armed conflict, these obligations must always be interpreted in light of the relevant norms of IHL. It was explained above that, in certain situations of armed conflict, IHL provides *lex specialis* rules which may modify or derogate from the general rules of HRL. In the conduct of hostilities, for example, the definition of an unlawful killing under HRL is essentially determined by the special rules of IHL,[123] with the result that the host state's obligation to prevent PMSC killings is less demanding in hostilities than in more stable contexts. On the other hand, where PMSCs perform ordinary law enforcement or security functions, the host state will be held to a more demanding standard which is

---

120 Ruggie, 'Protect, Respect and Remedy: A Framework for Business and Human Rights', UN Doc. A/HRC/8/5 (7 April 2008); Ruggie, 'Business and Human Rights: Towards Operationalizing the "Protect, Respect and Remedy" Framework', UN Doc. A/HRC/11/13 (22 April 2009); Ruggie, 'Business and Human Rights: Further Steps towards the Operationalization of the "Protect, Respect and Remedy" Framework', UN Doc. A/HRC/14/27 (9 April 2010) ('Ruggie Reports').
121 2009 Ruggie Report, para. 14.   122 Montreux Document, Part I, para. 10.
123 See *Nuclear Weapons* advisory opinion, para. 25.

primarily determined by the ordinary rules of HRL. In relation to the prohibition of torture and ill-treatment, the rules of IHL largely mirror the
rules of HRL, and consequently the substantive scope of the host state's
preventive obligation will not differ greatly between the two regimes.

Another factor complicating the analysis of the host state's preventive
obligations in armed conflict is that the state may have lost control over
parts of its territory, or it may simply lack the resources and/or institutional capacity to control PMSC behaviour effectively. Notwithstanding
these difficulties, the host state will remain obliged to exercise due diligence and take those measures that are reasonably within its power in
the circumstances. The ECtHR makes this clear in *Ilaşcu* v. *Moldova and
Russia,* holding that a state's

> positive obligations to take appropriate steps to ensure respect for those
> rights and freedoms within its territory . . . remain even where the exercise
> of the State's authority is limited in part of its territory, so that it has a
> duty to take all the appropriate measures which it is still within its power
> to take.[124]

The Court emphasised, however, that these positive obligations must not
be interpreted 'in such a way as to impose an impossible or disproportionate burden' on the state.[125]

Bearing these general considerations in mind, this section now examines three specific aspects of the preventive obligation that are particularly
pertinent to the host state of a PMSC, and identifies certain measures that
the state should take in order to fill these preventive obligations. It then
turns to examine the state's obligation to investigate, punish and redress
human rights violations committed in its territory.

Special measures targeting known sources of danger

Human rights bodies have recognised that states may need to take special
preventive measures targeting individuals who are known to be dangerous, taking into account the heightened risk that such individuals pose
to society.[126] Similarly, states may need to take more vigorous measures
to prevent the recurrence of a particular violation – measures that go
'beyond a victim-specific remedy' and 'may require changes in the State

---

124 *Ilaşcu* v. *Moldova and Russia* (App. No. 48787/99), ECHR, 8 July 2004, para. 313.
125 *Ibid.,* para. 332.
126 See *Mastromatteo* v. *Italy* (App. No. 37703/97), ECHR, 24 October 2002.

Party's laws or practices'.[127] These requirements reflect the general nature of the due diligence standard, discussed in Chapter 2, which demands a degree of diligence that is proportional to the degree of risk in the specific case.[128]

These principles are clearly relevant to the host state of a PMSC. Many PMSCs perform inherently dangerous activities involving the threat or use of force or coercion, and recent history has shown that the same type of misconduct tends to recur in the private security industry. Some companies are known to be particularly aggressive. For example, one journalist who spent a month with Blackwater personnel in Baghdad observed that '[t]hey're famous for being very aggressive. They use their machine guns like car horns.'[129] According to a House of Representatives report, Blackwater was involved in an average of 1.4 shooting incidents per week in Iraq in 2005–7.[130] The company fired the first shots in over 80 per cent of the incidents, despite the fact that its contract only authorised the defensive use of force, and over 80 per cent of the shooting incidents resulted in casualties or property damage. The report also highlights specific incidents in which Blackwater personnel killed apparently innocent civilian bystanders, culminating in the September 2007 Baghdad shootings in which, according to the US government, 'at least 34 unarmed Iraqi civilians, including women and children, were killed or injured without justification or provocation'.[131]

In light of the unique nature of the private security industry and the risk that PMSCs can pose to individual life, the obligation to protect life would seem to require states to develop preventive measures specially targeting PMSCs that operate in their territory, with particularly stringent preventive measures targeting companies that are known to be particularly aggressive.

---

127 General Comment 31, para. 17; see also *Neira Alegría v. Peru* (Merits), Judgment of 19 January 1995, IACtHR Ser. C No. 20, para. 19.

128 See, e.g., *Alabama Claims (US v. Britain)* (1871), 572–3, 613; International Law Commission Draft Articles on the Prevention of Transboundary Harm from Hazardous Activities with Commentaries (2001) *Yearbook of the International Law Commission*, vol. II(2), Commentary to Art. 3, para. 11; Curtis, 'The Law of Hostile Military Expeditions as Applied by the United States: Part 2' (1914) 8 *AJIL* 224, 233; Sibert, *Traité de Droit International Public*, 317.

129 Reid, 'Blackwater Loses Security License in Iraq', *Associated Press* (18 September 2007).

130 US House of Representatives Committee on Oversight and Governmental Reform, 'Additional Information about Blackwater USA' (1 October 2007), 1.

131 US Department of Justice Press Release 08-1068, 8 December 2008.

Protecting individuals whose lives are at risk

In addition to taking measures targeting known sources of danger, in certain circumstances the host state may have an obligation to take positive steps to protect particular individuals whose lives are at risk. In *Herrera Rubio v. Colombia*, for example, the Human Rights Committee found a violation of the right to life on the basis that the state had 'failed to take appropriate measures to prevent the disappearance and subsequent killings' of the applicant's parents, where there was clear evidence that the government knew or ought to have known of a risk to the victims from private parties.[132]

The ECtHR recognised a similar principle in *Osman v. UK*, holding that an obligation to take steps to protect the life of an individual will arise where the

> authorities knew or ought to have known at the time of the existence of a real risk to the life of an identified individual from the criminal acts of a third party and that they failed to take measures within the scope of their powers which, judged reasonably, might have been expected to avoid that risk.[133]

On the facts of the case, however, the Court found that there had been no breach of the right to life because the applicants were unable to establish that the UK knew or ought to have known of the risk to the victim's life. The Court reiterated this test in *Kaya v. Turkey*, again emphasising the need for actual or constructive state knowledge of a real risk to the life of an identified individual.[134]

In light of the strict *mens rea* required for state responsibility in these cases, it is difficult to see how this principle would apply to the host state of a PMSC; for although PMSCs working in armed conflict may at times pose a real risk to the life of individuals or groups, the host state will rarely be in a position to identify the potential victims in advance.

On the other hand, this obligation could be highly significant if the courts were to accept actual or constructive state knowledge of a particularly vulnerable *group* of individuals, or of a particular *location* that

---

132 *Herrera Rubio v. Colombia*, UNHRC, 2 November 1987, UN Doc. CCPR/C/OP/2 at 192, para. 11; see also *Delgado Paez v. Colombia*, UNHRC, 12 July 1990, UN Doc. A/45/40.

133 *Osman v. UK* (App. No. 23452/94), ECHR, 28 October 1998, para. 116.

134 *Kaya v. Turkey* (App. No. 22535/93), ECHR, 28 March 2000; see also *Akkoç v. Turkey* (App. No. 22947/93, 22948/93), ECHR, 10 October 2000.

was known to be at risk.[135] This would impose a heightened obligation on the host state to take more stringent preventive steps in relation to PMSCs working with that group or in that location. The IACtHR case of *Digna Ochoa and Plácido* v. *Mexico* provides an example of an analogous approach. In that case, the Court ordered the state to adopt all necessary measures not only to protect four identified human rights defenders who had received threats to their lives, but also to ensure that all persons visiting or working in the offices of their human rights centre could perform their duties without risk to their lives or personal safety.[136]

Special obligations relating to women and children

Like IHL, discussed in the first section of this chapter, HRL obliges states to take special steps to protect women and children, who can be particularly vulnerable in armed conflict and post-conflict environments. In these contexts, the host state should be mindful that some PMSC personnel (like national soldiers) may engage in sexual activities exploiting civilian women and/or children, as illustrated by the DynCorp 'sex-slave' scandal in post-conflict Bosnia.[137]

In relation to the exploitation of children, Article 34 of the Convention on the Rights of the Child provides:

> States Parties undertake to protect the child from all forms of sexual exploitation and sexual abuse. For these purposes, States Parties shall in particular take all appropriate national, bilateral and multilateral measures to prevent:
>
> (a) The inducement or coercion of a child to engage in any unlawful sexual activity;
>
> (b) The exploitative use of children in prostitution or other unlawful sexual practices;
>
> (c) The exploitative use of children in pornographic performances and materials.

In relation to women, Article 3 of the Convention on the Elimination of All Forms of Discrimination Against Women (CEDAW) prohibits gender

---

135 Hoppe gives the example of a crowded market-place in a conflict zone: see Hoppe, 'Passing the Buck: State Responsibility for Private Military Companies' (2008) 19(5) *EJIL* 989, 1003.

136 *Digna Ochoa and Plácido* v. *Mexico*, Order of 17 November 1999, IACtHR Ser. E No. 2.

137 See Human Rights Watch, 'Hopes Betrayed'; Maffai, 'Accountability for Private Military and Security Company Employees that Engage in Sex Trafficking and Related Abuses While under Contract with the United States Overseas'.

discrimination.[138] The CEDAW Committee has emphasised that the prohibition against gender discrimination 'includes gender-based violence',
which in turn includes 'acts which inflict physical, mental, or sexual
harm or suffering, threats of such acts, coercion or other deprivations
of liberty'.[139] In discussing such violence, the Committee has noted that
'[s]tates may also be responsible for private acts if they fail to act with due
diligence to prevent violations of rights or to investigate and punish acts
of violence, and to provide compensation'.[140]

It is possible to infer from these provisions a due diligence obligation
on the host state to prevent PMSC personnel from having sexual relations
with children and from committing violent or sexually exploitative acts
against women, and to punish such acts when they occur.

Positive action to discharge the preventive obligations

In order to fulfil the preventive obligations identified in this section, the
host state will clearly need to criminalise violations of the right to life
and the prohibition of torture and ill-treatment, and to investigate and
punish offenders. Such *ex post facto* punishment serves a critical preventive
function by reinforcing the state's prohibitory measures and deterring
other potential wrongdoers. The establishment of a licensing scheme for
PMSCs operating in state territory, as described in the first section of
this chapter and recommended in the Montreux Document,[141] would
complement these criminal measures by increasing overall transparency
and state control within the private security industry.

Obligations to investigate, punish and redress PMSC violations

HRL obliges states to investigate, punish and redress human rights violations within state jurisdiction. This section considers the sources of these
obligations, the circumstances in which they apply to the host state of a
PMSC in armed conflict, and the measures that the host state should take
to discharge its obligations.

---

138 Convention on the Elimination of All Forms of Discrimination Against Women (adopted
    18 December 1979, entered into force 3 September 1981), 1249 UNTS 13; 186 states have
    ratified this Convention, with the US being the only developed nation that is not a state
    party.
139 CEDAW Committee, General Recommendation 19 (30 January 1992), UN Doc. A/47/38,
    para. 6.
140 *Ibid.*, para. 9; see also Hakimi, 'State Bystander Responsibility' (2010) 21 *EJIL* 341.
141 Montreux Document, Part II, paras. 25–48.

Sources of states' obligations to investigate, punish and redress violations

States' obligations to investigate, punish and redress human rights violations within state jurisdiction essentially derive from a combination of three norms: first, the general obligation to ensure rights; secondly, the principle of effectiveness – that is, the need to interpret rights in a manner that is practical and effective as opposed to theoretical and illusory; and, thirdly, the specific obligations in the main human rights treaties to provide an effective remedy to victims of human rights violations.[142]

Article 2(3) of the ICCPR sets out a typical series of obligations relating to the provision of effective domestic remedies:

> (a) To ensure that any person whose rights or freedoms as herein recognized are violated shall have an effective remedy, notwithstanding that the violation has been committed by persons acting in an official capacity;

> (b) To ensure that any person claiming such a remedy shall have his right thereto determined by competent judicial, administrative or legislative authorities, or by any other competent authority provided for by the legal system of the State, and to develop the possibilities of judicial remedy;

> (c) To ensure that the competent authorities shall enforce such remedies when granted.

The Human Rights Committee has emphasised that the combination of Article 2(3) and the general obligation to ensure rights in Article 2(1) requires states to investigate, punish and redress human rights violations within state jurisdiction.[143]

The American Convention establishes a similar scheme, which the IACtHR has explained in the following terms:

> States Parties have an obligation to provide effective judicial remedies to victims of human rights violations (Art. 25), remedies that must be substantiated in accordance with the rules of due process of law (Art. 8 (1)), all in keeping with the general obligation of such States to guarantee the free and full exercise of the rights recognized by the Convention to all persons subject to their jurisdictions (Art. 1).[144]

---

142 Mowbray, *The Development of Positive Obligations under the ECHR by the European Court of Human Rights* (2004), 1–6; Roht-Arriaza, 'Sources in International Treaties of an Obligation to Investigate, Prosecute and Provide Redress', in Roht-Arriaza (ed.), *Impunity and Human Rights in International Law and Practice* (1995).

143 General Comment 31, para. 8.   144 *Velásquez Rodríguez v. Honduras*, para. 90.

The African Charter also has several provisions on remedies. Most significantly, Article 7 guarantees to every individual the right to have his cause heard, including 'the right to an appeal to competent national organs against acts violating his fundamental rights as recognized and guaranteed by conventions, laws, regulations and customs in force', and Article 26 imposes a duty on states parties to guarantee the independence of the courts and to allow the establishment and improvement of appropriate national institutions entrusted with the promotion and protection of rights. These provisions must be read in accordance with states' general obligation under Article 1 to adopt measures 'to give effect to' rights.

In the European context, Article 13 of the ECHR provides a right to 'an effective remedy before a national authority' for all violations of Convention rights, and Article 6(1) complements this provision by bestowing on individuals a procedural right of access to a fair hearing in the determination of their 'civil rights'. In addition to these general obligations, the ECtHR has implied into Article 2 (the right to life) and Article 3 (the prohibition of torture and ill-treatment) a procedural obligation to investigate alleged killings and incidents of ill-treatment. The Court considers these investigative obligations necessary to render the substantive rights effective in practice, in accordance with states' general duty to secure rights under Article 1.[145] Whilst the investigative obligations implicit in Articles 2 and 3 are conceptually distinct from the general obligation to provide effective domestic remedies set out in Article 13, there is considerable overlap between the two categories and in some cases a state may incur responsibility for a violation of both.[146]

Finally, the UNCAT imposes a number of remedial obligations on states in relation to torture and ill-treatment. States must ensure that their 'competent authorities' conduct 'a prompt and impartial investigation' wherever there is reasonable ground to believe that torture or ill-treatment has been committed within state jurisdiction,[147] as well as establishing procedures to hear individual complaints.[148] In addition, in relation to torture states have an obligation to ensure that the victim 'obtains redress

---

145 See *McCann* v. *UK*, para. 161; *Ilhan* v. *Turkey* (App. No. 22277/93), ECHR, 27 June 2000, para. 91; see also Mowbray, *The Development of Positive Obligations under the ECHR*, 27–40.

146 See, e.g., *Kaya* v. *Turkey*, paras. 109 and 126.   147 UNCAT, Art. 12.

148 *Ibid.*, Art. 13. Although Arts. 12 and 13 refer only to 'torture', Art. 16 provides that these obligations also apply to 'other forms of cruel, inhuman or degrading treatment or punishment'.

and has an enforceable right to fair and adequate compensation including the means for as full rehabilitation as possible'.[149]

When will these obligations arise in relation to PMSC violations in armed conflict?

The Ruggie Reports on human rights and transnational corporations confirm that the 'duty to protect' under HRL requires states to take appropriate steps to investigate, punish and redress corporate-related human rights abuses within their jurisdiction – in short, to provide access to remedies. Without such steps, the state's duty to protect could be rendered weak or even meaningless.[150]

The notion of an effective 'remedy' encompasses not only the punishment of offenders and the payment of compensation to victims, but also certain antecedent measures including the diligent investigation of allegations and the provision of adequate domestic procedures to hear individual complaints. When conceived in this way, the obligation to provide a remedy clearly cannot be dependent on any prior determination that a violation has in fact taken place. The ECtHR explained this conception of a remedy in *Klass* v. *Germany*, in relation to states' obligation under Article 13 to provide 'an effective remedy before a national authority' to any individual whose Convention rights 'are violated':

> This provision, read literally, seems to say that a person is entitled to a national remedy only if a 'violation' has occurred. However, a person cannot establish a 'violation' before a national authority unless he is first able to lodge with such an authority a complaint to that effect. Consequently . . . it cannot be a prerequisite for the application of Article 13 (art. 13) that the Convention be in fact violated.[151]

The Court concluded that a state's obligation to provide a remedy arises wherever an individual raises *an arguable claim* to have suffered a violation of his or her Convention rights within state jurisdiction.[152] Conversely, providing access to a remedy does not presume that an allegation represents a real abuse or a *bona fide* complaint.[153]

In situations of armed conflict, it is important to consider the rules of IHL as well as those of HRL when assessing whether the victim's claim is 'arguable'. Regarding the right to life in the context of hostilities, for

---

149 *Ibid.*, Art. 14.   150 See Ruggie Reports 2008–10.
151 *Klass* v. *Germany* (App. No. 5029/71), ECHR Ser. A No. 28 (1978), para. 164.
152 *Ibid.*; see also *Silver* v. *UK* (App. No. 5947/72), ECHR Ser. A No. 61 (1983), para. 113.
153 Ruggie Report 2008, para. 82.

example, the question of what is an 'arguable' violation of the right to life under HRL will be tied to the rules of IHL.[154] Killings that are clearly a lawful part of hostilities will not trigger the state's obligation to provide a remedy under HRL, whereas killings that *prima facie* appear to be the result of unlawful targeting or a failure of weapons to hit their targets may trigger the remedial obligation.[155]

Crucially for the present analysis, the jurisprudence of the main human rights tribunals indicates that the obligation to provide a remedy is *not* limited to allegations of human rights abuses committed by state agents and officials, but may also arise in some cases where an individual claims to have suffered a violation at the hands of a private actor such as a PMSC employee. For example, the Human Rights Committee stated in its General Comment 31:

> There may be circumstances in which a failure to ensure Covenant rights as required by article 2 would give rise to violations by States Parties of those rights, as a result of States Parties' *permitting or failing to take appropriate measures or to exercise due diligence to prevent, punish, investigate or redress the harm caused by such acts by private persons or entities*. States are reminded of the interrelationship between the positive obligations imposed under article 2 and the need to provide effective remedies in the event of breach under article 2, paragraph 3.[156]

Likewise, the IACtHR emphasised in *Velásquez Rodríguez* that the obligation to investigate and punish applies to violations committed by private persons as well as violations committed by state agents. A state's failure to take the necessary action in relation to private violations effectively 'allows private persons or groups to act freely and with impunity to the detriment of the rights recognized by the [American] Convention', and this amounts to a failure on the part of the state 'to comply with its duty to ensure the free and full exercise of those rights to the persons within its jurisdiction'.[157]

In the European context, the ECtHR has made it clear that the investigative obligations implicit in Articles 2 and 3 of the ECHR apply to violations committed by private actors as well as those committed by

---

154 See *Nuclear Weapons* advisory opinion, para. 25.
155 See Watkin, 'Controlling the Use of Force: A Role for Human Rights Norms in Contemporary Armed Conflict' (2004) 98(1) *AJIL* 1, 33.
156 General Comment 31, para. 8 (emphasis added).
157 *Velásquez Rodríguez v. Honduras*, para. 176; see also para. 182.

state agents.[158] In relation to victims' access to justice and civil remedies under the ECHR, the case of *Osman* v. *UK* suggests that the obligations in Articles 6(1) and 13 will arise wherever an individual seeks to sue state authorities for negligence for failing to prevent a private human rights violation in state jurisdiction. Article 6(1) provides that '[i]n the determination of his civil rights and obligations . . . everyone is entitled to a fair and public hearing within a reasonable time by an independent and impartial tribunal established by law'. This provision is more specific than the right to an effective remedy in Article 13, and therefore the general requirements of the latter are absorbed by the more stringent requirements of the former.[159] In *Osman*, the victim's family had sought to sue the police for failing to protect the victim from a private killing, but their claim was barred by virtue of the public policy immunity enjoyed by police when faced with negligence claims connected to the investigation or suppression of crime. The Court found that there had been no violation of the UK's duty to prevent violations of the right to life, nor had there been any failure to investigate and prosecute. Nonetheless, the Court unanimously found that there had been a breach of Article 6(1) on the basis that the victim's family members had been denied access to a tribunal for a determination of their civil rights and obligations.[160] Clapham asserts that this decision points to 'an internationally protected human right to sue the police authorities for negligence for failing to protect the right to life in the context of a killing by a private person'.[161]

Remedial action required of the host state

The host state's obligation under HRL to provide an effective remedy for human rights violations by PMSCs comprises both a procedural and a substantive element. On the procedural side, states must establish mechanisms to investigate claims of human rights abuses and provide adequate procedures for victims to have their claims heard by an impartial and competent tribunal. In relation to substantive redress, states must make reparation to victims, usually in the form of compensation, as well as punishing the perpetrators.

---

158 See *Secic* v. *Croatia* (App. No. 40116/02), ECHR, 31 May 2007, para. 53; *MC* v. *Bulgaria* (App. No. 39272/98), ECHR, 4 December 2003, para. 151; *Ergi* v. *Turkey* (App. No. 23818/94), ECHR 1998-IV, para. 82; *Kaya* v. *Turkey*, para. 108.

159 *Osman* v. *UK*, para. 158.   160 *Ibid.*, para. 154.

161 Clapham, 'The European Convention on Human Rights', in Scott (ed.), *Torture as Tort* (2001), 515–16.

Criminal investigation and prosecution   Human rights bodies have made it clear that, in cases involving serious violations such as torture, ill-treatment and arbitrary killings, the remedy must include a *criminal investigation and prosecution*. For example, the Human Rights Committee has emphasised that '[c]omplaints about ill-treatment must be investigated effectively by competent authorities' and '[t]hose found guilty must be held responsible'.[162] Thus, in *Bautista de Arellana* v. *Colombia* the Committee held that a combination of disciplinary sanctions and compensation did not constitute an effective remedy for a violation of the right to life; criminal investigation and prosecution were also required.[163] The ECtHR has likewise stressed that, in cases of serious violations, '[e]ffective deterrence is indispensable . . . and it can be achieved only by criminal-law provisions'.[164]

The ECtHR has articulated a number of institutional and procedural requirements of an 'effective' investigation. In particular, the persons responsible for and carrying out the investigation must be independent from those implicated in the events, the investigation must be reasonably expeditious and subject to public scrutiny, the authorities must take whatever reasonable steps they can to secure the evidence concerning the incident in order to establish the cause of death or injury and the person responsible, and the victim's family must be involved in the procedure to the extent necessary to safeguard his or her legitimate interests.[165] The Court has applied these requirements to situations of armed conflict.[166] Whilst it may not always be appropriate to demand a public investigation with full victim participation in the context of an ongoing armed conflict, it is clear that investigations must still comply with the requirements of independence and impartiality.[167]

---

162 Human Rights Committee, General Comment 7, UN Doc. HRI/GEN/1/Rev.1, para. 1.
163 *Bautista de Arellana* v. *Colombia*, UNHRC, 11 October 1994, UN Doc. CCPR/C/55/D/563/1993, para. 8.2.
164 *X and Y* v. *Netherlands* (App. No. 8978/80), ECHR Ser. A No. 91 (1985), para. 27, referring to a violation of the right to privacy in Art. 8.
165 See *Oğur* v. *Turkey* (App. No. 21594/93), ECHR, 20 May 1999, paras. 91–2; *Güleç* v. *Turkey* (App. No. 21593/93), ECHR 1998-IV, paras. 81–2; *Anguelova* v. *Bulgaria* (App. No. 38361/97), ECHR, 13 June 2002, para. 140; *Kelly* v. *UK* (App. No. 30054/96), ECHR, 4 May 2001, paras. 95–8; *McKerr* v. *UK* (App. No. 28883/95), ECHR, 4 May 2001, para. 113.
166 *Isayeva* v. *Russia*, paras. 208–13; see also *Myrna Mack-Chang* v. *Guatemala*, Judgment of 25 November 2003, IACtHR Ser. C No. 101; Human Rights Committee, 'Concluding Observations on Colombia' (5 May 1997), UN Doc. CCPR/C/79/Add 76, para. 32.
167 Droege, 'The Interplay between International Humanitarian Law and International Human Rights Law', 352.

The due diligence nature of the investigative obligation is clearly crucial in situations of armed conflict. As the IACtHR explained, '[t]he duty to investigate, like the duty to prevent, is not breached merely because the investigation does not produce a satisfactory result'. Nonetheless, even where the state faces significant obstacles, the investigation 'must be undertaken in a serious manner and not as a mere formality preordained to be ineffective'.[168] The ECtHR has likewise stressed that the investigative obligation continues to apply, albeit to a less onerous standard, where the state faces great practical difficulties in conducting its investigations. In *Kaya v. Turkey*, for example, in finding Turkey to be in violation of its investigative obligation implicit in the right to life, the ECtHR acknowledged 'the difficulties facing public prosecutors in the south-east region [of Turkey] at that time', but nonetheless found that 'it was incumbent on the authorities to respond actively and with reasonable expedition'.[169]

Even if the host state is able to conduct an effective investigation, it may face obstacles in prosecuting the contractors involved in the human rights violation. In particular, there may be an immunity agreement in place such as CPA Order No. 17 in Iraq, discussed in the third section of this chapter, which granted foreign contractors immunity from Iraqi laws in matters relating to their contracts. Where such immunity applies or the host state is otherwise unable to conduct an effective prosecution, the host state could fulfil its obligation by handing the PMSC employees over for trial to another state (such as their state of nationality) that has made out a *prima facie* case. On the other hand, where host state prosecution is barred by an immunity agreement but the state is unable to ensure that the contractors are held accountable in another forum, the state may be in violation of its obligations under HRL. States that undertake inconsistent international obligations must deal with the consequences if those obligations conflict.

Access to justice and compensation   Finally, where an individual claims that the host state failed to prevent, investigate or punish a human rights abuse by a PMSC, the host state must provide procedures to hear the victim's claim against state authorities and must pay compensation to the victim where appropriate. A comparable scenario was in issue in the

---

168 *Velásquez Rodríguez* v. *Honduras*, para. 177.
169 *Kaya* v. *Turkey*, para. 107; see also *Assenov* v. *Bulgaria* (App. No. 24760/94), ECHR 1998-VIII.

ECtHR case of *Osman* v. *UK*, where the family of the deceased victim had sought to sue the British police for negligence for failing to prevent the victim's murder by a private person.

Action taken by the host state to fulfil its obligation to provide an effective remedy could provide a crucial means for bringing wrongdoing PMSCs and/or their employees to account at the domestic level, providing victims with compensation for their injuries and, more generally, enabling the host state to assert its sovereignty over PMSC activities in its territory. On the other hand, a failure by the host state to take the necessary remedial action following an alleged PMSC violation could constitute a breach of the state's international obligations, quite independent of any responsibility for the state's own involvement in or failure to prevent the human rights violation in the first place.

4.3 How immunity agreements can undermine host state control over PMSCs

States ordinarily have jurisdiction over crimes that are committed in their territory, regardless of the nationality of the defendant. Such jurisdiction is a corollary of state sovereignty and is central to the host state's obligations – identified in the first two sections of this chapter – to prevent and punish PMSC misconduct in armed conflict. In some cases, however, an international agreement or other legal instrument may grant foreign contractors certain immunities from local laws, and this can seriously undermine the host state's ability to fulfil its international obligations of prevention and punishment.

A Status of Forces Agreement (SOFA) is an agreement concluded between a host country and a foreign state that is stationing forces in that country. Such agreements set forth rights and responsibilities between the sending state and the host government on various matters including criminal and civil jurisdiction, the wearing of uniforms, the carrying of arms, tax and customs relief, entry and exit of personnel and property, and the resolution of damage claims.[170] While the US has the largest number of troops deployed overseas and therefore has the most SOFAs, many other states, including the UK, France, Germany, Italy, Russia, Australia

---

170 See Mason, 'Status of Forces Agreement (SOFA): What Is It, and How Might One Be Utilized in Iraq?', US Congressional Research Service Report for Congress RL34531 (1 December 2008); Sari, 'The European Union Status of Forces Agreement' (2008) 13 *Journal of Conflict and Security Law* 353; Bruno, 'US Security Agreements and Iraq' (US Council on Foreign Relations, 23 December 2008).

and South Korea, also negotiate SOFAs with foreign states in which they maintain a military presence.

Most SOFAs recognise the right of the host government to primary jurisdiction over cases in which sending state personnel violate the host country's laws, except in relation to criminal offences committed by sending state personnel carrying out their official duty, in which case the sending state has a first right of prosecution. The NATO SOFA of 1951, for example, distinguishes between on-duty and off-duty offences and contains provisions for possible waiver of jurisdiction between the sending and host states in cases of joint jurisdiction.[171] Such an arrangement often benefits both the host nation and the sending state by facilitating the uniform application of law in a conflict or military environment.[172]

SOFAs must be negotiated, and the talks are often tough because sovereign states do not like the idea that foreigners who commit crimes in their territory will not be subject to their laws. In contrast, following the 2003 invasion of Iraq, the CPA unilaterally issued a sweeping directive granting foreign troops and contractors almost blanket immunity from Iraqi laws. The Iraqi government was required to accept this directive – known as Order No. 17 – as a condition of the transfer of power.[173] According to Paul Bremer, who was the administrator of the CPA, the order was intended as a substitute for a SOFA, which can be made only with a sovereign country.[174]

The key passage of Order No. 17 reads:

> Contractors shall not be subject to Iraqi laws or regulations in matters relating to the terms and conditions of their Contracts... Contractors shall be immune from Iraqi legal process with respect to acts performed by them pursuant to the terms and conditions of a Contract or any subcontract thereto... Certification by the Sending State that its Contractor acted pursuant to the terms and conditions of the Contract shall, in any Iraqi legal process, be conclusive evidence of the facts so certified.[175]

171 Agreement between the Parties to the North Atlantic Treaty Regarding the Status of their Forces (19 June 1951).
172 See US House of Representatives Committee on the Judiciary, Subcommittee on Crime, Terrorism, and Homeland Security Hearing 19 June 2007, 'War Profiteering and Other Contractor Crimes Committed Overseas', Statement of Scott Horton ('Horton Statement'), 54.
173 Dickey, 'The Rule of Order 17', *Newsweek* (29 June 2006); Engelhardt, 'Order 17', *The Nation* (24 September 2007).
174 Rubin and von Zielbauer, 'Blackwater Case Highlights Legal Uncertainties', *New York Times* (11 October 2007).
175 CPA Order No. 17 (27 June 2004), s. 4(2).

Order No. 17 is far more sweeping than standard US SOFAs as it places wrongdoing contractors beyond the reach of Iraqi civil and criminal law, rather than simply providing the US with a first right to prosecute in criminal cases. This is particularly extreme since Order No. 17 fails to provide any alternative arrangement for US prosecutions to be carried out on Iraqi soil (such as exists, for example, in the US–Korea SOFA[176]). This blanket immunity dramatically reduces victims' chances of receiving compensation for damage caused by PMSC misconduct and leaves only one avenue for justice in the case of PMSC crimes: removal to the US for prosecution under US law.[177]

The events that followed the September 2007 Blackwater shootings in Baghdad, in which 'at least 34 unarmed Iraqi civilians, including women and children, were killed or injured without justification or provocation',[178] highlight the inadequacy of this arrangement. Immediately after the incident, Iraqi Prime Minister Nouri al-Maliki announced that his government would revoke Blackwater's licence to operate in Iraq and would prosecute any foreign contractors found to have been involved in the killings. Nonetheless, Blackwater resumed its operations in Iraq five days later, leaving the Iraqi government powerless and doing little to develop public trust and confidence in the rule of law.[179] Order No. 17 impeded Iraq's attempts to prosecute the Blackwater contractors involved in the shootings, notwithstanding Iraqi investigators' *prima facie* conclusion that the shootings were crimes under domestic law,[180] and barred Iraqi plaintiffs from suing the company or its personnel under Iraqi law.[181] Five Blackwater employees were subsequently indicted in the US on several counts of manslaughter and attempted manslaughter arising from the

---

176 See Snyder, 'A Call for Justice and the US–ROK Alliance' (18 December 2002).
177 Horton Statement, 54.
178 US Department of Justice Press Release 08-1068, 8 December 2008.
179 Singer, 'Can't Win with 'Em, Can't Go to War without 'Em: Private Military Contractors and Counterinsurgency' (September 2007); Rubin and Kramer, 'Iraqi Premier Says Blackwater Shootings Challenge His Nation's Sovereignty', *New York Times* (24 September 2007).
180 Glanz and Rubin, 'Blackwater Shootings "Murder", Iraq Says', *New York Times* (8 October 2007).
181 This forced the plaintiffs to seek reparations in the US courts: see *In re Xe Services Alien Tort Litigation*, 665 F Supp 2d 569 (ED Va 2009); Gallagher, 'Civil Litigation and Transnational Business: An Alien Tort Statute Primer' (2010) 8 *Journal of International Criminal Justice* 745.

Baghdad shootings,[182] but in December 2009 a federal US judge dismissed the charges on the basis that the US government had misused statements made by the accused guards.[183] The dismissal of the case triggered reactions of anger, bitterness and disbelief amongst Iraqis.[184] Despite repeated efforts by the Iraqi government to expel Blackwater, the State Department renewed the company's contract in April 2008 and the company (or its successor Xe Services) continued to perform US contracts in Iraq in 2009 and 2010.[185]

Iraq's 2004 Transitional Administrative Law provided that the CPA's decrees would remain in force unless superseded by new legislation.[186] Following the transfer of authority from the interim Iraqi government to the new government, the Minister of Justice and other officials consistently challenged the validity and legality of Order No. 17,[187] and in October 2007 the Iraqi cabinet drafted a measure attempting to rescind the decree.[188] It was not until 2008, however, that the Iraqi and US governments finally renegotiated the status of foreign military forces and contractors in Iraq,[189] and on 1 January 2009 an Iraq–US SOFA took effect which recognised Iraq's primary right to exercise jurisdiction over US contractors.[190]

---

182 Zoepf, 'US Prosecutor in Blackwater Shooting Case Arrives in Baghdad', *New York Times* (7 December 2008); Sturcke, 'Blackwater Security Guards Face Manslaughter Charges', *Guardian* (8 December 2008).

183 'US Judge Dismisses Charges in Blackwater Iraq Killings', *BBC News* (31 December 2009).

184 Williams, 'Iraqis Angered as Blackwater Charges Are Dropped', *New York Times* (2 January 2010).

185 Baker and Murphy, 'Blackwater Out of Iraq? No, Not Yet', *Washington Times* (20 April 2009).

186 Law of Administration for the State of Iraq for the Transitional Period (8 March 2004); see also Katzman and Elsea, 'Iraq: Transition to Sovereignty'.

187 Horton Statement, 54.

188 'Iraq Moves to End Contractors' Immunity', *ABC News* (30 October 2007); Rubin, 'Iraqi Cabinet Votes to End Security Firms' Immunity', *New York Times* (31 October 2007).

189 Pallister, 'Foreign Security Teams to Lose Immunity from Prosecution in Iraq', *Guardian* (27 December 2008).

190 Agreement between the United States of America and the Republic of Iraq on the Withdrawal of United States Forces from Iraq and the Organization of Their Activities During Their Temporary Presence in Iraq (17 November 2008); see also Lee, 'Contracting under the SOFA: New Agreement Subjects Contractors to Iraqi Criminal and Civil Laws' (2009) 4(4) *Journal of International Peace Operations* 7; Mayer, 'Peaceful Warriors: Private Military Security Companies and the Quest for Stable Societies' (2010) 89 *Journal of Business Ethics* 387.

4.4 Conclusion

The host state of a PMSC is presumed to possess some capacity to control company activities by virtue of its sovereignty and control over the territory in which the company operates. Accordingly, IHL and HRL impose certain obligations on the host state to take diligent measures to prevent, investigate, punish and redress PMSC misconduct in armed conflict. These obligations could provide an important accountability mechanism to address PMSC misconduct, as the host state could incur responsibility for any failure to exercise due diligence in a particular case. Moreover, these obligations could play a key role in setting standards to guide the host state in developing its domestic laws and practices with a view to exercising greater control over PMSCs.

The obligation to ensure respect for IHL in Common Article 1 mandates a baseline level of positive action for all states in whose territory PMSCs operate, whether in international or non-international armed conflict. Although *prima facie* the vague terms of Common Article 1 might appear to render this obligation rather weak, a closer analysis reveals that it could provide a powerful tool for promoting greater host state control and accountability in the private security industry. More onerous obligations may also bind the host state in specific circumstances, but Common Article 1 will always provide a minimum yardstick to guide the state's actions in relation to PMSCs operating in its territory. HRL also requires the host state to take certain positive action to regulate PMSC behaviour in state territory. Since HRL provides a number of institutionalised procedures for hearing individual complaints, in many cases it will offer victims of PMSC abuse the best hope of securing an international remedy against the host state. The host state's obligation to provide an effective domestic remedy for human rights violations complements these international mechanisms by increasing the likelihood that victims will obtain redress at the domestic level.

Of course, a state in whose territory an armed conflict is taking place will frequently lack the capacity to ensure that PMSCs respect the full range of rights contained in the main human rights treaties. International law takes account of this reality in two ways. First, in certain situations the specific rules of IHL may modify the content of the host state's obligations under the general regime of HRL, effectively reducing the burden on the host state to ensure the rights of victims in its territory. Secondly, the due diligence standard is sufficiently flexible to take account of the practical difficulties that may confront the host state in attempting to control PMSCs operating in its territory, although the state will always be obliged to take those measures that are reasonably within its power in the circumstances.

The diligent implementation of measures to control PMSCs – such as a licensing scheme for PMSCs operating in state territory – would not only help the host state to fulfil its obligations to ensure respect for IHL and HRL; it could also help the state to regain and retain its sovereignty during and after the armed conflict in the face of a large presence of foreign troops and contractors.

5

Obligations of the hiring state

The recent boom in private security raises the concern that states may simply outsource military and security activities to PMSCs without taking adequate measures to promote company compliance with international norms. In relation to their national military forces, states have clear obligations to take positive steps to ensure that soldiers respect international law and to investigate, punish and redress any violations that soldiers commit in the field. But what international standards exist to guide states' actions in relation to PMSCs that they hire in armed conflict?

This chapter argues that clear international standards *do* in fact exist, in the form of the hiring state's obligations under international humanitarian law (IHL) and human rights law (HRL) to take positive steps to prevent, investigate, punish and redress PMSC misconduct in armed conflict. These obligations could provide an alternative pathway to state responsibility in cases of PMSC misconduct where the wrongdoing contractor is *not* acting as an agent of the hiring state – that is, where the contractor is neither part of the hiring state's armed forces, nor exercising governmental authority, nor acting under the hiring state's instructions, direction or control, when he or she engages in the misconduct. In such cases, although the PMSC misconduct is not itself attributable to the hiring state, the state may nonetheless incur international responsibility if it has failed to fulfil its obligation to take diligent preventive or remedial action. This 'backup' pathway to state responsibility could help to minimise the gap in the rules of attribution (identified in Chapter 3) between states that act through their national forces and states that act through PMSCs.[1] On a broader level, the hiring state's obligations to control PMSCs could guide future state behaviour by mandating a minimum threshold of positive action for all states that hire PMSCs in armed conflict.

---

1 See Hoppe, 'Passing the Buck: State Responsibility for Private Military Companies' (2008) 19(5) *EJIL* 989.

The first section of this chapter considers the preliminary question of whether international law constrains states' ability to hire PMSCs in the first place. The remainder of the chapter assumes that the hiring state is not *per se* prohibited from using a PMSC to perform a particular activity, and proceeds to identify the circumstances in which the state may have an obligation to take positive steps to control PMSC behaviour. The second section considers the hiring state's obligations under IHL, and the third section considers the state's obligations under HRL.

5.1 Constraints on states' ability to hire PMSCs in armed conflict?

There is no general obligation on states requiring them to use their public forces rather than private actors to carry out military and security functions in armed conflict. Indeed, international law includes only limited obligations with regard to the internal order of states, and the organisation of military and security functions is very much part of this *domaine réservé*. The UN Working Group on the Use of Mercenaries has developed a proposal for a possible international convention to limit and regulate the activities of PMSCs at the international level, but the draft legal instrument remains a long way from becoming law.[2] International law does, however, impose a small number of restrictions on the ability of states to use PMSCs to carry out certain activities in armed conflict. Two regimes are particularly pertinent in this context: international mercenary law and IHL.

Constraints on the hiring state under international mercenary law

It is often assumed that PMSC personnel qualify as mercenaries under international law and that states are therefore restricted in their ability to hire PMSCs. Such blanket assumptions are erroneous, however, for two reasons. First, the definition of a mercenary in international law is extremely narrow and excludes many of the PMSC personnel who would qualify as mercenaries within common (non-legal) conceptions of the term.[3] Secondly, there is no broad prohibition of mercenary activity in international law. There are two international conventions that prohibit mercenarism: the Organization of African Unity Convention for the

---

2 Report of the Working Group on the Use of Mercenaries as a Means of Violating Human Rights and Impeding the Exercise of the Right of Peoples to Self-Determination (2 July 2010), UN Doc. A/HRC/15/25.
3 See Chapter 1, section 1.3.

Elimination of Mercenarism in Africa of 1977 ('OAU Convention')[4] and the International Convention Against the Recruitment, Use, Financing and Training of Mercenaries of 1989 ('UN Convention').[5] However, the regional limitations and narrow scope of the OAU Convention and the low number of ratifications of the UN Convention render these instruments irrelevant to most contemporary PMSCs.

Nonetheless, there may be cases in which a state party to one of these conventions hires PMSC personnel who qualify as mercenaries under the relevant definition, in which case the state could incur international responsibility for mercenarism. It is therefore important to delineate the scope of states' obligations under these conventions and to assess how these obligations apply to PMSCs.

The definitions of a mercenary contained in the UN Convention and the OAU Convention essentially reflect the definition contained in Article 47 of the First Additional Protocol to the Geneva Conventions (Protocol I), with certain minor alterations as discussed below.[6] Article 47 does not prohibit mercenarism, nor does it impose any obligations on states in relation to mercenary activity; instead, it denies individual mercenaries the right to combatant and prisoner of war status in armed conflict. The two mercenary conventions go much further in that they criminalise mercenarism *per se* and impose a number of obligations on states in relation to mercenary activity.[7] Another key difference is that the definition in Article 47 is limited to international armed conflicts, whereas the definitions in the two mercenary conventions encompass both international and non-international conflicts. Since this book is concerned with the international obligations of *states* in relation to PMSCs in armed conflict, rather than the obligations of individual contractors or the potential negative consequences for those contractors of particular behaviour in armed conflict, the present discussion focuses on the two mercenary conventions rather than Article 47 of Protocol I.

---

4 Convention of the OAU for the Elimination of Mercenarism in Africa (adopted 3 July 1977, entered into force 22 April 1985), OAU Doc. CM/433/Rev.L.Annex 1.
5 International Convention Against the Recruitment, Use, Financing and Training of Mercenaries (adopted 4 December 1989, entered into force 20 October 2001), 29 ILM 91, UN Doc. A/Res/44/34.
6 First Additional Protocol to the Geneva Conventions of 12 August 1949, and relating to the Protection of Victims of International Armed Conflicts (adopted 8 June 1977, entered into force 7 December 1979), 1125 UNTS 3.
7 Art. 3 of the OAU Convention also denies mercenaries the right to combatant and prisoner of war status in armed conflict.

The obligations of states party to the UN Convention

The UN Convention of 1989 is the only universal instrument dedicated to addressing mercenary activity. The main weakness of the UN Convention is its extremely low rate of ratification: there are only thirty-two states parties and this list includes none of the major state powers.[8] Article 5 of the Convention provides that 'States Parties shall not recruit, use, finance or train mercenaries and shall prohibit such activities in accordance with the provisions of the present Convention'. This obligation is highly significant for states parties that hire PMSCs. The crucial factor in delineating the scope of this obligation is the definition of a mercenary in Article 1(1) as any person who:

> (a) Is specially recruited locally or abroad in order to fight in an armed conflict;
>
> (b) Is motivated to take part in the hostilities essentially by the desire for private gain and, in fact, is promised, by or on behalf of a party to the conflict, material compensation substantially in excess of that promised or paid to combatants of similar rank and functions in the armed forces of that party;
>
> (c) Is neither a national of a party to the conflict nor a resident of territory controlled by a party to the conflict;
>
> (d) Is not a member of the armed forces of a party to the conflict; and
>
> (e) Has not been sent by a State which is not a party to the conflict on official duty as a member of its armed forces.[9]

An individual must satisfy all five conditions in order to qualify as a mercenary. The definition of a mercenary in Article 1(1) essentially mirrors the definition in Article 47 of Protocol I, except that the former omits the requirement in Article 47(2)(b) that the person 'does, in fact, take a direct part in hostilities'. It makes sense for Article 47 to include this extra criterion, since the purpose of that provision is to deny prisoner

---

8 The states parties are: Azerbaijan, Barbados, Belarus, Belgium, Cameroon, Costa Rica, Croatia, Cuba, Cyprus, Georgia, Guinea, Honduras, Italy, Liberia, Libya, Maldives, Mali, Mauritania, Moldova, New Zealand, Peru, Qatar, Saudi Arabia, Senegal, Seychelles, Suriname, Syria, Togo, Turkmenistan, Ukraine, Uruguay and Uzbekistan.

9 Art. 1(2) provides an alternative definition of a mercenary, which encompasses individuals recruited to participate in 'a concerted act of violence' aimed at overthrowing a government or otherwise undermining the constitutional order or territorial integrity of a state. That definition is beyond the scope of the armed conflict scenario under consideration in this book.

of war status to mercenaries on the basis of their actual participation in the conflict. The UN Convention instead incorporates the need for actual participation as an element of the crime of individual mercenarism in Article 3. For the purpose of the *state's* obligation under Article 5, on the other hand, the Convention does not require actual participation in the conflict; it requires only that the state recruit, use, finance or train a mercenary with a view to future participation.

A close analysis of Article 1(1) reveals that some contemporary PMSC personnel could qualify as mercenaries thereunder, but the provision contains significant loopholes which would enable a hiring state to exclude individuals from the definition with relative ease.

Paragraph (a): recruited ... in order to fight   The first defining criterion of mercenaries under Article 1(1) of the UN Convention is that they are 'recruited ... in order to fight' in an armed conflict. An individual will 'fight' in an armed conflict if he or she takes a direct part in the hostilities.[10] This is implicit in the definition of a mercenary in Article 47 of Protocol I, which includes a second criterion (not included in the UN Convention) that the individual '[d]oes, in fact, take a direct part in the hostilities'.[11]

The requirement that the individual be 'recruited ... in order to fight' focuses upon the original scope and purpose of the PMSC's engagement: did the hiring state consider it reasonably likely that PMSC personnel would engage in acts that qualify as direct participation in hostilities? Whilst the contract of hire will of course be the primary point of reference for this assessment, in some cases it may be necessary to look past the written terms of the contract in order to discover the true intentions of the parties. The contract between the Croatian government and the American firm MPRI during the Balkans conflict of the 1990s, examined in Chapter 1, provides one example. Although the contract provided that MPRI was to provide general instruction in civil–military relations, in reality the company planned and commanded specific military operations of the Croatian army during its war against Serbia. Whatever the written terms of the contract, it is likely that the parties envisioned that

---

10 University Centre for International Humanitarian Law, 'Expert Meeting on Private Military Contractors' (Geneva, August 2005) ('UCIHL Expert Meeting'), 26–7; Doswald-Beck, 'Private Military Companies under International Humanitarian Law', in Chesterman and Lehnardt (eds.), *From Mercenaries to Market: The Rise and Regulation of Private Military Companies* (2007), 122–3.
11 Protocol I, Art. 47(2)(b).

MPRI's operations would go beyond mere classroom training.[12] Singer also notes that in some cases PMSC personnel hired as military advisers or trainers are actually present on the frontline, proffering excuses such as the need to see if their training is working. During the first Gulf war, for example, Vinnell employees reportedly accompanied their Saudi National Guard units into the battle of Khafji.[13]

Once the envisioned PMSC activities have been identified, the crucial question under paragraph (a) is whether those activities qualify as 'direct participation in hostilities'. There is no definition of this term in IHL, and its meaning is highly ambiguous. The Commentary to Protocol I states that 'direct participation means acts of war which by their nature or purpose are likely to cause actual harm to the personnel and equipment of the enemy armed forces'.[14] The ICRC's 'Interpretative Guidance on the Notion of Direct Participation in Hostilities under International Humanitarian Law' ('ICRC Guidance'), which was published in June 2009 following a series of expert meetings held between 2003 and 2008, provides a more detailed legal interpretation of this phrase.[15]

It is clear from the ICRC Guidance that a PMSC act must meet three criteria in order to qualify as direct participation in hostilities. First, the act must be 'likely' either 'to adversely affect the military operations or military capacity' of a party to the conflict or 'to inflict death, injury, or destruction on persons or objects protected against direct attack'.[16] The former threshold is generally more pertinent to PMSCs working for a state in armed conflict. Secondly, there must be 'a direct causal link between the act and the harm likely to result either from that act, or from a coordinated military operation of which that act constitutes an integral part'.[17] This test does *not* encompass PMSC acts that merely form part of the general effort to wage and sustain the war, such as the provision of general training or advice, since such acts cause only indirect harm. Also significant for PMSCs, a direct causal link is not necessarily dependent on the temporal or geographical proximity of the individual to the resulting harm. For

---

12 See UCIHL Expert Meeting, 26.
13 Singer, *Corporate Warriors: The Rise of the Privatized Military Industry*, updated edn (2008), 95.
14 Sandoz, Swinarski and Zimmermann (eds.), *Commentary to the Additional Protocols of 8 June 1977 to the Geneva Conventions of 12 August 1949* (1987) ('*ICRC Commentary to the Additional Protocol*'), para. 1944.
15 International Committee of the Red Cross, 'Interpretive Guidance on the Notion of Direct Participation in Hostilities under International Humanitarian Law' (June 2009).
16 *Ibid.*, 47–50.
17 *Ibid.*, 51–8; see also *ICRC Commentary to the Additional Protocols*, para. 1679.

example, a contractor who operates a remote-controlled missile is taking a direct part in hostilities, whereas a contractor who prepares food close to the frontline is not.[18] The third criterion identified by the ICRC is that the act must form an integral part of the hostilities, in the sense that it must be 'specifically designed to directly cause the required threshold of harm in support of a party to the conflict and to the detriment of another'.[19] If a contractor transporting medical supplies is subject to an unlawful attack by enemy forces, for example, an act of individual self-defence will *not* constitute direct participation as its purpose will not be to support a party to the conflict against another.[20]

How do these elements apply to specific PMSC services?[21] Chapter 1 classified PMSC services into four broad categories: offensive combat, military/security expertise, armed security and military support.[22] Each category will now be assessed in turn.

There is no doubt that offensive combat contracts envision direct participation in hostilities. The employees of Executive Outcomes and Sandline who were hired to provide offensive combat services during the 1990s were therefore 'recruited . . . in order to fight' within paragraph (a) of the mercenary definition. The operation of complex weapons systems also falls within this category. Singer notes that during the 2003 invasion of Iraq, US-hired contractors actually loaded weapons systems such as B-2 stealth bombers and helped to operate combat systems such as the army's Patriot missile batteries and the navy's Aegis missile defence system.[23] Such individuals clearly participated directly in hostilities.

The analysis is more complex in relation to PMSC contracts involving military or security expertise such as advice and training, the collection and analysis of intelligence, the maintenance of equipment, and the

---

18 ICRC Guidance, 55.   19 *Ibid.*, 58–64.   20 *Ibid.*, 61.

21 See Kidane, 'The Status of Private Military Contractors under International Humanitarian Law' (2010) 38(3) *Denver Journal of International Law and Policy*; de Nevers, 'Private Security Companies and the Laws of War' (2009) 40(2) *Security Dialogue* 169; Sossai, 'Status of Private Military Companies in the Law of War: The Question of Direct Participation in Hostilities' (European University Institute Working Paper 2009/6); Gillard, 'Business Goes to War: Private Military/Security Companies and International Humanitarian Law' (2006) 88(863) *International Review of the Red Cross* 525; Schmitt, 'Humanitarian Law and Direct Participation in Hostilities by Private Contractors or Civilian Employees' (2004–5) 5 *Chicago Journal of International Law* 511; Faite, 'Involvement of Private Contractors in Armed Conflict: Implications under International Humanitarian Law' (2004) 4(2) *Defence Studies* 166.

22 See Chapter 1, section 1.4.

23 Singer, 'Can't Win with 'Em, Can't Go to War without 'Em: Private Military Contractors and Counterinsurgency' (September 2007), 2.

clearance of mines. Whilst the *travaux préparatoires* indicate that the definition of a mercenary in Article 47 of Protocol I was not generally intended to include advisers, trainers and military technicians,[24] that intention was based on the assumption that such experts would not take a direct part in hostilities.[25] Military experts who are hired to perform functions that entail direct participation are 'recruited... in order to fight' within the mercenary definition. The ICRC Guidance distinguishes between general advice, training, intelligence and technical services, which do not entail direct participation, and such services 'carried out with a view to the execution of a specific hostile act', which do entail direct participation.[26] The training/advice provided by MPRI to the Croatian government may have qualified as direct participation, since it appeared to relate to specific tactical military operations.[27] This distinction can also be applied to the maintenance of complex weapons systems. General depot maintenance conducted away from the battlefield does not qualify as direct participation, nor does routine maintenance even if conducted near the front; but the preparation of equipment for a specific battle does generally entail direct participation.[28] Likewise, contractors who collect or analyse tactical intelligence are generally participating directly in hostilities, whereas contractors who provide such services on a strategic level are not.[29] The ICRC Guidance further states that the clearance of mines placed by the adversary – another common PMSC service – constitutes direct participation in hostilities.[30]

Turning to consider PMSC contracts for the provision of armed security, the question of whether these contractors are 'recruited... in order to fight' hinges on two factors: first, whether the persons or objects that the contractors are hired to guard constitute a military objective; and, secondly, whether the contractors are hired to guard those persons/objects

---

24 See *Official Records of the Diplomatic Conference on the Reaffirmation and Development of International Humanitarian Law Applicable in Armed Conflicts, Geneva (1974–1976)* (1978), Report of Committee III, para. 25.

25 See *ICRC Commentary to the Additional Protocols*, para. 1806 (in relation to Art. 47(2)(b)).

26 ICRC Guidance, 66; see also *ibid.*, 53; Schmitt, 'Humanitarian Law and Direct Participation in Hostilities by Private Contractors or Civilian Employees', 542–5.

27 See Chapter 1, section 1.4. Note that Croatia ratified the UN Mercenary Convention in 2000, several years after the MPRI operation.

28 Schmitt, 'Humanitarian Law and Direct Participation in Hostilities by Private Contractors or Civilian Employees', 544–5.

29 *Ibid.*; Gillard, 'Business Goes to War'; de Nevers, 'Private Security Companies and the Laws of War'.

30 ICRC Guidance, 48.

against enemy forces or merely against common criminals.[31] Article 52(2) of Protocol I provides that 'attacks shall be limited strictly to military objectives', and Article 49(1) defines 'attacks' as 'acts of violence against the adversary, whether in offence or defence'. It follows that, if a state hires a PMSC to defend a military objective, any act of violence by PMSC personnel in defence of that objective against enemy forces will constitute an 'attack' within Article 49(1). Since the hiring state envisions the PMSC personnel engaging in such defensive attacks where necessary, the contractors must be viewed as 'recruited . . . in order to fight' in an armed conflict. Conversely, if a state hires a PMSC to guard a civilian object, any attack on that object will be unlawful under IHL and the PMSC personnel may take certain limited action in self-defence and defence of other civilians without participating directly in hostilities.[32] Such PMSC personnel are not envisioned as taking a direct part in hostilities and therefore are not 'recruited . . . in order to fight'. In practice, of course, a considerable grey zone exists between these two scenarios, particularly in low-intensity conflicts where it is often difficult to distinguish enemy attacks from common criminality. A logical approach would be to assume that the hiring state envisions PMSC personnel defending against attacks by enemy forces if, at the time of hiring, the protected object is or is likely to become a military objective. Any rules of engagement issued to PMSC personnel would provide further assistance in discerning the intentions of the hiring state in these circumstances.[33]

The final category of PMSC contract identified in Chapter 1 entails military support such as the preparation of food, the transport of personnel and equipment, and the assembly and disassembly of military bases. PMSC personnel hired to provide these services are not generally envisioned as participating directly in hostilities and therefore are not 'recruited . . . in order to fight' within the mercenary definition in Article 1(1) of the UN Convention. However, there may be exceptions. One scenario that consistently arose during the expert meetings leading to the ICRC Guidance was that of the civilian truck driver 'Bob' who transports ammunition to an active firing position at the frontline.[34] The

---

31 See Doswald-Beck, 'Private Military Companies under International Humanitarian Law', 129; Sossai, 'Status of Private Military Companies in the Law of War', 12; de Nevers, 'Private Security Companies and the Laws of War', 179.

32 Faite, 'Involvement of Private Contractors in Armed Conflict', 174.

33 See UCIHL Expert Meeting, 27.

34 See, e.g., ICRC, 'Report of the First Expert Meeting on the Notion of Direct Participation in Hostilities' (September 2003), 4.

ICRC Guidance states that the driver in this scenario must be regarded as an integral part of ongoing combat operations and, therefore, as directly participating in hostilities.[35] On the other hand, the transport of ammunition from a factory to a port for further shipping to a storehouse in a conflict zone 'is too remote from the use of that ammunition in specific military operations to cause the ensuing harm directly', and therefore does not constitute direct participation in hostilities.[36]

Paragraph (b): motivated by private gain   Paragraph (b) is the 'crux' of mercenarism,[37] without which the definition would be meaningless.[38] In the context of Article 47 of Protocol I, this criterion is also commonly regarded as a serious flaw in the mercenary definition. It focuses on the *motivation* of the individual, identifying mercenaries not by reference to *what* they do, but *why* they do it. Yet monetary reward is often only one of several factors motivating an individual to take part in a conflict. For example, many national soldiers join the armed forces at least in part for the salary and benefits, whereas many irregular fighters are motivated by ideology or religion rather than financial gain. It is often difficult to identify the 'essential' motivation. According to the Diplock Report of 1976, the inclusion of this criterion renders the definition of a mercenary 'either . . . unworkable, or so haphazard in its application as between comparable individuals as to be unacceptable'.[39]

It is not surprising that this criterion is considered problematic in the context of Article 47, since the purpose of that provision is to deny combatant and prisoner of war status to individual mercenaries in an ongoing armed conflict. IHL is highly concerned to ensure that fighters are not unfairly or prematurely denied such status, and this is reflected in the requirement in Article 45 that, when in doubt, the holding party should presume prisoner of war status for any prisoner until such time as his status has been determined by a competent tribunal. This effectively restricts the holding party's freedom to draw inferences of financial motivation

---

35 ICRC Guidance, 56.   36 *Ibid.*
37 *ICRC Commentary to the Additional Protocols*, para. 1807.
38 See Percy, 'Mercenaries: Strong Norm, Weak Law' (2008) 61(2) *International Organization* 367; Taulbee, 'Myths, Mercenaries and Contemporary International Law' (1985) 15 *California Western International Law Journal* 339.
39 'Report of the Committee of Privy Counsellors Appointed to Inquire into the Recruitment of Mercenaries' (1976), para. 7; see also Burmester, 'The Recruitment and Use of Mercenaries in Armed Conflicts' (1978) 72 *AJIL* 37, 37–8; Kwakwa, 'The Current Status of Mercenaries in the Law of Armed Conflict' (1990) 14(1) *Hastings International and Comparative Law Review* 67, 71–2.

from the surrounding circumstances, thereby rendering the mercenary definition in Article 47 virtually 'unworkable' in practice.

In relation to the *state's* obligation not to hire mercenaries under Article 5 of the UN Convention, on the other hand, the requirement of financial motivation is far less problematic. It will frequently be possible to infer such motivation from the surrounding circumstances, particularly in the case of PMSC personnel who are openly engaged in the business of military and security provision. Where a state hires a PMSC to work in an armed conflict and the company personnel are relatively well paid, in the absence of evidence pointing to some other motivation it can reasonably be inferred that the contractors are financially motivated for the purpose of the state's obligation under Article 5.

Paragraph (c): nationality   Article 1(1)(c) of the UN Convention further limits the definition of a mercenary to 'any person who . . . [i]s neither a national of a party to the conflict nor a resident of territory controlled by a party to the conflict'. Both the UN Convention and Article 47 of Protocol I were intended to address individual mercenaries rather than mercenary groups as such, and it is plain from the wording of this criterion that it is the nationality of the individual person, rather than the nationality of the group to which he or she belongs, that is decisive. Thus, where the nationality of the PMSC differs from that of the PMSC employee in question, it is the nationality of the latter that should be considered under paragraph (c).[40] This leads to an unsatisfactory situation whereby certain members of a PMSC may be considered mercenaries and others not, even when performing the same tasks; but there is no other interpretation reasonably open on the wording of the provision.

The nationality criterion would exclude a significant number of modern PMSC personnel, such as the British and American contractors who worked in Iraq following the 2003 invasion and the large number of host state nationals currently working for foreign PMSCs in Afghanistan and Iraq. For other contractors, the hiring state could circumvent the nationality requirement by granting citizenship,[41] although it would be more

---

40 Doswald-Beck, 'Private Military Companies under International Humanitarian Law', 123; UCIHL Expert Meeting, 24–5.
41 See UK Foreign and Commonwealth Office Green Paper, 'Private Military Companies: Options for Regulation' (February 2002), 7; UN Commission on Human Rights, 'Report on the Question of the Use of Mercenaries as a Means of Violating Human Rights and

likely to exclude such individuals from the mercenary definition by incorporating them into the national armed forces, as discussed below. The nationality criterion in Article 1(1) therefore constitutes a loophole in the UN Convention as it permits the hiring state to evade its obligation not to hire mercenaries by taking action lying solely within its own control.

Paragraphs (d) and (e): forming part of the armed forces of the hiring state   Paragraphs (d) and (e) of Article 1(1) present the biggest loopholes in the definition of a mercenary insofar as that definition delineates the state's obligation not to hire mercenaries under Article 5. These criteria enable the hiring state easily to exclude individual fighters by enrolling them temporarily in its armed forces. Cassese describes this as 'the most crucial inadequacy' of the mercenary definition.[42] Similarly, the ICRC Commentary to Article 47 of Protocol I states:

> Perhaps with some justification it has been said that this clause made the definition of mercenaries completely meaningless... [as] each State has control over the composition of its armed forces subject to the provisions of Article 43, it is clear that enlistment in itself is sufficient to prevent the definition being met.[43]

In some cases, a state may hire a PMSC to work in an armed conflict to which the state is itself a party. Prominent examples include Executive Outcomes and Sandline hired by the governments of Sierra Leone and Angola during the civil wars in those countries, MPRI hired by the Croatian government during the Balkan conflict, and the various PMSCs hired by the US and the UK in Iraq following the 2003 invasion.[44] In such cases, the hiring state could exclude the contractors from paragraph (d) of the mercenary definition, which provides that a mercenary must not be a member of the armed forces of a party to the conflict, by incorporating them into its armed forces. Indeed, that was standard practice for Executive Outcomes and Sandline during the 1990s.[45]

Impeding the Exercise of the Right of Peoples to Self-Determination' (20 February 1997), UN Doc. E/CN4/1997/24, 80–1.

42 Cassese, 'Mercenaries: Lawful Combatants or War Criminals?' (1980) 40 *Zeitschrift für ausländisches öffentliches Recht und Völkerrecht* 1, 26.

43 *ICRC Commentary to the Additional Protocols*, para. 1813 (references omitted).

44 For an overview of these operations, see Chapter 1, section 1.4.

45 Dinnen, May and Regan (eds.), *Challenging the State: The Sandline Affair in Papua New Guinea* (1997), 163; Zarate, 'The Emergence of a New Dog of War: Private International

In other cases a state may hire a PMSC to work in an armed conflict to which the state is *not* itself a party. For example, a state may hire a PMSC to assist a foreign government fighting a civil war, or to work in a peacekeeping force, or to provide security for state officials working in a foreign conflict to which the hiring state is not a party. In such cases, the hiring state could exclude the PMSC personnel from paragraph (e) of the mercenary definition, which provides that a mercenary must not have been 'sent by a State which is not a party to the conflict on official duty as a member of its armed forces', by incorporating them into its armed forces.

Even in the absence of formal enlistment, if PMSC personnel are fighting alongside national soldiers in an international armed conflict, the hiring state could argue that they are in fact so highly integrated into its armed forces that they form part of those forces *de facto* pursuant to Article 43 of Protocol I (if applicable).[46] This provides yet another potential avenue for a state to evade responsibility for hiring mercenaries under the UN Convention.

The obligations of states party to the OAU Convention

In the African context, the OAU Convention provides another source of obligations that might limit states' freedom to hire PMSCs in armed conflict. The Convention was the culmination of several years of collaboration between OAU member states during the 1960s and 1970s to confront the destabilising effects of mercenaries in Africa, and consequently its terms are tailored to the particular problem of mercenarism in that context.[47] The regional nature of the OAU Convention further limits its impact, as it is binding only on those African states that have ratified it.

Article 1(1) of the OAU Convention adopts the same basic definition of a mercenary as Article 47 of Protocol I, and therefore contains all of the loopholes discussed above. Article 1(2) prohibits individuals, groups, associations, states or representatives of states from using or otherwise supporting mercenaries 'with the aim of opposing by armed violence a process of self-determination stability or the territorial integrity of

Security Companies, International Law, and the New World Disorder' (1998) 34 *Stanford Journal of International Law* 75, 124; UK Green Paper, para. 6.

46 See Chapter 3, section 3.1.

47 See Kufuor, 'The OAU Convention for the Elimination of Mercenarism in Civil Conflicts', in Musah and Fayemi (eds.), *Mercenaries: An African Security Dilemma* (2000); Milliard, 'Overcoming Post-Colonial Myopia: A Call to Recognize and Regulate Private Military Companies' (2003) 176 *Military Law Review* 1, 43–57.

another State'. This defines the crime of mercenarism narrowly according to the *purpose* of the actor in question. The result of this purposive approach is that a state could hire PMSC personnel who qualified as mercenaries under Article 1(1), and yet fail to satisfy the elements of the crime of mercenarism in Article 1(2) if it did not act with the specified purpose.

A number of commentators argue that OAU member states carefully constructed the crime of mercenarism in Article 1(2) to protect themselves and OAU-recognised national liberation movements from mercenary attacks, whilst retaining the option of using mercenaries against rebel groups within their own borders.[48] According to Cassese, OAU member states 'did not condemn every category of mercenary, but only such mercenaries as were fighting against national liberation movements or sovereign States'.[49] For example, the South African government (which was outside the OAU at the time) was prohibited from using mercenaries against the African National Congress, an OAU-recognised rebel group, whilst other states (such as Angola and Zaire) freely used mercenaries against dissident groups on their own soil.[50]

Whatever the exact motives of the drafting states, it is clear that the reference to 'a process of self-determination' in Article 1(2) was directed at the anti-colonial/anti-racist struggle of the time.[51] This raises the question of how 'a process of self-determination' should be construed in the modern context. The widely held view is that this phrase encompasses only internationally recognised national liberation movements, with the result that the OAU Convention does *not* prohibit states parties from hiring mercenaries to fight against dissident groups in their own territory.[52] On this understanding, Sierra Leone and Angola would not have violated Article 1(2) when they hired Executive Outcomes and Sandline to fight in their respective civil wars during the 1990s, even if they had not incorporated the PMSC personnel into their national armed forces. An alternative interpretation of Article 1(2) might construe 'a process of self-determination' more broadly to encompass certain

---

48 Cassese, 'Mercenaries'; Taulbee, 'Myths, Mercenaries and Contemporary International Law', 347; Zarate, 'The Emergence of a New Dog of War', 128; Singer, 'War, Profits, and the Vacuum of Law: Privatized Military Firms and International Law' (2004) 42 *Columbia Journal of Transnational Law* 521, 529.

49 Cassese, 'Mercenaries', 24.   50 Singer, 'War, Profits', 529; Cassese, 'Mercenaries', 3.

51 See, e.g., the Preamble to the Convention: 'Concerned with the threat which the activities of mercenaries pose to the legitimate exercise of the right of African People under colonial and racist domination to their independence and freedom ...'

52 See, e.g., Singer, 'War, Profits', 528–9; Zarate, 'The Emergence of a New Dog of War', 128; UK Green Paper, paras. 7–8; Milliard, 'Overcoming Post-Colonial Myopia', 54–7.

minority group struggles against the government. Kufuor notes, for example, that the meaning of the Convention is not entirely clear as to whether states themselves can use mercenaries against rebels on their own soil, since the struggle for liberation 'might not necessarily be limited to the anti-colonial/anti-racist struggle' but might also include 'the continuing struggle by the people of Africa against authoritarian and undemocratic regimes'.[53] Kufuor presents arguments for both interpretations and concludes that 'there is a need to redraft the Convention in order to clear the ambiguity in the text, or for the OAU to come out with a resolution specifying whether its members can or cannot use soldiers of fortune'.[54]

On balance, it would seem that Article 1(2) of the OAU Convention as presently drafted does *not* prohibit states parties from hiring mercenaries to fight rebels on state territory. Article 1(2) does, however, prohibit states parties from hiring mercenaries to fight against *another state*, and this could restrict the freedom of states parties to hire PMSCs in certain circumstances. For example, O'Brien notes that the Angolan MPLA government hired the PMSC AirScan in October 1997 and then just weeks later overthrew the democratically elected government in Congo-Brazzaville.[55] This scenario clearly raises questions as to Angola's responsibility for mercenarism under Article 1(2) of the OAU Convention.

In short, despite popular conceptions of PMSC personnel as mercenaries, various factors combine to render international mercenary law irrelevant to most contemporary private security activity. Nonetheless, there may be cases in which a state party to one of the two mercenary conventions hires PMSC personnel who fall within the definition of a mercenary, and this could give rise to the responsibility of the hiring state for a violation of its obligations under the relevant instrument.

Constraints on the hiring state under international humanitarian law

IHL provides only a small number of rules restricting states' ability to use PMSCs in international armed conflicts, and it places no such restrictions

---

53 Kufuor, 'The OAU Convention', 202. Such a construction would reflect a broader conception of the right of self-determination of peoples: see, e.g., the decision of the Supreme Court of Canada in *Reference re Secession of Quebec* [1998] 1 SCR 217; Haljan, 'A Constitutional Duty to Negotiate Amendments: *Reference re Secession of Quebec*' (1999) 48 *ICLQ* 447; Crawford, 'Right of Self-Determination in International Law', in Alston (ed.), *Peoples' Rights* (2005), 47–63.
54 Kufuor, 'The OAU Convention', 205.
55 O'Brien, 'Military-Advisory Groups and African Security: Privatized Peacekeeping?' (1998) 5(3) *International Peacekeeping* 78.

on states in non-international armed conflicts. The Geneva Conventions impose a direct obligation on states to use regular soldiers in two specific situations of international armed conflict. First, Article 39 of the Third Geneva Convention (GCIII) provides that '[e]very prisoner of war camp shall be put under the immediate authority of a responsible commissioned officer belonging to the regular armed forces of the Detaining Power'.[56] Secondly, Article 99 of the Fourth Geneva Convention (GCIV) imposes a similar, albeit less stringent, obligation in relation to places of internment: 'Every place of internment shall be put under the authority of a responsible officer, chosen from the regular military forces or the regular civil administration of the Detaining Power.'[57] Thus, if a state placed a prisoner of war camp under the immediate authority of a PMSC employee, or if it allowed a contractor to operate a place of internment without authoritative military oversight, the state would violate its obligations under these provisions.[58]

Having identified the few norms of international law that may restrict the freedom of states to hire PMSCs in the first place, the remainder of this chapter critically analyses the key obligations on the hiring state to take positive steps to control PMSC behaviour in armed conflict.

5.2 Obligations to control PMSCs under international humanitarian law

IHL imposes a number of obligations on the hiring state to take positive steps to control PMSCs in armed conflict. This section examines these obligations in five categories: first, the general duty to ensure respect for IHL in all circumstances; secondly, the duty to disseminate the Geneva Conventions and to instruct particular individuals working in armed conflict; thirdly, the duty to protect certain vulnerable groups in armed conflict; fourthly, the special obligations of an occupying power in the occupied territory; and, finally, the duty to repress or suppress violations of IHL.

---

56 Third Geneva Convention relative to the Treatment of Prisoners of War (adopted 12 August 1949, entered into force 21 October 1950), 75 UNTS 135.
57 Fourth Geneva Convention relative to the Protection of Civilian Persons in Time of War (adopted 12 August 1949, entered into force 21 October 1950), 75 UNTS 287.
58 See also Montreux Document on Pertinent International Legal Obligations and Good Practices for States Related to Operations of Private Military and Security Companies during Armed Conflict (17 September 2008), UN Doc. A/63/467-S/2008/636 ('Montreux Document'), Part I, para. 2.

The obligation to ensure respect for IHL

Chapter 4 critically analysed the obligation in Common Article 1 of the Geneva Conventions 'to ensure respect' for IHL 'in all circumstances', and concluded that it requires the host state of a PMSC to take diligent steps to ensure that company personnel comply with IHL.[59] The present chapter argues that the obligation in Common Article 1 is also highly pertinent to the hiring state of a PMSC. This discussion first addresses two specific questions which may arise in cases where a PMSC operates outside the territory of the hiring state. It then considers the measures that the hiring state should take to discharge its Common Article 1 obligation and the circumstances in which the state could incur responsibility for breach.

Does Common Article 1 bind the hiring state in relation to PMSCs operating outside state territory?

A key question in relation to the hiring state of a PMSC is whether Common Article 1 obliges states to take steps to control company behaviour *overseas*. As noted in Chapter 4, the obligation to ensure respect for IHL in Common Article 1 shares a number of features with the obligation to prevent and punish genocide in Article 1 of the Genocide Convention.[60] One important parallel is that neither Common Article 1 nor Article 1 of the Genocide Convention is territorially limited. The former applies to a state 'in all circumstances', whilst the latter applies to a state 'wherever it may be acting or may be able to act in ways appropriate to meeting the obligations in question'.[61] Thus, in *Nicaragua* the ICJ found that the US had violated its obligation to ensure respect for IHL by virtue of its encouragement of the rebel *contras* operating in the armed conflict in Nicaragua.[62] Similarly, in the *Genocide* case the Court found Serbia responsible for failing to prevent genocidal acts that had taken place outside Serbian territory.[63] The lack of any territorial limitation on Common Article 1 is clearly crucial for states that hire PMSCs to operate in armed

---

59 See Chapter 4, section 4.1.
60 Convention on the Prevention and Punishment of the Crime of Genocide (adopted 9 December 1948, entered into force 12 January 1951), 78 UNTS 277.
61 *Case Concerning the Application of the Convention on the Prevention and Punishment of the Crime of Genocide (Bosnia and Herzegovina v. Serbia and Montenegro)* (Merits) (26 February 2007), para. 183.
62 *Military and Paramilitary Activities In and Against Nicaragua (Nicaragua v. USA)* (Merits) ICJ Reports 1986, paras. 220 and 255.
63 *Genocide* case, para. 183.

conflict overseas, and this is all the more significant when compared with the strict jurisdictional limitations that apply in HRL, discussed in the third section of this chapter.

Chapter 4 also argued that, although Common Article 1 binds all states 'in all circumstances', in practice a state must have some capacity to influence a PMSC effectively before the state will be required to take positive measures to control company behaviour.[64] Conversely, a state may only incur responsibility for a failure to take action to ensure that a particular PMSC respect IHL if the state actually had some capacity to influence that company effectively. The ICJ implicitly adopted a similar approach to the obligation to prevent genocide in the *Genocide* case, noting that the measures required to discharge the obligation depend largely on the state's 'capacity to influence effectively the action of persons likely to commit, or already committing, genocide'.[65] This indicates that a state will not incur responsibility for a failure to take preventive action directed towards particular individuals unless the state in fact had the capacity to influence those individuals effectively.

The requirement that a state have the 'capacity to influence effectively' a PMSC translates the universal and somewhat vague terms of Common Article 1 into a concrete obligation on particular states to take positive action in relation to particular PMSCs. The hiring state of a PMSC has a clear means of influencing company behaviour through the contract of hire, even where the company operates overseas, and it follows that Common Article 1 obliges the hiring state to take positive action to ensure that the PMSC complies with IHL. This is reflected in the Montreux Document, which stipulates that hiring states 'have an obligation, within their power, to ensure respect for international humanitarian law by PMSCs they contract'.[66]

---

64 For a similar point in relation to the obligation to ensure respect by other states, see Kessler, 'The Duty to "Ensure Respect" under Common Article 1 of the Geneva Conventions: Its Implications on International and Non-International Armed Conflicts' (2001) 44 *German Yearbook of International Law* 498, 505; Levrat, 'Les Conséquences de l'Engagement Pris par le HPC de "Faire Respecter" les Conventions Humanitaires', in Kalshoven and Sandoz (eds.), *Implementation of International Humanitarian Law* (1989), 279; Gasser, 'Ensuring Respect for the Geneva Conventions and Protocols: The Role of Third States and the United Nations', in Fox and Meyer (eds.), *Effecting Compliance* (1993), 28; Kessler, 'Die Durchsetzung der Genfer Abkommen von 1949 in nicht-internationalen bewaffneten Konflikten auf Grundlage ihres gemeinsamen Art. 1' (2001) 132 *Veröffentlichungen des Walther-Schücking-Instituts für Internationales Recht an der Universität Kiel* 26, 118.

65 *Genocide* case, para. 430.

66 Montreux Document, Part I, para. 3. Part I of the Montreux Document sets out the understanding of the seventeen drafting states (Afghanistan, Angola, Australia, Austria,

Does Common Article 1 bind the hiring state if it is not a party to the conflict?

Another key question is whether the obligation 'to ensure respect' in Common Article 1 applies to *all* hiring states, or whether it applies only to those hiring states that are party to the armed conflict in question. In many cases where a state hires a PMSC to work in an armed conflict, the state will itself be a party to that conflict. For example, Executive Outcomes and Sandline fought for the governments of Sierra Leone and Angola in their respective civil wars, MPRI worked for the Croatian government during the Balkan conflict, and various PMSCs worked for the US and the UK in Iraq in 2003.[67] As there is widespread agreement that Common Article 1 was intended to impose obligations on states party to the conflict, there can be no doubt that a hiring state will be obliged to ensure PMSC respect for IHL in these circumstances.

There are also cases, however, where the hiring state is not a party to the conflict in which the PMSC operates. For example, a state may hire a PMSC to provide security for state officials working in a foreign conflict to which the state is not a party, or a state may send a PMSC to assist a foreign government fighting a civil war, or a state may send a PMSC as part of a peacekeeping mission. These scenarios raise the question of whether Common Article 1 imposes any obligations on so-called 'third states', which are not party to the conflict.

The ICRC has long answered this question in the affirmative, explaining in its Commentary to Common Article 1 that 'in the event of a Power failing to fulfil its obligations, each of the other Contracting Parties (neutral, allied or enemy) should endeavour to bring it back to an attitude of respect for the Convention'.[68] This interpretation of Common Article 1 encompasses *all* states, irrespective of whether they are party to the conflict in question.

Kalshoven takes issue with the ICRC's interpretation of Common Article 1, arguing in his comprehensive study of the *travaux préparatoires* that the ICRC's approach does not accord with the true intention of the

---

Canada, China, France, Germany, Iraq, Poland, Sierra Leone, South Africa, Sweden, Switzerland, the UK, Ukraine and the US) of the existing obligations of states, PMSCs and their personnel under international law in relation to PMSCs in armed conflict.

67 See Chapter 1, section 1.4.

68 Pictet (ed.), *Commentary to the Geneva Convention Relative to the Treatment of Prisoners of War* (1960), 18.

drafters.[69] In particular, Kalshoven notes that the drafters did not intend for Common Article 1 to impose an obligation on third states to take action to ensure that states party to the conflict ensure respect for IHL. Instead, according to Kalshoven, the provision was intended to oblige states party to the conflict to ensure respect for the Conventions by their own populations as well as by their agents and officials, in particular with a view to expanding the binding effect of the Conventions to insurgents in a civil war. Kalshoven's findings on this point suggest that, if a strict originalist interpretation were applicable today, Common Article 1 might not impose obligations on a state that hired a PMSC to work in a foreign conflict to which the state was not itself a party.

However, the original intent of the drafters is never conclusive as to the current status of a legal norm, since modern treaty interpretation also relies heavily on the 'subsequent practice in the application of the treaty which establishes the agreement of the parties regarding its interpretation'.[70] Although the drafters may have envisaged a somewhat restricted interpretation of Common Article 1, in the decades since 1949 this provision has been widely interpreted as imposing an obligation on *all* states – including third states – to take reasonable steps to ensure that the rules of IHL are respected by all, particularly by the parties to the conflict. In 1968, for example, delegates at the Tehran Conference on Human Rights passed a resolution affirming that *every* state has an obligation to use all means at its disposal to promote respect for IHL by all.[71] The UN Security Council,[72] the General Assembly[73] and numerous other international organisations including the Council of Europe, NATO, the OAU and the Organization of American States have since passed resolutions calling upon *all* member states to respect and ensure respect for IHL.[74]

---

69 Kalshoven, 'The Undertaking to Respect and Ensure Respect in All Circumstances: From Tiny Seed to Ripening Fruit' (1999) 2 *Yearbook of International Humanitarian Law* 3.

70 Art. 31(3) of the Vienna Convention on the Law of Treaties (adopted 23 May 1969, entered into force 27 January 1980), 1155 UNTS 331; see also Aust, *Modern Treaty Law and Practice* (2000).

71 Res. XXIII, International Conference on Human Rights, Tehran (12 May 1968), adopted with no opposing votes.

72 UNSC Res. 681 (20 December 1990), UN Doc. S/RES/681, para. 5.

73 See, e.g., UNGA Res. 32/91 A (13 December 1977), UN Doc. A/RES/32/91; UNGA Res. 37/123 A (16 December 1982), UN Doc. A/RES/37/123; UNGA Res. 38/180 A (19 December 1983), UN Doc. A/RES/38/180; UNGA Res. 43/21 (3 November 1988), UN Doc. A/RES/43/21; see also UNGA Res. 60/147 (16 December 2005), UN Doc. A/RES/60/147, para. 3.

74 See Henckaerts and Doswald-Beck (eds.), *Customary International Humanitarian Law* (2005) ('*ICRC Customary Law Study*'), vol. I, 510.

The ICJ confirmed this broad interpretation of Common Article 1 in its *Wall* advisory opinion of 2004, stating that every state party, 'whether or not it is a party to a specific conflict, is under an obligation to ensure that the requirements of the instruments in question are complied with'.[75]

It follows that all states that hire PMSCs in armed conflict will be obliged to take steps to ensure that those companies comply with IHL, including states that are not party to the conflict. This discussion now turns to consider the precise measures that the hiring state should take to fulfil this obligation.

Positive action to discharge the Common Article 1 obligation

Part I of the Montreux Document identifies three distinct components of the hiring state's obligation to ensure respect for IHL:

> 3. Contracting States have an obligation, within their power, to ensure respect for international humanitarian law by PMSCs they contract, in particular to:
>
> a) ensure that PMSCs that they contract and their personnel are aware of their obligations and trained accordingly;
>
> b) not encourage or assist in, and take appropriate measures to prevent, any violations of international humanitarian law by personnel of PMSCs;
>
> c) take measures to suppress violations of international humanitarian law committed by the personnel of PMSCs through appropriate means, such as military regulations, administrative orders and other regulatory measures as well as administrative, disciplinary or judicial sanctions, as appropriate.[76]

Each of these constituent positive obligations – the obligation to instruct and train, the obligation to prevent, and the obligation to suppress – entails a due diligence standard of conduct, which becomes more exacting as the state's capacity to influence the PMSC increases.[77] The hiring state will need to take a range of measures to meet this due diligence threshold. Part II of the Montreux Document sets out twenty-three 'good practices', which provide guidance as to the specific steps that the hiring state should

---

75 *Legal Consequences of the Construction of a Wall in the Occupied Palestinian Territory* (Advisory Opinion) ICJ Reports 2004, 158. Judge Kooijmans disagreed with the majority's conclusion that Common Article 1 imposes obligations on third states to take action in relation to other states: see Judge Kooijmans' separate opinion, para. 50 (citing Kalshoven's study of the *travaux préparatoires*).
76 Montreux Document, Part I, para. 3.   77 See Chapter 4, section 4.1.

take to discharge its international obligations in relation to PMSCs. In general, a failure by the hiring state to implement any one of these good practices will not, in itself, constitute a breach of Common Article 1, but a wholesale disregard for these standards will most likely point to state responsibility for a failure to exercise due diligence. Conversely, diligent efforts to implement the good practices identified in the Montreux Document will generally ensure that the hiring state meets not only its obligation to ensure respect for IHL, but also any applicable obligations under HRL discussed in the third section of this chapter.

Part I, paragraph 3, of the Montreux Document (set out above) characterises training of PMSC personnel as a concrete obligation deriving from Common Article 1, rather than a mere good practice. This reflects the ICRC position on this issue.[78] In international armed conflict, the hiring state's obligation to ensure that PMSC personnel are adequately trained and instructed in IHL is reinforced by the specific duties of instruction in the Geneva Conventions and Protocol I, discussed below. The PMSC personnel hired by the US to work as interrogators at Abu Ghraib prison in Iraq present an extreme example of deficient PMSC training standards. When the prisoner abuse scandal came to light in 2004, it emerged that approximately 35 per cent of the PMSC interrogators working at the prison lacked formal military training as interrogators, and neither their hiring firm CACI nor the US government had conducted adequate background investigations prior to their employment.[79] A more recent example of deficient training standards is the ArmorGroup operation to guard the US embassy in Kabul, which utilised a large number of guards who could not speak English and who had no security training or experience.[80]

As for the obligation to take 'appropriate measures to prevent' violations of IHL, set out above in paragraph 3(b), first and foremost the Montreux Document suggests that the hiring state take into account whether a particular service 'could cause PMSC personnel to become

---

78 See ICRC, Frequently Asked Questions: International Humanitarian Law and Private Military/Security Companies, available at www.icrc.org.

79 Fay, 'Investigation of the Abu Ghraib Detention Facility and 205th Military Intelligence Brigade' (August 2004) ('Fay Report'); Schooner, 'Contractor Atrocities at Abu Ghraib: Compromised Accountability in a Streamlined, Outsourced Government' (2005) 16 *Stanford Law and Policy Review* 549, 556–7; Gibson and Shane, 'Contractors Act as Interrogators', *Baltimore Sun* (4 May 2004).

80 Senate Committee on Homeland Security and Governmental Affairs, Subcommittee on Contracting Oversight, 'New Information about the Guard Force Contract at the US Embassy in Kabul' (June 2009).

involved in direct participation in hostilities'.[81] Whilst there is no general rule of international law prohibiting states from hiring PMSCs to take a direct part in hostilities, as discussed in the first section of this chapter, it would be wise for states to consider carefully their use of contractors in certain high-risk situations.

If a state chooses to hire a PMSC, it should ensure that company personnel are adequately vetted in order to exclude individuals who have been convicted of violent crimes from working in armed conflict, where they are likely to face abuse-prone situations. Good practices 5 to 13 recommend certain vetting procedures in order to take into account, within available means, the past conduct of the PMSC and its personnel. This responds to widespread criticisms amongst private security commentators, such as the following 2008 statement of the UN Working Group on Mercenaries:

> [A]mong the PMSC contractors there are South Africans now training and providing support to the Iraqi police who served earlier in the South African police and army during the former apartheid regime, some of whom have committed crimes against humanity.[82]

A failure to conduct adequate background investigations may increase the risk of contractor misconduct. In one incident in August 2009, for example, an ArmorGroup security guard allegedly shot and killed two fellow guards and wounded at least one Iraqi in Baghdad. It subsequently emerged that the guard had a criminal record and was described by one fellow contractor as 'a walking time-bomb'.[83] A thorough screening process should have excluded such an individual from employment as an armed guard in a conflict zone.

In addition, the hiring state should 'include contractual clauses and performance requirements that ensure respect for relevant national law, international humanitarian law and human rights law by the contracted PMSC'.[84] In fact, this is the most direct way by which the hiring state can impose conditions on PMSC personnel. Effective oversight of contractual performance is also crucial, and accordingly the Montreux

---

81 Montreux Document, Part II, para. 1.
82 Report of the Working Group on the Use of Mercenaries as a Means of Violating Human Rights and Impeding the Exercise of the Right of People to Self-Determination (9 January 2008), UN Doc. A/HRC/7/7, para. 47.
83 'Briton Held in Iraq over Shooting', *BBC News* (10 August 2009); Haynes and Ford, 'Briton Facing Iraq Murder Trial on Probation for Gun Offence', *Times* (13 August 2009).
84 Montreux Document, Part II, para. 14.

Document contains an elaborate description of good practice in contract monitoring.[85] The hiring state should ensure that it maintains high standards of oversight even where subcontracting arrangements weaken the state's relationship with the PMSC personnel who are ultimately performing the services in the field.[86]

Another important aspect of prevention under Common Article 1 relates to PMSCs that are hired to provide advice or training to military forces. Clearly a state that hires a PMSC to train/advise its own armed forces will be obliged to ensure that the PMSC's training/advice complies with IHL. A state should apply the same procedure when it hires a PMSC to train/advise *foreign* forces. In *Nicaragua*, the ICJ found that the US had supplied to the Nicaraguan rebels a training manual which discussed the possible necessity of shooting civilians who were attempting to leave a town and advised the 'neutralisation' of local judges and other officials.[87] This contributed to the Court's finding that the US had violated Common Article 1 by encouraging the *contras* to violate IHL.[88] Assuming that the obligation in Common Article 1 requires states to take positive steps to prevent violations of IHL, it is possible to stretch the *Nicaragua* scenario one step further. Let us say that the US government today hired a PMSC to train a foreign force such as the Iraqi army, but the US neither provided training guidelines nor supervised the training in any way. If the company trained the force using a manual similar to that used in *Nicaragua*, it does not seem too remote to suggest that the US might incur some responsibility if the foreign soldiers then violated IHL in accordance with their training. In such a case, the US would not be incurring responsibility directly for the violation of IHL committed by the foreign soldiers, but for its own failure to fulfil its obligation under Common Article 1 to ensure that the PMSC training/advice complied with IHL.

Finally, as set out in the Montreux Document, the obligation to ensure respect for IHL requires the hiring state to 'suppress' any PMSC violations that occur. In order to fulfil this aspect of the obligation, the hiring state should first criminalise violations of IHL in its domestic law, and then investigate any alleged incidents of wrongdoing and, where appropriate, prosecute the individuals in question. Indeed, the Appeals Chamber of the International Criminal Tribunal for the former Yugoslavia

85 *Ibid.*, Part II, para. 21.
86 See US Commission on Wartime Contracting Hearing, 'Subcontracting: Who's Minding the Store?' (26 July 2010).
87 *Nicaragua*, para. 122.   88 *Ibid.*, para. 255.

(ICTY) stated in the *Čelebići* case that the absence of domestic criminal legislation providing for the repression of violations of Common Article 3 'would, arguably, be inconsistent with the general obligation contained in common Article 1 of the Conventions'.[89] Individual contracts of hire should complement these criminal measures by stipulating contractual penalties in cases of violation. The hiring state should also take steps to prevent PMSC violations from recurring, for example by changing its hiring practices, issuing new instructions and introducing new training requirements for other PMSCs doing similar work in the field.

State responsibility for a violation of Common Article 1

A hiring state that fails to exercise due diligence to control PMSC behaviour could incur responsibility for a breach of Common Article 1 if a company employee acts in a way that violates IHL. In order to establish such a breach, it would not be necessary to prove that an exercise of due diligence by the hiring state would have in fact prevented the PMSC violation in question. This would be difficult to prove and in any event it is irrelevant to the breach of the state's due diligence obligation. Rather, it would suffice to prove that the hiring state failed to take those measures within its power that *might* have been expected to prevent the violation in the circumstances.[90]

If the PMSC employee was acting as an agent of the hiring state when he or she committed the violation, there would be no need to consider the state's obligation to ensure respect for IHL, since the PMSC violation would itself be an 'act of a state' giving rise to state responsibility. On the other hand, if the PMSC employee was not acting as an agent of the hiring state at the relevant time – meaning that he or she was not part of the state's armed forces, nor exercising governmental authority, nor acting under the hiring state's instructions, direction or control – the hiring state's obligation to ensure respect for IHL could provide an alternative pathway to state responsibility. This would be particularly important if one adopted the ICJ's 'effective control' test for attribution rather than the less stringent 'overall control' test favoured by the ICTY, as discussed

---

89 *Prosecutor* v. *Delalić*, Judgment, IT-96-21-A, Appeals Chamber, 20 February 2001 ('*Čelebići* case'), para. 167.

90 This reflects the test utilised by the ICJ in the *Genocide* case, para. 430, and by the European Court of Human Rights in assessing the obligation to safeguard the right to life in *Keenan* v. *UK* (App. No. 27229/95), ECHR, 3 April 2001, para. 89, and *Osman* v. *UK* (App. No. 23452/94), ECHR, 28 October 1998, para. 116.

in Chapter 3.[91] A similar situation faced the ICJ in the *Genocide* case, when Serbia's obligation to prevent genocide assumed central importance because the Court could not attribute the genocide itself to Serbia using the stringent 'effective control' test for attribution.[92]

In short, the obligation to ensure respect for IHL could help to maximise the responsibility of the hiring state for any PMSC misconduct committed in the field, thereby bridging the responsibility gap between states that act through PMSCs and states that act through their armed forces. More generally, Common Article 1 could play a valuable prospective role by setting a baseline level of obligatory conduct which *all* hiring states must satisfy in *all* circumstances, in addition to any more specific rules that may apply in a given case. In this way, Common Article 1 could play a similar role to Common Article 3 as 'a minimum yardstick'[93] against which a hiring state's conduct is to be assessed in both international and non-international armed conflicts. Having established this minimum standard of conduct for the hiring state, the remainder of this section examines four of the more specific IHL obligations that may bind the state in particular circumstances.

Duty to train and disseminate

States have clear obligations to instruct their national soldiers in IHL and to ensure that legal advisers are available to the armed forces, when necessary, to advise military commanders on the application of IHL.[94] Thus, in the rare case that a PMSC formed part of the hiring state's armed forces, the state would have an obligation to ensure that all company personnel had been trained in IHL.

Outside the context of the armed forces, IHL does not explicitly delineate any general obligation on states to instruct civilians in IHL. States are required to disseminate the Conventions and Protocol I as widely as possible, and to 'encourage' the study of these instruments by the civilian population. For example, Article 48 of GCII provides:

---

91 See Chapter 3, section 3.3.   92 *Genocide* case, paras. 425–50.
93 In *Nicaragua* (at para. 218), the ICJ stated that Common Article 3 constitutes 'a minimum yardstick' which applies in all armed conflicts, 'in addition to the more elaborate rules which are also to apply to international conflicts'; see also *Prosecutor* v. *Tadić*, Decision on the Defence Motion for Interlocutory Appeal on Jurisdiction, ICTY-94-1-AR72, Appeals Chamber, 2 October 1995, para. 102.
94 See, e.g., Convention Respecting the Laws and Customs of War on Land (adopted 18 October 1907, entered into force 26 January 1910), 205 Consol TS 277, Art. 1; GCIII, Art. 127(1); Protocol I, Arts. 80(2) and 82–3; *ICRC Customary Law Study*, vol. I, rules 141–2, 500–5.

> The High Contracting Parties undertake, in time of peace as in time of war, to disseminate the text of the present Convention as widely as possible in their respective countries, and, in particular, to include the study thereof in their programmes of military and, if possible, civil instruction, so that the principles thereof may become known to the entire population, *in particular to the armed fighting forces, the medical personnel and the chaplains.*[95]

A similar obligation appears in Article 47 of GCI[96] and Article 83 of Protocol I.[97] These provisions are not generally considered to impose a binding obligation on states to ensure that their entire civilian population is knowledgeable about IHL.[98] However, PMSCs can hardly be grouped with the general civilian population in this context; on the contrary, it is likely that the drafters would have grouped PMSCs with 'the armed fighting forces, the medical personnel and the chaplains'.[99] This interpretation is particularly persuasive when one reads these provisions in conjunction with the general duty to ensure respect for IHL in Common Article 1.

In addition to the obligation to disseminate the Conventions and Protocol I, in international armed conflict IHL imposes an explicit obligation on states to train individuals who assume responsibilities in respect of prisoners of war or protected persons. There are no equivalent provisions applicable in non-international armed conflict.

In relation to prisoners of war, Article 39 of GCIII provides:

> Every prisoner of war camp shall be put under the immediate authority of a responsible commissioned officer belonging to the regular armed forces of the Detaining Power. Such officer shall have in his possession a copy of the present Convention; *he shall ensure that its provisions are known to the camp staff and the guard and shall be responsible, under the direction of his government, for its application.*[100]

---

95 Second Geneva Convention for the Amelioration of the Condition of Wounded, Sick and Shipwrecked Members of Armed Forces at Sea (adopted 12 August 1949, entered into force 21 October 1950), 75 UNTS 85 (emphasis added).

96 First Geneva Convention for the Amelioration of the Condition of the Wounded and Sick in Armed Forces in the Field (adopted 12 August 1949, entered into force 21 October 1950), 75 UNTS 31.

97 See also *ICRC Customary Law Study*, vol. II, rule 143, 505.

98 Turns, 'Implementation and Compliance', in Wilmshurst and Breau (eds.), *Perspectives on the ICRC's Study on Customary International Humanitarian Law* (2007), 363–4; UCIHL Expert Meeting, 43.

99 Doswald-Beck, 'Private Military Companies under International Humanitarian Law', 132–3.

100 Emphasis added.

Article 127(2) strengthens this requirement by stating that '[a]ny military or other authorities, who in time of war assume responsibilities in respect of prisoners of war, must possess the text of the Convention and be specially instructed as to its provisions'. Although the drafters of this provision undoubtedly had *governmental* entities in mind when they used the term 'authorities', in modern times when so many functions once considered governmental are performed by non-governmental entities, such a reading of 'authorities' would be too narrow. It would be in keeping with the spirit of the provision to require it to be applied to all PMSCs that 'assume responsibilities' for prisoners of war. The Detaining Power's obligations under GCIII provide useful standards to guide states that hire PMSCs to work in prisoner of war camps. These obligations would not, however, alter the responsibility of the hiring state if a PMSC mistreated a prisoner of war, since a Detaining Power retains absolute responsibility for the treatment given to prisoners by virtue of Article 12 of GCIII.

GCIV provides a further obligation in relation to 'protected persons', which it defines in Article 4 as 'those who, at a given moment and in any manner whatsoever, find themselves, in case of a conflict, in the hands of a Party to the conflict or Occupying Power of which they are not nationals'. Article 144(2) of GCIV provides that '[a]ny civilian, military, police or other authorities, who in time of war assume responsibilities in respect of protected persons, must possess the text of the Convention and be specially instructed as to its provisions'. The inclusion of the phrase 'any civilian' clearly brings PMSCs within the scope of the obligation to instruct. Moreover, since the performance of some duties 'in respect of protected persons' (such as the duty to provide food and medical supplies) may *not* entail the exercise of 'governmental authority' within Article 5 of the International Law Commission's Articles on Responsibility of States for Internationally Wrongful Acts,[101] misconduct by PMSCs performing such duties would not necessarily be attributable to the hiring state.[102] The obligation to instruct PMSCs under Article 144(2) of GCIV could provide an alternative pathway to state responsibility in such cases.

Protection of civilians in international armed conflict

As discussed in Chapter 4 in relation to the host state of a PMSC, in international armed conflict Article 27 of GCIV imposes an obligation on

---

101 International Law Commission Articles on Responsibility of States for Internationally Wrongful Acts with Commentaries (2001) *Yearbook of the International Law Commission*, vol. II(2).
102 See generally Chapter 3, section 3.2.

states to take positive measures to protect civilians, particularly women and children.[103] Similarly, Article 76 of Protocol I obliges states to protect women 'in particular against rape, forced prostitution and any other form of indecent assault', and Article 77 obliges states to protect children 'against any form of indecent assault'.

These provisions effectively oblige the hiring state to exercise due diligence to control PMSCs performing activities that could threaten the civilian population, particularly women and children, and to minimise the risk that off-duty contractors will engage in unlawful sexual activities with women or children.[104] To fulfil these obligations, the hiring state should take steps to ensure not only that PMSC personnel are adequately vetted and trained, but also that the company has a clear policy of dismissing any contractors found to have engaged in activities that exploit women or children. Such measures could help to prevent a repeat of the DynCorp 'sex-slave' scandal that took place in Bosnia in 1999–2000, discussed in Chapter 4, in which employees of the US firm DynCorp working under contract with the US government were implicated in a prostitution ring involving girls as young as twelve, including trafficking victims.[105] Finally, the hiring state should ensure that any contractors found to have engaged in unlawful activities with civilian women or girls face disciplinary and, when the evidence merits, criminal proceedings.

Obligation to repress or suppress violations of IHL

The Geneva Conventions impose an explicit obligation on the hiring state of a PMSC, like other states, to 'repress' grave breaches[106] and to 'suppress' other breaches of IHL in international armed conflict.[107] These provisions clearly oblige the hiring state to enact legislation enabling criminal prosecution or extradition of PMSC personnel who commit grave breaches of IHL, whether in state territory or overseas, in the exercise of universal

---

103 See Chapter 4, section 4.1.
104 Hoppe, 'State Responsibility for Violations of International Humanitarian Law Committed by Individuals Providing Coercive Services under a Contract with a State' (2008), 43–4.
105 See Chapter 4, section 4.1; see also Human Rights Watch, 'Hopes Betrayed: Trafficking of Women and Girls to Post-Conflict Bosnia and Herzegovina for Forced Prostitution' (26 November 2002); Maffai, 'Accountability for Private Military and Security Company Employees that Engage in Sex Trafficking and Related Abuses While under Contract with the United States Overseas' (2008–9) 26 *Wisconsin International Law Journal* 1095.
106 GCI, Art. 49(1); GCII, Art. 50(1), GCIII, Art. 129(1); GCIV, Art. 146(1); see also Montreux Document, Part I, para. 5.
107 GCI, Art. 49(3); GCII, Art. 50(3), GCIII, Art. 129(3); GCIV, Art. 146(3).

jurisdiction. Grave breaches refer to certain serious offences including wilful killing, torture or inhuman treatment, and wilfully causing great suffering or serious injury to body or health.[108] The hiring state should also enact domestic legislation criminalising non-grave breaches of IHL – although it is not under an *explicit* obligation to do so – and should prosecute any offending PMSC personnel in the exercise of ordinary criminal jurisdiction.[109] The hiring state should combine its criminal legislation with other measures to suppress PMSC violations of IHL, such as ensuring that contractors are vetted and trained, including clear and appropriate terms in the contract, implementing procedures to monitor contractors in the field, and imposing contractual penalties for violations.

There are no specific provisions of this nature applicable in noninternational armed conflict, but a general obligation to suppress violations of IHL is implicit in the obligation to ensure respect for IHL in Common Article 1, as discussed above.[110]

Special obligations of an occupying power

In some situations of military occupation, the occupying power may hire a PMSC to work in the occupied territory. This was the case for the PMSCs hired by the Coalition Provisional Authority in Iraq, for example, following the 2003 invasion. In these situations, the hiring state will be bound by Article 43 of the Hague Regulations, which provides that the occupying power 'shall take all the measures in his power to restore, and ensure, as far as possible, public order and safety, while respecting, unless absolutely prevented, the laws in force in the country'.[111]

In the *Congo* case of 2005, the ICJ stated that Article 43 entails three distinct duties, namely, 'to secure respect for the applicable rules of international human rights law and international humanitarian law, to protect the inhabitants of the occupied territory against acts of violence, and not to tolerate such violence by any third party'.[112] Having concluded that

---

108 GCI, Art. 50; GCII, Art. 51; GCIII, Art. 130; GCIV, Art. 147.

109 See Pictet (ed.), *Commentary, Geneva Convention Relative to the Protection of Civilian Persons in Time of War* (1958), 593–4.

110 See also Montreux Document, Part I, para. 9(c); *Čelebići* case, paras. 163–7.

111 Regulations Respecting the Laws and Customs of War on Land, annexed to the Convention Respecting the Laws and Customs of War on Land (adopted 18 October 1907, entered into force 26 January 1910), 205 Consol TS 277.

112 *Case Concerning Armed Activities in the Territory of the Congo (DRC v. Uganda)* (Merits) ICJ Reports 2005, para. 178.

Uganda was an occupying power in Ituri at the relevant time, the Court found that

> Uganda's responsibility is engaged both for any acts of its military that violated its international obligations and for any *lack of vigilance* in preventing violations of human rights and international humanitarian law by other actors present in the occupied territory, including rebel groups acting on their own account.[113]

The Court therefore applied a standard of 'vigilance', synonymous with due diligence, to the obligation in Article 43 of the Hague Regulations. The Court's reference to 'other actors present in the occupied territory' would clearly encompass any PMSCs operating in the area.

It follows that an occupying power will have an obligation to take positive steps and exercise due diligence to prevent PMSC violations within the occupied territory, irrespective of whether the companies are working for the occupying power itself or for some other state or non-state actor. Where the occupying power is also the hiring state of the PMSC, the duty of vigilance to prevent violations of IHL will be even greater than that of Uganda in the *Congo* case, particularly when Article 43 is read in conjunction with the general duty to ensure respect for IHL in Common Article 1.[114]

5.3 Obligations to control PMSCs under human rights law

In certain circumstances HRL, like IHL, imposes important obligations on the hiring state to control PMSCs. Chapter 4 identified the principal foundations and objectives of HRL and discussed how this general framework differs from and relates to the more specialised framework of IHL.[115] It is widely accepted that HRL continues to apply during armed conflict, except to the extent that states have formally derogated from the particular human rights treaty in question.[116] Such derogations are permitted only to the degree strictly required by the exigencies of the situation, and not in relation to the specified non-derogable rights such as the right to life and freedom from torture.

---

113 *Ibid.*, para. 179 (emphasis added).
114 See also Montreux Document, Part I, para. 1.   115 See Chapter 4, section 4.2.
116 See International Covenant on Civil and Political Rights (adopted 16 December 1966, entered into force 23 March 1976), 999 UNTS 171 (ICCPR), Art. 4; European Convention on Human Rights (4 November 1950), CETS No. 005 (ECHR), Art. 15; American Convention on Human Rights (adopted 22 November 1969, entered into force 18 July 1978), 1144 UNTS 123 ('American Convention'), Art. 27.

The dual application of HRL alongside IHL has great potential to enhance the protection of individual rights in armed conflict.[117] Certain procedural rights are more strongly enshrined in HRL than IHL, particularly the right to an individual remedy and to an independent and impartial investigation. HRL also offers a number of sophisticated international procedures for individual complaint and redress – procedures that are not available under IHL – and victims may stand on their own rights without necessarily relying on the goodwill of their state to take up their case on the international plane. As discussed in Chapter 4, however, the concurrent application of IHL and HRL also complicates legal analysis as it necessitates a nuanced assessment of the relationship between the two regimes in the particular circumstances under consideration.

One significant limitation of HRL is that it imposes obligations on states only within their 'jurisdiction', and this notion of jurisdiction is primarily territorial.[118] This conception flows from the classic paradigm of HRL as a mechanism for protecting individuals from abuses by their governments. Where a PMSC operates within the hiring state's own territory – that is, where the hiring state is also the host state – the HRL analysis will essentially fall within Chapter 4. The present section, on the other hand, focuses on the situation where a state hires a PMSC to operate in a *foreign* conflict – that is, where the hiring state and the host state are different. The constraints on the extraterritorial applicability of HRL are clearly crucial in such cases. This section first considers the preliminary question of extraterritorial jurisdiction, and it then proceeds to assess the substantive content of the hiring state's obligations to prevent, investigate, punish and redress PMSC violations of human rights, assuming that HRL binds the hiring state in relation to the particular PMSC activities in question.

Extraterritorial scope of human rights law

In certain circumstances HRL may impose obligations on the hiring state in relation to PMSC activities overseas, but the precise scope of extraterritorial jurisdiction will depend on the specific wording of the human rights treaty in question. Each of the three main human rights treaties will be considered in turn.

117 See generally Provost, *International Human Rights and Humanitarian Law* (2002).
118 See, e.g., ECHR, Art. 1; American Convention, Art. 1; ICCPR, Art. 2(1); UN Convention Against Torture (adopted 10 December 1984, entered into force 26 June 1987) 1465 UNTS 85 (UNCAT), Art. 2(1), although note that the obligation to prosecute torture under Art. 7 of the UNCAT also applies to torture committed outside state jurisdiction.

International Covenant on Civil and Political Rights

On its face, the ICCPR presents the most difficult case for extraterritorial jurisdiction by virtue of its application clause in Article 2(1), which provides that each state party 'undertakes to respect and to ensure to all individuals *within its territory and subject to its jurisdiction* the rights recognised in the present Covenant'.[119] Nonetheless, very early in its existence the Human Rights Committee adopted a broad approach to the applicability of the ICCPR, essentially interpreting the terms 'territory' and 'jurisdiction' in Article 2(1) as disjunctive.[120]

The Human Rights Committee has equated the notion of 'jurisdiction' in Article 2(1) with power or effective control over the individual victim. In the 1981 case of *Lopez Burgos* v. *Uruguay*, for example, the Committee applied the ICCPR to the abduction, arrest, secret detention and torture of a Uruguayan citizen by Uruguay agents outside state territory, stating that

> [t]he reference . . . to 'individuals subject to its jurisdiction' is not to the place where the violation occurred, but rather to the relationship between the individual and the State in relation to a violation of any of the rights set forth in the Covenant, wherever they occurred.[121]

In the view of the Committee, it would be 'unconscionable' if a state could perpetrate violations of the Covenant in the territory of another state when it could not perpetrate such violations in its own territory.[122] More recently, the Committee's General Comment 31 confirms this broad interpretation of Article 2(1), emphasising that 'a State party must respect and ensure the rights laid down in the Covenant to *anyone within the power or effective control of that State Party, even if not situated within the territory of the State Party*'.[123] The Committee has applied this approach

---

119 Emphasis added.
120 For a detailed analysis of the extraterritorial application of the ICCPR, see McGoldrick, 'The International Covenant on Civil and Political Rights', and Scheinin, 'Extraterritorial Effect of the International Covenant on Civil and Political Rights', both in Coomans and Kamminga (eds.), *Extraterritorial Application of Human Rights Treaties* (2004).
121 *Lopez Burgos* v. *Uruguay*, UNHRC, 29 July 1981, UN Doc. A/36/40, 176, para. 12.2.
122 *Ibid.*, para. 12.3; see also *Delia Saldias de Lopez* v. *Uruguay* UNHRC, 29 July 1981, UN Doc. CCPR/C/OP/1, 88; *Celiberti de Casariego* v. *Uruguay*, UNHRC, 29 July 1981, UN Doc. Supp. No. 40 (A/36/40) at 185; *Mabel Pereira Montero* v. *Uruguay*, UNHRC, 31 March 1983, UN Doc. Supp. No. 40 (A/38/40) at 186.
123 Human Rights Committee, General Comment 31, UN Doc. CCPR/C/21/Rev.1/Add.13 (2004), para. 10 (emphasis added).

in a number of different contexts where a state takes measures which result in human rights violations overseas, including in situations of military occupation[124] and in relation to troops taking part in peacekeeping operations abroad.[125]

Where a state detains individuals overseas and hires a PMSC to work at the detention centre – as was the case when the US hired the PMSCs Titan and CACI to work at Abu Ghraib prison in Iraq – the state will clearly be bound by the ICCPR in relation to the company's operations. Yet the jurisprudence of the Human Rights Committee demonstrates that the ICCPR may also apply extraterritorially in situations that do *not* involve full control over the individual.[126] In the 'passport cases', for example, the Committee held that a state's control over its citizens' freedom of movement between foreign states gives rise to a positive obligation to issue a passport to its citizens overseas.[127] Another example is *Ibrahim Gueye* v. *France*, which concerned retired Senegalese soldiers of the French military forces who were living in Senegal but receiving a pension from France. As they received a lower pension than French retired solders in the same situation, the Committee found that they had suffered discrimination in violation of Article 26. The Committee noted that the Senegalese soldiers were 'not generally subject to French jurisdiction', but nonetheless considered it a sufficient basis for the extraterritorial application of the ICCPR that the soldiers 'rely on French legislation in relation to the amount of their pension rights'.[128]

The passport cases and *Ibrahim Gueye* v. *France* suggest that extraterritorial jurisdiction could derive from a state's exercise of control over a *particular aspect* of a person's life overseas, even if the person is not entirely within the power of the authorities. The victims in those cases

---

124 See Concluding Observations on: Cyprus, UN Doc. CCPR/C/79/Add39 (21 September 1994), para. 3; Israel, UN Doc. CCPR/CO/78/ISR (21 August 2003), para. 11; Israel, UN Doc. CCPR/C/79/Add93 (18 August 1998), para. 10; see also Meron, 'Applicability of Multilateral Conventions to Occupied Territories' (1978) 72 *AJIL* 542; Cohen, *Human Rights in the Israeli Occupied Territories* (1985).

125 See Concluding Observations on: Belgium, CCPR/CO/81/BEL (12 August 2004), para. 6; CCPR/C/79/Add99 (19 November 1998), para. 17; Netherlands, CCPR/CO/72/NET (27 August 2001), para. 8.

126 See Scheinin, 'Extraterritorial Effect of the ICCPR'.

127 *Nunez* v. *Uruguay*, UNHRC, 22 July 1983, UN Doc. Supp. No. 40 (A/38/40) at 225; *Mabel Pereira Montero* v. *Uruguay*, UNHRC, 31 March 1983, UN Doc. Supp. No. 40 (A/38/40) at 186; *Sophie Vidal Martins* v. *Uruguay*, UNHRC, 23 March 1982, UN Doc. Supp. No. 40 (A/37/40) at 157.

128 *Ibrahim Gueye* v. *France*, UNHRC, 6 April 1989, UN Doc. CCPR/C/35/D/196/1985, para. 9.4.

had a strong, long-term link to the state in question (citizenship in the passport cases and former membership of the armed forces and receipt of a state pension in *Ibrahim*); but could a more short-term exercise of state control suffice? For example, what if Iraqi civilians living in a particular compound relied exclusively on the US to provide security, and the US outsourced that task to a PMSC? Would the US be obliged to take steps to ensure that the PMSC personnel acted in accordance with HRL in their relations with the Iraqi civilians they were protecting? The broad conception of jurisdiction adopted by the Human Rights Committee provides some scope for arguments of this nature.

Both the US and Israel have objected to the Human Rights Committee's broad interpretation of the extraterritorial applicability of the ICCPR.[129] Michael Dennis, formerly of the US State Department, reflected the official US position in arguing in 2005 that states' human rights obligations were never intended to apply extraterritorially during periods of armed conflict.[130] Dennis propounded a strict interpretation of Article 2(1) of the ICCPR whereby both conditions must be met – that is, the victim of the violation must be 'within state territory' *and* 'subject to state jurisdiction' – before the Convention can apply extraterritorially. The Israeli government adopts by and large the same approach propounded by Dennis in rejecting the application of HRL in the occupied Palestinian territories, although the Israeli High Court of Justice has taken a different view in some of its judgments, most notably in the *Ma'arab* case of 2003.[131]

The ICJ has essentially adopted the approach of the Human Rights Committee in relation to the extraterritorial applicability of the ICCPR. In its *Wall* advisory opinion, the Court stated that the Covenant 'is applicable in respect of acts done by a state in the exercise of its jurisdiction outside its own territory' in concluding that the ICCPR, the International Covenant on Economic, Social and Cultural Rights[132] and the Convention on the

---

129 See, e.g., Second Periodic Report of Israel to the Human Rights Committee (4 December 2001), UN Doc. CCPR/C/ISR/2001/2, para. 8; Human Rights Committee, Consideration of Reports Submitted by States Parties under Article 40 of the Covenant, 2nd and 3rd Periodic Reports of the United States of America (28 November 2005), UN Doc. CCPR/C/USA/3, Annex I: 'Territorial Scope of the Application of the Covenant'.

130 Dennis, 'Application of Human Rights Treaties Extraterritorially in Times of Armed Conflict and Military Occupation' (2005) 99 *AJIL* 119.

131 *Ma'arab* v. *The IDF Commander in Judea and Samaria*, 57(2) PD 349, HCJ 3239/02.

132 International Covenant on Economic, Social and Cultural Rights (adopted 16 December 1966, entered into force 3 January 1976), 993 UNTS 3.

Rights of the Child[133] were all applicable within the occupied Palestinian territory.[134]

The ICJ appeared to take this approach one step further in the *Congo* case of 2005, stating that "'international human rights instruments are applicable in respect of acts done by a State in the exercise of its jurisdiction outside its own territory', *particularly in occupied territories*'.[135] The Court found Uganda to be in violation of its human rights obligations under the ICCPR and other instruments in relation to its conduct in the DRC, not only as an occupying power in the Ituri province but also in other locations (particularly the city of Kisangani) where it was not an occupying power.[136] This suggests that territorial control falling short of formal occupation, such as territorial control exercised temporarily by an invading force, could suffice to establish the applicability of human rights instruments. On this understanding, the ICCPR could bind the hiring state of a PMSC in relation to the company's activities in a foreign conflict, simply because the state's military forces exercised temporary control over the area in which the PMSC was operating; this would be highly significant indeed.

Inter-American system

In the Organization of American States, human rights are understood to be the rights set out in the American Convention on Human Rights in relation to the states parties thereto, and those set out in the American Declaration on the Rights and Duties of Man[137] in relation to the other member states that have not ratified the Convention.[138] The American Convention binds states parties in regard to 'all persons subject to their jurisdiction'.[139] The American Declaration, on the other hand, has no express jurisdictional scope and was not intended to function as a treaty. Nonetheless, it is important in the present context because most of the examples of the extraterritorial application of human rights instruments in the Inter-American system concern the US, which has not ratified the American Convention.

---

133 Convention on the Rights of the Child (adopted 20 November 1989, entered into force 2 September 1990), 1577 UNTS 3.

134 *Wall* advisory opinion, paras. 108–11.   135 *Congo* case, para. 216 (emphasis added).

136 *Ibid.*, paras. 206–7 and 220.

137 American Declaration of the Rights and Duties of Man (April 1948).

138 See Statute of the Inter-American Commission on Human Rights (October 1979), Art. 1.

139 American Convention, Art. 1.

The Inter-American Commission on Human Rights (IAComHR) has found that both the Convention and the Declaration can bind a state extraterritorially in relation to persons who are subject to the state's authority and control.[140] The Commission has adopted a very broad understanding of control in this context, particularly in relation to military operations. For example, in asserting jurisdiction over acts associated with the US invasion of Panama, the IAComHR did not consider it necessary to establish that the US had exercised effective control over the particular territory in which alleged killings and property damage by the US military took place, nor was it necessary to establish that the US had arrested the individual victims prior to the incidents.[141] The Commission simply stated that, 'where it is asserted that a use of military force has resulted in noncombatant deaths, personal injury, and property loss, the human rights of the noncombatants are implicated'.[142]

Continuing this trend, in *Alejandre* v. *Cuba* the IAComHR ruled that the capacity of Cuban military pilots to shoot down civilian planes over international waters was sufficient to ground jurisdiction, even though the pilots did not control the territory in which the incident occurred.[143] According to the IAComHR, whilst 'jurisdiction' in the American Convention usually refers to persons who are within the territory of a state, it can also encompass extraterritorial actions 'when the person is present in the territory of a state but subject to the control of another state, generally through the actions of that state's agents abroad'.[144]

These cases suggest that the extraterritorial violation of a negative obligation (such as an unlawful killing) by a state agent could itself ground jurisdiction, without the need to establish effective state control over the territory or the individual victim in question. This is highly significant for the US in the private security context, as it suggests that the American Declaration could bind the US in relation to human rights violations

---

140 See *Saldano* v. *Argentina*, Petition, IAComHR Rep. No. 38/99, 11 March 1999, paras. 18–19; *Coard* v. *US*, IAComHR Rep. No. 109/99, Case 10.951, 29 September 1999, para. 37; Cerna, 'Extraterritorial Application of the Human Rights Instruments of the Inter-American System', and Cassel, 'Extraterritorial Application of Inter-American Human Rights Instruments', both in Coomans and Kamminga (eds.), *Extraterritorial Application of Human Rights Treaties*; Pasqualucci, *The Practice and Procedure of the Inter-American Court of Human Rights* (2003).

141 *Salas* v. *US*, IAComHR Rep. No. 31/93, Case No. 10.573, 14 October 1993. The case was declared admissible in 1993 but is still pending a decision on the merits.

142 *Ibid.*, para. 6.

143 *Alejandre* v. *Cuba*, IAComHR Rep. No. 86/99, Case No. 11.589, 29 September 1999.

144 *Ibid.*, para. 23.

committed by PMSC personnel who are acting as state agents in the context of American military operations outside US territory.

A key uncertainty remains, however, in that the Inter-American system has never exercised jurisdiction over the acts of a member state perpetrated *outside the region*. In all of the IAComHR cases noted above, the relevant acts took place within the territory of a member of the Organization of American States. It is therefore difficult to assess whether the victims of human rights abuses committed by PMSCs hired by the US in Iraq or Afghanistan, for example, have any reasonable expectations or rights under the instruments of the Inter-American system. The preamble to the American Convention refers to the intention of states parties 'to consolidate *in this hemisphere*, within the framework of democratic institutions, a system of personal liberty and social justice based on respect for the essential rights of man'.[145] This might be construed as an implicit geographic limitation on jurisdiction.[146] On the other hand, the notion of 'authority and control' developed by the IAComHR is extremely broad, and there is no logical reason why such authority and control should be construed as limited to a particular geographic region. Why should the US be taken to be exercising authority and control over Iraqis detained at Guantanamo Bay,[147] but not over Iraqis detained at Abu Ghraib? Indeed, as Meron argued convincingly in 1995:

> Where agents of the state, whether military or civilian, exercise power and authority (jurisdiction or *de facto* jurisdiction) over persons outside national territory, the presumption should be that the state's obligation to respect the pertinent human rights continues.[148]

The IAComHR itself quoted Meron's statement in *Coard* v. *US*[149] in support of its holding that

> each American State is obliged to uphold the protected rights of any person subject to its jurisdiction. While this most commonly refers to persons within a state's territory, it may, under given circumstances, refer to conduct with an extraterritorial locus where the person concerned is present in the territory of one state, but subject to the control of another

---

145 Emphasis added.
146 See Hoppe, 'State Responsibility for Violations of International Humanitarian Law Committed by Individuals Providing Coercive Services under a Contract with a State', 996.
147 *Precautionary Measures Issued by the Inter-American Commission of Human Rights Concerning the Detainees at Guantanamo Bay, Cuba*, IAComHR, 13 March 2002.
148 Meron, 'Extraterritoriality of Human Rights Treaties' (1995) 89 *AJIL* 78, 81.
149 *Coard* v. *US*, note 6.

state – usually through the acts of the latter's agents abroad. *In principle, the inquiry turns not on the presumed victim's nationality or presence within a particular geographic area, but on whether, under the specific circumstances, the State observed the rights of a person subject to its authority and control.*[150]

To be sure, human rights bodies 'must draw the lines that circumscribe the limits on the exercise of their jurisdiction somewhere';[151] but the IAComHR has clearly and consistently drawn that line on the basis of state 'authority and control' rather than on the basis of rigid geographic boundaries.

European Convention on Human Rights

Article 1 of the ECHR provides that the Convention binds states in relation to 'everyone within their jurisdiction'. The European Court of Human Rights (ECtHR) has recognised a relational concept of extraterritorial jurisdiction, which is grounded on the state's exercise of effective control over a person or over territory.

In *Loizidou v. Turkey*, the Grand Chamber of the Court found the Convention to be applicable to individuals acting under the umbrella of Turkish officials in northern Cyprus.[152] The Court noted that Turkey's effective overall control over the territory in northern Cyprus gave rise not only to an obligation to respect human rights, but also to an obligation to take positive steps 'to secure, in such an area, the rights and freedoms set out in the Convention'.[153] In a series of subsequent cases, the Court emphasised that Turkey's effective overall control over northern Cyprus obliged it to secure in the relevant territory *the entire range* of substantive rights set out in the Convention.[154]

Against this background, it is perhaps surprising that the Grand Chamber adopted such a restrictive interpretation of the term 'jurisdiction' in its 2001 decision in *Bankovic v. Belgium*.[155] Relatives of four individuals who had been killed in the NATO attacks on a Belgrade broadcasting station had lodged a complaint against several NATO member states, alleging

---

150 *Ibid.*, para. 37 (emphasis added).
151 Cerna, 'Extraterritorial Application of the Human Rights Instruments of the Inter-American System', 170.
152 *Loizidou v. Turkey* (App. No. 15318/89), ECHR, 18 December 1996.
153 *Ibid.*, para. 62.
154 *Cyprus v. Turkey* (App. No. 25781/94), ECHR, 10 May 2001, para. 77; *Djavit An v. Cyprus* (App. No. 20652/92), ECHR, 20 February 2003, paras. 18–23; *Demades v. Turkey* (App. No. 16219/90), ECHR, 31 July 2003.
155 *Bankovic v. Belgium* (App. No. 52207/99), Inadmissibility Decision, ECHR, 12 December 2001.

violations of (*inter alia*) the right to life, the right to freedom of expression and the right to an effective legal remedy. The Court declared the case inadmissible on the basis that the applicants had not been within the jurisdiction of the states concerned at the relevant time. According to the Court, its case law

> demonstrates that its recognition of the exercise of extra-territorial jurisdiction by a Contracting State is exceptional: it has done so when the respondent State, through the effective control of the relevant territory and its inhabitants abroad as a consequence of military occupation or through the consent, invitation or acquiescence of the Government of that territory, exercises all or some of the public powers normally to be exercised by that Government.[156]

The Court also pointed out that the Convention is a regional treaty directed towards the 'European legal space' ('*espace juridique*'), rather than an instrument designed to be applied throughout the world. The Federal Republic of Yugoslavia was simply not a part of this legal space.[157] The notion of 'legal space' triggered considerable speculation. On a limited reading of the judgment, it was no more than a response to an argument raised by the applicants in relation to the specific facts of the case. On a broader reading, however, the notion of legal space implied that any act committed by a state party outside the geographic area covered by the Convention would fall outside the jurisdiction of the state.[158]

In more recent decisions, the ECtHR has implicitly moved away from *Bankovic's* narrow approach to jurisdiction and has reaffirmed that, although a state's jurisdictional competence is primarily territorial, the ECHR may apply extraterritorially where a state exercises effective overall control over territory (including such control falling short of formal occupation) or over an individual.

The leading authority on control over territory is the decision of the Grand Chamber in *Ilaşcu v. Moldova and Russia*, in which the Court found Russia to be responsible for human rights violations on the basis of its

---

156 *Ibid.*, para. 71. This contrasts with the IAComHR's decision in *Alejandre v. Cuba*, discussed above.

157 *Bankovic v. Belgium*, paras. 79–80.

158 Lawson, 'Life after Bankovic: On the Extraterritorial Application of the European Convention on Human Rights', in Coomans and Kamminga (eds.), *Extraterritorial Application of Human Rights Treaties*; Leach, 'The British Military in Iraq: The Applicability of the Espace Juridique Doctrine under the European Convention on Human Rights' (2005) *Public Law* 448; Condorelli, 'La Protection des Droits de l'Homme Lors d'Actions Militaires Menées à l'Etranger' (2005) 32 *Collegium* 89, 100.

effective overall control over Moldovan territory falling short of formal occupation.[159] The Court stated:

> According to the relevant principles of international law, a State's responsibility may be engaged where, as a consequence of military action – whether lawful or unlawful – it exercises in practice effective control of an area situated outside its national territory. The obligation to secure, in such an area, the rights and freedoms set out in the Convention derives from the fact of such control, whether it be exercised directly, through its armed forces, or through a subordinate local administration.[160]

The Court again recognised the possibility of extraterritorial jurisdiction based on control over territory falling short of occupation in *Issa* v. *Turkey*. Concerning a number of Iraqi shepherds who were shot and mutilated in northern Iraq at a time when there was a large-scale Turkish military operation into Iraq, the Court stated:

> The Court does not exclude the possibility that, as a consequence of this military action, the respondent State could be considered to have exercised, *temporarily, effective overall control of a particular portion of the territory* of northern Iraq. Accordingly, if there is a sufficient factual basis for holding that, at the relevant time, the victims were within that specific area, it would follow logically that they were within the jurisdiction of Turkey.[161]

Two aspects of this statement are particularly significant. First, the Court recognised that a state's *temporary* exercise of effective overall control over territory could bring individuals within the jurisdiction of the state, thereby implicitly rejecting the arguments put forward by the respondents in *Bankovic* that the notion of 'effective control' entails 'some form of structured relationship existing over a period of time'.[162] Secondly, the Court recognised that acts performed by agents of a state party *outside the European legal space* could entail state responsibility. Had Turkey exercised effective overall control over the portion of Iraqi territory in question, the individuals within that territory would have been within Turkish jurisdiction notwithstanding the fact that the area was outside the legal space of the contracting parties. On the evidence, however, the Court was not satisfied that Turkey did in fact exercise effective control over the relevant territory at the time of the victims' deaths.

---

159 *Ilaşcu* v. *Moldova and Russia* (App. No. 48787/99), ECHR, 8 July 2004.
160 *Ibid.*, para. 314.
161 *Issa* v. *Turkey* (App. No. 31821/96), ECHR, 16 November 2004, para. 74 (emphasis added).
162 *Bankovic* v. *Belgium*, para. 36.

A third highly significant aspect of the judgment in *Issa v. Turkey* is its recognition that the Convention may bind a state extraterritorially in relation to particular *individuals*, irrespective of any effective overall state control over territory. According to the Court, a state may incur responsibility where individuals, though in the territory of another state, are nonetheless under the former state's *authority and control* through its agents operating in the latter state.[163] Citing decisions of the IAComHR[164] and the Human Rights Committee,[165] among others, the ECtHR emphasised that 'Article 1 of the Convention cannot be interpreted so as to allow a State party to perpetrate violations of the Convention on the territory of another State, which it could not perpetrate on its own territory'.[166]

The Court adopted a similar approach in *Öcalan v. Turkey*, holding that the Convention bound Turkey in relation to the acts of Turkish forces in assuming custody over the leader of the Kurdish Workers' Party in Kenya before transferring him to Turkey.[167] The Court distinguished the circumstances from those in *Bankovic* on the grounds that the applicant was physically forced to return to Turkey by Turkish officials and was under their 'authority and control' following his arrest and return to Turkey.[168]

Thus, although the ECtHR continues to cite *Bankovic* as good authority, its post-*Bankovic* jurisprudence signals a clear shift towards a more flexible notion of jurisdiction based on 'effective overall control' over territory or 'authority and control' over an individual. This would appear to bring the Court closer to the Human Rights Committee and the IAComHR on the question of extraterritorial jurisdiction, and this in turn provides some hope to victims of human rights violations by PMSCs that are hired by an ECHR contracting state, wherever those victims may be located.

Having identified the circumstances in which a victim of PMSC abuse might fall within the jurisdiction of the hiring state for the purposes of HRL, the remainder of this section assumes the applicability of HRL as its starting point and proceeds to assess the substantive obligations on the hiring state to prevent, investigate, punish and redress PMSC violations of human rights in armed conflict.

---

163 *Issa v. Turkey*, para. 71.   164 *Coard v. US*, paras. 7, 39, 41 and 43.
165 *Lopez Burgos v. Uruguay*, para. 12.3; *Celiberti de Casariego v. Uruguay*, para. 10.3.
166 *Issa v. Turkey*, para. 71.
167 *Öcalan v. Turkey* (App. No. 46221/99), ECHR, 12 May 2005.   168 *Ibid.*, para. 91.

Obligation to prevent human rights violations by PMSCs

The obligation to ensure rights requires states to take positive steps to prevent, investigate, punish and redress private violations of human rights within state jurisdiction.[169] Part I of the Montreux Document thus provides that hiring states

> are responsible to implement their obligations under international human rights law, including by adopting such legislative and other measures as may be necessary to give effect to these obligations. To this end they have the obligation, in specific circumstances, to take appropriate measures to prevent, investigate and provide effective remedies for relevant misconduct of PMSCs and their personnel.[170]

More generally, the 2010 Report of John Ruggie, the UN special representative on the issue of human rights and transnational corporations and other business enterprises, emphasises that the 'duty to protect' requires states to consider human rights whenever they 'do business with business', as such transactions provide states with unique opportunities to help prevent adverse corporate-related human rights impacts.[171] The Ruggie Report also notes that states must 'foster corporate cultures respectful of rights at home and abroad' and 'devise innovative policies to guide companies operating in conflict-affected areas'.[172]

If the hiring state of a PMSC fails to take adequate measures to control company behaviour and a contractor violates human rights within state jurisdiction, the state could incur international responsibility. This pathway to state responsibility could assume central importance in cases where the wrongdoing contractor is *not* acting as an agent of the hiring state. As the IACtHR explains, '[a]n illegal act which violates human rights and which is initially not directly imputable to a State . . . can lead

---

169 Regarding the right to life, see *Velásquez Rodríguez* v. *Honduras* (Merits), Judgment of 29 July 1988, IACtHR Ser. C No. 4, paras. 174–5; Human Rights Committee, General Comment 6, UN Doc. A/37/40(1982), paras. 3–5; *LCB* v. *UK* (App. No. 23413/94), ECHR, 9 June 1998, para. 36. Regarding the prohibition of torture and ill-treatment, see *Costello-Roberts* v. *UK* (App. No. 13134/87), ECHR Ser. A No. 247-C (1993), paras. 26–8; *A* v. *UK* (App. No. 25599/94), ECHR 1998-VI, para. 22; *Z* v. *UK* (App. No. 29392/95), ECHR, 10 May 2001, para. 73; Human Rights Committee, General Comment 20, UN Doc. HRI/GEN/1/Rev.1, paras. 2 and 8; UNCAT, Arts. 1, 2, 4 and 16.

170 Montreux Document, Part I, para. 4.

171 Ruggie, 'Business and Human Rights: Further Steps towards the Operationalization of the "Protect, Respect and Remedy" Framework', UN Doc. A/HRC/14/27 (9 April 2010), paras. 26–32.

172 *Ibid.*, paras. 33–45.

to international responsibility of the State, not because of the act itself, but because of the lack of due diligence to prevent the violation'.[173]

In the context of an armed conflict, the substantive content of the hiring state's HRL obligations must be assessed by reference to the rules of IHL. Chapter 4 critically examined the relationship between IHL and HRL, and explained that in certain situations of armed conflict the rules of IHL may modify or derogate from the rules of HRL.[174] This is particularly important when assessing the obligations deriving from the right to life, since the notion of an 'arbitrary' deprivation of life differs between IHL and HRL.[175] Where PMSC personnel participate in hostilities, the scope of the hiring state's HRL obligation to prevent PMSC killings will essentially be tied to the rules of IHL. On the other hand, where PMSC personnel perform activities like law enforcement or the security of civilian objects, the hiring state's HRL obligation to prevent PMSC killings will be tied more closely to the ordinary rules of HRL. In relation to the prohibition of torture and ill-treatment, the rules of IHL largely mirror the rules of HRL, with the result that the substantive scope of the hiring state's preventive obligation will not differ greatly between the two regimes.

With these considerations in mind, this section critically analyses four specific elements of the hiring state's obligation to prevent PMSC violations of human rights within state jurisdiction, and it then identifies the specific measures that the hiring state should take in order to fulfil its obligations.

Special measures targeting known sources of danger

States have a heightened duty under HRL to take preventive action targeting known sources of danger, particularly with a view to minimising recurring violations[176] and controlling individuals who are known to pose a danger to society.[177] This reflects the general nature of the due diligence standard, which demands a degree of diligence that is proportional to the degree of risk in the specific case.[178] Chapter 4 argued that this heightened preventive duty applies in relation to PMSCs, particularly given the inherently dangerous nature of some PMSC activities, the *ad hoc* process

---

173 *Velásquez Rodríguez* v. *Honduras*, para. 172.   174 See Chapter 4, section 4.2.

175 See *Legality of the Threat or Use of Nuclear Weapons* (Advisory Opinion) ICJ Reports 1996, para. 25.

176 See Human Rights Committee, General Comment 31, para. 17; *Neira Alegría* v. *Peru* (Merits), Judgment of 19 January 1995, IACtHR Ser. C No. 20, para. 19.

177 See *Mastromatteo* v. *Italy* (App. No. 37703/97), ECHR, 24 October 2002.

178 See Chapter 2, section 2.4.

of their recruitment, and the fact that the same violations tend to recur within the private security industry.[179] It follows from this argument that states have an obligation to take special measures to control the PMSCs they hire, over and above the measures that would ordinarily be required in relation to other companies. PMSCs that are known to be particularly aggressive may require particularly stringent control mechanisms.

Planning and controlling security operations to minimise the risk to life

Also highly relevant to the hiring state is the obligation to take the utmost care when planning and carrying out operations that might involve the use of lethal force, in order to minimise any risk to life to the greatest extent possible. This entails a duty to choose means and methods that are proportionate to the legitimate aims of the operation, to take into account contingencies in planning, to allow for an appropriate margin of error, and to consider sufficient alternative options.

Both the IACtHR and the Human Rights Committee have emphasised the need for the means and methods used by state security forces to be proportionate to the aims of the operation. For example, *Neira Alegría v. Peru* involved a riot at a detention centre, during which the authorities delegated control over the centre to the armed forces and over 100 prisoners were subsequently killed. The IACtHR acknowledged that the rioters had been armed and highly dangerous, but nonetheless found that the means and methods employed by the armed forces were 'disproportionate' in the circumstances. The death of the three inmates in question therefore constituted a violation of the right to life. The Human Rights Committee likewise stressed the lack of proportionality in the means and methods used by state security forces in *Suarez de Guerrero v. Colombia*, leading to a finding that there had been a violation of the right to life.[180]

The ECtHR first recognised an implicit duty to plan and control security operations in *McCann v. UK*.[181] That case concerned an anti-terrorist operation in Gibraltar led by the British Special Air Service, during which the UK forces shot and killed three terrorist suspects. Both the majority and the minority of the Court evaluated the adequacy of the UK's

---

179 See Chapter 4, section 4.2.

180 *Suarez de Guerrero v. Colombia*, UNHRC, 31 March 1982, UN Doc. Supp. No. 40 (A/37/40) at 137.

181 *McCann v. UK* (App. No. 18984/91), ECHR Ser. A No. 324 (1995); see also Mowbray, *The Development of Positive Obligations under the ECHR by the European Court of Human Rights* (2004), ch. 2.

prospective planning and organisation of its security forces' operation in assessing whether there had been a violation of the right to life. The majority ultimately concluded that a violation had taken place. The Court once again evaluated a state's planning and organisation of its security operations in *Andronicou and Constantinou* v. *Cyprus*, focusing particularly on the authorities' decision to call in the special forces (who were trained to kill) to respond to a 'lovers' quarrel' in a domestic apartment, leading to the killing both of the hostage and the hostage taker.[182]

Whereas both *McCann* and *Andronicou* involved killings by state security forces, in *Ergi* v. *Turkey* the Court made it clear that the obligation to plan and control security operations may give rise to state responsibility for a failure to ensure the right to life, even where the killing in question is *not* attributable to the state.[183] The case of *Avsar* v. *Turkey* illustrates how this principle could apply to PMSCs.[184] In *Avsar*, the ECtHR applied the *Ergi* principle to civilian volunteers who were performing quasi-police functions in association with the full-time security forces in southeast Turkey. Finding that there had been a breach of the right to life, the Court acknowledged 'the risks attaching to the use of civilian volunteers in a quasi-police function', particularly since the volunteers 'were outside the normal structure of discipline and training applicable to gendarmes and police officers'. In these circumstances, it was not 'apparent what safeguards there were against wilful or unintentional abuses of position carried out by the village guards'.[185] These comments indicate that Turkey's failure to provide adequate training to the civilian volunteers and to subject them to effective discipline was central to the Court's finding that there had been a violation.

The application of these principles to the private security industry leads to the conclusion that states have an obligation, first, to consider carefully the military and security tasks that they outsource to private companies and, where they choose to hire PMSCs, to take diligent measures to control the use of force by company personnel so as to minimise the risk to life as far as possible.

Protecting the physical integrity of detainees

Another important aspect of the hiring state's preventive obligation is the duty to take special measures to protect the physical integrity of individuals in state custody, including a duty to prevent attacks by other

---

182 *Andronicou and Constantinou* v. *Cyprus* (App. No. 25052/94), ECHR 1997-VI.
183 *Ergi* v. *Turkey* (App. No. 23818/94), ECHR 1998-IV.
184 *Avsar* v. *Turkey* (App. No. 25657/94), ECHR, 10 July 2001.   185 *Ibid.*, para. 414.

detainees. Since the well-being of each detainee lies wholly, or in large part, within the exclusive knowledge of the detaining state, strong presumptions of fact will arise in respect of any injuries and deaths occurring during detention.[186] If a person is detained in good health and subsequently dies or suffers injury whilst in custody, the detaining state will be obliged to provide a satisfactory and convincing explanation for the detainee's injuries or death.[187] Thus, in the House of Lords case of *Al-Skeini*, the UK had an obligation to account for the death of one of the claimants in a British military prison in Iraq.[188] These obligations would apply equally if a PMSC were operating the detention centre rather than a state official, since a state 'cannot absolve itself from responsibility by delegating its obligations to private bodies or individuals'.[189]

It follows that, if a state hires a PMSC to work at a detention centre in armed conflict – just as the US hired the PMSCs Titan and CACI to provide interrogators and interpreters at Abu Ghraib prison in Iraq – the state must take steps to ensure, first, that the contractors do not themselves mistreat the detainees and, secondly, that the contractors protect detainees from attacks by other prisoners.

Special obligations to protect women and children

Lastly, Article 34 of the Convention on the Rights of the Child and Article 3 of the Convention on the Elimination of All Forms of Discrimination against Women, both discussed in Chapter 4, effectively impose an obligation on the hiring state to exercise due diligence to prevent PMSCs from having sexual relations with children or committing violent or sexually exploitative acts against women within state jurisdiction.[190]

Positive action to discharge the preventive obligations

To fulfil the various elements of its duty to prevent PMSC violations of human rights, the hiring state will need to take a range of measures to

---

186 *Neira Alegría* v. *Peru*; *Edwards* v. *UK* (App. No. 46477/99), ECHR, 14 March 2002; *Lantsova* v. *Russian Federation*, UNHRC, 26 March 2002, UN Doc. CCPR/C/74/D/763/1997; *Pantea* v. *Romania* (App. No. 33343/96), ECHR, 3 June 2003.

187 *Juan Humberto Sánchez* v. *Honduras*, Preliminary Objection (Merits), Reparations and Costs, Judgment of 7 June 2003, IACtHR Ser. C No. 99, para. 111; *Salman* v. *Turkey* (App. No. 21986/93), ECHR, 27 June 2000, para. 100; *Çakici* v. *Turkey* (App. No. 23657/94), ECHR, 8 July 1999, para. 85.

188 *Al-Skeini* v. *Secretary of State for Defence* [2007] UKHL 26; [2008] 1 AC 153.

189 *Costello-Roberts* v. *UK*, para. 27; *Storck* v. *Germany* (App. No. 61603/00), ECHR, 16 June 2005, para. 103.

190 See Chapter 4, section 4.2.

control PMSC activities in armed conflict. As noted above in relation to the obligation 'to ensure respect' for IHL, the 'good practices' section of the Montreux Document recommends a range of measures including vetting and training PMSC personnel, ensuring that their contracts contain clear and appropriate rules governing the use of force, and implementing procedures to monitor PMSCs in the field and to report any violations that take place.[191]

These measures are particularly important where a PMSC is hired to work in a coercive environment such as a detention centre. The Standard Minimum Rules for the Treatment of Prisoners emphasise the importance of hiring suitable personnel at the outset, stating that the prison administration 'shall provide for the careful selection of every grade of the personnel, since it is on their integrity, humanity, professional capacity and personal suitability for the work that the proper administration of the institutions depends'.[192] Moreover, '[b]efore entering on duty, the personnel shall be given a course of training in their general and specific duties and be required to pass theoretical and practical tests'.[193] The Basic Principles on the Use of Force and Firearms by Law Enforcement Officials likewise call for 'continuous and thorough professional training'.[194] Soft law instruments of this nature can play a useful role in refining and fleshing out states' obligations under HRL. Article 10 of the UNCAT incorporates these standards into a hard law obligation:

> Each State Party shall ensure that education and information regarding the prohibition against torture [or other acts of cruel, inhuman or degrading treatment or punishment[195]] are fully included in the training of law enforcement personnel . . . *and other persons* who may be involved in the custody, interrogation or treatment of any individual subjected to any form of arrest, detention or imprisonment.[196]

In relation to PMSC personnel hired as interrogators, states have an obligation to provide clear safeguards during interrogation and custody, and

---

191 See Montreux Document, Part II, paras. 1–23.
192 Standard Minimum Rules for the Treatment of Prisoners, Adopted by the First UN Congress on the Prevention of Crime and the Treatment of Offenders (Geneva, 1955) and approved by the Economic and Social Council by its Resolution 663 C (XXIV) of 31 July 1957 and 2076 (LXII) of 13 May 1977, Art. 46(1).
193 *Ibid.*, Art. 47(2).
194 Basic Principles on the Use of Force and Firearms by Law Enforcement Officials, Adopted by the 8th UN Congress on the Prevention of Crime and the Treatment of Offenders (Havana, 27 August–7 September 1990), para. 18.
195 See UNCAT, Art. 16.   196 Emphasis added.

to conduct regular reviews of procedures for detention and interrogation. Article 11 of the UNCAT provides:

> Each State Party shall keep under systematic review interrogation rules, instructions, methods and practices as well as arrangements for the custody and treatment of persons subjected to any form of arrest, detention or imprisonment in any territory under its jurisdiction, with a view to preventing any cases of torture [or other acts of cruel, inhuman or degrading treatment or punishment].

Both the Human Rights Committee[197] and the IACtHR[198] have also emphasised the need for special training programmes for prison, police and judicial officials in order to prevent torture and ill-treatment.

The Abu Ghraib prisoner abuse scandal of 2003–4 highlights the importance of these obligations for the hiring state. It was noted above that approximately 35 per cent of the contract interrogators working at the prison lacked formal military interrogation training, and neither CACI nor the US government had screened prospective employees effectively. These initial failures were exacerbated by the fact that 'there was no credible exercise of appropriate oversight of contract performance at Abu Ghraib', and in some cases contractors may have even 'supervised' public personnel rather than the other way around.[199]

Finally, if a PMSC repeatedly violates human rights within state jurisdiction, the hiring state may need to amend its hiring practices and supervisory procedures in relation to that particular company. One example of hiring state behaviour that would appear to fall short of this requirement is the US State Department's continuous use of Blackwater security guards in Iraq for several years following the 2003 invasion (assuming for the sake of this discussion that HRL applied extraterritorially in that particular case). An October 2007 report of the House of Representatives Committee on Oversight and Governmental Reform documented an extremely high rate of offensive shooting by Blackwater contractors hired to provide 'defensive' security in Iraq, with over 80 per cent of documented incidents resulting in casualties or property damage.[200] Despite this consistent practice, the report notes:

---

197 Human Rights Committee, General Comment 20, para. 11.
198 *Tibi* v. *Ecuador* (Preliminary Objections, Merits, Reparations and Costs), Judgment of 7 September 2004, IACtHR Ser. C No. 114, paras. 159–62.
199 Fay Report, 52; see also Schooner, 'Contractor Atrocities at Abu Ghraib', 556–7.
200 US House of Representatives Committee on Oversight and Governmental Reform, 'Additional Information about Blackwater USA' (1 October 2007), 1.

> There is no evidence in the documents that the Committee has reviewed that the State Department sought to restrain Blackwater's actions, raised concerns about the number of shooting incidents involving Blackwater or the company's high rate of shooting first, or detained Blackwater contractors for investigation.[201]

In fact, throughout this period Blackwater remained the State Department's company of choice for the provision of protective services in Iraq, receiving US$832 million from government contracts between 2004 and 2006.[202] In 2010, the CIA reportedly awarded a contract worth about US$100 million to Xe Services LLC – the company formerly known as Blackwater – to protect CIA installations in Afghanistan. This is in addition to a separate contract Xe has with the State Department to protect US officials in that country.[203]

Obligation to investigate, punish and redress PMSC violations

HRL also imposes obligations on states to investigate, prosecute and redress violations of human rights within state jurisdiction. Chapter 4 set out the main sources of these obligations, the circumstances in which the obligations will arise in relation to violations by PMSCs in armed conflict, and the remedial action required of a state in a particular case.[204] The present section applies that analysis to the hiring state of a PMSC in relation to violations of human rights committed by company personnel in armed conflict overseas. The discussion first considers the hiring state's obligation to investigate and prosecute PMSC violations of human rights, and then considers the obligation to ensure that victims can access adequate procedures to have their claims heard and to obtain compensation.

Criminal investigation and prosecution

Human rights bodies have consistently emphasised the importance of effective criminal investigations and prosecutions in relation to killings and ill-treatment within state jurisdiction. Criminal investigations that are capable of leading to the identification and punishment of the perpetrators are necessary not only to provide justice to individual victims as part of an effective remedy, but also more generally to ensure that domestic laws

---

201 *Ibid.*, 2.   202 *Ibid.*, 5.

203 Stein, 'CIA Gives Blackwater Firm New $100 Million Contract', *Washington Post* (23 June 2010); Hodge, 'CIA Retains Controversial Security Firm in Afghanistan', *Wall Street Journal* (27 June 2010).

204 See Chapter 4, section 4.2.

prohibiting killings and ill-treatment are enforced in order to render the substantive rights effective in practice.[205]

A state's obligation to investigate and (where appropriate) prosecute arises wherever an individual raises an arguable claim to have suffered a human rights violation within state jurisdiction, including violations by private actors such as PMSCs.[206] As explained in Chapter 4, in situations of armed conflict the notion of an 'arguable' claim must be assessed by reference to the relevant rules of IHL as well as HRL.[207] This is particularly important where it is alleged that a PMSC has violated the right to life of the victim, since the substantive content of the right to life differs considerably between IHL and HRL.[208]

Where a PMSC operates in an armed conflict outside the territory of the hiring state, it may be extremely difficult for that state to conduct an effective investigation into allegations of human rights abuses by company personnel. While these difficulties do not relieve the hiring state of its investigative obligations, they will of course be taken into account when assessing whether the state has met the due diligence standard. The measures taken by the US following the Blackwater shootings in Baghdad on 16 September 2007, in which at least thirty-four Iraqi civilians were killed or wounded,[209] provide an example of action that would go a long way towards fulfilling the hiring state's investigative obligation in this context (assuming, for the sake of the present discussion, that the US was bound by HRL in relation to Blackwater's conduct). The House of Representatives Committee on Oversight and Government Reform published a report on the incident on 1 October 2007, and the following day the Committee held a hearing in order to reassess Blackwater's continued presence in Iraq and to evaluate the State Department's response to the shootings.[210] A criminal investigation ensued, leading to the indictment of five Blackwater employees in December 2008 on several counts of manslaughter and attempted manslaughter.[211] A federal judge dismissed the charges in

---

205 See, e.g., *Assenov* v. *Bulgaria* (App. No. 24760/94), ECHR 1998-VIII, para. 102; *Labita* v. *Italy* (App. No. 26772/95), ECHR, 6 April 2000, para. 131.

206 See, e.g., *Secic* v. *Croatia* (App. No. 40116/02), ECHR, 31 May 2007, para. 53; *MC* v. *Bulgaria* (App. No. 39272/98), ECHR, 4 December 2003, para. 151; *Ergi* v. *Turkey*, para. 82; *Kaya* v. *Turkey* (App. No. 22535/93), ECHR, 28 March 2000, para. 108; *Velásquez Rodríguez* v. *Honduras*, paras. 176 and 182.

207 See Chapter 4, section 4.2.   208 See *Nuclear Weapons* advisory opinion, para. 25.

209 US Department of Justice Press Release 08-1068, 8 December 2008.

210 US House of Representatives Committee on Oversight and Governmental Reform, 'Additional Information about Blackwater USA' (1 October 2007).

211 Zoepf, 'US Prosecutor in Blackwater Shooting Case Arrives in Baghdad', *New York Times* (7 December 2008); Sturcke, 'Blackwater Security Guards Face Manslaughter Charges',

December 2009 on the basis of the misuse of statements made by the accused guards,[212] but the US government immediately announced that it would appeal the decision.[213]

Clearly the hiring state's investigation will only be capable of leading to a prosecution if the state has criminal jurisdiction over the PMSC activities in question. This can be complicated where the PMSC is operating outside state territory. Since civilians' crimes ordinarily fall within the jurisdiction of the state in which they are committed, a PMSC employee operating outside the territory of the hiring state would ordinarily face prosecution in the host state rather than the hiring state. Such prosecution may be unlikely, however, where the host state is engaged in an armed conflict on its territory, and in some cases foreign contractors may enjoy immunity from local criminal jurisdiction by virtue of an agreement like Coalition Provisional Authority (CPA) Order No. 17, which granted foreign contractors in Iraq immunity from local laws in matters relating to their contracts.[214]

An examination of the events following the Abu Ghraib prisoner abuse scandal of 2003–4 highlights the inadequacy of the US rules for extraterritorial criminal jurisdiction at that time, particularly when coupled with the contractor immunity granted by CPA Order No. 17. Investigators referred four contractors to the US Department of Justice after finding that they had contributed to the prisoner abuse, and two contractors for failing to report it. However, not all of those contractors could be prosecuted under the Military Extraterritorial Jurisdiction Act (MEJA),[215] and none was covered by the Uniform Code of Military Justice (UCMJ).[216] The US has since amended both the MEJA and the UCMJ in order to permit the prosecution, in certain circumstances, of PMSC employees who commit crimes overseas.

Guardian (8 December 2008); although there have been some suggestions of interference in the investigatory process: see Risen, 'Interference Seen in Blackwater Inquiry', *New York Times* (2 March 2010).

212 Savage, 'Judge Drops Charges from Blackwater Deaths in Iraq', *New York Times* (31 December 2009).

213 Shadid, 'Biden Says US Will Appeal Blackwater Case Dismissal', *New York Times* (24 January 2010).

214 See Chapter 4, section 4.3. Contractors' immunity from prosecution under Iraqi law was lifted on 1 January 2009: see Pallister, 'Foreign Security Teams to Lose Immunity from Prosecution in Iraq', *Guardian* (27 December 2008).

215 Military Extraterritorial Jurisdiction Act, 18 USC § 3261.

216 Uniform Code of Military Justice, 10 USC § 801; see Fay Report; Merle and McCarthy, '6 Employees from CACI International, Titan Referred for Prosecution', *Washington Post* (26 August 2004).

The MEJA provides one potential mechanism for the US to prose-cute crimes committed by PMSC personnel performing US government contracts in foreign conflicts.[217] It effectively establishes federal criminal jurisdiction over certain offences committed outside the US by individ-uals (including both US and non-US nationals) 'employed by or accom-panying the [US] armed forces' in situations where the host nation is unable or unwilling to prosecute.[218] The requirement that individuals be employed by or accompanying US forces encompasses contractors who are hired by the Department of Defense (DOD) or any other federal agency or any provisional authority, to the extent that they are employed in support of a DOD mission overseas.[219] The Act excludes, however, contractors who are nationals of or ordinarily resident in the host nation, thus excluding the large number of Iraqi and Afghan nationals who work for PMSCs accompanying the US forces in Iraq and Afghanistan.[220] The MEJA has been used in a range of contractor prosecutions. In January 2010, for example, two men were charged under the Act with crimes including murder, attempted murder and firearms offences allegedly com-mitted while working as contractors for a subsidiary of Xe (the company formerly known as Blackwater) under contract with the US DOD in Afghanistan.[221]

In 2010, draft legislation was introduced in each House of Congress for a Civilian Extraterritorial Jurisdiction Act, which would clarify and expand the jurisdiction of US courts over serious crimes committed by private contractors deployed abroad by the US. The proposed legislation would include anyone 'employed by or accompanying any department or agency of the United States'. It would therefore clearly and unambiguously encompass civilian contractors working for the Department of State, such as the Blackwater contractors who were involved in the September 2007 Baghdad shootings.[222]

---

217 See Chen, 'Holding "Hired Guns" Accountable: The Legal Status of Private Security Contractors in Iraq' (2009) 32 *Boston College International and Comparative Law Review* 101.

218 18 USC § 3261(b). The Act applies to federal criminal offences punishable by imprison-ment for more than one year: 18 USC § 3261(a).

219 18 USC § 3267(1)(A). 220 18 USC § 3267(1)(c) and (2)(c).

221 US Department of Justice Press Release, 'Two Individuals Charged with Murder and Other Offenses Related to Shooting Death of Two Afghan Nationals in Kabul, Afghanistan' (7 January 2010); Markon, 'Two Defense Contractors Indicted in Shooting of Afghans', *Washington Post* (8 January 2010).

222 Civilian Extraterritorial Jurisdiction Act of 2010, s. 2979, 111th Cong. (2010); Civilian Extraterritorial Jurisdiction Act of 2010, HR 4567, 111th Cong. (2010).

The UCMJ represents another promising tool for US prosecutors to hold wrongdoing PMSC personnel to account.[223] A January 2007 amendment to the UCMJ brought private contractors in contingency operations (such as Iraq and Afghanistan) within US courts martial jurisdiction.[224] In September 2007, the US Deputy Secretary of Defense issued a directive to senior officers in the Pentagon, reminding them that all DOD contractors are subject to UCMJ jurisdiction and that '[c]ommanders also have available to them contract and administrative remedies, and other remedies, including discipline and other possible criminal prosecution'.[225] The first prosecution of a PMSC employee under the UCMJ was conducted in June 2008, albeit for very minor offences.[226] Whilst the UCMJ is broader than the MEJA as applied to PMSC personnel, it still excludes contractors who are not serving with or accompanying US forces in the field. Moreover, given that the trial of civilians in military courts raises due process concerns under the US constitution, it is highly likely that the application of the UCMJ to private contractors will be challenged in the future.[227] Numerous federal court decisions have upheld military convictions of civilians accompanying US forces during declared war,[228] but the Supreme Court has found that subjecting civilians to the UCMJ in peacetime is unconstitutional.[229] It remains unclear whether court martial authority can be constitutionally extended to civilian contractors in contingency operations, which essentially fall between war and peace.

223 See generally Chapman, 'The Untouchables: Private Military Contractors' Criminal Accountability under the UCMJ' (2010) 63(4) *Vanderbilt Law Review* 1047; Chen, 'Holding "Hired Guns" Accountable'.

224 UCMJ, § 802(a)(10); see F. Stockman, 'Contractors in War Zones Lose Immunity', *Boston Globe* (7 January 2007).

225 US Deputy Secretary of Defense, 'Management of Department of Defense Contractors and Contractor Personnel Accompanying US Armed Forces in Contingency Operations Outside the US' (25 September 2007), 2.

226 *US* v. *Alaa 'Alex' Mohammed Ali* (22 June 2008).

227 Hamaguchi, 'Between War and Peace: Exploring the Constitutionality of Subjecting Private Civilian Contractors to the UCMJ during Contingency Operations' (2008) 86 *North Carolina Law Review* 1047; Govern and Bales, 'Taking Shots at Private Military Firms: International Law Misses Its Mark (Again)' (2008–9) 32 *Fordham International Law Journal* 55, 91–5.

228 See, e.g., *In re Berue*, 54 F Supp 252, 254 (SD Ohio 1944) (civilian merchant seaman accompanying the US army); *McCune* v. *Kilpatrick*, 53 F Supp 80, 89 (ED Va 1943) (civilian cook onboard a vessel used to transport troops and supplies); *In re Di Bartolo*, 50 F Supp 929, 933 (SDNY 1943) (civilian employee of an aircraft company in a combat zone).

229 See, e.g., *Reid* v. *Covert*, 352 US 77 (1956); *Kinsella* v. *Krueger*, 351 US 470 (1956); *McElroy* v. *US*, 361 US 281 (1960).

The recent amendments to the UCMJ bring it more into line with the equivalent UK legislation, pursuant to which civilians accompanying the British armed forces can be tried by court martial if they commit a criminal offence overseas.[230] Although the UK system does not raise the same constitutional issues as the UCMJ in the US, the trial of civilians by British military courts has long raised concerns about due process.[231] Jurisprudence of the ECtHR suggests that the trial of civilians by military courts may be incompatible with the defendant's right to a fair trial in Article 6 of the ECHR.[232] In *Ergin* v. *Turkey (No. 6)*, the Court stated that 'only in very exceptional circumstances could the determination of criminal charges against civilians in such courts be held to be compatible with Article 6'.[233] Other human rights bodies have expressed similar concerns.[234] Nonetheless, the House of Lords has rejected arguments that such trials are inherently lacking in independence and impartiality, and therefore incompatible with Article 6 of the ECHR.[235]

In short, both the US and the UK now have jurisdiction to prosecute certain human rights violations committed by PMSCs overseas. The key test for HRL will be whether the authorities exercise due diligence in pursuing these prosecutions in practice.

Access to justice and compensation

Finally, where an individual raises an arguable claim that the hiring state bears responsibility for a PMSC violation, either because the PMSC employee was acting as a state agent or because the state failed to exercise due diligence to prevent, investigate or punish the violation, the state must provide procedures to hear the victim's claim against state authorities and

---

230 See Army Act 1955, ss. 70(2) and 209(2); Air Force Act 1955, ss. 70(2) and 209(2); UK Law Commission, 'The Territorial and Extraterritorial Extent of the Criminal Law' (1978), 34–5.

231 See Borrie, 'Courts-Martial, Civilians and Civil Liberties' (1969) 32 *Modern Law Review* 35.

232 See *Incal* v. *Turkey* (App. No. 22678/93), ECHR, 9 June 1998, paras. 71–3; *Ciraklar* v. *Turkey* (App. No. 19601/92), ECHR, 28 October 1998, paras. 37–41; *Altay* v. *Turkey* (App. No. 22279/93), ECHR, 22 May 2001.

233 *Ergin* v. *Turkey (No. 6)* (App. No. 47533/99), ECHR, 4 May 2006, para. 44.

234 See, e.g., *Cantoral Benavides* v. *Peru*, Judgment of 18 August 2000, IACtHR Ser. C No. 69, para. 112; Human Rights Committee, General Comment 13, 13 April 1984, UN Doc. HRI/GEN/1/Rev.7/Add.1, para. 4; Human Rights Committee, Concluding Observations on Peru (15 November 2000), UN Doc. CCPR/CO/70/PER, para. 11; 4. African Commission on Human and Peoples' Rights, Principles and Guidelines on the Right to a Fair Trial and Legal Assistance in Africa, AU Doc. DOC/OS (XXX) 247.

235 *R* v. *Boyd and others* [2002] UKHL 31; [2002] 3 All ER 1074.

must pay compensation where appropriate.[236] This obligation increases the likelihood that victims of PMSC abuses will obtain redress and that wrongdoing PMSCs and/or their employees will be held to account at the domestic level.

5.4 Conclusion

International law imposes a number of obligations on the hiring state of a PMSC to exercise due diligence and take positive measures to prevent, investigate, punish and redress PMSC violations of international law. The contractual relationship between the hiring state and the PMSC places the state in an excellent position to influence the company's behaviour in the field, particularly in the case of highly developed states such as the US and the UK, which have the necessary resources and institutional capacity to meet a high threshold of diligence.

The obligation to ensure respect for IHL in Common Article 1 establishes a minimum threshold of mandatory regulation for all states that hire PMSCs. This serves as a residual obligation which binds the hiring state in both international and non-international armed conflict, in addition to any more specific IHL obligations that may apply in particular circumstances. The broad scope and universal applicability of this obligation render it a powerful tool for promoting greater state control and accountability in the private security industry, particularly in relation to PMSCs that operate outside the territory of their hiring state.

In certain circumstances, HRL also imposes important obligations on the hiring state to control PMSC behaviour, and these obligations could provide a key mechanism for victims of PMSC abuse to seek redress. However, constraints on extraterritorial applicability limit the utility of HRL in relation to PMSC operations outside the hiring state's territory. This reflects the traditional conception of human rights as protections for individuals against their own government. All of the main human rights treaties will bind the hiring state overseas where it is an occupying power or where it otherwise exercises effective control over the territory in which the PMSC operates or over the individual victim in question. The jurisprudence of the IAComHR indicates that the American Convention will bind the hiring state in relation to an even greater range of PMSC activities overseas, although it is not clear whether that Convention imposes obligations on states parties outside the Americas. In any case,

---

236 See Human Rights Committee, General Comment 31, para. 8; *Velásquez Rodríguez* v. *Honduras*, paras. 176 and 182; *Osman* v. *UK*; Clapham, 'The European Convention on Human Rights', in Scott (ed.), *Torture as Tort* (2001), 515–16; UNCAT, Art. 14.

where human rights obligations are applicable to the hiring state in armed conflict, HRL's sophisticated individual complaint procedures could provide an effective mechanism to scrutinise PMSC behaviour through the responsibility of the hiring state, and the state's obligation to provide an effective remedy could offer victims some hope of obtaining compensation and holding PMSCs to account under domestic law.

The hiring state's due diligence obligations under IHL and HRL could play a key role in establishing state responsibility for PMSC violations in cases where the wrongdoing PMSC employee is *not* acting as an agent or official of the hiring state – that is, where the contractor is neither part of the state's armed forces, nor exercising governmental authority, nor acting under the hiring state's instructions, direction or control. It follows that the relative importance of these obligations in enhancing state responsibility will depend on the scope given to the rules of attribution. The stricter the interpretation of those rules, the more difficult it will be to attribute PMSC misconduct directly to the hiring state and the greater the role for the state's due diligence obligations under IHL and HRL. Further discussion of these due diligence obligations could also play an important prospective role in setting minimum standards of conduct for all states that outsource their military and security activities to PMSCs. This in turn could enhance state control and transparency within the private security industry and improve overall respect for IHL and human rights in the field.

6

Obligations of the home state

International law has thus far been reluctant to impose any broad obligations on the home state of a multinational corporation to regulate the company's activities overseas. Indeed, a state is not generally responsible for the wrongful acts of its nationals abroad, unless of course such acts can be attributed to it under the rules of state responsibility, and there is no general obligation on a state to prevent harmful conduct by its nationals overseas. It follows that the home state of a PMSC – that is, the state in which the company is based or incorporated – will *not* automatically incur international responsibility for violations committed by that PMSC overseas merely by virtue of the territorial link between the state and the company.

Nonetheless, international law imposes a number of obligations on the home state of a PMSC to take certain positive steps to prevent the company from engaging in harmful conduct overseas and to punish any such conduct that occurs. Where an obligation of this nature applies and the home state fails to take the necessary measures, misconduct by the PMSC could give rise to the state's responsibility under international law. The state may fail to prevent local PMSCs from engaging in terrorist activities overseas, for example, or from providing military services to rebels attempting to overthrow the government of a foreign state; indeed, there have been reports of PMSCs providing these services in the past.[1] Responsibility in such cases arises neither from the attribution of the PMSC misconduct to the home state, nor from the state's complicity in that misconduct, but from the state's *own failure* to fulfil its obligation of prevention or punishment.[2]

---

1 See UK Foreign and Commonwealth Office Green Paper, 'Private Military Companies: Options for Regulation' (February 2002), 36–8; O'Brien, 'Military-Advisory Groups and African Security: Privatized Peacekeeping?' (1998) 5(3) *International Peacekeeping* 78.
2 Complicity would require positive state assistance in the commission of the activities: see *Case Concerning the Application of the Convention on the Prevention and Punishment of the*

The first section of this chapter discusses the general principle in the *Corfu Channel* case and assesses the extent to which it may apply to the modern private security industry. The subsequent four sections then examine four specific fields of international law which may impose pertinent obligations on the home state of a PMSC: the norm of non-intervention in the internal affairs of states, the law of neutrality, international humanitarian law (IHL) and human rights law (HRL).

6.1 General obligation to prevent private acts harmful to other states?

The ICJ recognised in the *Corfu Channel* case the 'general and well-recognised' principle that every state has an obligation 'not to allow knowingly its territory to be used for acts contrary to the rights of other states.'[3] This derives from the fundamental principle of state sovereignty, which not only grants to states the right to decide what acts shall or shall not be done in their territory, but which also imposes an obligation on states to take certain positive measures to secure, in their territory, respect for the sovereignty of other states.[4]

The *Corfu Channel* case involved Albanian responsibility for mine explosions which struck and damaged two British destroyers in Albanian territorial waters. Although the Court accepted that Albania had not laid the mines, it concluded from the evidence that the laying of the mines could not have been accomplished without the knowledge of the Albanian government. That knowledge gave rise to an obligation on the part of Albania to take specific measures to prevent the mines from causing harm to the vessels of other states, namely, to notify shipping generally of the existence of the minefield and to warn the approaching British ships of the imminent danger. Albania's failure to take those measures gave rise to its international responsibility for the damage caused to the British vessels by the explosion of the mines. The Court held that the obligation of prevention was based on

---

Crime of Genocide (Bosnia and Herzegovina v. Serbia and Montenegro) (Merits) (26 February 2007), para. 432; International Law Commission Articles on Responsibility of States for Internationally Wrongful Acts with Commentaries (2001) *Yearbook of the International Law Commission*, vol. II(2), Art. 16; Ago, 'Fourth Report on State Responsibility' (1972) *Yearbook of the International Law Commission*, vol. II, para. 65.

3 *Corfu Channel (UK v. Albania)* (Merits) ICJ Reports 1949, 22.

4 See W. E. Hall, *The Rights and Duties of Neutrals* (1874), 16–18; García-Mora, *International Responsibility for Hostile Acts of Private Persons Against Foreign States* (1962), 50–1; UN Secretariat, Survey of International Law, UN Doc. A/CN4/1 Rev.1 (1949), 34–5.

certain general and well-recognised principles, namely: elementary considerations of humanity, even more exacting in peace than in war; the principle of the freedom of maritime communication; and every state's obligation not to allow knowingly its territory to be used for acts contrary to the rights of other states.[5]

Although in the *Corfu Channel* case the damage to the injured state (the UK) took place in the territory of the state that harboured the initial source of danger (Albania), the same general principle could be applied to cases in which the damage took place in the territory of the injured state or a third state. As Brownlie explains,

> the principles at work in the *Corfu Channel* Case apply in those cases in which the harm to other states occurs beyond the boundaries of the state harbouring the source of danger. Activities of this class include the operations of armed bands and pirates, always assuming that the state is liable for failing to control rather than actual control or connivance.[6]

In relation to the prohibition of the use of force, which was in issue in the *Corfu Channel* case itself, it is widely accepted that states have an obligation to take positive steps to prevent private acts in state territory that are directed against the territorial integrity of another state.[7] Beyond the use of force context, the general principle on which the ICJ relied in the *Corfu Channel* case forms the basis for a number of more specific obligations, which can be broadly grouped together as obligations to prevent 'transboundary harm'.[8] Such obligations are well established in (*inter alia*) international environmental law,[9] the international law on terrorism,[10] the prohibition of intervention in the internal affairs of other states,[11] and the law of neutrality.[12] The latter two fields are particularly pertinent to this book and are examined in the second and third sections

---

5 *Corfu Channel*, 22.   6 Brownlie, *State Responsibility* (1983), 182.

7 See, e.g., UNGA Res. 2625 (XXV) (24 October 1970), UN Doc. A/8028.

8 See Bratspies and Miller (eds.), *Transboundary Harm in International Law* (2006).

9 See *Trail Smelter Arbitration* (1938) 2 RIAA 1905; International Law Commission Draft Articles on the Prevention of Transboundary Harm from Hazardous Activities with Commentaries (2001) *Yearbook of the International Law Commission*, vol. II(2); Francioni and Scovazzi (eds.), *International Responsibility for Environmental Harm* (1991); Gehring and Jachtenfuchs, 'Liability for Transboundary Environmental Damage: Towards a General Liability Regime?' (1993) 4 *EJIL* 92.

10 See UNGA Res. 49/60 (9 December 1994), UN Doc. A/RES/49/60.

11 See UNGA Res. 2625, para. 2.

12 See Convention Respecting the Rights and Duties of Neutral Powers and Persons in Case of War on Land (adopted 18 October 1907, entered into force 26 January 1910), 205 Consol TS 299 ('Hague V'), Art. 5.

of this chapter. In addition, specific duties of prevention are contained in a number of treaties in various contexts, such as the obligation to prevent genocide in Article 1 of the Genocide Convention.[13] Although in practice the lack of jurisprudence in other fields might appear to limit the scope of the general obligation enunciated in the *Corfu Channel* case, this lack of jurisprudence does not necessarily exclude the existence of a preventive duty in other contexts. In principle, the reasoning of the ICJ in the *Corfu Channel* case could certainly be applied in other fields, and this provides scope for the development of the traditional rules of international law to accommodate the modern private security industry.

Once it is shown that international law imposes an obligation on the home state to take positive steps to prevent a particular PMSC activity in state territory, two additional factors must be established before that state will incur responsibility for a violation of its obligation: first, there must be a failure by the state to take adequate preventive measures; and, secondly, there must be a specific instance of the prohibited PMSC activity in question. As explained in Chapter 2, a state's failure to take adequate preventive steps may result either from broad structural inadequacies in the state system or from the failure of individual state agents to *use* that system diligently to prevent PMSC misconduct in a particular case. Therefore a state cannot escape liability for failing to prevent a prohibited PMSC activity simply because it had previously failed to enact laws that would have enabled its administrative and judicial authorities to prevent or suppress that activity. In *Alabama Claims*, for example, Britain could not plead the insufficiency of its neutrality legislation to escape liability to the US for the violation by private individuals of British neutrality.[14]

Obligations of prevention generally entail a due diligence standard of conduct, requiring states to take all measures reasonably within their power to prevent the prohibited activities, as far as possible. Chapter 2 critically examined the notion of due diligence and noted that it entails a 'flexible reasonableness standard adaptable to the particular facts and

---

13 Convention on the Prevention and Punishment of the Crime of Genocide (adopted 9 December 1948, entered into force 12 January 1951), 78 UNTS 277.
14 *Alabama Claims (US* v. *Britain)* (1871); see also *Baldwin (US)* v. *Mexico* (11 April 1838) in J. B. Moore, *History and Digest of the International Arbitrations to which the US has been a Party* (1898), 2623; *Noyes* (1933) 6 RIAA 308, 311; *Kennedy* (1927) 4 RIAA 194, 198; W. E. Hall, *International Law*, 8th edn (1924), 641–2; Lauterpacht, 'Revolutionary Activities by Private Persons Against Foreign States' (1928) 22 *AJIL* 105, 128; Borchard, *Diplomatic Protection of Citizens Abroad* (1928), § 86.

circumstances'.[15] While the precise requirements of due diligence will depend on the particular obligation in question, factors relevant to the assessment may include the risk that the individual's activities will give rise to a violation of international law, the level of influence that the state exercises over the relevant PMSC, and the resources that are available to the state to take preventive measures.

Bearing in mind these general comments, the remaining four sections of this chapter examine four specific fields of international law – the prohibition of intervention, the law of neutrality, IHL and HRL – in order to identify the most pertinent obligations of prevention on the home state of a PMSC.

6.2 Obligation to prevent PMSC intervention into other states

It is a fundamental tenet of international law that a state must not intervene, directly or indirectly, in the affairs of another state. This principle not only prohibits interventions carried out by state agents and officials, but it also imposes an obligation on states to take certain positive steps to prevent or punish egregious interventions by private actors operating from state territory.

This section considers the application of the norm of non-intervention to the modern private security industry. In particular, it examines the situation where a PMSC based or incorporated in one state (the home state) is hired to provide military or security services in another state (the host state), in order to help fight a civil war or carry out a coup against the government of the host state. In such a scenario, the PMSC may be hired either by a third state or by a rebel group seeking to overthrow the host state government.

Although the majority of PMSCs denounce the provision of services to rebel groups seeking to overthrow a foreign government, there have been reports of PMSCs working for such groups in the past. For example, the UK Green Paper notes that Laurent Kabila's rebel forces allegedly hired Omega Support Ltd and International Defence and Security to fight against President Mobutu in the former Zaire in 1996–7.[16] After Kabila became president of the newly named Democratic Republic of the Congo, rebels fighting against his government reportedly hired SafeNet in 1998 to provide military services.[17] Similarly, the Florida-based PMSC AirScan

---

15 Barnidge, *Non-State Actors and Terrorism: Applying the Law of State Responsibility and the Due Diligence Principle* (2007), 138.
16 UK Green Paper, 36–7.   17 *Ibid.*, 38.

reportedly provided military support to rebels in Uganda in 1997–8,[18] and may have provided weapons to rebels in the Sudan.[19] There have also been reports of PMSCs being hired by the government of a state that is attempting to overthrow the government of another state. For example, O'Brien notes that the Angolan MPLA government hired AirScan in October 1997 and then just weeks later overthrew the democratically elected government in Congo-Brazzaville.[20] These incidents illustrate that disreputable PMSCs acting on the fringes of the industry could trigger the international responsibility of their home state for a failure to comply with the norm of non-intervention.[21]

This section first identifies the relevant obligations on the home state of a PMSC under the norm of non-intervention. It then considers the precise PMSC activities that the home state is obliged to prevent or punish, and identifies the positive action that the home state should take to discharge these obligations.

Sources of the norm of non-intervention

There are two main sources of rules governing the legality of intervention: the UN Charter and customary international law. The UN Charter contains a prohibition of the use of force by states and a prohibition of intervention by the UN, but it does not explicitly impose an obligation of non-intervention on states. Article 2(4) provides that all member states must 'refrain from the threat or use of force against the territorial integrity or political independence of any state, or in any other manner inconsistent with the purposes of the United Nations'. Article 2(7) prohibits the UN from intervening 'in matters which are essentially within the domestic jurisdiction of any state'. Although in its terms Article 2(7) is merely a rule of constitutional competence for an international organisation, it is commonly regarded as reflecting the general principle of non-intervention.[22] Article 2(1), concerning sovereign equality, and Article 1(2), concerning

---

18 *Ibid.*, 36.
19 Peck, 'Re-Militarizing Africa for Corporate Profit' (October 2000) *Z-Magazine*.
20 O'Brien, 'Military-Advisory Groups and African Security'.
21 In addition, in June 2007 the US charged eleven individuals with conspiring to overthrow the government of Laos. Although no PMSCs were involved, this incident demonstrates the potential market in the US for private actors to help overthrow a foreign government: see US Department of Justice Press Release 4 June 2007, www.usdoj.gov/usao/cae/press_releases/docs/2007/06-04-07JackPress Rlspdf.
22 See McGoldrick, 'The Principle of Non-intervention: Human Rights', in Lowe and Warbrick (eds.), *The UN and the Principles of International Law* (1994), 88.

the equal rights of peoples and their right of self-determination, provide further legal bases for the principle of non-intervention.[23]

The ICJ made it clear in *Nicaragua* that the prohibition of intervention also constitutes an essential principle of customary international law.[24] The Court expressly stated that the formulation in General Assembly Resolution 2625 (XXV) (1970) reflects the customary rule.[25] Paragraph 1 of that Resolution provides:

> No State or group of States has the right to intervene, directly or indirectly, for any reason whatever, in the internal or external affairs of any other State. Consequently, armed intervention and all other forms of interference or attempted threats against the personality of the state or against its political, economic and cultural elements, are in violation of international law.

Paragraph 2 provides:

> ... Also, no State shall organise, assist, foment, finance, incite *or tolerate* subversive, terrorist or armed activities directed towards the violent over-throw of the regime of another State, or interfere in civil strife in another State.[26]

The word 'tolerate' in paragraph 2 is crucial to the current analysis. According to the *Oxford English Dictionary*, to 'tolerate' X is 'to allow [X] to exist or to be done or practised *without authoritative interference*'.[27] It is generally accepted that the obligation not to tolerate the activities identified in Resolution 2625 requires states to take positive steps and exercise due diligence to prevent those activities in state territory.[28] Some earlier formulations of the obligation made this clear. For example, Article 1 of the 1928 Convention on the Duties and Rights of States in the Event of Civil Strife obliges the contracting parties 'to use all means at their disposal to prevent the inhabitants of their territories, nationals or aliens, from

---

23 See Sahovic, 'Non-Intervention in the Internal Affairs of States', in Sahovic (ed.), *Principles of International Law Concerning Friendly Relations and Cooperation* (1969), 249–50.

24 *Military and Paramilitary Activities In and Against Nicaragua (Nicaragua v. USA)* (Merits) ICJ Reports 1986, para. 202.

25 *Nicaragua*, para. 264.   26 Emphasis added.

27 Simpson and Weiner, *Oxford English Dictionary*, 2nd edn (1989), 200 (emphasis added).

28 See Wright, 'Subversive Intervention' (1960) 54 *AJIL* 521, 531; A. V. W. Thomas and A. J. Thomas Jr, 'International Legal Aspects of the Civil War in Spain, 1936–39', in Falk (ed.), *The International Law of Civil War* (1971), 154; Lin, 'Subversive Intervention' (1963) 25 *University of Pittsburgh Law Review* 35, 38; García-Mora, *International Responsibility for Hostile Acts of Private Persons Against Foreign States*.

participating in, gathering elements, crossing the boundary or sailing from their territory for the purpose of starting or promoting civil strife'.[29]

Prohibited PMSC activities

PMSC involvement in 'subversive, terrorist or armed activities directed towards the violent overthrow of the regime of another State' is a pre-condition to the international responsibility of the home state of that PMSC.

'[S]ubversive, terrorist or armed activities'

The term 'subversive activities' in Resolution 2625 refers to acts that are intended or likely to incite revolt against the government. It is usually discussed in the context of propaganda against a foreign government or infiltration into the political organisations of another state, a context which is not pertinent to this book.[30] The norm of non-intervention does not generally require states to prevent criticism of, or propaganda directed against, other states or governments on the part of private persons; indeed, such a requirement would undermine the fundamental right of freedom of expression.[31] States are required, however, to exercise due diligence to suppress private propaganda that *directly* incites the overthrow of the government of another state, at least where there exists a 'clear and present danger' that such incitement will succeed.[32] Contracts involving the provision of military advice/training by a PMSC based or incorporated in one state to rebel forces operating in another state could constitute 'subversive activities' if that advice/training was intended or likely to *directly* incite revolt against the government of the host state. Other PMSC services, however, would be unlikely to fall within the scope of 'subversive activities' for the purposes of Resolution 2625.

The term 'terrorist activities' covers a wide range of diverse criminal acts linked to the rather elusive notion of 'terrorism'.[33] The basic element

---

29 Convention on the Duties and Rights of States in the Event of Civil Strife (20 February 1928), 134 LNTS 25.
30 See, e.g., Wright, 'Subversive Intervention', 529–33; Lauterpacht, 'Revolutionary Activities by Private Persons Against Foreign States', 126.
31 Jennings and Watts (eds.), *Oppenheim's International Law*, 9th edn (1992), 393, 403–6; Wright, 'Subversive Intervention', 530–1.
32 Wright, 'Subversive Intervention', 531.
33 For a detailed analysis of states' obligations to prevent terrorism, see Barnidge, *Non-State Actors and Terrorism*, chs. 4–5.

of terrorism is that it is done with some kind of political motive, as reflected in one definition in General Assembly Resolution 49/60 (1994): 'Criminal acts intended or calculated to provoke a state of terror in the general public, a group of persons or particular persons for political purposes.'[34] Yet it has proved virtually impossible to pin down the precise elements that distinguish terrorism from ordinary criminal activity and to express those elements in an internationally accepted legal definition.[35] Higgins discussed this difficulty in 1997 and concluded that terrorism is 'a term without any legal significance . . . a convenient way of alluding to activities, whether of states or of individuals, widely disapproved of and in which either the methods used are unlawful, or the targets protected, or both'.[36]

Notwithstanding the absence of any agreed definition of terrorism in international law, there is now widespread agreement on how to identify certain specific terrorist activities, and the duty of due diligence in the context of terrorism has been developed through treaties and the activities of the UN.[37] International efforts to define and criminalise terrorist activities increased dramatically following the attacks of 11 September 2001 and the adoption of Security Council Resolution 1373, which calls on states to become parties to the various international instruments on terrorism.[38] Around two-thirds of UN member states have either ratified or acceded to at least ten of the sixteen international counter-terrorism instruments.[39] These instruments require states to suppress various activities linked to terrorism including terrorist financing,[40]

---

34 UNGA Res. 49/60 (9 December 1994), UN Doc. A/RES/49/60. Cassese considers this to be 'an acceptable definition of terrorism': see Cassese, *International Law*, 2nd edn (2005), 449.

35 See generally Saul, *Defining Terrorism in International Law* (2006).

36 Higgins, 'The General International Law of Terrorism', in Higgins and Flory (eds.), *Terrorism and International Law* (1997) 13, 28; see also Baxter, 'A Sceptical Look at the Concept of Terrorism' (1974) 7(2) *Akron Law Review* 380.

37 See Pejić, 'Terrorist Acts and Groups: A Role for International Law?' (2004) 75 *British Yearbook of International Law* 71, 95–6; Dupuy and Hoss, 'Trail Smelter and Terrorism', in Bratspies and Miller (eds.), *Transboundary Harm in International Law* (2006); Dubuisson, 'Vers un Renforcement des Obligations de Diligence en Matière de Lutte Contre le Terrorisme', in K. T. Bannelier, O. Corten Christakis and B. Delcourt (eds.), *Le Droit International Face au Terrorisme* (2002).

38 UNSC Res. 1373 (28 September 2001), UN Doc. S/RES/1373.

39 See UN Security Council Counter-Terrorism Committee: www.un.org/sc/ctc/laws.html.

40 International Convention for the Suppression of the Financing of Terrorism (adopted 9 December 1999, entered into force 10 April 2002), UN Doc. A/RES/54/109.

aircraft hijacking,[41] hostage taking,[42] unlawful acts against the safety of maritime navigation,[43] unlawful acts against the safety of civil aviation[44] or of airports serving international civil aviation,[45] the theft of nuclear material,[46] the use of plastic explosives,[47] attacks on diplomats,[48] nuclear terrorism[49] and terrorist bombings.[50] Thus, states have preferred to adopt a piecemeal approach to this problem by drawing up a number of separate conventions aimed at suppressing specific terrorist activities, rather than articulating a general international definition of terrorism as such.

In relation to the norm of non-intervention, a sensible approach would be to construe the term 'terrorist activities' in Resolution 2625 as encompassing the commission, attempted commission or conspiracy to commit any of the core activities defined in the sixteen international counter-terrorism instruments mentioned above, as well as the provision of direct material support (such as money, weapons, or expert advice or training)

---

41 Convention on Offences and Certain Other Acts Committed on Board Aircraft (adopted 14 September 1963, entered into force 4 December 1969), 704 UNTS 219; Convention for the Suppression of Unlawful Seizure of Aircraft (adopted 16 December 1970, entered into force 14 October 1971), 860 UNTS 105.

42 International Convention Against the Taking of Hostages (adopted 17 December 1979, entered into force 3 June 1983), UN Doc. A/C.6/34/L.23.

43 Convention for the Suppression of Unlawful Acts Against the Safety of Maritime Navigation (adopted 10 March 1988, entered into force 1 March 1992), 27 ILM 672; Protocol to the Convention for the Suppression of Unlawful Acts Against the Safety of Maritime Navigation (adopted 14 October 2005); Protocol for the Suppression of Unlawful Acts Against the Safety of Fixed Platforms Located on the Continental Shelf (adopted 10 March 1988, entered into force 1 March 1992), 27 ILM 685; Protocol to the Protocol for the Suppression of Unlawful Acts Against the Safety of Fixed Platforms Located on the Continental Shelf (adopted 14 October 2005).

44 Convention for the Suppression of Unlawful Acts Against the Safety of Civil Aviation (adopted 23 September 1971, entered into force 26 January 1973), 974 UNTS 178.

45 Protocol for the Suppression of Unlawful Acts of Violence at Airports Serving International Civil Aviation (adopted 24 February 1988, entered into force 6 August 1989), 27 ILM 627.

46 Convention on the Physical Protection of Nuclear Material (adopted 26 October 1979, entered into force 8 February 1987), TIAS 11080; Amendments to the Convention on the Physical Protection of Nuclear Material (adopted 8 July 2005).

47 Convention on the Marking of Plastic Explosives for the Purpose of Detection (adopted 1 March 1991, entered into force 21 June 1998).

48 Convention on the Prevention and Punishment of Crimes Against Internationally Protected Persons, Including Diplomatic Agents (adopted 14 December 1973, entered into force 20 February 1977), 1035 UNTS 167.

49 International Convention for the Suppression of Acts of Nuclear Terrorism (adopted 13 April 2005, entered into force 7 July 2007), UN Doc. A/RES/59/290.

50 International Convention for the Suppression of Terrorist Bombings (adopted 15 December 1997, entered into force 23 May 2001), UN Doc. A/52/653.

for those activities.[51] This conception would encompass PMSCs contracted to provide military/security services to help a client plan or carry out any of the core activities prohibited by the sixteen counter-terrorism instruments.

Finally, 'armed activities' in Resolution 2625 is a more general term which essentially encompasses any organised activities that utilise weapons with the intention of causing serious damage to persons or property. A PMSC would seem to fall within the term 'armed activities' for the purposes of the state's obligation in Resolution 2625 if it provided military or security services to help a client plan or carry out activities of this nature.

'[D]irected towards the violent overthrow of'

In assessing whether a particular PMSC activity may give rise to the responsibility of the home state, it is also necessary to examine the *purpose* towards which that activity is directed, since Resolution 2625 imposes on states a duty to prevent only those activities that are 'directed towards the violent overthrow of the regime of another state'. Indeed, this unlawful objective is the very essence of the prohibition of intervention.

Where a PMSC based or incorporated in one state (the home state) enters into a contract with a rebel group that is seeking to overthrow the government of another state (the host state) in a violent manner, and the PMSC is aware of that objective, the activities of the PMSC under the contract will be 'directed towards the violent overthrow' of the regime of the host state. Such knowledge may be inferred from the surrounding circumstances, particularly in the context of a military coup or civil war against the incumbent government. On the other hand, where the PMSC enters into a contract with the government of a third state (the hiring state), rather than a rebel group, the overall objective of the operation may be less clear. The third state may deny that it is attempting to overthrow the government of the host state, or it may claim that it has been invited by the government of the host state to assist in quelling internal unrest. In such cases, the objective of attempting violently to overthrow the government of another state would need to be reasonably clear from the terms of the

---

51 In relation to material support see, e.g., Council of Europe Convention on the Prevention of Terrorism 2006 (adopted 16 May 2005, entered into force 1 June 2007), CETS No. 196, Art. 7; UK Terrorism Act 2006, s. 6; US Patriot Act 2001, s. 805; US Intelligence Reform and Terrorism Prevention Act 2004, s. 6603.

contract or the nature of the operation, or both, in order to fall within the formulation in Resolution 2625.

'[T]he regime of another state'

As the obligation not to 'tolerate' applies only to activities directed towards the violent overthrow of the regime of another state, it is necessary to determine how to identify a particular regime as the government. A regime is generally recognised as the legitimate government of a state when it exercises *de facto* control over state territory.[52] Whereas a widely recognised government has the sovereign right to request foreign assistance to suppress internal unrest or simply to enhance its military strength,[53] the provision of aid to a rebel group is unequivocally unlawful – even after a full-scale civil war has erupted and control over state territory is divided between the warring parties.[54] Some commentators contend that aid to the government is also prohibited after the conflict has reached the threshold of a civil war,[55] whereas others argue that such aid must be frozen at pre-civil war levels.[56] Regardless of whether it retains the sovereign right to request outside assistance, the government of a state generally continues to represent the state in its international relations well beyond the moment that it loses control of the country and until the time that another, identifiable group has gained control.[57] For example, in the 1990s President Kabbah's government continued to represent

---

52 See, e.g., 'US Statement of 1977', in Harris (ed.), *Cases and Materials on International Law*, 6th edn (2004); UK Statement of 1980 (1980) 51 *British Yearbook of International Law* 367; Warbrick, 'The New British Policy on Recognition of Governments' (1981) 30 *ICLQ* 568; Talmon, 'Recognition of Governments: An Analysis of the New British Policy and Practice' (1992) 63 *British Yearbook of International Law* 231.

53 UNSC Res. 387 (31 March 1976), UN Doc. S/RES/387; UNGA Res. 3314 (XXIX) (14 December 1974), UN Doc. A/9631, Art. 3(e); *Nicaragua*, para. 246.

54 *Nicaragua*, para. 246.

55 See, e.g., W. E. Hall, *International Law*, 346; Wright, 'US Intervention in the Lebanon' (1959) 53 *AJIL* 112, 121–2.

56 See, e.g., Farer, 'Harnessing Rogue Elephants: A Short Discourse on Foreign Intervention in Civil Strife' (1969) 82 *Harvard Law Review* 511; J. N. Moore, 'Intervention: A Monochromatic Term for a Polychromatic Reality', in Falk (ed.), *The Vietnam War and International Law* (1969); Friedmann, 'Intervention, Civil War and the Role of International Law' (1965) 59 *American Society of International Law and Procedure* 67; Wippman, 'Change and Continuity in Legal Justifications for Military Intervention in Internal Conflicts' (1996) 27 *Columbia Human Rights Law Review* 435, 439–40.

57 Doswald-Beck, 'The Legal Validity of Military Intervention by Invitation of the Government' (1985) 56 *British Yearbook of International Law* 189, 197–200.

Sierra Leone in the General Assembly even after he had fled to Guinea.[58] Thus, once a regime is widely recognised as the government of a state by virtue of its exercise of *de facto* control over state territory, that regime will continue to qualify as 'the regime of' the state for the purposes of the norm of non-intervention, even after the outbreak of a civil war and until the time that another single regime has itself been recognised as the new government.

Positive action to discharge the obligation

The obligation not to tolerate the activities identified in Resolution 2625 requires states to exercise due diligence and take all measures reasonably within their power to prevent those activities in state territory. In order to fulfil this obligation, states will first need to ensure that they have adequate legislative, administrative and judicial arrangements in place to prevent, detect, restrain and punish the prohibited activities. States will then need to exercise due diligence to prevent particular prohibited activities and to detect, investigate and punish such activities where they occur or are about to occur.[59] Of course, the notion of 'tolerance' clearly implies some degree of state knowledge or wilful blindness. It follows that, for the home state to incur responsibility for tolerating PMSC activities that violate the norm of non-intervention, it must be shown that the state was aware or ought to have been aware that the activities were occurring or that there was a serious risk that they would occur in the future.[60] Such knowledge may be inferred from the circumstances, as occurred in the *Corfu Channel* case.[61]

There have been sporadic reports of PMSCs providing services to clients attempting to challenge the government of a foreign state, and there is a serious risk that disreputable firms operating at the fringes of the industry will provide services to such clients in the future. It is highly likely that some of those firms will be based in states with a flourishing private

---

58 See UN Press Release SC/6481, 'Security Council Stresses Need for Immediate Restoration of Democratically Elected Government to Sierra Leone' (26 February 1998).

59 See generally Pisillo-Mazzeschi, 'The Due Diligence Rule and the Nature of the International Responsibility of States' (1992) 35 *German Yearbook of International Law* 9, 26–30; Borchard, *Diplomatic Protection of Citizens Abroad*, § 86; UNGA Res. 60/147 (16 December 2005), UN Doc. A/RES/60/147, paras. 2–3.

60 Hampson, 'Mercenaries: Diagnosis before Proscription' (1991) 3 *Netherlands Yearbook of International Law* 1, 22.

61 *Corfu Channel*, 18.

security industry but little or no governmental regulation, such as the UK. The British government's 2002 Green Paper entitled 'Private Military Companies: Options for Regulation' demonstrates its knowledge of the risks posed by PMSCs and of the need to regulate the local industry. Due diligence would therefore appear to require the government to take special measures of prevention targeting the local industry. More recent governmental policy papers, however, indicate a preference for non-binding self-regulation rather than a formal regulatory regime.[62] This reflects the broader problem that the UK, 'despite being closely associated with the world of private security, since at least the 1970s... has an unfortunate pattern of dealing with the problems caused by private force in civil wars abroad after they occur'.[63] In these circumstances, if a British PMSC were to undertake one of the prohibited activities identified in Resolution 2625, the UK would risk incurring international responsibility for 'tolerating' private interventions into the internal affairs of another state.

One possible means for states to discharge their obligations under Resolution 2625 would be to establish a licensing scheme for PMSCs based or incorporated in state territory. The envisaged scheme would require all local PMSCs initially to register with the government and subsequently to obtain a governmental licence for each and every contract that they concluded with a foreign client for the provision of military or security services. Such a scheme would incorporate considerations of intervention law into the criteria against which PMSC contracts were assessed, thereby enabling the government to refuse to license PMSC contracts that may involve the activities prohibited by Resolution 2625. Any PMSCs that provided military or security services without governmental approval would incur sanctions and could be barred from operating in the home state altogether.

Licensing schemes of this nature currently operate in the US[64] and South Africa.[65] The British government recommended the establishment

---

62 See UK Foreign and Commonwealth Office Consultation Paper, 'Consultation on Promoting High Standards of Conduct by Private Military and Security Companies Internationally' (April 2009); UK Foreign and Commonwealth Office Impact Assessment, 'Promoting High Standards of Conduct by Private Military and Security Companies Internationally' (April 2009).

63 Percy, 'Private Security Companies and Civil Wars' (2009) 11(1) *Civil Wars* 57, 66.

64 Arms Export Control Act 1976; International Traffic in Arms Regulations 22 CFR Parts 120–30.

65 Prohibition of Mercenary Activities and Regulation of Certain Activities in Country of Armed Conflict Act 2007; see also Caparini, 'Licensing Regimes for the Export of Military Goods and Services', in Chesterman and Lehnardt (eds.), *From Mercenaries to Market: The Rise and Regulation of Private Military Companies* (2007), 158; Taljaard, 'Implementing

of a similar scheme in its 2002 Green Paper, but then failed to take any further action.[66] The 'good practices' section of the 2008 Montreux Document, which was discussed in earlier chapters of this book, recommends that home states 'consider establishing' an authorisation system for the provision of military and security services abroad.[67] The Montreux Document also recommends the harmonisation of export authorisation systems with other states, possibly through 'regional approaches',[68] a suggestion which was intended to allow room for the adaptation of the approach used in the European Arms Export Code[69] to the export of military and security services.[70] The implementation of a licensing scheme for local PMSCs would help to ensure that the home state fulfils not only its obligations under the norm of non-intervention, but also its obligations under the law of neutrality and IHL, discussed below.

6.3 Obligations to control PMSCs under the law of neutrality

In certain contemporary international armed conflicts, the law of neutrality imposes obligations on neutral states to control private military and security activities originating from their territory. The law of neutrality is redundant in respect of non-international armed conflicts, however, as it has been subsumed within the prohibition of intervention in the affairs of other states.[71]

This section examines how the law of neutrality may be relevant to the modern private security industry, particularly in international armed conflicts in which the home state of a PMSC is neutral whereas the

South Africa's Regulation of Foreign Military Assistance Act', in Bryden and Caparini (eds.), *Private Actors and Security Governance* (2006).

66 See UK Green Paper, 24–5; Foreign Affairs Committee Ninth Report, 'Private Military Companies' (October 2002).

67 Montreux Document on Pertinent International Legal Obligations and Good Practices for States Related to Operations of Private Military and Security Companies during Armed Conflict (17 September 2008), UN Doc. A/63/467-S/2008/636 ('Montreux Document'), Part II, para. 54.

68 *Ibid.*, Part II, para. 56.

69 European Union Code of Conduct for Arms Exports (8 June 1998).

70 See Cockayne, 'Regulating Private Military and Security Companies: The Content, Negotiation, Weaknesses and Promise of the Montreux Document' (2009) 13(3) *Journal of Conflict and Security Law* 401, 413.

71 Higgins, 'International Law and Civil Conflict', in Luard (ed.), *The International Regulation of Civil Wars* (1972), 171; Gomulkiewicz, 'International Law Governing Aid to Opposition Groups in Civil War: Resurrecting the Standards of Belligerency' (1988) 63 *Washington Law Review* 42, 48; *Santissima Trinidad*, 20 US (7 Wheat) 283 (1822), 337–8; Layeb, 'Mercenary Activity: United States Neutrality Laws and Enforcement' (1989) 10 *New York Law School Journal of International and Comparative Law* 269, 291–2.

hiring state is a belligerent. It first discusses the general applicability of the law of neutrality to modern international armed conflicts. It then considers the obligations on the home state in relation to PMSCs, the steps that the home state should take to discharge these obligations, and the particular PMSC activities that may jeopardise the home state's neutrality.

Applicability of the law of neutrality to modern conflicts

The traditional law of neutrality

Whilst the basic notion of neutrality as non-participation in war has a long history, the conception of neutrality as a formal legal status involving defined rights and duties appeared to emerge only in the eighteenth century.[72] By the nineteenth century, it had developed into a sophisticated and well-defined system of rights and obligations applicable in wartime.

The Hague Conventions of 1907 codified the customary rules of neutrality in the earliest formalised international laws of war in the modern state system. Under the Hague Conventions and customary law, the applicability and operation of the law of neutrality were relatively clear. Belligerents would first notify third states of the existence of a state of war,[73] and third states then had a duty to choose a status of either co-belligerent or neutral and to declare their decision formally. That declaration established a legal relationship of neutrals and belligerents, and brought into operation the entire system of neutrality law, which then remained in operation until the official termination of the war or until either a belligerent or a neutral chose to assume an active belligerent status towards the other.[74]

The law of neutrality post-1945

The efforts to outlaw war following World War I, which culminated in Article 2(4) of the UN Charter, called into question the very philosophy

72 See P. C. Jessup, F. Deák, W. Alison Phillips, A. H. Reede and E. W. Turlington, *Neutrality, Its History, Economics and Law* (1935), vol. I, 4, 20–1 and 249; Wright, 'The Future of Neutrality' (1928–9) 12 *International Conciliation* 353, 363; Lauterpacht (ed.), *Oppenheim's International Law*, 7th edn (1952), vol. I, 626–7.

73 Convention Relative to the Opening of Hostilities (adopted 18 October 1907, entered into force 26 January 1910), 205 Consol TS 263 ('Hague III'), Art. 2.

74 See Norton, 'Between the Ideology and the Reality: The Shadow of the Law of Neutrality' (1976) 17 *Harvard International Law Journal* 249, 250; Lauterpacht (ed.), *Oppenheim's International Law*, 7th edn, vol. I, 653–4 and 666–72.

underlying the law of neutrality. 'The foundation of the doctrine of neutrality was the absolute right of the state to resort to war',[75] but Article 2(4) of the Charter effectively outlawed war by prohibiting the threat or use of force by states. In the legal order envisaged by the Charter, the Security Council would adopt a binding Chapter VII resolution designating the aggressor in any armed conflict. All or some member states (as determined by the Security Council pursuant to Article 48) would then be bound to participate in any subsequent collective military action, and all member states would be bound by Articles 2(5) and 25 to support the action and to refrain from taking any measures to impede it.[76]

In certain circumstances, the collective security system established by the Charter supersedes the traditional law of neutrality. Specifically, where the Security Council has made an authoritative determination of the aggressor or wrongdoer in an armed conflict, Articles 2(5) and 25 impose an obligation on member states *not* to adopt a strict neutral stance in the traditional sense, at least to the extent that such a stance involves the granting of belligerent rights to the aggressor.[77] This obligation takes precedence over states' other international obligations by virtue of Article 103. In such cases, states wishing to remain neutral may only adopt a stance of 'qualified' neutrality, which involves non-participation in the hostilities but which does not require absolute impartiality towards both parties to the conflict. This non-participation does *not* bring into play the traditional law of neutrality, as that system contemplates only two relations: belligerency and strict neutrality.[78]

75 Lauterpacht, 'The Revision of the Law of War' (1952) 29 *British Yearbook of International Law* 360, 369; see also Brownlie, *International Law and the Use of Force by States* (1963), 402–4; Schwarzenberger, *International Law as Applied by International Courts and Tribunals* (1968), 664–6.

76 Art. 39 authorises the Security Council to determine the existence of any threat to the peace, breach of the peace or act of aggression and to make recommendations or decide what measures shall be taken to maintain or restore international peace and security. The Security Council may then take binding measures falling short of the use of force under Art. 41, or it may authorise the use of force under Art. 42. Art. 25 obliges all members to comply with Security Council decisions.

77 The Security Council has in some cases made a binding determination as to which party in a conflict is the aggressor: see, e.g., UNSC Res. 454 (2 November 1979), UN Doc. S/RES/454 (South African aggression against Angola) and UNSC Res. 573 (4 October 1985), UN Doc. S/RES/573 (Israeli aggression against Tunisia).

78 W. E. Hall, *Neutrals*, 14. A number of treaties concluded since 1945 implicitly accept that non-participation in hostilities is a valid position that is distinct from strict neutrality: see, e.g., GCIII, Arts. 4B(2) and 122; Protocol I, Arts. 9(2)(a), 19 and 31.

The UN Charter did not render the traditional law of neutrality entirely redundant, however, since in the overwhelming majority of cases the Security Council does not authoritatively designate the wrongdoing party. This leaves third states free to make their own determinations at their own risk.[79] Third states may assist the victim state in an exercise of collective self-defence under Article 51, in which case the dual requirements of necessity and proportionality strictly limit the scope of the operation, or they may adopt lesser forms of discrimination against the aggressor. Alternatively, third states may adopt a position of strict neutrality in the conflict, thereby bringing into play the system of rights and obligations of neutrality law. Indeed, states have expressly declared themselves 'neutral' in a number of conflicts since 1945.[80] The US adopted a position of neutrality in the 1967 Arab–Israeli war, but abandoned that position in the 1973 war.[81] In the Iran–Iraq conflict (1980–8), although the parties never officially declared war, the US, the UK, the Soviet Union and China all characterised the conflict as war and stated that they would remain neutral.[82] This state practice indicates that strict neutrality remains a possible status in a considerable number of situations. The fact that many modern military manuals refer to the law of neutrality supports this conclusion.[83]

Circumstances in which the law of neutrality applies today

Whilst there appears to be widespread agreement that the law of neutrality retains vitality in some modern situations, the precise circumstances in which it applies are not entirely clear. The traditional law hinged upon the existence of a state of war in the legal sense, which required both the

---

79 Brownlie, *Use of Force*, 404.
80 For an analysis of state practice, see Norton, 'Between the Ideology and the Reality', 254–78; Greenwood, 'The Concept of War in Modern International Law' (1987) 36 *ICLQ* 283, 290–4; Petrochilos, 'The Relevance of the Concepts of War and Armed Conflict to the Law of Neutrality' (1998) 31 *Vanderbilt Journal of Transnational Law* 575, 583–601.
81 See Norton, 'Between the Ideology and the Reality', 301.
82 Petrochilos, 'The Relevance of the Concepts of War and Armed Conflict to the Law of Neutrality', 594. From the outbreak of hostilities in September 1980 until October 1985, the UK government spoke of the 'Iran–Iraq War' and proclaimed 'neutrality' in that war; but, from October 1985, the government spoke of 'the conflict between Iran and Iraq' and described the UK position as one of 'impartiality': see Gray, 'The British Position in Regard to the Gulf Conflict' (1988) 37 *ICLQ* 420, 421.
83 See, e.g., Fleck, *The Handbook of Humanitarian Law in Armed Conflicts* (1995), ch. 11; UK Ministry of Defence, *The Manual of the Law of Armed Conflict* (2004), paras. 1.42–1.43; US Army, *Field Manual 27-10: The Law of Land Warfare* (1956), ch. 9.

objective existence of armed hostilities and a subjective intent on the part of one or both of the parties to conduct a war.[84] Such intent was usually manifested by a formal declaration of war, but it could also be inferred from the circumstances.[85] Article 2 of Hague III thus provides:

> The existence of a state of war must be notified to the neutral Powers without delay, and shall not take effect in regard to them until after the receipt of a notification, which may, however, be given by telegraph. Neutral Powers, nevertheless, cannot rely on the absence of notification if it is clearly established that they were in fact aware of the existence of a state of war.

Since belligerents in modern conflicts rarely declare war, there is rarely any clear manifestation of the intent to wage war. Nonetheless, numerous examples exist of states adopting a neutral stance in conflicts in the absence of any declaration of war. In the Falklands conflict of 1982, for example, many states adopted a formal neutral stance, even though the UK positively denied the existence of a state of war.[86] Furthermore, as Brownlie notes, '[s]ince 1920 draftsmen of treaties have usually avoided "war" as a term of art' and have referred instead to factual phenomena such as the use of force, armed attack and armed aggression.[87] The application of the Geneva Conventions, for example, hinges upon the factual existence of an 'armed conflict'.[88] In light of this practice, many commentators agree that the sensible view is that the law of neutrality can apply to any conflict that constitutes a war in the material sense – in other words, neutrality is a permissible stance in any 'armed conflict'.[89]

Nonetheless, it is not clear whether a neutral stance is entirely voluntary or whether it is mandatory in certain circumstances. Many modern

---

84 Greenwood, 'The Concept of War in Modern International Law'; Brownlie, *Use of Force*, 38; Fleck *Handbook of Humanitarian Law*, para. 1106; Castren, *The Present Law of War and Neutrality* (1954), 31.

85 Norton, 'Between the Ideology and the Reality', 250; Lauterpacht (ed.), *Oppenheim's International Law*, 7th edn, vol. I, 653–4 and 666–72.

86 See Marston, 'UK Materials in International Law' (1982) 53 *British Yearbook of International Law* 519, 519–20; Statement of Prime Minister Thatcher, 22 Parl. Deb., HC 616 (1982); Petrochilos, 'The Relevance of the Concepts of War and Armed Conflict to the Law of Neutrality', 599–601; Brownlie, *Use of Force*, 395.

87 Brownlie, *Use of Force*, 393–4.

88 Art. 2 common to the four Geneva Conventions of 1949; see also Greenwood, 'The Concept of War in Modern International Law', 294–303.

89 See, e.g., Lauterpacht, 'The Revision of the Law of War', 293; Brownlie, *Use of Force*, 395–6; Greenspan, *The Modern Law of Land Warfare* (1959), 531; Briggs, *The Law of Nations*, 2nd edn (1952), 975.

commentators assert that the law of neutrality continues to apply automatically to all third states in cases of declared war, as in the past.[90] Yet most conflicts today are not declared to be 'war', and as Oppenheim explains 'it is not clear to what extent an undeclared war of this nature imposes upon third states the *obligations* of neutrality'.[91] The simplest approach to this dilemma would be to assert that all third states are automatically neutral in all armed conflicts and are therefore automatically subject to neutral obligations.[92] However, there is little evidence in state practice or in the literature to support that assertion.[93]

An alternative approach would be to stipulate that third states may *voluntarily* assume a neutral status in any armed conflict, but cannot have that status imposed upon them except in a declared war.[94] According to Oppenheim, third states arguably 'retain freedom of action' in cases where there has been no declaration of war.[95] Stone notes more decisively that 'it is clear from the practice' that, where war is not openly intended by the parties, 'third states are free ... either to treat the hostilities as a war and assume a neutral attitude, or to take the attitude of the belligerents at its face value and act as far as they can as if no war exists'.[96] This approach appears to accord most closely with state practice. Norton observes that belligerents since 1945 have tended only to assert rights against non-belligerent states in declared wars (such as the Arab–Israeli and India–Pakistan wars) and in other conflicts in which non-belligerent states formally declared themselves neutral (such as the US and South Vietnamese invasions of Cambodia).[97] Greenwood also notes that, in cases where a third state has not voluntarily assumed the status of a neutral, '[a]ttempts to exercise belligerent rights under the

---

90 Although Greenwood points out the illogical and unsatisfactory nature of this position: see Greenwood, 'The Concept of War in Modern International Law'. In any case, this does not affect the right of third states to assist the victim state in an exercise of collective self-defence: see Brownlie, *Use of Force*, 403.

91 Lauterpacht (ed.), *Oppenheim's International Law*, 7th edn, vol. II, 293, note 1 (emphasis added).

92 See the remarks of Carl Salans (then Deputy Legal Adviser to the US Department of State) [1968] *American Society of International Law Proceedings* 76.

93 Greenwood, 'The Concept of War in Modern International Law', 300.

94 See Norton, 'Between the Ideology and the Reality', 308; Greenwood, 'The Concept of War in Modern International Law', 298–301; Stone, *Legal Controls of International Conflict* (1954), 313; Schindler, 'Aspects Contemporains de la Neutralité' (1967) 121 *Recueil des Cours* 221, 288.

95 Lauterpacht (ed.), *Oppenheim's International Law*, 7th edn, vol. II, 293.

96 Stone, *Legal Controls of International Conflict*, 313.

97 Norton, 'Between the Ideology and the Reality', 257–78.

law of neutrality in conflicts falling short of war have generally met with widespread international resistance'.[98]

This analysis is consistent with the general framework of the Geneva Conventions. Common Article 2 provides that the Conventions shall apply 'to all cases of declared war or of any other armed conflict which may arise between two or more of the High Contracting Parties, even if the state of war is not recognised by one of them'. Article 4B of GCIII refers to 'neutral or non-belligerent Powers' for the purpose of granting prisoner of war protection to individuals from both categories of states, and thus appears implicitly to accept that non-participation in hostilities is a valid position that is distinct from strict neutrality. Similarly, Article 9(2)(b) of Protocol I refers to 'a neutral or other State which is not a Party to that conflict'.[99] This supports the argument that strict neutrality is voluntary in armed conflicts that do not constitute declared wars; for if neutrality were obligatory for all third states in all armed conflicts, there would be no possibility of a third status of non-belligerency.[100]

On balance, the current state of the law appears to be that all third states are automatically neutral in declared wars, but in other armed conflicts the law of neutrality applies only where third states voluntarily assume an official neutral stance. In both declared and undeclared wars, third states retain the right to assist the victim state in an exercise of collective self-defence.

Content of the law of neutrality

The two-dimensional nature of the law of neutrality

The law of neutrality is often described as two-dimensional in nature.[101] The first dimension governs the rights and duties of neutral *states* vis-à-vis belligerent *states*. It obliges neutrals to adopt an attitude of complete impartiality towards belligerents and thus to refrain from committing

---

98 One example is the hostile reaction to French claims in the Algerian conflict: see Greenwood, 'The Concept of War in Modern International Law', 298.

99 First Additional Protocol to the Geneva Conventions of 12 August 1949, and relating to the Protection of Victims of International Armed Conflicts (adopted 8 June 1977, entered into force 7 December 1979), 1125 UNTS 3; see also Arts. 19 and 31.

100 This interpretation does not diminish the protection granted to individuals from non-belligerent states, but merely imposes additional obligations on neutral states in relation to the conflict (e.g. GCIV, Arts. 9, 11, 24, 36, 61 and 140, and ch. XII) and removes certain protections for neutral individuals found in belligerent territory (e.g. GCIV, Art. 4).

101 See, e.g., W. E. Hall, *Neutrals*, 20–1.

any act that directly or indirectly favours one belligerent's prosecution of the war. In addition, the first dimension obliges belligerents to respect the sovereignty of neutrals. The second dimension of neutrality law, on the other hand, governs the relationship between neutral *individuals* and belligerent *states*. As states and individuals were not, and could not be, bound by obligations to each other under classic international law, the law of neutrality does not impose direct obligations on neutral individuals and belligerent states *vis-à-vis* each other.[102] Instead, neutrality law regulates the relationship between neutral individuals and belligerent states *indirectly*, by imposing obligations on neutral states to control certain private activities that may favour one belligerent in the war.

The second dimension of the law of neutrality obliges neutral states not to allow their territory to be used as a base for hostile operations by belligerents. Articles 4, 5 and 6 of the Convention Respecting the Rights and Duties of Neutral Powers and Persons in Case of War on Land (Hague V), which represent customary law, provide:

> 4. Corps of combatants cannot be formed nor recruiting agencies opened on the territory of a neutral Power to assist the belligerents.
>
> 5. A neutral Power must not allow any of the acts referred to in Articles 2 to 4 to occur on its territory. It is not called upon to punish acts in violation of its neutrality unless the said acts have been committed on its own territory.[103]
>
> 6. The responsibility of a neutral Power is not engaged by the fact of persons crossing the frontier separately to offer their services to one of the belligerents.

Thus, Article 4 prohibits states from officially forming or recruiting corps of combatants to assist a belligerent, whilst Article 5 requires states to take positive steps to prevent such activities on the part of private individuals in state territory. The Report presented by the Second Commission of the Hague Conference describes Article 5 as 'the logical and necessary counterpart of Articles 2 to 4'.[104]

Although it is not explicitly stated in Article 5, it is generally accepted that this provision obliges a neutral state to exercise due diligence to

---

102 *Ibid.*, 21.
103 Arts. 2 and 3 prohibit *belligerents* from carrying out certain activities on neutral state territory.
104 J. B. Scott (ed.), *Reports to the Hague Conferences of 1899 and 1907* (1917), 541; see also Brownlie, 'Volunteers and the Law of War and Neutrality' (1956) 5 *ICLQ* 570, 571.

prevent the private activities in question.[105] As Stone explains, the duty of prevention on a neutral state 'is not absolute, but according to his power';[106] it is an obligation of diligent conduct, not one of result. Article 6 makes it clear, however, that Hague V imposes no duty on neutral states to prevent individuals from departing the state in an unorganised fashion ('separately' or '*isolément*') to fight for a belligerent.[107] Individuals may be considered to be crossing state borders separately 'when there exists between them no bond of a known or obvious organisation, even when a number of them pass the frontier simultaneously'.[108] Moreover, consistent with the two-dimensional nature of neutrality law, Hague V imposes no duty on neutral individuals themselves.

The law of neutrality and modern PMSCs

It follows from the above analysis that neutral states in international armed conflict are under a duty to prevent, in state territory, the organ-isation and recruitment of PMSC personnel to work as combatants for a belligerent. PMSC personnel will fall within this formulation if they are hired by a belligerent to provide services that are reasonably likely to entail direct participation in hostilities. Chapter 5 critically examined the question of when PMSC personnel will qualify as taking a direct part in hostilities, with reference to the four categories of PMSC contract iden-tified in Chapter 1.[109] Applying that analysis to the present context, a neutral home state's preventive obligation under Article 5 of Hague V will apply to all PMSC contracts for offensive combat services, as well as armed security contracts where the protected object is or is likely to become a military objective. The preventive obligation will not ordinarily apply to contracts involving military/security expertise (such as advice, training,

---

105 See Kelsen, *Principles of International Law* (1952), 161; Kunz, 'Sanctions in Interna-tional Law' (1956) 50 *AJIL* 514, 527; Borchard, *Diplomatic Protection of Citizens Abroad*, §§ 86–7, 107; Thomas and Thomas, 'International Legal Aspects of the Civil War in Spain, 1936–39', 154–6; Curtis, 'The Law of Hostile Military Expeditions as Applied by the United States' (1914) 8 *AJIL* 1, 35; see also the cases in J. B. Moore, *US Arbitrations*, 4027–56.
106 Stone, *Legal Controls of International Conflict*, 391.
107 Lauterpacht (ed.), *Oppenheim's International Law*, 8th edn (1955), 704; Brownlie, 'Vol-unteers and the Law of War and Neutrality', 571.
108 J. B. Scott (ed.), *Reports to the Hague Conferences of 1899 and 1907*, 542.
109 See Chapter 5, section 5.1. That discussion related to the question of whether an indi-vidual is 'recruited . . . in order to fight' in an armed conflict (for the purposes of inter-national mercenary law), which is essentially analogous to the question of whether an individual is recruited as a combatant in an armed conflict (for the purposes of neutrality law).

intelligence and weapons maintenance), unless the services relate directly to a specific tactical operation. Finally, military support contracts will not generally entail direct participation in hostilities and therefore will not trigger the home state's preventive obligation under Hague V.[110]

This analysis raises the interesting question of what constitutes recruitment and organisation of PMSC personnel 'on the territory of' a neutral power for the purposes of Hague V. As discussed in Chapter 1, PMSCs often use a database of names to recruit and organise a team of contractors from around the world in order to perform a particular contract. Many foreign contractors may not even enter the home state of the PMSC, but may travel straight from their own home state to the state in which the contract is to be performed (the host state). Nonetheless, for the purposes of the preventive obligation in Article 5 of Hague V, the organisation and recruitment of the PMSC personnel can be said to occur on the territory of the home state if the contract is concluded by a PMSC that is based or incorporated in that state.

Like the obligation not to 'tolerate' certain egregious interventions, discussed in the second section of this chapter, the obligation not to 'allow' a particular non-neutral activity arises at the moment that the state becomes aware, or ought to become aware, that the activity is occurring or that there is a serious risk that the activity will occur in the future. In certain cases, actual knowledge may be inferred from the surrounding circumstances.[111]

Article 8 of Hague XIII imposes a further duty on neutral states, which may be relevant to the home state of a PMSC:

> A neutral Government is bound to employ the means at its disposal to prevent the fitting out or arming of any vessel within its jurisdiction which it has reason to believe is intended to cruise, or engage in hostile operations, against a Power with which that Government is at peace. It is also bound to display the same vigilance to prevent the departure from its jurisdiction of any vessel intended to cruise, or engage in hostile operations, which had been adapted entirely or partly within the said jurisdiction for use in war.[112]

---

110 In rare cases, however, military support services may entail direct participation in hostilities, such as the transportation of ammunition to an active firing position at the frontline: see ICRC, 'Interpretive Guidance on the Notion of Direct Participation in Hostilities under International Humanitarian Law' (June 2009).

111 See Brownlie, 'Volunteers and the Law of War and Neutrality', 574; Stone, *Legal Controls of International Conflict*, 570.

112 Convention Concerning the Rights and Duties of Neutral Powers in Naval War (adopted 18 October 1907, entered into force 26 January 1910), 205 Consol TS 395 ('Hague XIII').

This effectively obliges neutral states to prevent PMSCs from servicing the military vessels (including naval vessels and aircraft) of belligerents in state territory.

Aside from the two duties identified above, the Hague Conventions demand very little of neutral states in the way of control over private individuals. They impose no duty on states to prevent individuals from providing *indirect* assistance to belligerents, such as the loan of money or the provision of commercial services to belligerents. They do not require neutral states to prevent individuals in state territory from transporting enemy troops for commercial purposes,[113] nor do they require neutral states to prevent their licensed pilots from working on belligerent warships.[114] The neutral state bears no responsibility under international law for these private, non-neutral acts.[115] Moreover, although the Hague Conventions prohibit neutral states from officially delivering war materials to belligerents, they do not require neutral states to prohibit such delivery by private persons.[116]

Positive action to discharge the obligations

In the past, states usually discharged their obligations under neutrality law by enacting domestic neutrality legislation, which stipulated the acts that states believed would compromise their neutrality and equipped states with the means of prosecuting and punishing those who committed such acts.[117] Although a large number of states still have neutrality legislation on their statute books, such as the US Neutrality Act 1794 and the UK Foreign Enlistment Act 1870, that legislation is outdated and ineffective in dealing with the modern private security industry. There has never been a successful prosecution in connection with enlistment or recruitment

This obligation originated from the Treaty of Washington (8 May 1871) (applied in the *Alabama Claims* arbitrations between the US and Britain), which imposed an obligation on neutral states to use due diligence to prevent the specified activities.

113 Lauterpacht (ed.), *Oppenheim's International Law*, 7th edn, vol. I, 746–7.

114 Hague XIII, Art. 11.

115 See Hague V, Art. 18; Hague XIII, Art. 7; Fenwick, *The Neutrality Laws of the US* (1913), 120–5; Lauterpacht (ed.), *Oppenheim's International Law*, 7th edn, vol. I, 652–61, 739–45.

116 See Hague V, Arts. 7 and 18; Hague XIII, Art. 7; Fenwick, *The Neutrality Laws of the US*, 120–5; Lauterpacht (ed.), *Oppenheim's International Law*, 7th edn, vol. I, 652–61, 739–45. Cf Fleck, *Handbook of Humanitarian Law*, 497–8, who argues that state practice has modified this rule under customary law such that mere state *permission* of arms exports is to be considered a non-neutral act.

117 Fenwick, *The Neutrality Laws of the US*, 14; Deâk and Jessup, *A Collection of Neutrality Laws, Regulations and Treaties of Various Countries* (1974).

under the UK neutrality legislation,[118] and the US has generally pursued a policy of non-enforcement of its neutrality laws relating to enlistment or recruitment.[119] A more effective means for neutral states to discharge their obligations would be to establish a licensing scheme of the kind outlined in the second section of this chapter, and to incorporate considerations of neutrality law (among others) into the criteria against which PMSC contracts are assessed.

6.4 Obligations to control PMSCs under international humanitarian law

Chapters 4 and 5 argued that *all* states – including states not party to the armed conflict – have an obligation under Common Article 1 of the Geneva Conventions and customary law to take positive steps to ensure respect for IHL by private actors under their influence or control.[120] This obligation is binding on states 'in all circumstances', including times of peace as well as times of armed conflict. The home state of a PMSC, like the host state and the hiring state, will ordinarily have some capacity to influence the company's behaviour in the field, and it follows that the home state has an obligation to take steps within its power to promote company respect for IHL.

This obligation is reflected in Part I of the Montreux Document:

> 14. Home States have an obligation, within their power, to ensure respect for international humanitarian law by PMSCs of their nationality, in particular to:
>
> a) disseminate, as widely as possible, the text of the Geneva Conventions and other relevant norms of international humanitarian law among PMSCs and their personnel;
>
> b) not encourage or assist in, and take appropriate measures to prevent, any violations of international humanitarian law by personnel of PMSCs;

---

118 See Mockler, *The Mercenaries* (1969); Foreign Affairs Committee, *Sierra Leone* (First Report, 1998–9), para. 92; 'Report of the Committee of Privy Counsellors Appointed to Inquire into the Recruitment of Mercenaries' (1976).

119 See Layeb, 'Mercenary Activity'; Lobel, 'The Rise and Decline of the Neutrality Act: Sovereignty and Congressional War Powers in US Foreign Policy' (1983) 24 *Harvard International Law Journal* 1. In 2007, the US used the Neutrality Act to prosecute offences relating to the overthrow of the government of Laos, but those offences did not relate to the obligations of the US under the law of neutrality.

120 See Chapter 4, section 4.1, and Chapter 5, section 5.2.

c) take measures to suppress violations of international humanitarian law committed by the personnel of PMSCs through appropriate means such as administrative or other regulatory measures as well as administrative, disciplinary or judicial sanctions, as appropriate.[121]

Part II of the Montreux Document sets out a number of 'good practices' to guide the home state in fulfilling its obligations. As noted in the second section of this chapter in relation to the norm of non-intervention, the principal recommendation is that states consider establishing a licensing scheme for PMSCs based or incorporated in state territory.[122] A regulatory regime of this nature would help the home state to fulfil its obligation to ensure respect for IHL, particularly since the government could stipulate minimum screening and training requirements for PMSC personnel and could revoke its authorisation if company personnel misbehaved in the field.

The home state, like other states, also has a specific obligation under the Geneva Conventions to search for and prosecute or extradite persons suspected of grave breaches of IHL (in the exercise of universal jurisdiction),[123] as well as an obligation to 'suppress' non-grave breaches of IHL in international armed conflict.[124] These obligations apply over and above the general obligation to ensure respect for IHL in Common Article 1, which includes an obligation to suppress violations of IHL in both international and non-international armed conflict.[125] To be effective, the home state's suppression of non-grave breaches should generally entail (*inter alia*) the enactment of domestic criminal legislation and the prosecution of offenders in the exercise of the state's ordinary criminal jurisdiction over its nationals overseas.[126] The Montreux Document further suggests that states 'consider establishing ... corporate criminal responsibility for crimes committed by the PMSC',[127] as well as providing for 'non-criminal accountability mechanisms for improper and unlawful conduct of PMSCs and their personnel'.[128]

---

121 Montreux Document, Part I, para. 14.   122 *Ibid.*, Part II, para. 54.

123 GCI, Art. 50; GCII, Art. 51; GCIII, Art. 130; GCIV, Art. 147; see also Montreux Document, Part I, para. 16.

124 GCI, Art. 49(3); GCII, Art. 50(3); GCIII, Art. 129(3); GCIV, Art. 146(3); Protocol I, Art. 86.

125 See Montreux Document, Part I, para. 14(c) (quoted above).

126 Pictet (ed.), *Commentary, Geneva Convention Relative to the Protection of Civilian Persons in Time of War* (1958), 593–4.

127 Montreux Document, Part II, para. 70.   128 *Ibid.*, Part II, para. 71.

6.5 Obligations to control PMSCs under human rights law

General human rights law

As discussed in Chapter 5, the HRL obligation to 'ensure' rights is binding on states only within their jurisdiction, and this notion of jurisdiction is primarily territorial.[129] The home state of a PMSC therefore has no general obligation under HRL to take positive steps to prevent the company from violating the rights of individuals overseas, unless the home state exercises effective control over the foreign territory in which the company operates or over the particular individual in question. Some commentators have argued that home states should be under an obligation to exercise control to prohibit companies that are based or incorporated in their territory from violating peremptory norms of international law when abroad.[130] Whatever the merits of these arguments, they do not represent the current state of the law.[131]

In his reports to the Human Rights Council, the UN special representative on the issue of human rights and transnational corporations and other business enterprises, John Ruggie, confirms that states have a duty under HRL to protect against corporate-related human rights abuse.[132] Ruggie notes that states 'are not required to regulate the extraterritorial activities of businesses incorporated in their jurisdiction, nor are they generally prohibited from doing so provided there is a recognized

---

129 See Chapter 5, section 5.3.
130 See, e.g., McCorquodale and Simons, 'Responsibility Beyond Borders: State Responsibility for Extraterritorial Violations by Corporations of International Human Rights Law' (2007) 70(4) *Modern Law Review* 598, 615–23; Sornarajah, 'Linking State Responsibility for Certain Harms Caused by Corporate Nationals Abroad to Civil Recourse in the Legal Systems of Home States', in C. Scott (ed.), *Torture as Tort: Comparative Perspectives on the Development of Transnational Human Rights Litigation* (2001), ch. 18; de Arechega and Tanzi, 'International State Responsibility', in Bedjaoui (ed.), *International Law: Achievements and Prospects* (1991), 359.
131 See de Schutter, 'The Accountability of Multinationals for Human Rights Violations in European Law', in Alston (ed.), *Non-State Actors and Human Rights* (2005), 235–7; van den Herik and Letnar Cernic, 'Regulating Corporations under International Law: From Human Rights to International Criminal Law and Back Again' (2010) 8 *Journal of International Criminal Justice* 725.
132 Ruggie, 'Protect, Respect and Remedy: A Framework for Business and Human Rights', UN Doc. A/HRC/8/5 (7 April 2008); Ruggie, 'Business and Human Rights: Towards Operationalizing the "Protect, Respect and Remedy" Framework', UN Doc. A/HRC/11/13 (22 April 2009); Ruggie, 'Business and Human Rights: Further Steps towards the Operationalization of the "Protect, Respect and Remedy" Framework', UN Doc. A/HRC/14/27 (9 April 2010) ('Ruggie Reports').

jurisdictional basis, and that an overall test of reasonableness is met'.[133] Ruggie emphasises, however, that there are strong policy reasons for home states to encourage their companies to respect rights abroad, as 'such encouragement gets home States out of the untenable position of being associated with possible overseas corporate abuse'. Moreover, home state regulation 'can provide much-needed support to host States that lack the capacity to implement fully an effective regulatory environment on their own'.[134]

The UN Convention Against Torture

In rare cases, a contractor working for a local PMSC might commit acts falling within the UN Convention Against Torture (UNCAT), giving rise to an obligation on the home state to prosecute the contractor if he or she entered any territory under the state's jurisdiction.[135] The strict definition of torture in Article 1 of the UNCAT is limited to those acts 'by which severe pain or suffering, whether physical or mental, is intentionally inflicted on a person . . . by or at the instigation of or with the consent or acquiescence of a public official or other person acting in an official capacity'. The Titan and CACI contractors implicated in the Abu Ghraib prisoner abuse scandal operated alongside and with the consent and acquiescence of US soldiers, thus illustrating how PMSC personnel could fall within the UNCAT in extreme cases.[136]

This scenario raises a further question in relation to the provision of effective remedies for victims. Specifically, would the home state have an obligation under Article 14 of the UNCAT to provide domestic procedures by which the victims of PMSC torture committed overseas could sue the hiring state for its involvement in the torture? Article 14 provides:

> Each State Party shall ensure in its legal system that the victim of an act of torture obtains redress and has an enforceable right to fair and adequate compensation including the means for as full rehabilitation as possible.

133 Ruggie 2009 Report, para. 15.   134 Ibid., para. 16.
135 UN Convention Against Torture (adopted 10 December 1984, entered into force 26 June 1987), 1465 UNTS 85, Art. 7.
136 See Fay, 'Investigation of the Abu Ghraib Detention Facility and 205th Military Intelligence Brigade' (August 2004). A class action brought against CACI and Titan under the Alien Tort Statute charged the companies with torture and other heinous and illegal acts committed against Iraqi detainees. On 11 September 2009, in a 2–1 decision, a panel of the Court of Appeals for the District of Columbia affirmed the dismissal of all claims against Titan and, reversing the decision of the District Court, also dismissed all claims against CACI: see Saleh v. Titan, 580 F 3d 1.

> In the event of the death of the victim as a result of an act of torture, his
> dependants shall be entitled to compensation.

Unlike other provisions of the UNCAT, Article 14 contains no explicit territorial limitation. An initial draft of the provision included the phrase 'committed in any territory under its jurisdiction' after the word 'torture', but this phrase had disappeared from the text by the time of adoption of the final version of the draft Convention in 1982, and the *travaux préparatoires* contain no explanation for its removal.[137] The UN Committee Against Torture, the body established under the Convention to review compliance by states parties with their treaty obligations, has interpreted Article 14 as requiring states parties to provide a procedure permitting victims to obtain reparations from those responsible for torture regardless of where it was committed.[138] However, both the UK House of Lords[139] and the Court of Appeal of Ontario[140] have taken a different view.[141] The state of the law is thus unclear and perhaps the best that can be said is that universal civil jurisdiction for torture under Article 14 of the UNCAT is permissive, but not mandatory.[142]

6.6 Conclusion

A state that turns a blind eye to PMSCs based or incorporated in its territory does so at its own risk, for in certain circumstances the acts of a PMSC overseas may give rise to the responsibility of the company's home state for a failure to take adequate measures to control company

137 See Byrnes, 'Civil Remedies for Torture Committed Abroad', in C. Scott (ed.), *Torture as Tort* (2001), 545–6.

138 UN Committee Against Torture, Conclusions and Recommendations, 34th Sess., UN Doc. CAT/C/CR/34/CAN (7 July 2005), paras. 4(g) and 5(f); see also C. Hall, 'The Duty of States Parties to the Convention Against Torture to Provide Procedures Permitting Victims to Recover Reparations for Torture Committed Abroad' (2008) 18(5) *EJIL* 921; Nowak and McArthur, *The United Nations Convention Against Torture: A Commentary* (2008), 490–505.

139 *Jones v. Ministry of Interior Al-Mamlaka A-Arabiya AS Saudiya (the Kingdom of Saudi Arabia)* [2006] UKHL 26.

140 *Bouzari v. Islamic Republic of Iran* [2004] OJ No. 2800 Docket No C38295 (Court of Appeal of Ontario).

141 See also *Al-Adsani v. UK* (App. No. 35763/97), ECHR, 21 November 2001.

142 For a discussion of the use of the Alien Tort Statute to bring torture claims in US courts, see Staino, 'Suing Private Military Contractors for Torture: How to Use the Alien Tort Statute Without Granting Sovereign Immunity-Related Defenses' (2010) 50 *Santa Clara Law Review* 1277; Gallagher, 'Civil Litigation and Transnational Business: An Alien Tort Statute Primer' (2010) 8 *Journal of International Criminal Justice* 745; Isenberg, 'Speaking Hypothetically: What to Do When a PMC Tortures', *Huffington Post* (27 July 2010).

behaviour. Three factors must be established for the home state of a PMSC to incur responsibility in this way: first, an obligation on the state to prevent or punish a particular PMSC activity; secondly, a failure on the part of the state to take the requisite preventive or penal measures; and, thirdly, a specific instance of the prohibited PMSC activity.

Both the norm of non-intervention and the law of neutrality impose due diligence obligations on the home state to prevent the PMSC from undertaking certain activities from state territory and to punish such activities where they occur. The obligation to ensure respect for IHL imposes a further due diligence obligation on the home state to promote PMSC compliance with IHL in the field. Notwithstanding the existence of these obligations, a number of key states – most notably the UK – continue to close their eyes to PMSCs operating from their territory. Diligent measures such as the establishment of a licensing scheme for local PMSCs would help to increase transparency and state control over local PMSCs, whilst also promoting general PMSC compliance with international law in the field. State inaction, on the other hand, would represent a conscious failure to prevent harmful PMSC activities overseas, and in certain circumstances this could give rise to the responsibility of the home state under international law.

~

Conclusion

The extensive use of PMSCs in recent armed conflicts challenges the conventional wisdom that military and security functions are most effectively and appropriately performed through public forces. In practice, this may reduce the ability of states to control violence and to ensure accountability for misconduct in armed conflict. Yet the widespread outsourcing of military and security activities to PMSCs has *not* entirely undermined the capacity of states to control violence in the international arena, nor has it rendered the traditional state-centred frameworks of international law irrelevant in this context. Certain states retain the capacity to exert significant influence over PMSCs operating in armed conflict, and this enables international law to regulate PMSC activities *indirectly* using states as an intermediary.

The hiring state, the host state and the home state of a PMSC are in a particularly strong position to influence PMSC behaviour in armed conflict. Accordingly, international law imposes a range of obligations on these states to take positive steps to regulate PMSC activities. Inappropriate or harmful conduct by a PMSC employee in armed conflict may, in certain circumstances, give rise to the international responsibility of any or all of these three states. There are essentially two ways in which such responsibility may arise.

The first pathway to state responsibility involves the direct attribution of wrongful PMSC conduct to the hiring state. Aside from those rare cases in which the contractor forms part of the armed forces of the hiring state, such attribution will ordinarily depend upon either Article 5 or Article 8 of the International Law Commission's Articles on Responsibility of States for Internationally Wrongful Acts ('ILC Articles').[1] Article 5 encompasses contractors who are empowered by the law of the hiring state to exercise governmental authority, provided that they are 'acting in that capacity

hiring state

---

1 ILC Articles on Responsibility of States for Internationally Wrongful Acts with Commentaries (2001) *Yearbook of the International Law Commission*, vol. II(2).

in the particular instance'. Even where that is not the case, the PMSC activities may fall within Article 8, which encompasses contractors who are in fact acting on the instructions or under the direction or control of the hiring state. A close contextual analysis leads to the conclusion that a large proportion of PMSC activities in armed conflict will fall within one of these two provisions.

The second pathway to state responsibility does not involve the direct attribution of PMSC misconduct to a state, nor does it involve state complicity in PMSC misconduct. Rather, it derives from a state's failure to take adequate steps to prevent, investigate, punish or redress the PMSC misconduct. The hiring state, the host state and/or the home state of an errant PMSC may incur responsibility in this way, provided that there is a pre-existing obligation on the relevant state to prevent, investigate, punish or redress the PMSC misconduct in question. Various fields of international law impose pertinent obligations of this nature on states.

As the regime specially tailored to situations of armed conflict, international humanitarian law (IHL) is naturally the first port of call for any consideration of states' obligations to control PMSCs in this context. Of particular importance is the obligation 'to ensure respect' for IHL in Common Article 1 of the Geneva Conventions, which requires the hiring state, the host state and the home state to take diligent steps within their power to promote PMSC compliance with IHL. This serves as a residual obligation mandating a baseline level of positive state action, over and above any more specific obligations that may bind a particular state in a particular case.

The more general regime of human rights law (HRL) also imposes a number of important obligations on states to take diligent measures to control PMSCs within state jurisdiction. In the unique context of an armed conflict, these general human rights obligations must be interpreted by reference to the more specific rules of IHL. Whilst HRL is applicable primarily to the host state of a PMSC or the occupying power of that state, the hiring state may also be subject to human rights obligations in certain situations where it exercises effective control over PMSC activities. States' human rights obligations may be particularly important for victims of PMSC abuses, since HRL offers more advanced procedural safeguards than IHL, coupled with a range of sophisticated international procedures for individual complaint and redress.

In relation to the home state of a PMSC, there is no general obligation on states to regulate the activities of companies based or incorporated in state territory. Nonetheless, in certain situations international law requires positive state action to prevent local companies from engaging in activities that are harmful to other states. In particular, the law of neutrality obliges the home state of a PMSC not to 'allow' non-neutral PMSC activities in international armed conflicts in which the state is neutral, whilst the norm of non-intervention obliges the home state not to 'tolerate' PMSC activities that intervene in the internal affairs of another state. These obligations apply in addition to the general duty 'to ensure respect' for IHL in Common Article 1, which sets a minimum threshold of home state regulation in relation to PMSCs operating in armed conflict. States that turn a blind eye to PMSCs based or incorporated in their territory therefore run the risk of violating their obligations under international law.

In legal terms, international responsibility arises automatically upon the commission of an internationally wrongful act by a state. In practice, however, such responsibility must be invoked by the injured state or some other interested party, such as an individual applicant before a human rights tribunal. The ILC Articles deal only with the invocation of state responsibility by another state or states, but they emphasise that obligations may also exist towards entities other than states, as in the case for 'human rights violations and other breaches of international law where the primary beneficiary of the obligation breached is not a State'.[2] The procedures for the presentation and settlement of interstate claims largely resemble those that exist for civil claims in domestic legal systems. Whilst the available means of settling interstate disputes include binding legal procedures such as international arbitration and adjudication, the overwhelming majority of these disputes are resolved through diplomatic negotiations. Parties are often heavily influenced throughout such negotiations by their perceptions of their legal rights and obligations, and a clear articulation by the claimant state of the other state's obligations can therefore play a critical role in the informal dispute resolution process.

This book may facilitate the resolution of disputes arising from PMSC misconduct by articulating and critically analysing the content of states' obligations and the principles that govern state responsibility in such cases. This in turn could help to promote broader accountability within the private security industry. Of course, state responsibility is not sufficient in itself to address the accountability concerns surrounding PMSCs, particularly since it cannot address the accountability of contractors or companies *per se* and it lacks powerful enforcement mechanisms. Any

2 *Ibid.*, Commentary to Art. 28, para. 3; see also Art. 33(2).

effective response to the private security industry should not simply rely on the existing accountability frameworks of international law, but should also develop new domestic and international frameworks targeting a variety of actors including states, PMSCs and their personnel. Nonetheless, this book has demonstrated that the law of state responsibility remains vitally relevant in this area, and a close analysis of states' international obligations and responsibility should constitute a core component of any strategy to address the burgeoning private security industry.

Yet the value of this book does not lie solely in facilitating the assessment of state responsibility *ex post facto* in relation to particular instances of PMSC misconduct. Ultimately, this analysis could also play an important *prospective* role in promoting PMSC compliance with international law. The obligations discussed in this book serve to establish basic standards of state conduct in relation to PMSCs operating in armed conflict. These standards could guide states in the development of effective internal laws and policies to regulate the private security industry, helping states to scrutinise compliance and rectify deviance from within. International law routinely frames debates and informs domestic laws and policies, as well as providing principles and mechanisms for resolving disputes; but this is only possible if the content of the relevant international legal principles is clear in the first place. By drawing attention to states' international obligations to regulate PMSCs in armed conflict, critically analysing the content of those obligations, and evaluating recent state practice, this book provides the necessary clarity to assist states in formulating their internal laws and policies on private security in accordance with international law. The onus is now on states to implement, promote and enforce the existing rules, whilst also working to develop new regulatory regimes at the national and international level.

BIBLIOGRAPHY

Article, books, reports and conferences

Abdullah, I., 'Bush Path to Destruction: The Origin and Character of the Revolutionary United Front/Sierra Leone' (1998) 36(2) *Journal of Modern African Studies* 203

Abresch, W., 'A Human Rights Law of Internal Armed Conflict: The European Court of Human Rights in Chechnya' (2005) 16(4) *European Journal of International Law* 741

Adams, C., 'Straw to Back Controls over British Mercenaries', *Financial Times* (2 August 2002)

Ago, R., 'Fourth Report on State Responsibility' (1972) *Yearbook of the International Law Commission*, vol. II

'Seventh Report on State Responsibility' (1978) *Yearbook of the International Law Commission*, vol. II(2)

Akehurst, M., 'The Hierarchy of the Sources of International Law' (1974–5) 47 *British Yearbook of International Law* 273

Aldrich, G., 'New Life for the Laws of War' (1981) 75 *American Journal of International Law* 764

Alexander, D., 'US Says 16 Guards Removed in Afghan Embassy Scandal', *New York Times* (10 September 2009)

Alston, P. (ed.), *Non-State Actors and Human Rights* (Oxford, Oxford University Press, 2005)

Amerasinghe, C., *Diplomatic Protection* (Oxford, Oxford University Press, 2008)

'Americans Mutilated after Iraqi Ambush', *Washington Post* (4 April 2004)

Annan, K. (then UN Secretary-General), Ditchley Foundation Lecture, Ditchley Park, United Kingdom (26 June 1998)

Ashworth, M., 'PNG's Private Army Spurs Australia into Action', *Independent* (13 March 1997)

Askin, K., 'Prosecuting Wartime Rape and Other Gender-Related Crimes under International Law: Extraordinary Advances, Enduring Obstacles' (2003) 21 *Berkeley Journal of International Law* 288

Aust, A., *Modern Treaty Law and Practice* (Cambridge, Cambridge University Press, 2000)

Australian Law Reform Commission, Report No. 24, 'Foreign State Immunity' (1984)

Avant, D., 'From Mercenaries to Citizen Armies: Explaining Change in the Practice of War' (2000) 54(1) *International Organization* 41

'Privatizing Military Training' (2000) 5(17) *Foreign Policy in Focus*

The Market for Force: The Consequences of Privatizing Security (Cambridge, Cambridge University Press, 2005)

'NGOs, Corporations, and Security Transformation in Africa' (2007) 29(2) *International Relations* 143

Avant, D., and Sigelman, L., 'Private Security and Democracy: Lessons from the US in Iraq' (2010) 19(2) *Security Studies* 230

Azzam, F., 'The Duty of Third States to Implement and Enforce International Humanitarian Law' (1997) 66 *Nordic Journal of International Law* 55

Baker, M., and Murphy, B., 'Blackwater Out of Iraq? No, Not Yet', *Washington Times* (20 April 2009)

Barnidge, R., *Non-State Actors and Terrorism: Applying the Law of State Responsibility and the Due Diligence Principle* (Cambridge, Cambridge University Press, 2007)

Barstow, D., 'Security Companies: Shadow Soldiers in Iraq', *New York Times* (19 April 2004)

Baxter, R., 'So-Called "Unprivileged Belligerency": Spies, Guerillas, and Saboteurs' (1951) 28 *British Yearbook of International Law* 323

'A Sceptical Look at the Concept of Terrorism' (1974) 7(2) *Akron Law Review* 380

Ben-Naftali, O., and Shany, Y., 'Living in Denial: The Application of Human Rights in the Occupied Territories' (2003–4) 37 *Israel Law Review* 17

Best, G., *Humanity in Warfare: The Modern History of the International Law of Armed Conflicts* (London, Weidenfeld & Nicolson Ltd, 1980)

Bianco, A., and Anderson Forest, S., 'Outsourcing War', *Business Week* (15 September 2003)

Boisson de Chazournes, L., and Condorelli, L., 'Quelques Remarques à propos de l'Obligation des Etats de "Respecter et Faire Respecter" le Droit International Humanitaire en Toutes Circonstances', in C. Swinarski (ed.), *Studies and Essays on International Humanitarian Law and Red Cross Principles in Honour of Jean Pictet* (Geneva/The Hague, ICRC/Martinus Nijhoff, 1984)

'Common Article 1 of the Geneva Conventions Revisited: Protecting Collective Interests' (2000) 837 *International Review of the Red Cross* 67

Bonn International Center for Conversion, *Global Disarmament, Demilitarization and Demobilization* (Baden-Baden, Nomos Verlagsgesellschaft, 2003)

Borchard, E., *Diplomatic Protection of Citizens Abroad* (New York, Banks Law Publishing, 1928)

Borgen, C., 'Resolving Treaty Conflicts' (2005) 37 *George Washington International Law Review* 573

Borger, J., 'Cooks and Drivers Were Working as Interrogators', *Guardian* (7 May 2004)

Borrie, G., 'Courts-Martial, Civilians and Civil Liberties' (1969) 32 *Modern Law Review* 35

Bothe, M., 'The Historical Evolution of International Humanitarian Law, International Human Rights Law, Refugee Law and International Criminal Law', in H. Fischer, U. Froissart, W. Heintschel von Heinegg and C. Raap (eds.), *Crisis Management and Humanitarian Protection* (Berlin, Berliner Wissenschafts-Verlag, 2004)

Bothe, M., Partsch, K., and Solf, W., *New Rules for Victims of Armed Conflict: Commentary on the Two 1977 Protocols Additional to the Geneva Conventions of 1949* (The Hague, Martinus Nijhoff, 1982)

Bratspies, R., and Miller, R. (eds.), *Transboundary Harm in International Law* (Cambridge, Cambridge University Press, 2006)

Briggs, H., *The Law of Nations*, 2nd edn (London, Stevens, 1952)

Brinkley, J., 'Private Contractor Use Violated US Army's Policy', *New York Times* (12 June 2004)

'Briton Held in Iraq over Shooting', *BBC News* (10 August 2009)

Brodsky, R., 'Inherently Governmental Rule Sparks Little Consensus', *Government Executive* (3 June 2010)

Brooks, D., 'Write a Cheque, End a War' (2000) 6 *Conflict Trends*

Brooks, D., 'Help for Beleaguered Peacekeepers', *Washington Post* (2 June 2003)

Brownlie, I., 'Volunteers and the Law of War and Neutrality' (1956) 5 *International and Comparative Law Quarterly* 570

   International Law and the Use of Force by States (Oxford, Clarendon Press, 1963)

   State Responsibility (Oxford, Clarendon Press, 1983)

   Principles of Public International Law, 7th edn (Oxford, Clarendon Press, 2008)

Bruno, G., 'US Security Agreements and Iraq' (US Council on Foreign Relations, 23 December 2008)

Buchanan, A., *Justice, Legitimacy and Self-Determination: Moral Foundations for International Law* (Oxford, Oxford University Press, 2004)

Burmester, H. C., 'The Recruitment and Use of Mercenaries in Armed Conflicts' (1978) 72 *American Journal of International Law* 37

Byrnes, A., 'Civil Remedies for Torture Committed Abroad', in C. Scott (ed.), *Torture as Tort* (Oxford, Hart, 2001)

Caparini, M., 'Licensing Regimes for the Export of Military Goods and Services', in S. Chesterman and C. Lehnardt (eds.), *From Mercenaries to Market: The Rise and Regulation of Private Military Companies* (Oxford, Oxford University Press, 2007)

Caron, D., 'The ILC Articles on State Responsibility: The Paradoxical Relationship between Form and Authority' (2002) 96 *American Journal of International Law* 857

Cassese, A., 'Mercenaries: Lawful Combatants or War Criminals?' (1980) 40 *Zeitschrift für ausländisches öffentliches Recht und Völkerrecht* 1

  'On the Current Trends towards Criminal Prosecution and Punishment of Breaches of International Humanitarian Law' (1998) 9(1) *European Journal of International Law* 2

  International Law, 2nd edn (Oxford, Oxford University Press, 2005)

  International Criminal Law, 2nd edn (Oxford, Oxford University Press, 2008)

Castren, E., *The Present Law of War and Neutrality* (Helsinki, Suomalainen Tiedeakatemia, 1954)

Cawthra, G., 'The Security Forces in Transition', in G. Cawthra, J. Cilliers and P.-B. Mertz, *The Future of Security and Defence in South Africa* (Mowbray, Institute for a Democratic Alternative for South Africa, 1998)

Chapman, K., 'The Untouchables: Private Military Contractors' Criminal Accountability under the UCMJ' (2010) 63(4) *Vanderbilt Law Review* 1047

Chen, D., 'Holding "Hired Guns" Accountable: The Legal Status of Private Security Contractors in Iraq' (2009) 32 *Boston College International and Comparative Law Review* 101

Chesterman, S., '"We Can't Spy ... If We Can't Buy!": The Privatization of Intelligence and the Limits of Outsourcing "Inherently Governmental Functions"' (2008) 19(5) *European Journal of International Law* 1055

Clapham, A., 'The European Convention on Human Rights', in C. Scott (ed.), *Torture as Tort* (Oxford, Hart, 2001)

  Human Rights Obligations of Non-State Actors (Oxford, Oxford University Press, 2006)

Cockayne, J., *Commercial Security in Humanitarian and Post-Conflict Settings: An Exploratory Study* (New York, International Peace Academy, 2006)

  'Regulating Private Military and Security Companies: The Content, Negotiation, Weaknesses and Promise of the Montreux Document' (2009) 13(3) *Journal of Conflict and Security Law* 401

Cockayne, J. (ed.), with Speers Mears, E., Cherneva, I., Gurin, A., Oviedo, S., and Yaeger, D., *Beyond Market Forces: Regulating the Global Security Industry* (International Peace Institute, New York 2009)

Cohen, E., *Citizens and Soldiers: The Dilemmas of Military Service* (New York, Cornell University Press, 1985)

  Human Rights in the Israeli Occupied Territories (Manchester, Manchester University Press, 1985)

Cohen, R., 'US Cooling Ties to Croatia after Winking at Its Buildup', *New York Times* (28 October 1995)

Cole, A., 'Firm Fires US Embassy Guards in Kabul', *Wall Street Journal* (5 September 2009)

Combacau, J., 'Obligations de Résultat et Obligations de Comportement: Quelques Questions et Pas de Réponse', in *Mélanges Offerts à P. Reuter* (Paris, Pedone, 1981)

Combacau, J., and Alland, D., '"Primary" and "Secondary" Rules in the Law of State Responsibility: Categorising International Obligations' (1985) 16 *Netherlands Yearbook of International Law* 81

Condorelli, L., 'La Protection des Droits de l'Homme Lors d'Actions Militaires Menées à l'Etranger' (2005) 32 *Collegium* 89

Conforti, B., 'State Responsibility for Breach of Positive Obligations', in M. Fitzmaurice and D. Sarooshi (eds.), *Issues of State Responsibility before International Judicial Institutions* (Oxford, Hart, 2004)

'Contractors in Combat: Firefight from a Rooftop in Iraq', *Virginia Pilot* (25 July 2006)

Coomans, F., and Kamminga, M. (eds.), *Extraterritorial Application of Human Rights Treaties* (Oxford, Intersentia, 2004)

Cottier, M., 'Elements for Contracting Private Military and Security Companies' (2006) 88(863) *International Review of the Red Cross* 637

Cowell, A., 'Pretoria Announces an End to Unit Accused in Slayings', *New York Times* (1 August 1990)

'Conflict in the Balkans', *New York Times* (1 August 1995)

Crawford, J., 'Execution of Judgments and Foreign Sovereign Immunity' (1981) 75 *American Journal of International Law* 820

'International Law and Foreign Sovereigns: Distinguishing Immune Transactions' (1983) 54 *British Yearbook of International Law* 74

'Revising the Draft Articles on State Responsibility' (1999) 10 *European Journal of International Law* 436

'Right of Self-Determination in International Law', in P. Alston (ed.), *Peoples' Rights* (Oxford, Oxford University Press, 2005)

Crawford J., and Olleson, S., 'The Continuing Debate on a UN Convention on State Responsibility' (2005) 54 *International and Comparative Law Quarterly* 959

'Croatia: Tudjman's New Model Army', *Economist* (11 November 1995) 148

Curtis, R. E., 'The Law of Hostile Military Expeditions as Applied by the United States' (1914) 8 *American Journal of International Law* 1

'The Law of Hostile Military Expeditions as Applied by the United States: Part 2' (1914) 8 *American Journal of International Law* 224

Daragahi, B., 'Use of Private Security Firms in Iraq Draws Concerns', *Washington Times* (10 June 2003)

Deâk, F., and Jessup, P. C., *A Collection of Neutrality Laws, Regulations and Treaties of Various Countries* (Westport, CT, Greenwood Press, 1974)

De Arechega, J., and Tanzi, A., 'International State Responsibility', in M. Bedjaoui (ed.), *International Law: Achievements and Prospects* (London, Martinus Nijhoff, 1991)

De Bustamente, A., 'The Hague Convention Concerning the Rights and Duties of Neutral Powers and Persons in Land Warfare' (1908) 2 *American Journal of International Law* 95

De Nevers, R., 'Private Security Companies and the Laws of War' (2009) 40(2) *Security Dialogue* 169

'(Self) Regulating War?: Voluntary Regulation and the Private Security Industry' (2009) 18(3) *Security Studies* 479

'The Effectiveness of Self-Regulation by the Private Military and Security Industry' (2010) 30(2) *Journal of Public Policy* 219

De Schutter, O., 'The Accountability of Multinationals for Human Rights Violations in European Law', in P. Alston (ed.), *Non-State Actors and Human Rights* (Oxford, Oxford University Press, 2005)

Del Prado, J., 'Private Military and Security Companies and the UN Working Group on the Use of Mercenaries' (2009) 13(3) *Journal of Conflict and Security Law* 429

Dennis, M., 'Application of Human Rights Treaties Extraterritorially in Times of Armed Conflict and Military Occupation' (2005) 99 *American Journal of International Law* 119

Dickey, C., 'The Rule of Order 17', *Newsweek* (29 June 2006)

Dickinson, L., 'Public Law Values in a Privatized World' (2006) 31 *Yale Journal of International Law* 383

'Accountability of Private Security Contractors under International and Domestic Law' (2007) 11(31) *American Society of International Law Insights*

Dinnen, S., May, R., and Regan, A. (eds.), *Challenging the State: The Sandline Affair in Papua New Guinea* (Canberra, National Centre for Development Studies, 1997)

Dinstein, Y., 'The International Law of Inter-State Wars and Human Rights' [1977] *Israel Yearbook of Human Rights* 148

The Conduct of Hostilities under the Law of International Armed Conflict (Cambridge, Cambridge University Press, 2004)

Dörmann, K., 'Legal Situation of "Unlawful/Unprivileged Combatants"' (2003) 849 *International Review of the Red Cross* 46

Doswald-Beck, L., 'The Legal Validity of Military Intervention by Invitation of the Government' (1985) 56 *British Yearbook of International Law* 189

'Private Military Companies under International Humanitarian Law', in S. Chesterman and C. Lehnardt (eds.), *From Mercenaries to Market: The Rise and Regulation of Private Military Companies* (Oxford, Oxford University Press, 2007)

Doswald-Beck, L., and Vité, S., 'International Humanitarian Law and Human Rights Law' (1993) 293 *International Review of the Red Cross* 94

Douglas, I., 'Fighting for Diamonds: Private Military Companies in Sierra Leone', in J. Cilliers and P. Mason (eds.), *Peace, Profit or Plunder? The Privatisation of Security in War-Torn African Societies* (Johannesburg, Institute for Security Studies, 1990)

Droege, C., 'Private Military and Security Companies and Human Rights: A Rough Sketch of the Legal Framework', Workshop of the Swiss Initiative on PMCs/PSCs (Küsnacht, January 2006)

'The Interplay between International Humanitarian Law and International Human Rights Law' (2007) 40 *Israel Law Review* 310

Dubuisson, F., 'Vers un Renforcement des Obligations de Diligence en Matière de Lutte Contre le Terrorisme', in K. Bannelier, T. Christakis, O. Corten and B. Delcourt (eds.), *Le Droit International Face au Terrorisme* (Paris, Pedone, 2002)

Dupuy, P.-M., 'Due Diligence in the International Law of State Responsibility', in *Legal Aspects of Transfrontier Pollution* (Paris, Organisation for Economic Co-operation and Development, 1977)

'Reviewing the Difficulties of Codification: On Ago's Classification of Obligations of Means and Obligations of Result in Relation to State Responsibility' (1999) 10 *European Journal of International Law* 371

Dupuy, P.-M., and Hoss, C., 'Trail Smelter and Terrorism', in R. Bratspies and R. Miller (eds.), *Transboundary Harm in International Law* (Cambridge, Cambridge University Press, 2006)

Duquesne, A., 'La Responsabilité Solidaire des Etats aux Termes de l'Article 1 des Conventions de Genève' (1966) 15 *Annales de Droit International Médical* 83

Eagar, C., 'Invisible US Army Defeats Serbs', *Observer* (5 November 1995)

Elsea, J., Schwartz, M., and Nakamura, K., 'Private Security Contractors in Iraq: Background, Legal Status and Other Issues', Congressional Research Service Report for Congress RL 32419 (updated 25 August 2008)

'Embassy Guard Photos Evoke Abu Ghraib Comparison', *New York Times* (14 September 2009)

Engelhardt, T., 'Order 17', *The Nation* (24 September 2007)

'Equatorial Guinea Coup Plotters Receive Long Jail Terms', *Times* (26 November 2004)

'Erez Crossing Will Be Operated by Private Company Starting Thursday', *Haaretz* (18 January 2006)

European Commission for Democracy through Law, 'Report on Private Military and Security Firms and Erosion of the State Monopoly on the Use of Force' (Venice, 12–13 June 2009)

Evans, M., *International Law*, 2nd edn (Oxford, Oxford University Press, 2006)

'Ex-Managers: Security Firm Cut Corners at Embassy', *New York Times* (11 September 2009)

Faite, A., 'Involvement of Private Contractors in Armed Conflict: Implications under International Humanitarian Law' (2004) 4(2) *Defence Studies* 166

Farer, T. J., 'Harnessing Rogue Elephants: A Short Discourse on Foreign Intervention in Civil Strife' (1969) 82 *Harvard Law Review* 511

Farrell, N., 'Attributing Criminal Liability to Corporate Actors: Some Lessons from the International Tribunals' (2010) 8 *Journal of International Criminal Justice* 873

Fay, G. R., 'Investigation of the Abu Ghraib Detention Facility and 205th Military Intelligence Brigade' (August 2004)

Fenwick, C., *The Neutrality Laws of the US* (Washington DC, Carnegie Endowment for International Peace, 1913)

Fidler, S., and Catan, T., 'Private Military Companies Pursue the Peace Divide', *Financial Times* (23 July 2003)

Fleck, D., *The Handbook of Humanitarian Law in Armed Conflicts* (Oxford, Oxford University Press, 1995)

　'International Accountability for Violations of the Ius in Bello: The Impact of the ICRC Study on Customary International Humanitarian Law' (2006) 11 *Journal of Conflict and Security Law* 182

Fletcher, G., 'On the Crimes Subject to Prosecution in Military Commissions' (2007) 5 *Journal of International Criminal Justice* 39

Foundation for Middle East Peace, 'Settlement Time Line' (2006) 16(2) *Report on Israeli Settlement in the Occupied Territories* 5

Fowler, K. A., 'War and Change in Late Medieval France and England', in K. A. Fowler (ed.), *The Hundred Years War* (London, Macmillan, 1971)

　Medieval Mercenaries (Oxford, Blackwell, 2001), vol. I

Fox, H., *The Law of State Immunity* (Oxford, Oxford University Press, 2002)

Fox, R., 'Fresh War Clouds Threaten Ceasefire', *Sunday Telegraph* (15 October 1995)

France, J. (ed.), *Mercenaries and Paid Men: The Mercenary Identity in the Middle Ages* (Leiden, Brill, 2008)

Francioni, F., and Scovazzi, T. (eds.), *International Responsibility for Environmental Harm* (London, Graham & Trotman, 1991)

Freeman, A. V., 'Responsibility of States for Unlawful Acts of Their Armed Forces' (1956) 88 *Recueil des Cours* 261

Friedmann, W., 'Intervention, Civil War and the Role of International Law' (1965) 59 *American Society of International Law Proceedings* 67

Gallagher, K., 'Civil Litigation and Transnational Business: An Alien Tort Statute Primer' (2010) 8 *Journal of International Criminal Justice* 745

García-Mora, M. R., *International Responsibility for Hostile Acts of Private Persons Against Foreign States* (The Hague, Martinus Nijhoff, 1962)

Gasser, H.-P., 'Agora: The US Decision Not to Ratify Protocol I to the Geneva Conventions in the Protection of War Victims' (1987) 81 *American Journal of International Law* 912

Gasser, H.-P., 'Ensuring Respect for the Geneva Conventions and Protocols: The Role of Third States and the United Nations', in H. Fox and M. Meyer (eds.), *Effecting Compliance* (London, British Institute of International and Comparative Law, 1993)

Gehring, T., and Jachtenfuchs, M., 'Liability for Transboundary Environmental Damage: Towards a General Liability Regime?' (1993) 4 *European Journal of International Law* 92

Gettleman, J., '4 From US Killed in Ambush in Iraq: Mob Drags Bodies', *New York Times* (1 April 2004)

Gibson, G., and Shane, S., 'Contractors Act as Interrogators', *Baltimore Sun* (4 May 2004)

Gillard, E.-C., 'Reparation for Violations of International Humanitarian Law' (2003) 851 *International Review of the Red Cross* 529

'Business Goes to War: Private Military/Security Companies and International Humanitarian Law' (2006) 88(863) *International Review of the Red Cross* 525

Giustozzi, A., 'The Privatization of War and Security in Afghanistan: Future or Dead End?' (2007) 2(1) *Economics of Peace and Security Journal*

Glanz, J., and Rubin, A., 'Blackwater Shootings "Murder", Iraq Says', *New York Times* (8 October 2007)

Gomulkiewicz, R., 'International Law Governing Aid to Opposition Groups in Civil War: Resurrecting the Standards of Belligerency' (1988) 63 *Washington Law Review* 42

Gooch, J., *Armies in Europe* (London, Routledge and Kegan Paul, 1980)

Gordon, M., 'Civilians to Take US Lead after Military Leaves Iraq', *New York Times* (18 August 2010)

Goulet, Y., 'Mixing Business with Bullets', *Jane's Intelligence Review* (September 1997)

Govern, K., and Bales, E., 'Taking Shots at Private Military Firms: International Law Misses Its Mark (Again)' (2008–9) 32 *Fordham International Law Journal* 55

Gray, C., 'The British Position in Regard to the Gulf Conflict' (1988) 37 *International and Comparative Law Quarterly* 420

Greenspan, M., *The Modern Law of Land Warfare* (Berkeley, University of California Press, 1959)

Greenwood, C., 'The Concept of War in Modern International Law' (1987) 36 *International and Comparative Law Quarterly* 283

Grundy, K., 'On Machiavelli and the Mercenaries' (1968) 6(3) *Journal of Modern African Studies* 295

Hakimi, M., 'State Bystander Responsibility' (2010) 21 *European Journal of International Law* 341

Haljan, D. P., 'A Constitutional Duty to Negotiate Amendments: Reference re Secession of Quebec' (1999) 48 *International and Comparative Law Quarterly* 447

Hall, C., 'The Duty of States Parties to the Convention Against Torture to Provide Procedures Permitting Victims to Recover Reparations for Torture Committed Abroad' (2008) 18(5) *European Journal of International Law* 921

Hall, W. E., *The Rights and Duties of Neutrals* (London, Longmans, Green, 1874) *International Law*, 8 edn (Oxford, Clarendon Press, 1924)

Hamaguchi, C., 'Between War and Peace: Exploring the Constitutionality of Subjecting Private Civilian Contractors to the UCMJ During Contingency Operations' (2008) 86 *North Carolina Law Review* 1047

Hampson, F. J., 'Mercenaries: Diagnosis Before Proscription' (1991) 3 *Netherlands Yearbook International Law* 1

Hanes, S., 'Private Security Contractors Look to Africa for Recruits', *Christian Science Monitor* (8 January 2008)

Haynes, D., and Ford, R., 'Briton Facing Iraq Murder Trial on Probation for Gun Offence', *Times* (13 August 2009)

Heintze, H.-J., 'On the Relationship between Human Rights Law Protection and International Humanitarian Law' (2004) 86(856) *International Review of the Red Cross* 789

Henckaerts, J.-M., and Doswald-Beck, L. (eds.), *Customary International Humanitarian Law* (Cambridge, Cambridge University Press, 2005), vol. I: Rules
(eds.), *Customary International Humanitarian Law* (Cambridge, Cambridge University Press, 2005), vol. II: Practice

Hessbruegge, J. A., 'The Historical Development of the Doctrines of Attribution and Due Diligence in International Law' (2004) 36 *New York University Journal of International Law and Policy* 265

Higgins, R., 'International Law and Civil Conflict', in E. Luard (ed.), *The International Regulation of Civil Wars* (London, Thames & Hudson Ltd, 1972)
Problems and Process: International Law and How We Use It (Oxford, Clarendon Press, 1994)
'The General International Law of Terrorism', in R. Higgins and M. Flory (eds.), *Terrorism and International Law* (London, Routledge, 1997)

Hirsch, J., *Sierra Leone: Diamonds and the Struggle for Democracy* (London, Lynne Rienner, 2001)

Hodge, N., 'CIA Retains Controversial Security Firm in Afghanistan', *Wall Street Journal* (27 June 2010)
'Doubling the State Department's Private Army in Iraq?', *Wall Street Journal* (12 July 2010)

Holmquist, C., 'Private Security Companies: The Case for Regulation' (Stockholm, Stockholm International Policy Research Institute, 2005)

Hooper, J., 'Peace in Sierra Leone: A Temporary Outcome?' (February 1997) *Jane's Intelligence Review* 91

Bloodsong: An Account of Executive Outcomes in Angola (London, Collins, 2002)

Hoppe, C., 'Passing the Buck: State Responsibility for Private Military Companies' (2008) 19(5) *European Journal of International Law* 989

'State Responsibility for Violations of International Humanitarian Law Committed by Individuals Providing Coercive Services under a Contract with a State' (Centre for Studies and Research of The Hague Academy of International Law, 2008)

Howe, H., 'Private Security Forces and African Stability: The Case of Executive Outcomes' (1998) 36(2) *Journal of Modern African Studies* 307

Human Rights First, 'Private Security Contractors at War: Ending the Culture of Impunity' (2008)

Human Rights Watch, 'Hopes Betrayed: Trafficking of Women and Girls to Post-Conflict Bosnia and Herzegovina for Forced Prostitution' (26 November 2002)

Hunt, A., 'The Council of Europe Convention on the Prevention of Terrorism' (2006) 12(4) *European Public Law* 603

Huntington, S. P., *The Soldier and the State: The Theory and Politics of Civil-Military Relations* (New York, Random House, 1957)

International Committee of the Red Cross, 'Report of the First Expert Meeting on the Notion of Direct Participation in Hostilities' (Geneva, September 2003)

'Report of the Third Expert Meeting on the Notion of Direct Participation in Hostilities' (Geneva, October 2005)

'Interpretive Guidance on the Notion of Direct Participation in Hostilities under International Humanitarian Law' (June 2009)

'Iraq Moves to End Contractors' Immunity', *ABC News* (30 October 2007)

Isenberg, D., 'A Fistful of Contractors: The Case for a Pragmatic Assessment of Private Military Companies in Iraq', British–American Security Information Council Research Report (September 2004)

'Challenges of Security Privatisation in Iraq', in A. Bryden and M. Caparini (eds.), *Private Actors and Security Governance* (Berlin, LIT Verlag, 2007)

'Dogs of War: Blue Helmets and Bottom Lines', www.upi.com (17 February 2009)

Speaking Hypothetically: What To Do When a PMC Tortures', *Huffington Post* (27 July 2010)

Jennings, R., and Watts, A. (eds.), *Oppenheim's International Law*, 9th edn (Harlow, Longman, 1992)

Jessup, P. C., Deâk, F., Alison Phillips, W., Reede, A. H., and Turlington, E. W., *Neutrality, Its History, Economics and Law* (Columbia University Press, New York 1935)

Kaleck, W., and Saage-Maaß, M., 'Corporate Accountability for Human Rights Violations Amounting to International Crimes: The Status Quo and Its Challenges' (2010) 8 *Journal of International Criminal Justice* 699

Kalshoven, F., 'State Responsibility for Warlike Acts of the Armed Forces' (1991) 40 *International and Comparative Law Quarterly* 827

'The Undertaking to Respect and Ensure Respect in All Circumstances: From Tiny Seed to Ripening Fruit' (1999) 2 *Yearbook of International Humanitarian Law* 3

Kamenov, T., 'The Origin of State and Entity Responsibility for Violations of International Humanitarian Law in Armed Conflicts', in F. Kalshoven and Y. Sandoz (eds.), *Implementation of International Humanitarian Law* (Dordrecht, Martinus Nijhoff, 1989)

Katzman, K., and Elsea, J., 'Iraq: Transition to Sovereignty', Congressional Research Service Report for Congress RS21820 (21 July 2004)

Keefe, P. R., 'Don't Privatize Our Spies', *New York Times* (25 June 2007)

Kelsen, H., *Principles of International Law* (New York, Rinehart, 1952)

Kessler, B., 'Die Durchsetzung der Genfer Abkommen von 1949 in nicht-internationalen bewaffneten Konflikten auf Grundlage ihres gemeinsamen Art. 1' (2001) 132 *Veröffentlichungen des Walther-Schücking-Instituts für Internationales Recht an der Universität Kiel* 26

'The Duty to "Ensure Respect" under Common Article 1 of the Geneva Conventions: Its Implications on International and Non-International Armed Conflicts' (2001) 44 *German Yearbook of International Law* 498

Kidane, W., 'The Status of Private Military Contractors under International Humanitarian Law' (2010) 38(3) *Denver Journal of International Law and Policy*

Kinsey, C., *Corporate Soldiers and International Security: The Rise of Private Military Companies* (London, Routledge, 2006)

Krahmann, E., *States, Citizens and the Privatisation of Security* (Cambridge, Cambridge University Press, 2010)

Krasner, S. D., 'Sovereignty: An Institutional Perspective', in J. A. Caporaso (ed.), *The Elusive State: International and Comparative Perspectives* (Newbury Park, CA, Sage, 1989)

Kremnitzer, M., 'A Possible Case for Imposing Criminal Liability on Corporations in International Criminal Law' (2010) 8 *Journal of International Criminal Justice* 909

Krieger, H., 'A Conflict of Norms: The Relationship between Humanitarian Law and Human Rights Law in the ICRC Customary Law Study' (2006) 11(2) *Journal of Conflict and Security Law* 265

Kunz, J., 'Sanctions in International Law' (1956) 50 *American Journal of International Law* 514

Kwakwa, E., 'The Current Status of Mercenaries in the Law of Armed Conflict' (1990) 14(1) *Hastings International and Comparative Law Review* 67

Lauterpacht, H., 'Revolutionary Activities by Private Persons Against Foreign States' (1928) 22 *American Journal of International Law* 105

'The Revision of the Law of War' (1952) 29 *British Yearbook of International Law* 360

(ed.), *Oppenheim's International Law*, 7th edn (London, Longmans, 1952), vol. I

(ed.), *Oppenheim's International Law*, 7th edn (London, Longmans, 1952), vol. II

(ed.), *Oppenheim's International Law*, 8th edn (London, Longmans, Green, 1955)

Layeb, A., 'Mercenary Activity: United States Neutrality Laws and Enforcement' (1989) 10 *New York Law School Journal of International and Comparative Law* 269

Leach, P., 'The British Military in Iraq: The Applicability of the Espace Juridique Doctrine under the European Convention on Human Rights' (2005) *Public Law* 448

Leander, A., 'Drafting Community: Understanding the Fate of Conscription' (2004) 30(4) *Armed Forces and Society* 571

'The Market for Force and Public Security: The Destabilizing Consequences of Private Military Companies' (2005) 42 *Journal of Peace Research* 605

'Eroding State Authority? Private Military Companies and the Legitimate Use of Force' (Rome, Centro Militare di Studi Strategici, 2006)

Lee, T., 'Contracting under the SOFA: New Agreement Subjects Contractors to Iraqi Criminal and Civil Laws' (2009) 4(4) *Journal of International Peace Operations* 7

Legg, T., and Ibbs, I., 'Report of the Sierra Leone Arms Investigation', Return to an Address of the Honourable the House of Commons (27 July 1998)

Lehnardt, C., 'Private Military Companies and State Responsibility', in S. Chesterman and C. Lehnardt (eds.), *From Mercenaries to Market: The Rise and Regulation of Private Military Companies* (Oxford, Oxford University Press, 2007)

Levrat, N., 'Les Conséquences de l'Engagement pris par le HPC de "Faire Respecter" les Conventions Humanitaires', in F. Kalshoven and Y. Sandoz (eds.), *Implementation of International Humanitarian Law* (Dordrecht, Martinus Nijhoff, 1989)

Lin, F., 'Subversive Intervention' (1963) 25 *University of Pittsburgh Law Review* 35

Lindroos, A., 'Addressing Norm Conflicts in a Fragmented Legal System: The Doctrine of Lex Specialis' (2005) 74 *Nordic Journal of International Law* 27

Luckey, J., Grasso, V., and Manuel, K., 'Inherently Governmental Functions and Department of Defense Operations: Background, Issues, and Options for Congress', Congressional Research Service Report for Congress R40641 (22 July 2009)

Lynch, C., 'UN Embraces Private Military Contractors', *Foreign Policy* (17 January 2010)

Lynch, T., and Walsh, A. J., 'The Good Mercenary' (2000) 8(2) *Journal of Political Philosophy* 133

MacAskill, E., 'CIA Hired Blackwater for Al-Qaida Assassination Programme, Sources Say', *Guardian* (20 August 2009)

Maffai, M., 'Accountability for Private Military and Security Company Employees That Engage in Sex Trafficking and Related Abuses While under Contract with the United States Overseas' (2008–9) 26 *Wisconsin International Law Journal* 1095

Malan, M., and Cilliers, J., 'Mercenaries and Mischief: The Regulation of Foreign Military Assistance Bill' (Institute for Security Studies Occasional Paper No. 25, 1997)

Mallaby, S., 'Mercenaries Are No Altruists, But They Can Do Good', *Washington Post* (4 June 2001)

'Think Again: Renouncing Use of Mercenaries Can Be Lethal', *Washington Post* (5 June 2001)

Mallett, M. E., *Mercenaries and Their Masters: Warfare in Renaissance Italy* (London, The Bodley Head, 1974)

Markon, J., 'Two Defense Contractors Indicted in Shooting of Afghans', *Washington Post* (8 January 2010)

Marston, G., 'UK Materials in International Law' (1982) 53 *British Yearbook of International Law* 519

Mason, R. C., 'Status of Forces Agreement (SOFA): What Is It, and How Might One Be Utilized in Iraq?', US Congressional Research Service Report for Congress RL34531 (1 December 2008)

Maxwell, M., and Watts, S., 'Unlawful Enemy Combatant: Status, Theory of Culpability or Neither?' (2007) 5 *Journal of International Criminal Justice* 19

Mayer, D., 'Peaceful Warriors: Private Military Security Companies and the Quest for Stable Societies' (2010) 89 *Journal of Business Ethics* 387

Mazzetti, M., 'CIA Sought Blackwater's Help to Kill Jihadists', *New York Times* (19 August 2009)

McCormack, T., 'The "Sandline Affair": Papua New Guinea Resorts to Mercenarism to End the Bougainville Conflict' (1998) 1 *Yearbook of International Humanitarian Law* 292

McCorquodale, R., and Simons, P., 'Responsibility Beyond Borders: State Responsibility for Extraterritorial Violations by Corporations of International Human Rights Law' (2007) 70(4) *Modern Law Review* 598

McGoldrick, D., *The Human Rights Committee: Its Role in the Development of the International Covenant on Civil and Political Rights* (Oxford, Clarendon Press, 1991)

'The Principle of Non-Intervention: Human Rights', in A. V. Lowe and C. Warbrick (eds.), *The UN and the Principles of International Law* (London, Routledge, 1994)

McNeill, W., *The Pursuit of Power: Technology, Armed Force, and Society Since AD 1000* (Oxford, Blackwell, 1982)

Merle, R., and McCarthy, E., '6 Employees from CACI International, Titan Referred for Prosecution', *Washington Post* (26 August 2004)

Meron, T., 'Applicability of Multilateral Conventions to Occupied Territories' (1978) 72 *American Journal of International Law* 542

'Extraterritoriality of Human Rights Treaties' (1995) 89 *American Journal of International Law* 78

'International Criminalization of Internal Atrocities' (1995) 89 *American Journal of International Law* 554

'The Humanization of Humanitarian Law' (2000) 94 *American Journal of International Law* 239

Meyrovitz, H., 'Le Droit de la Guerre et les Droits de l'Homme' (1972) 88 *Revue de Droit Public et de la Science Politique* 1059

Milliard, T. S., 'Overcoming Post-Colonial Myopia: A Call to Recognize and Regulate Private Military Companies' (2003) 176 *Military Law Review* 1

Mlinarcik, J. T., 'Private Military Contractors and Justice: A Look at the Industry, Blackwater and the Fallujah Incident' (2006) 4 *Regent Journal of International Law* 129

Mockler, A., *The Mercenaries* (London, MacDonald, 1969)

The New Mercenaries (London, Sidgwick & Jackson, 1985)

Moeckli, D., 'The US Supreme Court's "Enemy Combatant" Decisions: A "Major Victory for the Rule of Law"?' (2005) 10 *Journal of Conflict and Security Law* 75

Moore, J. B., *History and Digest of the International Arbitrations to Which the US Has Been a Party* (Washington DC, Government Printing Office, 1898)

Moore, J. N., 'Intervention: A Monochromatic Term for a Polychromatic Reality', in R. Falk (ed.), *The Vietnam War and International Law* (Princeton, NJ, Princeton University Press, 1969)

'The Control of Foreign Intervention in Internal Conflict' (1969) 9 *Virginia Journal of International Law* 205

Mowbray, A., *The Development of Positive Obligations under the European Convention on Human Rights by the European Court of Human Rights* (Oxford, Hart, 2004)

Musah, A.-F., and Fayemi, J. K. (eds.), *Mercenaries: An African Security Dilemma* (London, Pluto Press, 2000)

Nagl, J., and Fontaine, R., 'Contracting in Conflicts: The Path to Reform' (Center for a New American Security, June 2010)

Nollkaemper, A., 'Concurrence between Individual Responsibility and State Responsibility in International Law' (2003) 52 *International and Comparative Law Quarterly* 615

Norton, P. M., 'Between the Ideology and the Reality: The Shadow of the Law of Neutrality' (1976) 17 *Harvard International Law Journal* 249

Nowak, M., and McArthur, E., *The United Nations Convention Against Torture: A Commentary* (Oxford, Oxford University Press, 2008)

O'Brien, K., 'Freelance Forces: Exploiters of Old or New-Age Peacebrokers?' (August 1998) *Jane's Intelligence Review* 42

'Military-Advisory Groups and African Security: Privatized Peacekeeping?' (1998) 5(3) *International Peacekeeping* 78

'What Should and What Should Not Be Regulated?', in S. Chesterman and C. Lehnardt (eds.), *From Mercenaries to Market: The Rise and Regulation of Private Military Companies* (Oxford, Oxford University Press, 2007)

Official Records of the Diplomatic Conference on the Reaffirmation and Development of International Humanitarian Law Applicable in Armed Conflicts, Geneva (1974–6) (Bern, Federal Political Department, 1978)

Ortiz, C., *Private Armed Forces and Global Security: A Guide to the Issues* (Santa Barbara, CA, Praeger, 2010)

Østensen, A. G., *Outsourcing Peace?: The United Nations' Use of Private Security and Military Companies* (Saärbrucken, VDM Verlag, 2009)

Pallister, D., 'Foreign Security Teams to Lose Immunity from Prosecution in Iraq', *Guardian* (27 December 2008)

Palwankar, U., 'Measures Available to States for Fulfilling Their Obligation to Ensure Respect for International Humanitarian Law' (1994) 298 *International Review of the Red Cross* 9

'Papua New Guinea Hires Mercenaries', *Washington Times* (28 February 1997)

Parker, J., *The Gurkhas: The Inside Story of the World's Most Feared Soldiers* (London, Headline, 2005)

Parks, W. H., 'Remarks, Customary Law and Additional Protocol I to the Geneva Conventions for Protection of War Victims' (1987) 81 *American Society of International Law Proceedings* 27

Partlow, J., 'Karzai Wants Private Security Firms Out of Afghanistan', *Washington Post* (17 August 2010)

Pasqualucci, J., *The Practice and Procedure of the Inter-American Court of Human Rights* (Cambridge, Cambridge University Press, 2003)

Patterson, M., *Privatising Peace: A Corporate Adjunct to United Nations Peacekeeping and Humanitarian Operations* (New York, Palgrave Macmillan, 2009)

Pauwelyn, J., *Conflict of Norms in Public International Law: How WTO Law Relates to Other Rules of International Law* (Cambridge, Cambridge University Press, 2003)

'Payout Ends Mercenary War', *Australian* (1 May 1999)

Pech, K., and Beresford, D., 'Corporate Dogs of War Grow Fat in Africa', *Guardian Weekly* (26 June 1997)

Peck, J., 'Remilitarizing Africa for Corporate Profit' (October 2000) *Z-Magazine*

Pejić, J., 'Terrorist Acts and Groups: A Role for International Law?' (2004) 75 *British Yearbook of International Law* 71

Percy, S., *Regulating the Private Security Industry* (Adelphi Paper No. 384, 2006)

  Mercenaries: The History of a Norm in International Relations (Oxford, Oxford University Press, 2007)

    'Morality and Regulation', in S. Chesterman and C. Lehnardt (eds.), *From Mercenaries to Market: The Rise and Regulation of Private Military Companies* (Oxford, Oxford University Press, 2007)

    'Mercenaries: Strong Norm, Weak Law' (2008) 61(2) *International Organization* 367

    'Private Security Companies and Civil Wars' (2009) 11(1) *Civil Wars* 57

Petrochilos, G., 'The Relevance of the Concepts of War and Armed Conflict to the Law of Neutrality' (1998) 31 *Vanderbilt Journal of Transnational Law* 575

Pfanner, T., 'Interview with Andrew Bearpark' (2006) 88(863) *International Review of the Red Cross* 449

Philpott, D., *Revolutions in Sovereignty: How Ideas Shaped Modern International Relations* (Princeton, NJ, Princeton University Press, 2001)

Phinney, D., 'Department of Defense Tightening Contracting Rules after Iraqi Prison Scandals', *Federal Times* (7 June 2004)

Pictet, J. (ed.), *Commentary to the Geneva Convention Relative to the Protection of Civilian Persons in Time of War* (Geneva, International Committee of the Red Cross, 1958)

  (ed.), *Commentary to the Geneva Convention Relative to the Treatment of Prisoners of War* (Geneva, International Committee of the Red Cross, 1960)

  Humanitarian Law and the Protection of War Victims (Geneva, Henry Dunant Institute, 1975)

Pincus, W., 'Lawmakers Want More Data on Contracting Out Intelligence', *Washington Post* (7 May 2006)

Pisillo-Mazzeschi, R., *'Due diligence' e Responsabilita Internazionale Degli Stati* (Milan, Giuffrè, 1989)

  'The Due Diligence Rule and the Nature of the International Responsibility of States' (1992) 35 *German Yearbook of International Law* 9

  'International Obligations to Provide for Reparation Claims', in A. Randelzhofer and C. Tomuschat (eds.), *State Responsibility and the Individual: Reparation in Instances of Grave Violations of Human Rights* (London, Martinus Nijhoff Publishers, 1999)

'PNG Pays up to Mercenaries', *BBC News* (1 May 1999)

Porch, D., *The French Foreign Legion: A Complete History* (London, Macmillan, 1991)

Posen, B., 'Nationalism, the Mass Army, and Military Power' (1993) 18(2) *International Security* 80

Power, S., *et al.*, 'The Croatian Army's Friends' *US News and World Report* (21 August 1995)

Price, R., 'A Genealogy of the Chemical Weapons Taboo' (1995) 49(1) *International Organization* 73

Priest, D., 'Private Guards Repel Attack on US Headquarters', *Washington Post* (6 April 2004)

Project on Government Oversight, Letter to Secretary of State Hillary Clinton Regarding US Embassy in Kabul (1 September 2009), available at www.pogo.org/pogo-files/letters/contract-oversight/co-gp-20090901.html

Provost, R., *International Human Rights and Humanitarian Law* (Cambridge, Cambridge University Press, 2002)

Ranganathan, S., 'Between Complicity and Irrelevance? Industry Associations and the Challenge of Regulating Private Security Contractors' (2010) 41(2) *Georgetown Journal of International Law*

Ratner, S., 'Foreign Occupation and International Territorial Administration: The Challenges of Convergence' (2005) 16 *European Journal of International Law* 696

Reid, R. H., 'Blackwater Loses Security License in Iraq', *Associated Press* (18 September 2007)

Reno, W., 'Privatising War in Sierra Leone' (1997) 97 *Current History* 610

'Report of the Committee of Privy Counsellors Appointed to Inquire into the Recruitment of Mercenaries' (London, Her Majesty's Stationery Office, 1976)

Rimli, L., and Schmeidl, S., 'Private Security Companies and Local Populations: An Exploratory Study of Afghanistan and Angola' (Geneva, Swiss Peace Foundation, 2007)

Risen, J., 'Interference Seen in Blackwater Inquiry', *New York Times* (2 March 2010)

Roberts, A., 'Implementation of the Laws of War in Late 20th Century Conflicts' (1998) 29(2) *Security Dialogue* 137

Rogers, A., 'Combatant Status', in E. Wilmshurst and S. Breau (eds.), *Perspectives on the ICRC Study on Customary International Humanitarian Law* (Cambridge, British Institute of International and Comparative Law, 2007)

Roht-Arriaza, N., 'Sources in International Treaties of an Obligation to Investigate, Prosecute and Provide Redress', in N. Roht-Arriaza (ed.), *Impunity and Human Rights in International Law and Practice* (Oxford, Oxford University Press, 1995)

Rothenberg, G., *The Art of Warfare in the Age of Napoleon* (London, BT Batsford, 1977)

Rubin, A., 'Iraqi Cabinet Votes to End Security Firms' Immunity', *New York Times* (31 October 2007)

'Karzai Orders Guard Firms to Disband', *New York Times* (17 August 2010)

Rubin, A., and Kramer, A., 'Iraqi Premier Says Blackwater Shootings Challenge His Nation's Sovereignty', *New York Times* (24 September 2007)

Rubin, A., and von Zielbauer, P., 'Blackwater Case Highlights Legal Uncertainties', *New York Times* (11 October 2007)

Rubin, E., 'An Army of One's Own' (February 1997) *Harper's Magazine* 44

Sahovic, M., 'Non-Intervention in the Internal Affairs of States', in M. Sahovic (ed.), *Principles of International Law Concerning Friendly Relations and Cooperation* (New York, Oceana Publications, 1969)

Principles of International Law Concerning Friendly Relations and Cooperation (New York, Oceana Publications, 1972)

Salans, C. (then Deputy Legal Adviser to the US Department of State) [1968] *American Society of International Law Proceedings* 76

Sandoz, Y., 'Private Security and International Law', in J. Cilliers and P. Mason (eds.), *Peace, Profit, or Plunder: The Privatisation of Security in War-Torn African Societies* (Pretoria, Institute for Security Studies, 1999)

Sandoz, Y., Swinarski, C., and Zimmermann, B. (eds.), *Commentary on the Additional Protocols of 8 June 1977 to the Geneva Conventions of 12 August 1949* (Geneva, International Committee of the Red Cross, 1987)

Sari, A., 'The European Union Status of Forces Agreement' (2008) 13 *Journal of Conflict and Security Law* 353

Saul, B., *Defining Terrorism in International Law* (Oxford, Oxford University Press, 2006)

Savage, C., 'Judge Drops Charges from Blackwater Deaths in Iraq', *New York Times* (31 December 2009)

Scahill, J., *Blackwater* (London, Serpent's Tail, 2007)

Schindler, D., 'Aspects Contemporains de la Neutralité' (1967) 121 *Recueil des Cours* 221

Schmitt, M., 'Humanitarian Law and Direct Participation in Hostilities by Private Contractors or Civilian Employees' (2004–5) 5 *Chicago Journal of International Law* 511

Schooner, S. L., 'Contractor Atrocities at Abu Ghraib: Compromised Accountability in a Streamlined, Outsourced Government' (2005) 16 *Stanford Law and Policy Review* 549

Schreier, F., and Caparini, M., *Privatising Security: Law, Practice and Governance of Private Military and Security Companies* (Geneva, Centre for the Democratic Control of Armed Forces, 2005)

Schreuer, C., *State Immunity: Some Recent Developments* (Cambridge, Grotius, 1988)

Schwartz, M., 'Department of Defense Contractors in Iraq and Afghanistan: Background and Analysis', Congressional Research Service Report for Congress R40764 (2 July 2010)

Schwarzenberger, G., *International Law as Applied by International Courts and Tribunals* (London, Stevens, 1968)

Scott, J. B. (ed.), *Reports to the Hague Conferences of 1899 and 1907* (Oxford, Clarendon Press, 1917)

Seegers, A., *The Security Forces and the Transition in South Africa: 1986–1994* (Cape Town, University of Cape Town, 1995)

Sevastopulo, D., 'Iraqis Pull Security Contractor's Licence', *Financial Times* (17 September 2007)

Seybold, T. B., 'Major Armed Conflicts', in *Stockholm International Peace Research Institute Yearbook 2000* (Oxford, Oxford University Press, 2000)

Shadid, A., 'Biden Says US Will Appeal Blackwater Case Dismissal', *New York Times* (24 January 2010)

Shearer, D., *Private Armies and Military Intervention* (Adelphi Paper No. 316, 1998)

Shelton, D., *Remedies in International Human Rights Law* (Oxford, Oxford University Press, 1999)

Sherman, J., and DiDomenico, V., 'The Public Cost of Private Security in Afghanistan' (New York, Center on International Cooperation, New York University, September 2009)

Sibert, M., *Traité de Droit International Public* (Paris, Dalloz, 1951)

Silber, L., and Little, A., *Yugoslavia: Death of a Nation* (New York, Penguin Books, 1997)

Silverstein, K., 'Privatising War: How Affairs of States Are Outsourced to Private Corporations', *The Nation* (28 July 1997) 4

Private Warriors (London, Verso, 2000)

Simpson, J., and Weiner, E., *Oxford English Dictionary*, 2nd edn (Clarendon Press, Oxford 1989)

Sinclair, I., 'The Law of Sovereign Immunity: Recent Developments' (1980) 167(ii) *Recueil des Cours* 113

Singer, P., 'The Private Military Industry and Iraq: What Have We Learned and Where to Next?' (Geneva, Geneva Centre for the Democratic Control of the Armed Forces, 2004)

'War, Profits, and the Vacuum of Law: Privatised Military Firms and International Law' (2004) 42 *Columbia Journal of Transnational Law* 521

'Outsourcing War' *Foreign Affairs* (1 March 2005)

'Can't Win With 'Em, Can't Go to War Without 'Em: Private Military Contractors and Counterinsurgency' (Washington DC, Brookings Institution, September 2007)

Corporate Warriors: The Rise of the Privatized Military Industry, updated edn (London, Cornell University Press, 2008)

Snyder, S., 'A Call for Justice and the US–ROK Alliance' (Pacific Forum, Center for Strategic and International Studies, 18 December 2002)

Sornarajah, M., 'Problems in Applying the Restrictive Theory of Sovereign Immunity' (1982) 31 *International and Comparative Law Quarterly* 661

'Linking State Responsibility for Certain Harms Caused by Corporate Nationals Abroad to Civil Recourse in the Legal Systems of Home States', in C. Scott (ed.), *Torture as Tort: Comparative Perspectives on the Development of Transnational Human Rights Litigation* (Oxford, Hart, 2001)

Sossai, M., 'Status of Private Military Companies in the Law of War: The Question of Direct Participation in Hostilities' (European University Institute Working Paper 2009/6)

Spearin, C., 'Private Security Companies and Humanitarians: A Corporate Solution to Securing Humanitarian Spaces?' (2001) 8(1) *International Peacekeeping* 20

Special Inspector-General for Iraq Reconstruction, 'Field Commanders See Improvements in Controlling and Coordinating Private Security Contractor Missions in Iraq' SIGIR 09-022 (28 July 2009)

Spicer, T., *An Unorthodox Soldier: Peace and War and the Sandline Affair* (Edinburgh, Mainstream, 1999)

Spinedi, M., 'Private Contractors: Responsabilité Internationale des Entreprises ou Attribution à l'Etat de la Conduite des Personnes Privées?' (2005) 7 *Forum du Droit International* 273

Staino, E., 'Suing Private Military Contractors for Torture: How to Use the Alien Tort Statute Without Granting Sovereign Immunity-Related Defenses' (2010) 50 *Santa Clara Law Review* 1277

Steele, D., 'Last Stop Before Iraq', *Army* (1 May 2004)

Stein, J., 'CIA Gives Blackwater Firm New $100 Million Contract', *Washington Post* (23 June 2010)

Stockman, F., 'Contractors in War Zones Lose Immunity', *Boston Globe* (7 January 2007)

Stoddard, A., Harmer, A., and DiDomenico, V., *The Use of Private Security Providers and Services in Humanitarian Operations* (London, Overseas Development Institute, 2008)

Stone, J., *Legal Controls of International Conflict* (London, Stevens, 1954)

Sturcke, J., 'Blackwater Security Guards Face Manslaughter Charges', *Guardian* (8 December 2008)

Suter, W. K., 'An Enquiry into the Meaning of the Phrase "Human Rights in Armed Conflicts"' (1976) 15 *Revue de Droit Pénal Militaire et Droit de la Guerre* 393

Symonides, J. (ed.), *Human Rights: International Protection, Monitoring, Enforcement* (Aldershot/Paris, Ashgate/UNESCO, 2003)

Taljaard, R., 'Implementing South Africa's Regulation of Foreign Military Assistance Act', in A. Bryden and M. Caparini (eds.), *Private Actors and Security Governance* (Geneva, Geneva Centre for the Democratic Control of the Armed Forces, 2006)

Talmon, S., 'Recognition of Governments: An Analysis of the New British Policy and Practice' (1992) 63 *British Yearbook of International Law* 231

Taulbee, J., 'Myths, Mercenaries and Contemporary International Law' (1985) 15 *California Western International Law Journal* 339

Tavernise, S., 'US Contractor Banned by Iraq over Shootings', *New York Times* (18 September 2007)

Statement of Prime Minister Thatcher, 22 Parl. Deb., HC 616 (1982)

'Thatcher and a Very African Coup', *Guardian* (26 August 2004)

'Thatcher's Son Pleads Guilty in Coup Plot, Avoiding Prison', *New York Times* (14 January 2005)

Thomas, A. V. W., and Thomas, A. J., Jr, 'International Legal Aspects of the Civil War in Spain, 1936–39', in R. Falk (ed.), *The International Law of Civil War* (Baltimore, MD, Johns Hopkins University Press, 1971)

Thompson, G., and Landler, M., 'Company Kept Kabul Security Contract Despite Record', *New York Times* (11 September 2009)

Thompson, M., 'Generals for Hire', *Time* (15 January 1996) 34

Thomson, J. E., *Mercenaries, Pirates, and Sovereigns: State-Building and Extraterritorial Violence in Early Modern Europe* (Princeton, NJ, Princeton University Press, 1994)

Traynor, I., 'The Privatisation of Warfare', *Guardian* (10 December 2003)

Trooboff, P., 'Foreign State Immunity: Emerging Consensus of Principles' (1986) 200 *Recueil des Cours* 235

Turns, D., 'Implementation and Compliance', in E. Wilmshurst and S. Breau (eds.), *Perspectives on the ICRC's Study on Customary International Humanitarian Law* (Cambridge, British Institute of International and Comparative Law, 2007)

UK Foreign Affairs Committee, Ninth Report, 'Private Military Companies' (October 2002)

UK Foreign and Commonwealth Office, Green Paper, 'Private Military Companies: Options for Regulation' (February 2002)

Consultation Paper, 'Consultation on Promoting High Standards of Conduct by Private Military and Security Companies Internationally' (April 2009)

Impact Assessment, 'Promoting High Standards of Conduct by Private Military and Security Companies Internationally' (April 2009)

UK Law Commission, Report No. 19, 'The Territorial and Extraterritorial Extent of the Criminal Law' (1978)

UK Ministry of Defence, *The Manual of the Law of Armed Conflict* (Oxford, Oxford University Press, 2004)

UK Statement of 1980 (1980) 51 *British Yearbook of International Law* 367

University Centre for International Humanitarian Law, Expert Meeting on Private Military Contractors (Geneva, August 2005)

US Air Force, *International Law: The Conduct of Armed Conflict and Air Operations*, AFP11-31 (1976)

US Army, *Field Manual 27-10: The Law of Land Warfare* (1956)

US Army, *Operational Law Handbook* (2004)

USCENTCOM, 2nd Quarterly Contractor Census Report (May 2009)

US Commission on Wartime Contracting, 'At What Cost? Contingency Contracting in Iraq and Afghanistan: Interim Report to Congress' (10 June 2009)

Hearing, 19 April 2010, 'Reliance on Contingency Services Contracts: Where Is the Management and Oversight?'

Hearing, 18 June 2010, 'Are Private Security Contractors Performing Inherently Governmental Functions?'

Hearing, 26 July 2010, 'Subcontracting: Who's Minding the Store?'

US Congressional Budget Office, 'Contractors' Support of US Operations in Iraq' (August 2008)

US Department of Defense, *Dictionary of Military and Associated Terms*, JP-102 (12 April 2001, as amended through April 2010)

Working Group Report on Detainee Interrogations in the Global War on Terrorism (2003)

Instruction 3020.41, 'Contractor Personnel Authorized to Accompany the US Armed Forces' (3 October 2005)

Directive 2311.01 E, 'DoD Law of War Program' (9 May 2006)

Instruction 1100.22, 'Guidance for Determining Workforce Mix' (7 September 2006)

Instruction 3020.50, 'US Government Private Security Contractors Operating in a Designated Area of Combat Operations' (22 June 2009)

US Department of Justice, Fact Sheet, 'Major US Export Enforcement Prosecutions During the Past Two Years' (28 October 2008)

Press Release, 'Two Individuals Charged with Murder and Other Offenses Related to Shooting Death of Two Afghan Nationals in Kabul, Afghanistan' (7 January 2010)

US Deputy Secretary of Defense, 'Management of Department of Defense Contractors and Contractor Personnel Accompanying US Armed Forces in Contingency Operations Outside the US' (25 September 2007)

'US Firm to Rebuild Iraqi Army', *BBC News* (26 June 2003)

US Government Accountability Office, 'Rebuilding Iraq: DOD and State Department Have Improved Oversight and Coordination of Private Security Contractors in Iraq, But Further Actions Are Needed to Sustain Improvements', GAO-08-966 (31 July 2008)

'DOD Needs to Address Contract Oversight and Quality Assurance Issues for Contracts Used to Support Contingency Operations', GAO-08-1087 (26 September 2008)

'Contingency Contracting: DOD, State, and USAID Contracts and Contractor Personnel in Iraq and Afghanistan', GAO-09-19 (1 October 2008)

'Contingency Contracting: Improvements Needed in Management of Contractors Supporting Contract and Grant Administration in Iraq and Afghanistan', GAO-10-357 (April 2010)

US House of Representatives Report No. 94-1487 (1976) 15 ILM 1398

US House of Representatives Committee on the Judiciary, Subcommittee on Crime, Terrorism, and Homeland Security Hearing, 19 June 2007, 'War Profiteering and Other Contractor Crimes Committed Overseas', Statement of Scott Horton

US House of Representatives Committee on Oversight and Governmental Reform, 'Additional Information about Blackwater USA' (1 October 2007)

US Joint Chiefs of Staff, Joint Publication 3-0 Doctrine for Joint Operations A-2 (2 September 2001)

'US Judge Dismisses Charges in Blackwater Iraq Killings', *BBC News* (31 December 2009)

US Naval Academy, Stockdale Center for Ethical Leadership, Symposiums and Seminars: McCain Conference 2009

US Office of Management and Budget, Circular No. A-76 (Revised), 'Performance of Commercial Activities' (29 May 2003)

Proposed Policy Letter, 'Work Reserved for Performance by Federal Government Employees' (31 March 2010)

US Office of the Secretary of Defense, Memorandum for Mr John McNeill, Assistant General Counsel (International), '1977 Protocols Additional to the Geneva Conventions: Customary International Law Implications' (8 May 1969)

US Office of the Under Secretary of Defense for Acquisition, Technology and Logistics, 'Contractor Support of US Operations in the USCENTCOM Area of Responsibility, Iraq, and Afghanistan' (May 2010)

US Senate, Report on Intelligence Authorization Act for Fiscal Year 2002 (14 September 2001)

US Senate Committee on Homeland Security and Governmental Affairs, Subcommittee on Contracting Oversight, 'New Information about the Guard Force Contract at the US Embassy in Kabul' (June 2009)

US Senate Select Committee on Intelligence Hearing, 5 February 2008, 'Annual Worldwide Threat Assessment'

'US Statement of 1977', in D. Harris (ed.), *Cases and Materials on International Law*, 6th edn (London, Sweet & Maxwell, 2004)

Van Den Herik, L., and Letnar Cernic, J., 'Regulating Corporations under International Law: From Human Rights to International Criminal Law and Back Again' (2010) 8 *Journal of International Criminal Justice* 725

Van Niekerk, P., 'Africa's Diamond Dogs of War', *Observer* (13 August 1995)

Venter, A., 'Sierra Leone's Mercenary War Battle for the Diamond Fields' (1995) 28 *International Defence Review* 65

Vest, H., 'Business Leaders and the Modes of Individual Criminal Responsibility under International Law' (2010) 8 *Journal of International Criminal Justice* 851

Vinuesa, R. E., 'Interface, Correspondence and Convergence of Human Rights and International Humanitarian Law' (1998) 1 *Yearbook of International Humanitarian Law* 69

Vogt, H., 'Karzai Decree Ousts Private Security Firms', *Washington Times* (17 August 2010)

Walker, C., and Whyte, D., 'Contracting Out War?: Private Military Companies, Law and Regulation in the United Kingdom' (2005) 54 *International and Comparative Law Quarterly* 651

Warbrick, C., 'The New British Policy on Recognition of Governments' (1981) 30 *International and Comparative Law Quarterly* 568

Warrick, J., 'CIA Assassination Program Had Been Outsourced to Blackwater, Ex-Officials Say', *Los Angeles Times* (20 August 2009)

Watkin, K., 'Controlling the Use of Force: A Role for Human Rights Norms in Contemporary Armed Conflict' (2004) 98(1) *American Journal of International Law* 1

Waugh, P., '"Mercenaries as Peacekeepers" Plan under Fire', *Independent* (14 February 2002)

Weber, M., *The Theory of Social and Economic Organization* (New York, Free Press, 1964)

    Economy and Society: An Outline of Interpretive Sociology (London, University of California Press, 1978)

'We're the Good Guys These Days', *Economist* (29 July 1995) 32

White House Office of the Press Secretary, 'Government Contracting: Memorandum for the Heads of Executive Departments and Agencies' (4 March 2009)

White, N., and MacLeod, S., 'EU Operations and Private Military Contractors: Issues of Corporate and Institutional Responsibility' (2008) 19(5) *European Journal of International Law* 965

Williams, T., 'Iraqis Angered as Blackwater Charges Are Dropped', *New York Times* (2 January 2010)

Wills, S., *Protecting Civilians: The Obligations of Peacekeepers* (Oxford, Oxford University Press, 2009)

Wilson, H., *International Law and the Use of Force by National Liberation Movements* (Oxford, Clarendon Press, 1988)

Wippman, D., 'Change and Continuity in Legal Justifications for Military Intervention in Internal Conflicts' (1996) 27 *Columbia Human Rights Law Review* 435

Wright, Q., 'The Future of Neutrality' (1928–9) 12 *International Conciliation* 353

'US Intervention in the Lebanon' (1959) 53 *American Journal of International Law* 112

'Subversive Intervention' (1960) 54 *American Journal of International Law* 521

Zarate, J. C., 'The Emergence of a New Dog of War: Private International Security Companies, International Law, and the New World Disorder' (1998) 34 *Stanford Journal of International Law* 75

Zegveld, L., 'Remedies for Victims of Violations of International Humanitarian Law' (2003) 851 *International Review of the Red Cross* 497

Zoepf, K., 'US Prosecutor in Blackwater Shooting Case Arrives in Baghdad', *New York Times* (7 December 2008)

Documents of international organisations

American Declaration of the Rights and Duties of Man, OAS Res. XXX, Adopted by the Ninth International Conference of American States (April 1948), reprinted in Basic Documents Pertaining to Human Rights in the Inter-American System, OEA/Ser.L.V/II.82 doc.6 rev.1, at 17 (1992)

Basic Principles on the Use of Force and Firearms by Law Enforcement Officials, Adopted by the 8th UN Congress on the Prevention of Crime and the Treatment of Offenders (Havana, 27 August–7 September 1990)

Committee on the Elimination of All Forms of Discrimination Against Women, General Recommendation 19 (30 January 1992), UN Doc. A/47/38

European Union Code of Conduct for Arms Exports (8 June 1998)

International Law Commission,1306th Meeting, 9 May 1975, 'State Responsibility' (1975) *Yearbook of the International Law Commission*, vol. I

Draft Articles on Jurisdictional Immunities of States and Their Property, with Commentaries (1991) 30 ILM 1554

Draft Code of Crimes against the Peace and Security of Mankind, UN Doc. A/SI/10 (1996)

Articles on Responsibility of States for Internationally Wrongful Acts with Commentaries (2001) *Yearbook of the International Law Commission*, vol. II(2)

Draft Articles on the Prevention of Transboundary Harm from Hazardous Activities with Commentaries (2001) *Yearbook of the International Law Commission*, vol. II(2)

International Law Commission Study Group on Fragmentation of International Law, 'Difficulties Arising from Diversification and Expansion of International Law' (29 July 2005), UN Doc. A/CN.4/L.676

Koskenniemi, M., Preliminary Report by the Chairman of the Study Group Submitted for Consideration during the 2004 Session of the International Law Commission, 'Study on the Function and Scope of the Lex Specialis Rule and the Question of "Self Contained Regimes"' (2004), UN Doc. ILC(LVI)/SG/FIL/CRD.1 and Add.1

Montreux Document on Pertinent International Legal Obligations and Good Practices for States Related to Operations of Private Military and Security Companies During Armed Conflict (17 September 2008), UN Doc. A/63/467-S/2008/636

Report of the Ad Hoc Committee on the Drafting of an International Convention Against the Recruitment, Use, Financing and Training of Mercenaries (June 1982), UN Doc. A/37/43

Report of the Secretary-General, 'Responsibility of States for Internationally Wrongful Acts: Compilation of Decisions of International Courts, Tribunals and Other Bodies' (1 February 2007), UN Doc. A/62/62

Report of the Secretary-General, 'Responsibility of States for Internationally Wrongful Acts: Comments and Information Received from Governments' (9 March 2007), UN Doc. A/62/63

Report of the UN Conference on Environment and Development (Rio de Janeiro, 3–14 June 1992), UN Doc. A/CONF.151/26/Rev.l, vol. I: Resolutions Adopted by the Conference, Res. 1, Annex I

Report of the Working Group on the Use of Mercenaries as a Means of Violating Human Rights and Impeding the Exercise of the Right of Peoples to Self-Determination (23 December 2005), UN Doc. E/CN.4/2006/11

Report of the Working Group on the Use of Mercenaries as a Means of Violating Human Rights and Impeding the Exercise of the Right of Peoples to Self-Determination (24 August 2007), UN Doc. A/62/301

Report of the Working Group on the Use of Mercenaries as a Means of Violating Human Rights and Impeding the Exercise of the Right of People to Self-Determination (9 January 2008), UN Doc. A/HRC/7/7

Report of the Working Group on the Use of Mercenaries as a Means of Violating Human Rights and Impeding the Exercise of the Right of People to Self-Determination (21 January 2009), UN Doc. A/HRC/10/14

Report of the Working Group on the Use of Mercenaries as a Means of Violating Human Rights and Impeding the Exercise of the Right of Peoples to Self-Determination (2 July 2010), UN Doc. A/HRC/15/25

Report on the Question of the Use of Mercenaries as a Means of Violating Human Rights and Impeding the Exercise of the Right of Peoples to Self-Determination' (20 February 2007), UN Doc. E/CN.4/1997/24

Resolution XXIII, International Conference on Human Rights, Tehran (12 May 1968)

Ruggie, J., Special Representative of the UN Secretary-General on Business and Human Rights, 'Protect, Respect and Remedy: A Framework for Business and Human Rights', UN Doc. A/HRC/8/5 (7 April 2008)

Special Representative of the UN Secretary-General on Business and Human Rights, 'Business and Human Rights: Towards Operationalizing the "Protect, Respect and Remedy" Framework', UN Doc. A/HRC/11/13 (22 April 2009)

Special Representative of the UN Secretary-General on Business and Human Rights, 'Business and Human Rights: Further Steps towards the Operationalization of the "Protect, Respect and Remedy" Framework', UN Doc. A/HRC/14/27 (9 April 2010)

Second Periodic Report of Israel to the Human Rights Committee (4 December 2001), UN Doc. CCPR/C/ISR/2001/2

Standard Minimum Rules for the Treatment of Prisoners, Adopted by the First UN Congress on the Prevention of Crime and the Treatment of Offenders (Geneva, 1955) and approved by the Economic and Social Council by its Resolutions 663 C (XXIV) of 31 July 1957 and 2076 (LXII) of 13 May 1977

Statute of the Inter-American Commission on Human Rights, Adopted by the Organization of American States General Assembly, Res. No. 448 (October 1979)

Statute of the International Court of Justice

Summary Legal Position of the Government of Israel, Annex I to the Report of the Secretary-General Prepared Pursuant to GA Res. ES-10713 (24 November 2003), UN Doc. A/ES-10/248

Summary Record of the 2380th Meeting: USA, 2 (27 July 2006), UN Doc. CCPR/C/SR2380

UN Committee Against Torture, Conclusions and Recommendations (7 July 2005), UN Doc. CAT/C/CR/34/CAN

UNGA Res. 498 (V) (1 February 1951), UN Doc. A/1775/Add.1

UNGA Res. 2131 (XX) (21 December 1965), UN Doc. A/6014

UNGA Res. 2625 (XXV) (24 October 1970), UN Doc. A/8028

UNGA Res. 2675 (XXV) (9 December 1970), UN Doc. A/2675

UNGA Res. 3074 (XXVIII) (3 December 1973), UN Doc. A/3074

UNGA Res. 3314 (XXIX) (14 December 1974), UN Doc. A/3314

UNGA Res. 32/91 A (13 December 1977), UN Doc. A/RES/32/91

UNGA Res. 37/123 A (16 December 1982), UN Doc. A/RES/37/123

UNGA Res. 38/180 A (19 December 1983), UN Doc. A/RES/38/180

UNGA Res. 43/21 (3 November 1988), UN Doc. A/RES/43/21

UNGA Res. 49/60 (9 December 1994), UN Doc. A/RES/49/60

UNGA Res. 56/83 (10 December 2001), UN Doc. A/RES/56/83

UNGA Res. 59/35 (2 December 2004), UN Doc. A/RES/59/35

UNGA Res. 60/147 (16 December 2005), UN Doc. A/RES/60/147

UNGA Res. 62/61 (6 December 2007), UN Doc. A/RES/62/61

UN Human Rights Committee, Concluding Observations on Belgium (19 November 1998), UN Doc. CCPR/C/79/Add99

Concluding Observations on Belgium (12 August 2004), UN Doc. CCPR/CO/81/BEL

Concluding Observations on Colombia (5 May 1997), UN Doc. CCPR/C/79/Add 76

Concluding Observations on Cyprus (21 September 1994), UN Doc. CCPR/C/79/Add39

Concluding Observations on Israel (18 August 1998), UN Doc. CCPR/C/79/Add93

Concluding Observations on Israel (21 August 2003), UN Doc. CCPR/CO/78/ISR

Concluding Observations on Peru (15 November 2000), UN Doc. CCPR/CO/70/PER

Consideration of Reports Submitted by States Parties under Article 40 of the Covenant, 2nd and 3rd Periodic Reports of the United States of America (28 November 2005), UN Doc. CCPR/C/USA/3

General Comment 6, UN Doc. A/37/40 (1982)

General Comment 7, UN Doc. HRI/GEN/1/Rev.1 at 7(1994)

General Comment 13, 13 April 1984, UN Doc. HRI/GEN/1/Rev.7/Add.1

General Comment 20, UN Doc. HRI/GEN/1/Rev.1 at 30 (1994)

General Comment 31, UN Doc. CCPR/C/21/Rev.1/Add.13 (2004)

UN Human Rights Committee Executive Committee, 'Operationalizing the "Ladder of Options"' (27 June 2000), UN Doc. EC/50/SCINF.4

UN Legislative Series, Materials on Jurisdictional Immunities of States and Their Property (ST/LEG/SER.B/20, 1982)

UNSC Res. 387 (31 March 1976), UN Doc. S/RES/387

UNSC Res. 454 (2 November 1979), UN Doc. S/RES/454

UNSC Res. 573 (4 October 1985), UN Doc. S/RES/573

UNSC Res. 681 (20 December 1990), UN Doc. S/RES/681

UNSC Res. 1132 (8 October 1997), UN Doc. S/RES/1132

UNSC Res. 1373 (28 September 2001), UN Doc. S/RES/1373

UN Secretariat, Survey of International Law, UN Doc. A/CN4/1 Rev.1 (1949)

Universal Declaration of Human Rights (adopted 10 December 1948), UNGA Res. 217 A (III), UN Doc. A/810 at 71 (1948)

Other sources

Agreement for the Provision of Military Assistance between the Independent State of Papua New Guinea and Sandline International (31 January 1997), available at: www.c-r.org/our-work/accord/png-bougainville/key-texts14.php

Armorgroup website: www.armorgroup.com

Brigade of Gurkhas website: www.army.mod.uk/brigade_of_gurkhas/index.htm

British Association of Private Security Companies website: www.bapsc.org.uk

CACI website: www.caci.com/fcc/isis.shtml

DynCorp International websites: www.dyn-intl.com

Erinys website: www.erinys.net

Executive Outcomes website in 1999: www.eo.com (accessed by D. Avant on
        14 January 1999)
French Foreign Legion website: www.legion-etrangere.com
Global Group website: www.globalgroup.com
International Peace Operations Association website: ipoaworld.org/eng/
Landmine Monitor website: www.icbl.org/lm/
Milsearch website: www.milsearch.com.au
MPRI website: www.mpri.com
Private Security Company Association of Iraq website: www.pscai.org
Ronco Consulting Corporation website: www.roncoconsulting.com
UNSC Counter-Terrorism Committee website: www.un.org/sc/ctc/laws.html
Xe Services LLC website: www.xecompany.com

INDEX

294

CAMBRIDGE STUDIES IN INTERNATIONAL AND COMPARATIVE LAW

Books in the series

State Control over Private Military and Security Companies in Armed Conflict
Hannah Tonkin

The UN and Human Rights: Who Guards the Guardians? Guglielmo Verdirame

Sovereign Defaults before International Courts and Tribunals Michael Waibel

Making the Law of the Sea: A Study in the Development of International Law
James Harrison

'Fair and Equitable Treatment' in International Investment Law Roland Kläger

Legal Aspects of Transition from Illegal Territorial Regimes in International Law
Yaël Ronen

Access to Asylum: International Refugee Law and the Globalisation of Migration Control
Thomas Gammeltoft-Hansen

Trading Fish, Saving Fish: The Interaction between Regimes in International Law
Margaret Young

*The Individual in the International Legal System: State-Centrism, History and Change in
International Law* Kate Parlett

*The Participation of States in International Organisations: The Role of Human Rights and
Democracy* Alison Duxbury

*Theatre of the Rule of Law: The Theory, History and Practice of Transnational Legal
Intervention* Stephen Humphreys

*'Armed Attack' and Article 51 of the UN Charter: Evolutions in Customary Law and
Practice* Tom Ruys

*Science and Risk Regulation in International Law: The Role of Science, Uncertainty and
Values* Jacqueline Peel

The Public International Law Theory of Hans Kelsen: Believing in Universal Law
Jochen von Bernstorff

Vicarious Liability in Tort: A Comparative Perspective Paula Giliker

Legal Personality in International Law Roland Portmann

Legitimacy and Legality in International Law: An Interactional Account
Jutta Brunnée and Stephen J. Toope

The Concept of Non-International Armed Conflict in International Humanitarian Law
Anthony Cullen

Lightning Source UK Ltd.
Milton Keynes UK
UKOW03f0947020114

223859UK00012B/568/P